D1134846

The Animated
Peter Lorre

The Animated Peter Lorre

by Matthew Hahn

BearManor Media 2020

Published in the USA by:
BearManor Media
1317 Edgewater Dr #110
Orlando, FL 32804
www.bearmanormedia.com

Printed in the United States.

Cover: Peter Lorre in *Hollywood Steps Out* (1941), author's collection.
TheAnimatedPeterLorre.Tumblr.Com

Typesetting and layout by Darlene Swanson • van-garde.com

ISBN: 978-1-62933-459-2 (paperback)
          978-1-62933-460-8 (hardback)

Previously by Matthew Hahn

The Animated Marx Brothers

ZaSu on her folded towel/bed.

Dedication

To my beloved Tonkinese cat, ZaSu, who knew that when Papa was writing this book, her place was on the folded towel/bed on the corner of his desk. She also taught this to her sister and littermate, Thelma. ZaSu was truly the Lioness of Literature. She passed the day after I finished my first draft, suddenly but peacefully, at home, sleeping in the sun, with her sister and me close by. We should all be so lucky.

Lorre Tune ('lô-rē-ˌtjuːn) n. 1. an animated cartoon featuring the likeness and/or sound of Peter Lorre, either in human form or as an anthropomorphic animal, plant, or object. 2. BROADLY: a cartoon that references Peter Lorre.

Table of Contents

Acknowledgements

Cheryl Morris wrote the book, or at least the epilogue, on Peter Lorre's "posthumous career" in Stephen D. Youngkin's *The Lost One: A Life of Peter Lorre*. That was a jumping off point for this volume. Cheryl was my first contact when I got the contract to write this, and she has been a constant source of encouragement, information, and help. Others who supplied me with titles of cartoons include Benny Drinnon, Mark Pawlick, Kim Newman, and Chris Signore. Kevin Fitzpatrick, Michael Dickson, and Felipe Ondera did some recon for me.

My wife, Cheri, proofread this manuscript. Mistakes are my own.

I would also like to thank the staffs of the Anne Arundel County Public Library, Baltimore's Enoch Pratt Library, Johns Hopkins University Library, William McDaniel College Library, and Maryland Institute College of Art Library; as well as Interlibrary Loan and Marina.

Prologue

"In the early twentieth century, motion picture exhibitors generally preferred to book cartoons that featured popular characters or caricatures of well-known stars," writes Miriam Petty. Peter Lorre is perhaps the celebrity most frequently caricatured (likeness and/or voice) in the history of animation, with over 700 theatrical cartoons, TV episodes, commercials, web movies, and even video games. It is not hard to see why. He falls into the same "sweet spot" as other frequently caricatured celebs, like the Marx Brothers, Laurel and Hardy, and Jimmy Durante. Animators love to draw him, and voice actors love to play him. The enormous, heavy-lidded eyes; rotten teeth, baby face, and small body of the pre-1941 Lorre made him catnip to Warner Bros. animators, and Mel Blanc played him with a high-pitched, nasal voice and an insane giggle. This set the template for all later portrayals, regardless of what Lorre actually looked like after his teeth were fixed and his weight fluctuated. He appeared in more original Warner Bros. Merrie Melodies and Looney Tunes than fan favorites like Michigan J. Frog and Marvin the Martian. Warner Bros. acknowledged its debt to Lorre by putting him into *Looney Tunes: Back in Action* (2003) (qv).

Ren Höek, the goggle-eyed Chihuahua of *The Ren & Stimpy Show* (1991) (qv) was visually and aurally modeled on Lorre by creator John Kricfalusi, although Billy West would later put his own spin on the character's voice. Robin Williams, who made arcane references to Lorre in his standup act, did a Lorre imitation as Genie in *Aladdin* (1992) (qv). Paul Frees played Beatle George Harrison as Lorre. Lorre has also been portrayed as a pig, a duck, a fish, a mole, a fox, a toad, a chameleon, a maggot, a weevil, a ghost, an evil spirit, a monster, a robot, a cyborg, a lamp, and the cereal mascot Boo Berry.

The crème de la crème of voice actors has played him: Blanc, Frees, West, Stan Freberg, Maurice LaMarche, Robert Easton, Bill Scott, Daws Butler, Don Messick, Howard Morris, Rob Paulsen, and Frank Welker. He was even portrayed by "Peter Lorre Jr.", also known as Eugene Weingand.

In addition to Warner Bros., Lorre has made animated appearances in cartoons from Disney, Columbia, Hanna-Barbera, 20th Century Fox Television, Paramount Television, and Rankin/Bass.

Creators of Lorre Tunes (directors, writers, and/or animators) include Tex Avery, Friz Freleng, Robert McKimson, Robert Clampett, Michael Maltese, Tim Burton, Steven Spielberg, and Tom Ruegger.

Who was this man who has inspired so much imitation?

Born László Löwenstein on June 26, 1904, he ran away from home at age 17 and worked at a bank while receiving stage training in Vienna before making his acting debut in Zurich. He played all sorts of parts, including Asians in "yellowface", on stage and in movies before German director Fritz Lang made him a film star as child killer Hans Beckert, who whistles "In the Hall of the Mountain King" from Peer Gynt Suite I, Op. 46 in *M* (1931), and who is identified by the chalk "M" on his jacket. Lorre fled Germany in 1933 when the Nazis took power and eventually ended up in London, where he played a villain in Alfred Hitchcock's *The Man Who Knew Too Much* (1934) by learning the English lines phonetically. The day after shooting completed, he sailed to America with his first wife on visitors' visas. He settled in Hollywood and received a contract from Columbia Pictures.

On a loan-out to Metro-Goldwyn-Mayer, he played an insane doctor in *Mad Love* (1935). After a starring role in Hitchcock's *Secret Agent* (1936) in London, he returned to Hollywood and took a contract with 20th Century Fox, starring in a series of Mr. Moto movies–back to yellowface. He made a comeback of sorts when John Huston cast him as Joel Cairo in *The Maltese Falcon* (1941). Although this Dashiell Hammett story had been filmed twice previously, this version is the one that became an enduring classic, with Humphrey Bogart's famous last line, "The, uh, stuff that dreams are made of." It led Peter Lorre to a contract with Warner Bros. and a "partnership" with Sydney Greenstreet, who played Cairo's associate, Kasper Gutman. The pair have nine common movies, including *Casablanca* (1942), in which they have no scenes together, but where Lorre utters his deathless line to Bogart, "You despise me, don't you?" Lorre and Greenstreet even appeared in a musical, *Hollywood Canteen* (1944). *The Maltese Falcon* (1941) and *Casablanca* (1942) are frequent targets of cartoon parody, and animated surrogates for Greenstreet abound in Lorre Tunes. After Greenstreet died, Lorre continued to work with his friend Bogart in pictures such as *Rope of Sand* (1949).

Lorre would play another doctor, the dipsomaniacal Herman Einstein in *Arsenic and Old Lace* (1944). His cartoon counterparts often play mad doctors or scientists. Often, his animated avatars are cast as a mad scientist's deformed assistant in an "Igor"-type role–somewhat oddly, since Lorre never played this type of part in real life. This character originated with Peggy Webling's unproduced stage adaptation of *Frankenstein* (1927), later adapted by John L. Balderston into the 1931 movie of the same name. The character does not appear in the novel, and in the play and movie, he is called "Fritz". The first use of "Igor" or "Ygor" comes from the film *Mystery of the Wax Museum* (1933) and the name was later used in two sequels to *Frankenstein* (1931), including *Son of Frankenstein* (1939), in which Peter Lorre was originally cast as Dr. Frankenstein! Neither "Igor" is an assistant, and neither is disfigured in the way "Igors" usually are. It is not known how the name "Igor" came to be associated with the disfigured assistant character. Even more strangely, in at least one cartoon, Daffy Duck plays a vampire's assistant as a fly eating madman, like Renfield in *Dracula* (1931), but with a Peter Lorre voice. Peter Lorre never played this part either, and in fact, the roles of both Fritz and Renfield were portrayed in the same year by the same man, the great character actor Dwight Frye.

In the years before his death, Peter Lorre alternated between small roles in big-budget movies like *Around the World in 80 Days* (1956) and *Voyage to the Bottom of the Sea* (1961), where he played a submarine officer who kept a shark onboard; guest shots on television, and starring roles in low-budget horror movies like *Tales of Terror* (1962). He was also a favorite among comics. "I am without a question of a doubt the most imitated man in night clubs," he once said. As this book hopes to show, he is also the most imitated man in animated cartoons.

Chapter 1:
Theatrical Lorre Tunes

NB: ALL LORRE TUNES HEREIN are rated for their portrayal of our subject on a scale of one to five Insane Giggles. Five Giggles is for an excellent visual and aural imitation. Zero Giggles indicates that a movie, although it may be considered Lorre Tunes canon by some, does not really seem to caricature him at all. Zero Giggles for looks may mean a character sounds like Peter Lorre but does not resemble him. Extra points are given for degree of difficulty and imaginative use of Lorre's countenance as a robot, object, animal, etc.

Porky's Movie Mystery (March 11, 1939)

Warner Bros. Directed by Robert Clampett. Written by Ernest Gee (story). Cast: Mel Blanc, Billy Bletcher.

"Warner Bros. was the cartoon studio, more than any other, that specialized in parodying celebrities," says animation historian Keith Scott. "Friz Freleng said that was because most of the people who worked there were old show biz buffs themselves. Friz Freleng was an old Vaudeville buff."

Warner Bros. animators were not limited to the stars under contract to the studio, and many others made frequent appearances, like the Marx Brothers and Laurel and Hardy. However, Warner Bros. did like to use its own stable of stars such as Humphrey Bogart, Edward G. Robinson, James Cagney, Hugh Herbert, and, of course, Peter Lorre, although he was not under contract to them until 1943. Warner Bros. is still making cartoons with Peter Lorre well into the twenty-first century, suggesting it feels an ongoing proprietorship.

Under the guidance of Hugh Harman and Rudolf Ising, Warner Bros. had tried and failed to make animation stars of Bosko, "a Negro boy", and

Buddy, "Bosko in whiteface." After Harman and Ising left after a dispute over money with producer Leon Schlesinger, new directors came in, including Friz Freleng, Robert Clampett, Tex Avery, and Chuck Jones. Warner Bros. launched a new series with animals in an Our Gang-type premise. They expected that Beans the Cat would rise to the top, but it was Mel Blanc as Porky Pig who became their first breakout star. Blanc, "The Man of a Thousand Voices", had come to the studio in 1936 and would eventually play Porky, Daffy Duck, Elmer Fudd, Bugs Bunny, Tweety Bird, Sylvester the Cat, Yosemite Sam, Foghorn Leghorn, Marvin the Martian, Pepe Le Pew, Speedy Gonzales, Wile E. Coyote, Road Runner, the Tasmanian Devil—all the major male characters in Warner Bros. cartoons.

A Looney Tunes cartoon. Looney Tunes were generally more plot-based than some of the Merrie Melodies that followed. The card after the titles reads, "Any resemblance this picture has to the original story from which it was stolen is purely coincidental." An expository radio broadcast by "Walter Windshield" (a parody of real-life correspondent Walter Winchell) informs us of a mysterious phantom on the lot of Warner Bros. The headline screams, "STUDIO POLICE HUNT PHANTOM". A tiny policeman interrogates Frankenstein's monster, but he won't talk. We see the Phantom slip into a dressing room marked "The Invisible Man". He takes off his cloak and he is—wait for it—invisible. He is bitter that he only starred in one picture. A headline blares, "AROUSED PEOPLE DEMAND MR. MOTTO". Another says, "SORRY, MOTTO ON VACATION". The head of the Studio PD demands Motto anyhow.

Motto (played by Porky Pig in round glasses with a thick Japanese accent) is reached on a desert island reading a book on jujitsu. He uses an outboard motor to take the island to a waiting plane, which he crashes through the roof of the Studio PD. He goes hunting for clues with his oversized magnifier, which has no actual glass in it. The Invisible Man, wearing only shoes and a hat, poses next to a poster of a (fictitious) Warner Bros. picture, *Great Guns*, starring Lotta Dimples. Mr. Motto walks on by, and The Invisible Man kicks him in the butt and then swings an axe at him. Mr. Motto uses jujitsu and decks him, then sprays him with anti-invisible juice, revealing him as Hugh Herbert, who utters his trademark, "Hoo hoo! Hoo hoo!"

FUN FACT: Herbert previously played a detective in *Sh! The Octopus* (1937), featuring a spectacular unmasking of the titular villain, which this cartoon may be referencing. Or not.

GIGGLE RATING: One Giggle. Blanc, who two years hence would basically invent the Peter Lorre imitation, here does a generic Japanese accent. Other than glasses, no attempt is made to make Porky look like Peter Lorre.

AVAILABILITY: On the Laserdisc *Guffaw and Order, Looney Tunes Fight Crime* (1993?)

Hollywood Steps Out (May 24, 1941)

Warner Bros. Directed by Tex Avery. Animated by Rod Scribner. Written by Melvin Millar. Music: Carl W. Stalling. Produced by Leon Schlesinger. Cast: Dave Barry (Cary Grant/Clark Gable/James Cagney/Bing Crosby/Lewis Stone/Ned Sparks/Groucho Marx), Sara Berner (Greta Garbo/Coat Check Girl/Henry Fonda's Mother/Dorothy Lamour), Mel Blanc (Jerry Colonna/Peter Lorre), Kent Rogers (Jimmy Stewart/Mickey Rooney/Henry Fonda).

From the Merrie Melodies series. This is the Duesenberg of 1940s "Who's that star?" celebrity caricature cartoons.

At Ciro's nightclub in Hollywood, Cary Grant says, "What a place! What a place! Why, it's as pretty as a picture! But if I ever told my favorite wife the awful truth, I'd land right on the front page," referencing several of his movie titles. Cigarette girl Greta Garbo sells him a pack of smokes and lights one by striking a match on her really big shoe. Many of these movies make jokes based on the mistaken notion that Garbo had large feet.

Edward G. Robinson asks Ann Sheridan, "The Oomph Girl", how she is, and she answers, "Oomph oomph oomph oomph oomph oomph oomph oomph oomph oomph. Oomph."

The camera pans past Leon Schlesinger and his assistant, Henry Binder. Johnny Weissmuller checks his coat, revealing himself in only his Tarzan outfit. Sally Rand, the famous stripper, checks her fur, presumably leaving herself naked. James Cagney, Humphrey Bogart, and George Raft pitch pennies. Raft was known for flipping a coin in *Scarface* (1932).

Harpo Marx gives Greta Garbo a hotfoot, and we all know how big those feet are. However, she barely reacts. Bing Crosby introduces longhair conductor Leopold Stokowski, whose orchestra strikes up a conga. The music does something to Dorothy Lamour, who wants to dance with Jimmy Stewart. Stewart runs away, leaving a sign on the table that says, "Mr. Smith Goes to Washington" (the title of one of his movies). Tyrone Power dances with Winter Olympic medal-winner Sonja Henie, who is wearing ice skates. Frankenstein's monster does the Robot. The Three Stooges smack and poke each other. Oliver Hardy is so fat, he dances with two women.

Mickey Rooney as Andy Hardy is dining with Judy Garland and gets the tab. He asks his movie father, Judge Hardy (Lewis Stone) for a heart-to-heart. They end up washing dishes.

Der Bingle introduces the stripper "Sally Strand", who changed her name since she checked her coat to avoid a lawsuit. Sally performs her bubble dance. William Powell, Spencer Tracy, Ronald Colman, Errol Flynn, Wallace Beery, and C. Aubrey Smith wolf-whistle at her. Peter Lorre purrs, "I haven't seen such a beautiful bubble since I was a child."

Finally, Harpo Marx literally bursts her bubble with a slingshot, revealing that she is wearing a barrel.

Clark Gable, who has been following a comely blonde all night, finally catches up with her and asks her for a kiss. It is Groucho Marx in drag. In the original ending, Gable kisses Groucho anyhow. This was cut when Gable complained it would hurt his career. This bit was used earlier in *The CooCoo Nut Grove* (1936), but Harpo un-wigged Groucho.

GIGGLE RATING: Five Giggles. The gold standard of Lorre impersonations and caricatures, it set the bar for all time.

AVAILABILITY: *Looney Tunes Golden Collection, Volume 2* (2004), Disc 4. This short is in the public domain and available on many VHS compilations in poor quality. There is a 4K restoration on YouTube at this writing.

Horton Hatches the Egg (April 11, 1942)

Warner Bros. Directed by Robert Clampett. Writing Credits (in alphabetical order): Michael Maltese, Dr. Seuss (book). Produced by Leon Schlesinger.

Producer: Henry Binder. Music by Carl W. Stalling. Effects animator: Robert McKimson. Animator: Bill Melendez. Cast: Sara Berner (Maysie/Baby) (uncredited), Mel Blanc (Mouse/Hunters/Audience Member) (uncredited), Robert Clampett (Various voices) (uncredited), Frank Graham (Narrator) (uncredited), Kent Rogers (Horton/Peter Lorre Fish) (uncredited).

Leon Schlesinger bought the rights to Dr. Seuss' book *Horton Hatches the Egg* at Bob Clampett's assistance, but, said Clampett, "Leon's argument was that if I filmed the book exactly as written, it would cause a big silent smile in the theaters, but wouldn't get any laughs. So, he gave me the go-ahead only on the condition that I would guarantee some theater laughs. By the time all the arrangements had been made, Mike Maltese and I only had about two sessions in which to gag the story. We didn't even have a storyboard on Horton, but sketched the added ideas right on my copy of the book. Then, as of a Friday night, I told my animators, who were all struggling to draw Bugs Bunny alike, 'Guess what, boys? First thing Monday morning I want you all to draw like Dr. Seuss!'"

Maysie the lazy bird searches for a sucker to sit on her egg, and finds one in Horton, a pink elephant, singing "The Hut-Sut Song". She persuades him to do it, saying she will be right back, and then takes off for Palm Beach, where she decides not to return. "Rally I won't," she says, imitating Katharine Hepburn.

Horton sits on the nest, rain or shine, and all through the winter. "I meant what I said, and I said what I meant. An elephant's faithful, one hundred percent." Come spring, he is taunted by the other animals. Three hunters approach with an elephant gun, but Horton stares them down. They decide to take him alive and sell him to the circus. They put him, tree and egg and all, on a ship. A Peter Lorre fish does a take upon spying this. "Well, now I've seen everything." Then he shoots himself in the head.

At the circus, Maysie flies by. She decides to go to the show. "Rally I will." She flies right into Horton just as the egg is hatching. Maysie kicks him out of the tree. The egg hatches, and a tiny elephant bird pops out. The circus sends Horton and his elephant bird home, where they sing "The Hut-Sut Song".

GIGGLE RATING: Five Giggles. Kent Rogers played several roles in *Hollywood Steps Out* (1941). He became a Navy Ensign in World War II and died in a training accident in 1944 at age twenty.

AVAILABILITY: On DVD: *The Best of Dr. Seuss* (2000)
Looney Tunes Golden Collection, Volume 6 (2008)

Hair-Raising Hare (May 25, 1946)

Warner Bros. Directed by Chuck Jones (as Charles M. Jones). Written by Tedd Pierce (story). Cast: Mel Blanc.

Bugs Bunny made his first appearances, unnamed, in Porky Pig cartoons before breaking out on his own in Tex Avery's *A Wild Hare* (1940) and becoming one of the greatest animated stars of all time.

Bugs pokes his head out of his hole and says, "Didja evah have the feelin' you was bein' watched?" The camera pulls back to show mad Dr. Lorre watching him on his telescreen. A monster is trying to break down the door of his cell. Lorre promises him a rabbit dinner, and sends out a female rabbit robot to lure Bugs. Bugs follows the robot back to Lorre's castle, which has a flashing neon sign that says, "Evil Scientist". The robot falls apart, and Bugs tries to leave, but is stopped by Lorre, who says he has another little friend who wants to meet Bugs. When Bugs sees the monster trying to break down the door, he tries to leave again. Lorre releases the monster, who has orange hair and was later called Gossamer. Bugs is unable to leave the castle, and Gossamer pursues him. Bugs is unable to flee when a trap door opens, so he pretends to be a manicurist and starts working on Gossamer's nails.

"My, I bet you monsters lead interesting lives. I said to my girlfriend just the other day, 'I'll bet monsters are interesting,' I said. The places you must go and the things you must see, my stars. And I'll bet you meet a lot of interesting people, too. I'm always interested in meeting interesting people. Now let's dip our patties in the water."

The water bowls have mousetraps in them, which snap shut on Gossamer's fingers. Bugs flees. Gossamer watches Bugs through eyes cut out on a painting.

Bugs pokes him in the eyes. Gossamer sees a painting of Bugs and tries to poke Bugs' eyes, but Bugs pokes him first. Bugs clobbers Gossamer, who is hiding behind the wall, with a mallet, and tries to exit again, but Gossamer is waiting for him disguised in a suit of armor. Bugs hits Gossamer with a lance, turning him into Canned Monster. Bugs tries to leave again, but Gossamer grabs him by the throat. Bugs asks him, "Didja evah have the feelin' you was bein' watched?" and points to the theatrical audience. Gossamer runs away. The reconstituted robot rabbit gives Bugs a kiss and he decides to go off with her even if she is mechanical.

FUN FACT: At the beginning, Bugs sings "Sweet Dreams, Sweetheart" from *Hollywood Canteen* (1944).

GIGGLE RATING: Five Giggles.

AVAILABILITY: On the following DVD: *Looney Tunes Golden Collection, Volume 1* (2003), Disc 3
Looney Tunes Golden Collection, Volume 4 (2006), Disc 2 (as part of the special feature "Bugs Bunny: Superstar Part 2")
Looney Tunes Golden Collection, Volume 3 (2005), Disc 3 (as part of the special feature "What's Up, Doc: A Salute to Bugs Bunny, Part 2")
The Essential Bugs Bunny (2010), Disc 1

Racketeer Rabbit (September 14, 1946)
Warner Bros. Directed by Friz Freleng (as I. Freleng). Written by Michael Maltese. Cast: Mel Blanc, Dick Nelson.

Bugs comes upon the abandoned Hotel Friz. He drills a rabbit hole in the floor and goes to sleep. Rocky (this Rocky is a caricature of Edward G. Robinson) and Hugo (a caricature of Peter Lorre) pull up one step ahead of the cops, with whom they have a shootout. Hugo's machine gun propels him across the room and Rocky pushes him back. "We got rid of those mugs," says Rocky. "They make me laugh," says Hugo.

Rocky divvies up the money with Hugo. Bugs steps in several times and takes many shares, then opens the door to leave. Rocky is on the other side with a gun. "Rocky's a little too smart for ya. Myeah." Rocky tries to get

Bugs to say what he's done with the money, but Bugs won't talk, so Rocky tells Hugo to take him for a ride. Bugs returns alone.

Rocky says, "I'm givin' ya two seconds to give me the dough, see?" Bugs says, "Okay, okay. But foist ya gotta close your eyes." Rocky says, "I'll count to ten and you better give it to me, see?" Bugs mixes up some dough with milk and flour and gives it to Rocky, right in the kisser.

Bugs goes through a door and Rocky opens it. Bugs is on the other side, dressed as a gangster and flipping a coin like George Raft. "It's coitains for you, Rocky." He hangs curtains on Rocky's head. "Oh, they're adorable."

Bugs pretends to be the cops, then hides Rocky in a trunk. He hands Rocky his "watch" (a time bomb), and pretends to fight with the cop. The bomb explodes as Bugs finishes his "fight." Rocky runs after the cops, begging them to take him away. "Some guys just can't take it, see? Myeah. Myeah. Myeah. Myeah."

GIGGLE RATING: Five Giggles.

AVAILABILITY: A bonus feature on the DVD of the documentary *Public Enemies, The Golden Age of Gangster Film* (2008).

Cockatoos for Two (February 1947)

Columbia. Directed by Bob Wickersham. Written by Robert Clampett. Cast: Stan Freberg, Cal Howard.

In 1945, Stan Freberg arrived in Hollywood, and with his voluminous talent, almost immediately landed a job at Warner Bros., often working with Mel Blanc. Bob Clampett had been preparing to leave for some time. When Leon Schlesinger sold his studio to Warner Bros., his assistant Henry Binder and Ray Katz became producers at Screen Gems, and hired Clampett as a creative supervisor and story head. Clampett wrote his own stories and got Freberg to come over and do voices.

Birth of a Notion (1947) was started before *Cockatoos for Two* (1947), but released after, perhaps because Clampett left and the cartoon had to be finished by Robert McKimson. Freberg plays Lorre in both cartoons, but differently. In the former, he plays Lorre like the insane doctor in *Mad Love* (1935) and in the latter, he plays Lorre like the funny doctor in *Arsenic and Old Lace* (1944).

Freberg would go on to have a voiceover career spanning more than seven decades in cartoons, puppetry, TV, film, radio, recordings, and commercials.

Mr. Sidney (Freberg as Lorre), who lives at 531 Greenstreet in Horrowood, California, is tired of "steaks, chops, caviar, etc." and desires a new taste sensation. His prayers seem to be answered when his butler delivers a letter from his friend, who is sending Sidney her $57,000 pet cockatoo, instructing him to "Keep him warm and feed well." Sidney fantasizes about roasting the bird and feeding himself.

The doorbell rings and Sidney rushes to answer it, thinking it is his cockatoo. Alas, it is only a homing pigeon looking for a place to crash for the night. Sidney literally kicks him out. The pigeon sees the cockatoo being delivered and after reading the instructions, "FEED WELL KEEP WARM", literally kicks the cockatoo to the curb.

The pigeon, wearing one of the cockatoo's tail feathers on his head, is delivered to an excited Sidney, who notes that the "cockatoo" needs fattening up. The pigeon kisses him.

Lorre has a lavish buffet prepared, and the pigeon eats it all, but is upset that he no longer has his girlish figure. Sidney has just the thing: "a Turkish bath." He places the bird into a roasting pan in the oven and turns the heat up to "Atomic". The real cockatoo arrives just in time with his barrister, who says the pigeon is an impostor, which he readily cops to and makes his exit.

Outside, the pigeon wonders how he would have tasted, so he takes a bite. "Woulda served him right," he says of the flavor.

GIGGLE RATING: Five Giggles. A superb rendering of Lorre, and Freberg's imitation is every bit as good as Blanc's.

AVAILABILITY: Lost for many years, recently partially restored and at this writing is available online.

Birth of a Notion (April 12, 1947)

Warner Bros. Directed by Robert McKimson. Written by Warren Foster (story). Cast: Mel Blanc, Stan Freberg.

Daffy Duck, like Bugs Bunny, started out as an anonymous co-star of Porky Pig. He got his name in his second movie, *Daffy Duck and Egghead*

(1938). He began life as a madcap, whose "Woo-hoo! Woo-hoo!" was reportedly based on Hugh Herbert's "Hoo hoo! Hoo hoo!"

Daffy has a strategy to avoid flying south for the winter. He lays a bone on the front porch of a house, opens the door and whistles for the dog, then hides. When the dog, Leopold, comes out and tries to eat the bone, Daffy tells him it is poison. Leopold is grateful to Daffy for saving his life and asks if there is anything he can do for him. "How about a home for the winter?" Leopold says his master is busy with a scientific experiment and would kick them both out if he found Daffy.

Meanwhile, Dr. Lorre is going over the formula for his experiment, which requires a duck wishbone. "I'll have to get a duck somewhere."

Leopold hides Daffy in a closet, telling him to stay there and Leopold will bring him food and water all winter. "I have no duck, Leopold, to complete my experiment," says Lorre. "I need that wishbone very badly."

Daffy overhears. "My wishbone! That little monster!" He prepares to throw a vase at Lorre, but is stopped by Leopold. Daffy throws a baseball bat at Lorre. Leopold catches it just as it hits Lorre in the head. "Why did you hit me in the head, Leopold? Don't you know that might make me very angry? Now, I will do terrible, horrible things to you." He snaps the bat into halves, then quarters, then eighths.

Lorre goes to bed, and Daffy attacks him with a knife. Lorre protects himself with a shield which blunts the blade. Daffy finally escapes. Lorre thinks maybe he can make do with a dog wishbone.

Daffy tries to find another house to stay in for the winter, but the one he chooses has a Joe Besser duck living there. "Not so faaaaaast. I'm workin' this side of the streeeeet. Ya craaaazy," and kicks him south. He is joined in flight by Leopold.

GIGGLE RATING: Five Giggles.

AVAILABILITY: On the following DVD: *Looney Tunes Golden Collection, Volume 6* (2008), Disc 1
Looney Tunes Spotlight Collection, Volume 6 (2008), Disc 1

Water, Water Every Hare (April 19, 1952)

Warner Bros. Directed by Chuck Jones (as Charles M. Jones). Written by Michael Maltese. Cast: Mel Blanc, John T. Smith.

Rain floods Bugs Bunny's rabbit hole and his mattress floats downriver to the Evil Scientist's castle, helpfully marked with a neon sign. The Evil Scientist, who is green and sounds more like Boris Karloff or Vincent Price than Peter Lorre, is looking for a brain for his mechanical masterpiece when Bugs floats by. He hooks Bugs just before he goes over the falls. Bugs awakens to find himself surrounded by mummies, robots, and a green man and runs away.

Meanwhile, Gossamer, the orange monster, tries to burst out of his cell. The Evil Scientist lets him out with the key. The Evil Scientist promises Gossamer some spider goulash if he catches the rabbit. Bugs flees, but is stopped by a moat with alligators. Behind him is Gossamer. "Uh oh. Think fast, rabbit."

"My stars, wherever did you get that awful hairdo? It doesn't become you at all," says Bugs as a gay hairdresser. "Lemme fix it up. Look how stringy and messy it is. What a shame. Such an interesting monster, too. My stars. If an interesting monster can't have an interesting hairdo, then I don't know what things are coming to. In my business, you meet so many interesting people–bobby pins, please–but the most interesting ones are the monsters. Oh, dear, that'll never stay. We'll just have to have a permanament." Bugs puts dynamite in Gossamer's hair and lights the fuse. "So, I've gotta give an interesting old lady a manicure, but I'll be back before you're done." He runs off and the dynamite explodes.

Bugs pours vanishing fluid on himself and disappears. He sneaks up on Gossamer and hits him with a mallet. Then he pours reducing oil on him, which makes him tiny. He goes to live in a mouse hole, kicking out the mouse and hanging out a sign that says, "I QUIT". The mouse says, "I quit, too," and gets rid of his bottle of hooch.

The Evil Scientist makes Bugs reappear with Hare Restorer. "Never send a monster to do the work of an evil scientist," he says. "Now be a cooperative bunny and let me have your brain." "Sorry doc, but I need what little I've got," says Bugs. The Evil Scientist hurls an axe at him. It hits a bottle of ether, which knocks the Evil Scientist out. Bugs makes it back to his rabbit hole before he conks out. He wakes up and says, "It musta been a night-mare." Gossamer rows by in a tiny boat. "Oh yeah? That's what you think."

GIGGLE RATING: Zero Giggles. Any similarity to Lorre is apparently unintentional.

AVAILABILITY: On the DVD *Looney Tunes Golden Collection, Volume 1* (2003), Disc 1.

Hyde and Hare (August 27, 1955)

Warner Bros. Directed by Friz Freleng (as I. Freleng). Written by Warren Foster (story). Cast: Mel Blanc, Jack Edwards.

Every day in the park, old ladies feed the birds and a mild-mannered little man feeds Bugs Bunny carrots. Bugs says, "Look, Doc, we go through dis every day. Gets me up early, gets you up early. What do you say you adopt me as a pet?" The little man agrees and takes Bugs home.

The man agrees. "It's strange that you should call me Doc. I happen to be a doctor." His shingle reads, "Dr. Jekyll". Dr. Jekyll goes into the lab to get Bugs a carrot and sees a potion there. He drinks it, although he knows he shouldn't, and turns into Mr. Hyde, a green-skinned monster with red eyes. Bugs imitates Liberace and plays "The Minute Waltz". He thinks Mr. Hyde is a patient and goes to get the Doc. Hyde tries to kill him with an axe. Bugs flees and Mr. Hyde changes back to Dr. Jekyll. Bugs tells him about the green monster, and Dr. Jekyll changes back into Mr. Hyde. Bugs flees, but Mr. Hyde turns back into Dr. Jekyll, and Bugs barricades them in a room and gives Dr. Jekyll a gun. He turns into Mr. Hyde again, and Bugs runs away, only for Mr. Hyde to change back to Dr. Jekyll. They go into a dark closet and Dr. Jekyll changes back, as we can see the color change in his eyes. Bugs escapes to the laboratory. Mr. Hyde changes back and Dr. Jekyll follows him into the lab. He asks Bugs if Bugs drank the formula, and Bugs is offended. He goes back to the park and turns into a monstrous green rabbit and frightens away the little old ladies and the birds. "Well, what's eatin' dem? You'd tink dey nevah saw a rabbit before!"

GIGGLE RATING: Zero Giggles. No similarity to Lorre at all.

AVAILABILITY: On the DVD *Looney Tunes Golden Collection, Volume 2* (2004).

Around the World in 80 Days (1956)

Michael Todd Company. Directed by Michael Anderson. Written by James Poe & John Farrow & S.J. Perelman (screenplay), Jules Verne (book). Produced by Michael Todd. Cast: David Niven (Phileas Fogg), Cantinflas (Passepartout), Shirley MacLaine (Princess Aouda), Robert Newton (Inspector Fix), Charles Boyer (Monsieur Gasse–Thomas Cook Paris Clerk), Joe E. Brown (Fort Kearney Station Master), Martine Carol (Girl in Paris Railroad Station), John Carradine (Col. Stamp Proctor–San Francisco Politico), Charles Coburn (Steamship Company Hong Kong Clerk), Ronald Colman (Great Indian Peninsular Railway Official), Melville Cooper (Mr. Talley–Steward, R. M. S. Mongolia), Noël Coward (Roland Hesketh-Baggott–London Employment Agency Manager), Finlay Currie (Andrew Stuart), Reginald Denny (Bombay Police Inspector), Andy Devine (First Mate of the S. S. Henrietta), Marlene Dietrich (Barbary Coast Saloon Owner), Luis Miguel Dominguín (Bullfighter), Fernandel (French Coachman), John Gielgud (Foster–Fogg's Ex-Valet), Hermione Gingold (Sporting Lady), José Greco (Flamenco Dancer), Sir Cedric Hardwicke (Sir Francis Cromarty–Bombay to Calcutta Train), Trevor Howard (Denis Fallentin–Reform Club Member), Glynis Johns (Sporting Lady's Companion), Buster Keaton (Train Conductor–San Francisco to Fort Kearney), Evelyn Keyes (Tart–Paris), Beatrice Lillie (Leader of London Revivalist Group), Peter Lorre (Japanese Steward–S. S. Carnatic), Edmund Lowe (Engineer of the S. S. Henrietta), Victor McLaglen (Helmsman of the S. S. Henrietta), Col. Tim McCoy (U.S. Cavalry Colonel), Mike Mazurki (Drunk in Hong Kong Dive), John Mills (London Carriage Driver), Robert Morley (Ralph–Bank of England Governor), Alan Mowbray (British Consul–Suez), Edward R. Murrow (Prologue Narrator), Jack Oakie (Captain of the S. S. Henrietta), George Raft (Barbary Coast Saloon Bouncer), Gilbert Roland (Achmed Abdullah), Cesar Romero (Achmed Abdullah's Henchman), Frank Sinatra (Barbary Coast Saloon Pianist), Red Skelton (Drunk in Barbary Coast Saloon).

For his first motion picture, producer Mike Todd wanted something that would showcase Todd-AO, his widescreen, 70 mm film format, although he later had to sell it to finance the film. Alexander Korda suggested a property he had bought years ago, a stage musical version of *Around the World in Eighty Days* called *Around the World* (1946). Coincidentally, Todd had been involved with this show and its creator, Orson Welles, in its early stages, but pulled out when Welles failed to produce a script. Todd decided to base his movie on the original Verne novel. Phileas Fogg of London and his valet, Passepartout, attempt to circle the globe in just under twelve weeks on a £20,000 wager set by his friends at the Club. (WARNING! SPOILERS AHEAD!) He returns to the club at the last possible moment and wins the bet. His wife-to-be, Princess Aouda, appears in the doorway and Fogg tells her not to come in, saying it could mean the end of the British Empire. Suddenly, Passepartout opens the windows and enters. A painting falls to the ground. "This is the end," says the Governor of the Bank of England.

Todd began the movie with Edward R. Murrow delivering a monotonal monologue on Jules Verne and technology, and then went right into the story, with no opening titles. The titles came at the end of the film in a six-minute animated mini-movie designed by Saul Bass and executed by Shamus Culhane Productions that parodied the events of the film and caricatured the characters. Most sources credit Bass with the idea, but Mike Todd's son ascribes it to Todd. In any case, it got Todd out of a jam.

Never one to do anything small, he had cast many small and even non-speaking roles with huge movie stars–knights, Oscar-winners, legendary icons–and paid most of them scale, making the gig more alluring by calling the bit parts "cameos", thus coining that now-familiar term. He said a cameo was a "a gem carved in celluloid by a star." How to bill them all? This problem was solved by listing the actors' names more or less in order of their appearance. Audiences used to jumping up and leaving at the end of a film stayed to watch all the credits and even applauded. Author Brian Sibley says, "The limited animation technique used here in contrast to the full-blown Disney style was originally pioneered in the postwar era by studios such as UPA, home of Mister Magoo (qv)." Other films followed suit with similar sequences, many by Bass, creating a new opportunity for animators as the production of theatrical cartoons was dying. At $65,000, "the cost of a B picture," the titles were the most expensive ever made at the time. Mike Todd made millions on the movie and still beat Shamus Culhane out of $3000 New York State sales tax.

Peter Lorre had a cameo as a Japanese steward on an American ship. In the titles, we see a close-up of his face. A butterfly lands on his nose, causing him to cross his eyes. The camera pulls back, and his portrait is rendered in the Oriental style, complete with sword.

GIGGLE RATING: Looks, Five Giggles; Voice, N/A.

AVAILABILITY: On the DVD *Around the World in 80 Days* [1956] *Special Edition* (2004).

Boston Quackie (June 22, 1957)

Warner Bros. Directed by Robert McKimson. Written by Tedd Pierce. Cast: Mel Blanc, June Foray.

Boston Blackie was a jewel thief and a yegg in the pulps: "Enemy to those who make him an enemy, friend to those who have no friend." In the movies, he was turned into a detective, with a friendly adversary named Inspector Faraday.

In this parody, Boston Quackie (Daffy Duck), "Friend to those who need no friends, enemy to those who have no enemies," is a secret agent on vacation with his girlfriend, Mary, when Inspector Faraway (Porky Pig) asks him to deliver a briefcase to the consulate in West Slobovia. "Every spy in the country will try to steal it from you." A man in a green hat immediately steals it and gets away in a car. Quackie, Mary, and Faraway follow in Mary's car. The man in the green hat gets on a train at the station and so does Quackie. The man ties Quackie in a mailbag and drops him off the train, but then the man falls off and Mary gets the briefcase.

Quackie delivers the briefcase to His Excellency at the Embassy, a Peter Lorre sound-alike. It contains Acme House Instant Girl ("Add WATER and POUR"). The Consul reconstitutes himself a date for the Embassy Ball. "You know, there just might be a market for this."

GIGGLE RATING: Five Giggles.

AVAILABILITY: On the LaserDisc *Guffaw and Order, Looney Tunes Fight Crime* (1993?). Also on the DVD *Stars of Space Jam, Daffy Duck* (2018), but time-compressed. Caveat emptor.

Happy Go Loopy (March 2, 1961)

Hanna-Barbera Studios. Directed by Joseph Barbera, William Hanna. Written by Warren Foster (story). Cast: Daws Butler (Loopy), Hal Smith.

William Hanna and Joseph Barbera were hired by Harman and Ising at the MGM cartoon studio in 1939 within weeks of each other. They worked on several shorts in the Tom and Jerry series and the Droopy series. In 1957, MGM decided to close the cartoon studio and Hanna and Barbera failed to persuade MGM to do their proposed animated TV series. With the backing of live-action director George Sidney, they started their own studio, and Sidney got a distribution deal from Screen Gems, Columbia Pictures' TV subsidiary.

Daws Butler and Don Messick did many of the voices. Daws Butler was a prolific voice actor who also played Snooper and Blabber, Quick Draw McGraw, Yogi Bear (all qv), and a host of other characters in his career, which spanned over three decades. He was also well known for his imitations, including Groucho Marx and Peter Lorre. Don Messick was another distinguished voice actor whose credits include Toad in *Drak Pack* (1980) and Scooby-Doo (both qv).

Hanna-Barbera's first show was *The Ruff and Reddy Show* (1957), followed by *The Huckleberry Hound Show* (1958), about a dog with a Southern accent; *The Quick Draw McGraw Show* (1959) (qv), *The Flintstones* (1960) (qv), and *The Yogi Bear Show* (1961) (qv). Loopy de Loop was their only theatrical cartoon series, and it was distributed by Columbia.

Loopy De Loop is a French-Canadian wolf who goes around in a toque trying to do good deeds to show people that wolves are not bad. His name is a triple pun on "loop the loop" (a 360-degree back flip performed by stunt pilots), "Canis lupus" (the scientific name for the gray wolf), and "loopy" (crazy). Loopy sees a lady with a cat up a tree, so he gets a ladder to get the cat down. Unfortunately, a painter is standing on top of the ladder and he falls to the ground. The lady sees the wolf and runs away. The painter colors Loopy's face aquamarine.

Loopy comes upon a costume party. The cigar-chomping host in a bear suit mistakes him for his friend Charlie, and asks him to "do the Omaha routine." Loopy says, "I do not know, uh, what this Omaha routine is, and I am not one of those Hollywood wolves." The crowd guffaws. "But I will do the impressions of the wolf who goes to Hollywood." The crowd applauds. Loopy does Maurice Chevalier, and then his "friend, Peter [Lorre]."

"Thank you for calling me your friend. I don't make friends very easily. I don't know why." He giggles insanely.

He also does Ed Sullivan and Jimmy Durante. The crowd carries him around on their shoulders and sings "For He's a Jolly Good Fellow". Loopy wins "1st Prize for Best Costume". The host tries to remove Loopy's "mask", which, of course, doesn't come off. The host realizes he is an actual wolf and kicks him out.

"Well, that's show business," philosophizes Loopy. "Sometimes you are a hit, sometimes you get hit. But always, you carry on with a smile." Loopy smiles, revealing he is now missing a tooth.

GIGGLE RATING: Five Giggles. Butler performs the difficult task of playing a character playing Peter Lorre and pulls it off. Loopy turns away from the audience and turns back, like a 1950s impressionist, and he also resembles Lorre.

AVAILABILITY: On the DVD *Loopy De Loop, The Complete Collection* (2014).

Mad Monster Party? (September, 1967)

Rankin/Bass Productions, Videocraft Productions. Directed by Jules Bass, Kizo Nagashima. Written by Len Korobkin, Harvey Kurtzman, Forrest J. Ackerman, Arthur Rankin Jr. Produced by Arthur Rankin Jr., Joseph E. Levine, Larry Roemer. Cast: Boris Karloff (Baron Boris von Frankenstein), Allen Swift (Felix Flankin/Yetch/Dracula/The Invisible Man/Dr. Jekyll/Mr. Hyde/The Werewolf/Fang [The Monster]/Mailman/Mr. Cronkite/Captain/Chef Machiavelli/Ship's Mate), Gale Garnett (Francesca), Phyllis Diller (The Monster's Mate).

Filmed in Animagic, using stop-motion animation with 3-D puppets, this was the third and last theatrical release produced by Rankin/Bass with

Joseph E. Levine for Embassy Pictures, and the most popular. Jack Davis designed the characters, as he did for *The King Kong Show* (1966) (qv).

Baron Boris von Frankenstein lives on the Isle of Evil with his secretary, Francesca; Yetch, a Peter Lorre-esque zombie dressed in a white dinner jacket; Fang, Frankenstein's monster; and Fang's Mate. Boris develops a formula to destroy matter and invites to the Isle of Evil all the monsters: Dracula, The Invisible Man (who is fat and sounds like Sydney Greenstreet), Dr. Jekyll, Mr. Hyde, The Werewolf, The Mummy, The Creature (of the Black Lagoon), and The Hunchback of Notre Dame, along with his nephew, Felix Flankin, who sounds but does not look like Jimmy Stewart. He pointedly does not invite "It". When everyone assembles, he plans to announce that he is retiring and turning over the family business to his nephew.

Dr. Frankenstein tells his zombie servants he doesn't want anyone losing his head. Yetch loses his head and puts it on backward. "I'm so excited, Doctor. I haven't seen all of our old friends in years." He bumps into Francesca. "You beautiful, adorable, lovable creature. How much I've wanted to touch you." Francesca gives him a jujitsu flip. "She noticed me for the first time."

Later, Yetch sees Francesca and says, "It's me, your Don Juan." Francesca says, "I Don Juan to look at you," and hits him on the head. Yetch says, "I love your eyes, I love your chin/I love the shape they put you in/And when I get to feel your touch/I ache for you so very much." Yetch enters the kitchen of Chef Machiavelli. "Hey Yetch, whaddya doin' in my kitchen? You-a no good snake in-a grass, you dirty swine, you ugly rat!" Yetch says, "Thank you for those kind words. I hope I can live up to them."

Francesca conspires with Dracula to eliminate Felix so she can inherit the business. Dracula tries to double-cross her by conspiring with Fang and Fang's Mate to eliminate Francesca. Francesca is rescued by Felix and they fall in love and try to get off the island together. "It", who looks like Kong, grabs all the monsters. Dr. Frankenstein destroys them all and himself with his antimatter formula and Felix and Francesca get away. Francesca reveals she is not human, she is a creation of Dr. Frankenstein. Felix, borrowing Joe E. Brown's final line from *Some Like It Hot* (1959), says, "Nobody's perfect," in a robotic voice that skips.

FUN FACT: Dell put out a comic book version of the movie.

GIGGLE RATING: Five Giggles. Allen Swift would go on to reprise many of these voices, but not Yetch, in the prequel *The Mad, Mad, Mad Monsters* (1972). There, the Baron's assistant is named Igor, but he is not a Peter Lorre-wannabe.

AVAILABILITY: Anchor Bay released a DVD on August 19, 2003, then re-released it on August 23, 2005 with additional features. On September 8, 2009, it was released as a Special Edition DVD by Lionsgate. It was released on Blu-ray on September 4, 2012.

Aladdin (November 25, 1992)

Walt Disney Pictures. Directed by Ron Clements, John Musker. Writing Credits: Ron Clements & John Musker and Ted Elliott & Terry Rossio (screen-play), Burny Mattinson and Roger Allers & Daan Jippes & Kevin Harkey & Sue C. Nichols (as Sue Nichols) & Francis Glebas & Darrell Rooney & Larry Leker & James Fujii & Kirk Hanson & Kevin Lima & Rebecca Rees & David S. Smith & Chris Sanders & Brian Pimental & Patrick A. Ventura (story). Produced by Ron Clements. Music by Alan Menken. Cast: Scott Weinger (Aladdin), Robin Williams (Genie/Peddler), Linda Larkin (Jasmine), Jonathan Freeman (Jafar), Frank Welker (Abu/Cave of Wonders/Rajah), Gilbert Gottfried (Iago), Douglas Seale (Sultan), Charles Adler (Gazeem/Melon Merchant/Nut Merchant) (as Charlie Adler), Jack Angel (Additional Voices), Corey Burton (Prince Achmed/Necklace Merchant), Philip L. Clarke (Additional Voices) (as Philip Clarke), Jim Cummings (Razoul/Farouk).

"One of my favorite actors of all time, although he doesn't necessarily play villains, is Peter Lorre," said Robin Williams. "I once asked him 'Mr. Lorre, what is it like to act?' and he says [Peter Lorre impression], 'I don't act, I just make faces.' But him with those eyes, him in *M* [1931], oh God, that's one of the greatest portrayals ever."

In the late seventies, on an HBO comedy special, Williams walks up to a young lady while whistling "In the Hall of the Mountain King". Imitating Lorre, he asks her, "You don't find me unattractive, do you?"

Aladdin, trapped in a dark pit, rubs a lamp and the Genie appears and grants him three wishes. "Any three wishes I want, right?" asks Aladdin. The Genie morphs into William F. Buckley Jr.: "Almost. There are a few provisos, a couple of quid pro quos." Rule number one, he can't kill anybody; rule number two, he can't make anybody fall in love with anybody else; and rule number three (here he morphs into Peter Lorre), "I can't bring people back from the dead. It's not a pretty picture. I DON'T LIKE DOING IT!"

Aladdin wishes for the Genie to make him a Prince so he can court the lovely Princess Jasmine, who must be wed in three days. Meanwhile, the Royal Vizier, Jafar, is scheming to marry Jasmine himself and has Aladdin dropped off a cliff into the water. He is rescued by the Genie and returns to the palace to confront Jafar. Jafar is arrested, but escapes.

He gets his parrot, Iago, to steal the lamp for him and his first wish is to be made Sultan and he disrupts the Sultan's announcement of the wedding of Aladdin and Jasmine. His second wish is to be made a sorcerer and he sends Aladdin to "the ends of the earth." Aladdin gets back to Agrabah on his magic carpet. He tricks Jafar into wishing to become a genie and traps him in his own lamp. Aladdin uses his last wish to free the Genie. Aladdin and Jasmine get engaged.

In addition to Lorre and Buckley, Williams impersonates Arnold Schwarzenegger, Ed Sullivan, Señor Wences, Robert De Niro, Carol Channing, Arsenio Hall, Walter Brennan, Mary Hart, Ethel Merman, Rodney Dangerfield, Jack Nicholson, and Groucho Marx.

FUN FACTS: The casting of Williams marked the beginning of the transition in animation from trained voice actors to celebrities.

Frequent Peter Lorre imitators Gilbert Gottfried, Frank Welker, Corey Burton, and Jim Cummings are in the cast.

GIGGLE RATING: Five Giggles. Williams did not do the first sequel, but he reprised the role multiple times.

AVAILABILITY: On October 5, 2004, the film was rereleased onto VHS and for the first time released onto DVD, as part of Disney's Platinum Edition line. The DVD release featured retouched and cleaned-up animation, and a second bonus disc. The DVD went into moratorium in January

2008. A Blu-ray was released in a few select European countries in March 2013. The Belgian edition was a one-disc version with its extras ported over from the Platinum Edition DVD. The same disc was released in the United Kingdom on April 14, 2013. Walt Disney Studios Home Entertainment released the film on a Diamond Edition Blu-ray on October 13, 2015. The film was released on Digital HD on September 29, 2015.

Carrotblanca (August 25, 1995)

Warner Bros. Directed by Douglas McCarthy. Writing Credits: Tim Cahill (story) (as Timothy Cahill) & Julie McNally Cahill (story) (as Julie McNally). Music by Richard Stone. Produced by Tim Cahill (as Timothy Cahill). Cast (in credits order): Joe Alaskey (Sylvester/Daffy Duck), Bob Bergen (Tweety as Usmarte), Greg Burson (Bugs Bunny/Pepe Le Pew as Louie/ Foghorn Leghorn as Radio Dispatcher), Maurice LaMarche (Yosemite Sam as General Pandemonium), Tress MacNeille (Penelope as Kitty).

This is the only Looney Tunes short produced by the writing team of *Animaniacs* (1993) and the Warner Bros. Feature Animation division. It was included on the special edition DVD as well as the HD DVD and Blu-ray of *Casablanca* (1942), which it pays homage to and parodies. Looney Tunes regulars, including frequent Peter Lorre imitators Maurice LaMarche and Joe Alaskey, play characters from the film, with varying results.

A German scientist has been knocked unconscious by a large frying pan, according to Radio Dispatcher Foghorn Leghorn, and important documents have been stolen. General Pandemonium (Yosemite Sam) gets the message and hurries by car to Carrotblanca, where the "Eleanor Roosevelt All-Girl Revue" is playing.

Usmarte (Tweety Bird parodying Peter Lorre as Ugarte) flies into Rick's Café Au Lait Americain. The joint is hopping, with Gossamer and others enjoying Daffy's rendition of "Knock on Wood" wherein he hits himself on the head with a mallet. Daffy is parodying Dooley Wilson as Sam. Usmarte asks Bugs (parodying Humphrey Bogart as Rick) to hide a document. "Dat wouldn't happen to be the document stolen from dat poor German sucka, now would it?" asks Bugs. "I'm sure I wouldn't know," says Tweety, and giggles insanely. Bugs isn't interested until he hears there's a dame involved.

Just then, Kitty (Penelope parodying Ingrid Bergman as Ilsa) walks in with her husband, Laszlo (Sylvester parodying Paul Henreid as Victor). "I tought I taw two putty tats," says Tweety, and giggles insanely. Louie (Pepe Le Pew parodying Claude Rains as Captain Renault) tries to make love to Kitty, but is scratched and thrown up against the wall by her.

At that moment, General Pandemonium comes through the door of the club in his car. "I got word you have that important document, ya dinner jacket-wearin' varmint!" "Where'd ya hear dat?" asks Bugs. "Let's just say a little birdie told me," replies General Pandemonium, who pulls Tweety out of his jacket. "You despise me, don't you?" asks Tweety. Bugs throws a paper through the door and the General runs to fetch it like a dog. Bugs slams the door behind him.

Laszlo goes away to get some "rafraîchissement" and Kitty asks Daffy, "Please play it for me." "I hope you don't mean that 'Knock On Wood' song. I've got a splitting headache," he says. "You know, my favorite song," says Kitty. Sam plays one note on the piano, and Bugs appears. "I tought I told you nevah to play that song."

"You think I wanted to play that?" asks Daffy, and jumps onto Kitty's table, pointing. "SHE MADE ME DO IT! IT WAS HER, HER, HER!" Bugs sees Kitty and has a flashback.

Bugs and Kitty drive through the country, his arm around her; Bugs and Kitty dance at The Coconut Grove (sadly, not The CooCoo Nut Grove); Bugs and Kitty toast at a romantic candlelit dinner. Then Bugs waits for her at the train station. Daffy delivers a letter from Kitty saying, "Dear Bugs, I cannot go with you. We're different, you and I. Remember, we'll always have Pongo Pongo, Helsinki, Pismo Beach, and Timbuktu. Love, Kitty".

Bugs hits the carrot juice hard. "Of all de juice joints in all de towns in all de countries in all de woild, she picks dis one." Kitty walks in and Daffy tells her, "Hit the road, sister." Kitty scratches him and kicks him out the door. She asks Bugs for help. General Pandemonium thinks Laszlo knows something about the stolen document and has arrested him. "I stick my cottontail out for no one," says Bugs. Kitty starts to cry. Bugs looks at the camera and turns into a lollipop labeled "SUCKER."

At Le Police, General Pandemonium is interrogating Laszlo. Bugs comes in and starts interrogating General Pandemonium, playing an Irish cop, a little boy accuser, the boy's mother, and a judge. General Pandemonium pleads guilty and locks himself in a prison cell with a large, apparently gay Black man. Bugs says, "Mr. Laszlo's got a plane to catch."

At the airport, Bugs gives Laszlo the document. It is a technical drawing of Groucho glasses. "This is gonna make me rich!" says Laszlo. He cuts short Bugs' speech to Kitty and yanks her onto the plane.

Onboard, Laszlo is admiring his Groucho glasses in the mirror when Louie approaches with the drinks cart. "Coffee, tea–or moi?" he says and tries to kiss her. Kitty dives out of the plane. Since she is a cat, she lands on her feet, and since this is a cartoon, she lands next to Bugs. They embrace, and Kitty's parachute pops open, covering them. "Here's lookin' for you, kid."

GIGGLE RATING: Three Giggles. Usmarte sounds sometimes more like Lorre, sometimes more like Tweety, instead of playing Tweety as Lorre. Bob Bergen's other credits include *Looney Tunes: Back in Action* (2003) and *Duck Dodgers* (2003) (both qv).

AVAILABILITY: On the DVD *The Essential Bugs Bunny* (2010). On DVD and Blu-ray: *Casablanca* [1942] *70th Anniversary Special Edition* (2003).

Looney Tunes: Back in Action (November 14, 2003)

Warner Bros. Directed by Joe Dante. Written by Larry Doyle. Produced by Bernie Goldmann, Joel Simon, Paula Weinstein. Music by Jerry Goldsmith. Cast: Brendan Fraser (DJ Drake/Himself/Voice of Tasmanian Devil and She-Devil), Jenna Elfman (Kate Houghton), Steve Martin (Mr. Chairman), Timothy Dalton (Damien Drake), Joe Alaskey (Bugs Bunny/Daffy Duck/Beaky Buzzard/Sylvester/Mama Bear), Jeff Bennett (Yosemite Sam/Foghorn Leghorn/Nasty Canasta) (as Jeff Glenn Bennett), Billy West (Elmer Fudd/Peter Lorre), Eric Goldberg (Tweety Bird/Marvin the Martian/Speedy Gonzalez), Bruce Lanoil (Pepe Le Pew), June Foray (Granny), Bob Bergen (Porky Pig), Casey Kasem (Shaggy), Frank Welker (Scooby-Doo), Danny Chambers (Cottontail Smith), Stan Freberg (Baby Bear), Will Ryan (Papa Bear), Danny Mann (Robo Dog & Spy Car), Mel Blanc (Gremlin Car) (archive footage).

Technically the last traditionally animated Warner Brothers film, although it also contains computer animation and live action.

Studio executive Kate Houghton (Jenna Elfman) fires Daffy Duck and tells security guard DJ Drake (Brendan Fraser) to escort him off the Warner Bros. lot. Daffy escapes and sets off a series of unfortunate events that result in the destruction of the Warner Bros. water tower and Houghton's car, so Houghton fires DJ.

At home, DJ realizes his movie star father, Damien, is actually a super-secret agent who has been kidnapped by the Acme Corporation's Chairman (Steve Martin), and DJ goes off to rescue Damien. Daffy tags along. Kate and Bugs follow to try to get Daffy to come back.

Peter Lorre has a machine that makes Damien slap himself in his own face. Mr. Chairman activates it. Lorre giggles insanely. "Give him a good zap once in awhile," he says. "My pleasure," answers Lorre.

DJ rescues Damien, vanquishes Mr. Chairman, and gets the girl, and all live happily ever after, except the movie's failure caused Warner Bros. to hold back the release of new completed Looney Tunes shorts and to cancel those in production.

FUN FACT: The cast includes Peter Lorre imitators Mel Blanc, Stan Freberg, Joe Alaskey, Frank Welker, Bob Bergen, and Casey Kasem.

GIGGLE RATING: Five Giggles. An update of the classic Warner Bros. image of Dr. Lorre and a good imitation of him by Billy West. Oddly enough, when John Kricfalusi stopped playing the Lorre-inspired Ren on *The Ren & Stimpy Show* (1993) (qv), West dropped the Lorre imitation and played Ren differently. Billy West is known for playing classic characters like Bugs and Elmer, but he prefers to create voices for new characters.

AVAILABILITY: Warner Home Video released the film on VHS and DVD on March 2, 2004. It was rereleased on DVD in separate widescreen and full screen editions on September 7, 2010. It was also released on Blu-ray with bonus features on December 2, 2014. A double DVD and Blu-ray release was released on June 7, 2016.

Corpse Bride (September 23, 2005)

Warner Bros. Pictures, Tim Burton Productions, Laika Entertainment, Patalex Productions, Will Vinton Studios. Directed by Michael Johnson, Tim Burton (Co-Directors). Written by John August, Caroline Thompson, Pamela Pettler. Produced by Tim Burton, Allison Abbate. Executive Producers: Jeffrey Auerbach, Joe Ranft. Cast: Johnny Depp (Victor Van Dort), Helena Bonham Carter (Emily), Emily Watson (Victoria Everglot), Tracey Ullman (Nell Van Dort/Hildegarde), Paul Whitehouse (William Van Dort/Mayhew/Paul), Joanna Lumley (Maudeline Everglot), Albert Finney (Finnis Everglot), Richard E. Grant (Barkis Bittern), Christopher Lee (Pastor Galswells), Michael Gough (Elder Gutknecht), Jane Horrocks (Black Widow Spider/Mrs. Plum), Enn Reitel (Maggot/Town Crier).

A British-American stop-motion animated musical fantasy film set in late-Victorian England. William Van Dort, a nouveau riche fishmonger; Nell, his obese wife; and Victor, their son, get into a carriage driven by the consumptive Mayhew to Victor's wedding rehearsal. It is a marriage of convenience to Victoria Everglot. Victoria's parents, Finnis and Maudeline, are land-rich but cash-poor and see this union as their only way out of poverty. Victor and Victoria have never met before, but when they do, by accident, it is clear they are soul mates.

The rehearsal is crashed by Lord Barkis, whom no one recalls actually inviting. The nervous Victor turns the rehearsal into a disaster, accidentally setting his future mother-in-law's dress on fire. The Pastor sends Victor away until he learns his vows.

Victor flees to the woods, where he practices. He puts the ring on what he thinks is a tree root and recites his vows. The root runs out to be the finger of Emily, the corpse bride, who rises from her grave thinking they are now married and brings him to the underworld for their wedding feast. A maggot, who looks and sounds like Peter Lorre, says, "Wedding feast? I'm salivating." It is explained in song that Emily was to elope with the man of her dreams, who murdered her, took her riches, and buried her. Victor flees again, and meets a Black Widow Spider.

The Town Crier announces that Victor was seen with a "mystery woman." The Van Dorts ask they be given until dawn to find him.

Meanwhile, Emily is looking for Victor. "If you ask me," says Maggot, "your boyfriend is kinda jumpy." He promises to "keep an eye out for him," pushing out Emily's eyeball. "There he goes! There he goes! He's getting away! Quick, quick!"

Emily finally catches Victor and he tricks her into taking him "upstairs" to meet his parents. Elder Gutknecht of the Land of the Dead sends them there using a Ukrainian haunting spell, and says when they want to come back, they must say, "Hopscotch." Victor actually goes to Victoria's house and tells Emily to wait outside. "This is the voice of your conscience," says Maggot. "Listen to what I say. I have a bad feeling about that boy." "I'm sure he has a perfectly good reason for waiting so long," says Emily. "Why don't you go ask him?" says Maggot.

Victor reunites with Victoria, but Emily surprises them and says, "Hopscotch," sending them back to the underworld. Maggot and Black Widow Spider try to cheer up Emily by singing her a song.

Upstairs, Lord Barkis tells the Everglots that he was once betrothed, but his bride died. The Everglots decide to marry Victoria to him and tell their maid, Hildegard, to make Victoria presentable. Meanwhile, Barkis plots to murder Victoria after the wedding. As the Van Dorts take their carriage home, Mayhew dies. He runs into Victor in the underworld and fills him in on what's going on upstairs.

Elder Gutknecht tells Emily there is a complication with her marriage. "Let me tell her. Please let me tell her," says Maggot, who giggles insanely. Her marriage is invalid because she is already dead. "There must be something you can do," she says. "We have to keell him," says Maggot, and giggles insanely. Victor has to repeat his vows in the land of the living and drink from the Wine of Ages, which will stop his heart forever. Victor agrees. Even Maggot cries at the news. Black Widow Spider picks him up, and off they go, with all the corpses, to the wedding.

The dead wedding party crashes the live one. "Excuse me, you don't know me," says Maggot, "but I used to live in your dead mother." Lord Barkis tells Victoria they must take her dowry and leave. Victoria says she has no dowry and walks out. The dead make their way to the church, where Emily sees Victoria and stops Victor from drinking the Wine of Ages. "I was a bride. My dreams were taken from me. Well, now, now I've stolen them from someone else." Victor, Victoria, and Emily join hands.

Barkis enters and says, "She's still my wife!" Emily recognizes Barkis as the man who killed her. Barkis pulls a sword; Victor, a fork; and they duel. Emily gets the sword and tells Barkis to get out. He toasts her with the Wine of Ages. "Let me at him," says Maggot, who is stopped by Elder Gutknecht. "We must abide by their rules. We are amongst the living." Barkis drinks the Wine of Ages and dies. "Not any more," says Maggot.

Emily gives Victor back his ring. "You set me free. Now I can do the same for you." She tosses her bouquet, which is first caught by Hildegard. Maggot, on Hildegard's shoulder, giggles insanely, causing her to throw the bouquet, which is caught by Victoria. Emily turns into butterflies and lives happily ever after. Or something.

GIGGLE RATING: Five Giggles. "He's inspired by Peter Lorre–an homage to the old horror films," explains co-director Mike Johnson. "He's kind of a twisted Jiminy Cricket-type voice of wisdom; when she's troubled, he pops out of her eye socket and offers some advice." Enn Reitel's credits include *Family Guy* (1998) (qv).

AVAILABILITY: The film was released on DVD and HD DVD on January 16, 2006; and on Blu-ray September 26, 2006.

Frankenweenie (October 5, 2012)

Walt Disney Pictures. Directed by Tim Burton. Written by John August. Based on the Original Short Written by Lenny Ripps and Tim Burton. Produced by Tim Burton, Allison Abbate, Don Hahn. Cast: Charlie Tahan (Victor Frankenstein), Winona Ryder (Elsa van Helsing), Catherine O'Hara (Mrs. Frankenstein/Weird Girl/Gym Teacher), Martin Short (Mr. Frankenstein/Nassor/Mr. Bergermeister), Martin Landau (Mr. Rzykruski), Robert Capron (Bob), Atticus Shaffer (Edgar), James Hiroyuki Liao (Toshiaki), Conchata Ferrell (Bob's Mom), Tom Kenny (Fire Chief/Soldier/Townsfolk).

A black and white 3-D stop-motion animated fantasy comedy horror film, a remake of Tim Burton's 1984 live-action short of the same name, and a parody of and homage to *Frankenstein* (1931).

Victor Frankenstein is a student in New Holland who makes films with his dog, Sparky, and wants to enter the science fair. "You'll be my partner, right Victor? You have to have a partner for the science fair," his classmate, Edgar 'E' Gore, a hunchbacked young Peter Lorre, asks. "We could make a death ray." Victor points out that the science fair prohibits death rays. "Who else will be your partner? You don't have friends, and neither do I." Victor says he likes to work alone.

Mr. Frankenstein, Victor's dad, will only let him do the science fair if he plays baseball. In his first game, Victor hits a home run, but Sparky chases the ball and is hit and killed by a car. The family buries Sparky in the pet cemetery.

Mr. Rzykruski, Victor's science teacher, shows how a dead frog can be stimulated with electricity. Victor digs up Sparky and reanimates him. Sparky gets out of his attic hiding place and Edgar sees him. "I know!" he tells Victor. "Your dog is alive!" and he giggles insanely. "You did it, you did it! . . . Show and tell, Victor. You show, and I won't tell."

Edgar buys a dead fish from the pet store and he and Victor reanimate it. Edgar promises not to tell, but he crosses his fingers. He ends up telling classmates Nassor, who looks like Frankenstein's monster; Toshiaki, Bob, and Weird Girl. They break into Victor's house while Victor and his parents are searching for Sparky, who has escaped. "It has something to do with the lightning," says Edgar. "I don't really understand it."

Weird Girl tries to reanimate a dead bat, which fuses with her live cat into a hideous hybrid monster. The batcat and Sparky end up fighting in a windmill, which is set on fire and kills them. The townspeople revive Sparky with their car batteries.

GIGGLE RATING: Five Giggles. Atticus Shaffer was born in 1998, and began his acting career in 2006.

AVAILABILITY: The film was released on DVD, Blu-ray, and Blu-ray 3D on January 8, 2013.

Untitled Ren & Stimpy Short

Paramount Animation, Nickelodeon Movies, Spümcø. Directed by John Kricfalusi. Written by Wendell Morris. Produced by Bruce Knapp. Cast: Eric Bauza (Stimpy), Chris Edgerly (Ren), Adrienne Alexander, Nancy Cartwright, Ben Giroux.

This short was to be a test for a Ren & Stimpy reboot in the form of a new TV series or a theatrical film. It has been canceled.

FUN FACT: On the episode "The Burns Cage" of *The Simpsons* (1989), Nancy Cartwright played Ralph Wiggum as Peter Lorre as Ugarte.

GIGGLE RATING: N/A. Chris Edgerly previously played Ren in *Nicktoons MLB* (2011), and his other credits include *Duck Dodgers* (2003), *Harvey Birdman: Attorney at Law* (2000), and *The Simpsons* (1989) (all qv).

AVAILABILITY: An animatic is online.

Chapter 2:
Television Lorre Tunes

The Quick Draw McGraw Show [Snooper and Blabber] (1959)
Hanna-Barbera Studios. Directed and Produced by Joseph Barbera, William Hanna. Written by Michael Maltese (story). Cast: Daws Butler (Snooper/Blabber/Evil Scientist), Jean Vander Pyl (Mrs. Scientist).

Quick Draw McGraw was an anthropomorphic horse (played by Daws Butler) who usually appeared as a sheriff. Snooper and Blabber was another segment on *The Quick Draw McGraw Show* (1959), along with the segment Augie Doggie and Doggie Daddy, about son and father dachshunds. Super Snooper, a cat, runs the Super Snooper Detective Agency. Blabbermouse is his loyal apprentice. Perennially hard-up for money, they will take most any job, even if it isn't in the normal purview of a private dick. Daws Butler played Snooper as an imitation of Ed Gardner's character Archie from *Duffy's Tavern* (1941).

Season 1
Episode 5 (October 27, 1959)
"Big Diaper Caper"
Snooper eagerly accepts a job to babysit a child for $1000. He and Blab arrive at the address, a scary mansion, with the name "Mr. & Mrs. Evil Scientist" on the mailbox. Snooper rings the bell, a button nose of a skull and crossbones. The bell makes a terrifying noise. Inside are Mr. and Mrs. Scientist. They are green-skinned and dressed in black. She is tall and slender, smokes a cigarette in a holder, and sounds somewhat like Tallulah Bankhead. He is short and squat and his teeth are uneven. He talks like

31

Peter Lorre and has an insane giggle. They are going to see a movie, Rock Crusher in *Boy Meets Ghoul.*

"You shouldn't have any trouble with [Junior]," says Mrs. Scientist. Snooper and Blabber go into the nursery to check Junior out. He is sound asleep. On their way out, Snooper sees lab glassware full of Hyde Bitters and Jekyll Juice.

Junior, who mostly just says, "Wop wop wop wop wop," saws his way out of the crib, mixes the two potions together and drinks it. The cocktail turns him into a huge monster. He sneaks up on Snooper and Blabber, who are watching TV, snatches Blabber, and puts him into the fishbowl, where Snooper finds him.

The monster puts his head through the back of the TV and shows up on the screen in black and white. This scares Blabber, who jumps into the fishbowl.

Blabber goes to check on Junior, who is not in his crib. Blabber sees the huge monster and tells Snooper. Meanwhile, the monster changes back to a baby. Snooper tries to put him in his crib, but he turns into a huge monster again. Snooper runs away with the monster in pursuit, but the monster turns back into a baby. "I oughta take you over me knee," says Snooper. Junior morphs into a huge monster again and chases them into another room, and a crocodile chases them back out. They duck into another room and a five-legged "octopus" chases them out. They run out the door just as the Scientists are walking in. "Junior, how many times have I told you never to bring your pets in the living room?" she asks. "No wonder we can't keep a babysitter." "But remember, darling," says Mr. Scientist, who now has a row of sharp teeth, "we've never paid one yet," and giggles insanely.

FUN FACT: Frequent Lorre Tune writer Michael Maltese left Warner Bros. circa 1958 and was replaced by John W. Dunn.

Episode 19 (February 2, 1960)
"Snap Happy Saps"

Snooper is offered "five grand thousand" to take baby pictures. He and Blabber pull up to the address, the corner of Banshee Boulevard and Scary Square. Blabber is scared, but Snooper rationalizes, "What's to be scared? Where there's a cuddly baby, there's bound to be peace and tranquilizers."

The mailbox now reads "Mr. & Mrs. Evil J. Scientist". This minor change is enough to fool Snooper and Blabber, who never seem to make the connection to the episode "The Big Diaper Caper". This house has a normal doorbell. Mr. Scientist and his family have pale skin, and his teeth are crooked, but he sounds like the same guy. Mrs. Scientist looks much more glamorous in this episode. Junior is taking his afternoon nap, but he bangs on the barred door to signify he's ready to get up. Junior imitates Blabber, and then a puppy dog, ending by biting Snooper on the leg.

While Snooper sets up the camera, Blabber follows Junior into his soda fountain. Junior makes himself a malted with Wolf Man Extract, and turns into a wolf. Mr. Scientist makes Junior turn himself back.

Blabber tells Junior to get his pet so they can be photographed together.

The pet is a crocodile, who eats Blab. Snoop hits the croc with a rolled up newspaper, and he spits out Blab, but chases Snoop around the house. Junior takes pictures of Snoop, the croc, Blab, and Mr. and Mrs. Evil. At the end of the session, Junior gives Snoop and Blab malteds which turn them into werewolves for a month. Snoop decides to specialize in wolf disguises in the meantime.

Season 2
Episode 13 (December 3, 1960)
"Surprised Party"

Snooper is offered $50,000 to guard a birthday party. The mailbox reads "Mr. & Mrs. J. Evil Scientists", which is enough to throw them off the scent once more. The doorbell is again the nose of a skull and crossbones, and emits a horrible scream. Our old friend Mr. Scientist answers the door. His skin is still pale but his teeth are now sharp again. When he says with an insane giggle that he shrinks heads, Blab tries to run away, but is stopped by Snoop. Mrs. Scientist has green skin again, and in the next shot, so does Mr. Scientist. "We're going to a scary movie. It's called *Ben-Horror*," a reference to the remake of *Ben-Hur* (1959). Snooper asks about other guests, and is told there are none. He balks, but Mrs. Scientist offers to pay him $60,000.

Junior emerges from a trap door in his play penitentiary, followed by a crocodile, which he clubs on the noggin. Snoop toots a squawker blowout into Junior's face, and Junior blows one into his. It has a gun on the end, which goes off. In the confusion, Junior feeds the cake to the crocodile, which grabs Snoop by the tail. "Run for your life, Blab!" he says. When Blab mentions the $60,000, Snoop pauses and decides to stay.

Junior opens one of his presents, a "DO IT YOURSELF MONSTER KIT". Snoop figures that will keep Junior busy until his folks come home, but in no time, Junior has assembled a killer robot. Snoop and Blab flee, passing Mr. and Mrs. Scientist. "They didn't even wait for their $60,000 fee," says Mrs. Scientist.

"Too bad," says Mr. Scientist. "I wanted to tell them what a great movie *Ben-Horror* was. Especially the chariot race. What a pileup!" An untrue rumor, which persists to this day, holds that a stuntman was killed in the making of *Ben-Hur* (1959).

Season 3
Episode 6 (October 20, 1961)
"Chilly Chiller"

The opening graphics, with the tic-tac-toe game and the word "CHILLER", parodies the credits of the contemporaneous Boris Karloff horror anthology series *Thriller* (1960). Snooper (and sometimes Blabber) narrate the program as Karloff did.

A Ghost (uncredited, sounds like Bill Thompson as Wally Wimple but may be Don Messick imitating Thompson) calls Snoop and asks him to come to Creepy Mountain House right away. Snoop says he doesn't sound like he needs help, so the Ghost yells, "HEEEEELLLLLP!"

Snoop and Blab go to Creepy Mountain House, and are met by the Ghost outside. He has hired them to get rid of some unwanted tenants who have scared him out of his haunted house.

Inside, Mrs. Scientist knits a spider web sweater for Junior and Mr. Scientist relaxes with a Gruesome Comics book. Their appearance is similar to that in the last cartoon. The "door chime", an eerie scream, sounds, and Mr. Scientist goes to answer. "Who is it, darling?" asks Mrs. Scientist. "Just some gentlemen who insist we move out," says Mr. Scientist, who giggles insanely. "We're not moving, and that's that," Mrs. Scientist says to Snoop and Blab. "Now run along."

Snoop and Blab decide to start by moving the furniture out, beginning with Junior's crib, which still contains Junior, who presses a button which electrocutes Snoop. While Snoop and Blab are rolling up the rug, Junior activates a trap door, and Snoop falls through. "Where's Snoop?" asks Blab. Junior points down the cellar stairs. Snoop appears, fighting off another "octopus." We can't see all of his legs, but he has at least four.

Junior mixes a potion and feeds it to a mosquito, who grows to the size of a VW Beetle. Snoop fends him off with a sword before ducking into a room and closing the door. The mosquito's proboscis pierces the door, and Blab bends it with a hammer so the mosquito can't escape.

Junior is watching *The Wolf Monster Program* on TV as Snoop and Blab try to remove the TV. Junior takes off the screen and releases the Wolf Monster, who chases Snoop and Blab through the house until Mr. Scientist, unable to get any reading done, tells Junior to go to his room and take the Wolf Monster.

Outside, the Ghost says, "What'll I do now? I'll be a homeless ghost." Snoop tries to sell his life story to TV and hires the Ghost to ghostwrite it.

FUN FACT: Unusually for supporting characters, the Scientists had their own comic book, which came out around Halloween every year from 1963-66.

GIGGLE RATING: Five Giggles.

AVAILABILITY: "Chilly Chiller" is available on the DVD *Saturday Morning Cartoons, 1960s Volume 2* (2009).

Rocky and His Friends (1959)

Jay Ward Productions. Directed by Bill Hurtz, Ted Parmelee, Gerry Ray, Gerard Baldwin, Jim Hiltz, Rudy Zamora, Dun Roman. Written by Bill Scott. Produced by Jay Ward, Bill Scott. Cast: Bill Scott (Bullwinkle J. Moose/Mr. Big/Fearless Leader/Gidney), June Foray (Rocket J. Squirrel/Natasha Fatale), Paul Frees (Boris Badenov/Peter Peachfuzz/Cloyd), William Conrad (General/Narrator).

The second all-new cartoon show to air on network television. The show was broadcast under the titles of *Rocky and His Friends* from 1959 to 1961, *The Bullwinkle Show* from 1961 to 1964, and *The Rocky and Bullwinkle Show* (or *The Adventures of Rocky and Bullwinkle* or *The Adventures of Bullwinkle and Rocky*) in syndication. Bullwinkle J. Moose and Rocket J. Squirrel of

Frostbite Falls, Minnesota, "Pop. 48", tangle with Pottsylvanian spies Boris Badenov and Natasha Fatale. Bill Scott played Bullwinkle (an imitation of Red Skelton's prizefighter character, Willie Lump-Lump), Moon Man Gidney, and also the Peter Lorre-esque Mr. Big. Scott had a career as a writer and voiceover artist that spanned five decades, and he previously voiced Peter Lorre on *The Watts Gnu Show* (1959), which used puppets. He also was a writer on *Time for Beany* (1949) (qv) and General Mills commercials. Paul Frees played Peter Peachfuzz (an Ed Wynn sound-alike), Moon Man Cloyd, and Boris. The series had limited animation, even for TV in its time, and was the first show to farm out the drawing to another country, in this case, Mexico. What it lacked in production values it made up in smart, punny writing with topical references. It was sometimes called a radio show with pictures. Characters frequently spoke with the narrator and otherwise broke the fourth wall. The Adventures of Rocky and Bullwinkle was a serialized story. Each episode would contain two installments (which were called "episodes" as well). The other three segments would rotate among Dudley Do-Right, Fractured Fairy Tales, Peabody's Improbable History, and others. Daws Butler sometimes appeared on Fractured Fairy Tales.

Season 2
"Upsidaisium" (Omnibus title for the serial)
Episode 1 (September 11, 1960)
"Upsidaisium"/"Big Bomb at Frostbite Falls or The Exploding Metropolis"

Episode 2 (September 18, 1960),
"The Road to Ruin or Mine Over Matter"/"Two Flying Ghosts or High Spirits"

Episode 3 (September 25, 1960),
"Crash Drive or Oedipus Wrecks"/"Fender Benders or The Asphalt Bungle"

Episode 4 (October 2, 1960)
"Burning Sands or The Hot Foot"/"Death in the Desert or A Place in the Sun"

Episode 5 (October 9, 1960)

"The Boy Bounders or Plane Punchy"/"A Peek at the Peak or Your Climb Is My Climb"

Episode 6 (October 16, 1960)

"You've Got a Secret or Out of Sight, Out of Mine"/"Boss and the Blade or Sheik, Rattle and Roll"

Episode 7 (October 23, 1960)

"Sourdough Squirrel or Hardrock Rocky"/"A Creep at the Switch or Sudden Pacific"

Episode 8 (October 30, 1960)

"The Train on the Plain or The Overland Express"/"Danger in the Desert or Max Attacks"

Episode 9 (November 6, 1960),

"The Missing Mountain or Peek-a-Boo Peak"/"Go Down Mooses or The Fall Guy"

Episode 10 (November 13, 1960)

"Rocky and the Rock or Braver and Boulder"/"Mountain Mover or Boris Sneaks a Peak"

Episode 11 (November 20, 1960)

"Bullwinkle's Rise or This Goon for Higher"/"Boris Bites Back or A Rebel without a Pause"

Episode 12 (November 27, 1960)

"Bullwinkle at the Bottom or Mish-Mash Moose!"/"Double Trouble or The Moose Hangs High"

Episode 13 (December 4, 1960)

"Jet Jockey Rocky or The One Point Landing"/"Plots And Plans or Two Many Crooks"

Episode 14 (December 11, 1960)

"The Cliff Hanger or Taken for Granite"/"Supersonic Boom or The Old Mount's A-Moverin'"

Episode 15 (December 18, 1960)

"The Big Blast or A Many Splintered Thing"/"The Steal Hour or A Snitch In Time"

Episode 16 (December 25, 1960)

"Verse and Worse or Crime without Rhyme"/"Truckdrivers in the Sky or Follow the Fleet"

Episode 17 (January 1, 1961)

"The Squirrel Next Door or High Neighbor"/"The Spell Binders or Hex Marks the Spot"

Episode 18 (January 8, 1961)

"Battle of the Giants or It Takes Two to Tangle"/"Bye-Bye, Boris or Farewell, My Ugly"

From his late Uncle Dewlap, Bullwinkle inherits a claim to a mine on the slopes of Mt. Flatten. This news makes the postmaster faint. Indeed, as they make their way there, Boris tries to thwart them at every turn, either by killing them or conning them out of the deed.

Rocky and Bullwinkle end up stranded in the desert, but they are picked up in a helicopter by Captain Peter "Wrongway" Peachfuzz, who is the head of the secretive government agency G-2, and who tells them that their claim is for an upsidaisium mine. The chopper crashes, and Rocky and Bullwinkle wander the desert again. They get to the spot where Mt. Flatten should be, but isn't. Then they realize the mountain is up in the air. Upsidaisium makes things float.

Rocky sends a message to Peachfuzz via smoke signals, which are read by Indians, and soon the whole country is aware of upsidaisium. Boris, posing as a grizzled prospector, weasels his way into Rocky and Bullwinkle's good graces and goes with them to the mountain in the sky, which he tries to steal.

In Pottsylvania, Fearless Leader tells Boris that the job is too big for him to handle and he is sending out Mr. Big. Boris decides to double-cross Mr. Big: "What kind of schnook you take me for?" "I give up, Badenov," says Mr. Big, who is represented as a huge shadow. "What kind?"

Alone with Peter Peachfuzz, Rocky tells him the mountain is made of upsidaisium. He doesn't know Mr. Big is listening in, and Big tries to kill them with a boulder. They see his large shadow. Rocky decides to fly Mt. Flatten to Washington, DC. The mountain makes it and the upsidaisium is mined. Mr. Big comes up with a plan to steal it. It fails, and Rocky and Bullwinkle reveal Mr. Big to actually be a tiny man. He escapes toward the upsidaisium vault. "At last I have arrived at my goal. The world's entire supply of upsidaisium." Rocky tries to capture him, but Mr. Big takes him hostage and steals an ingot of upsidaisium. The ingot carries him off into the sky. "It's mine!"

"Metal-Munching Mice" (Omnibus title for the serial)
Episode 19 (January 15, 1961)

"Metal-Munching Mice"/"Bullwinkle Bites Back or Nothing but the Tooth"

Episode 20 (January 22, 1961)

"Knock on Wood or Bullwinkle Takes the Rap"/"A Knock for the Rock or The Lamp is Low"

Episode 21 (January 29, 1961)

"Window Pains or The Moosetrap"/"Doorway to Danger or Doom in the Room"

Episode 22 (February 5, 1961),

"Boris Makes His Move or The Miceman Cometh"/"Big Cheese Boris or I'd Rather Be Rat"

Episode 23 (February 12, 1961)

"The Space Rat or Of Mice and Menace"/"The Shot Heard Round the World or The First National Bang"

Episode 24 (February 19, 1961)

"Bucks For Boris or Rocky Pays the Piper"/"The Rat Pack Attacks or Sharrup You Mouse"

Episode 25 (February 26, 1961)

"Fright Flight or A Rocky to the Moon"/"Bullwinkle Bellows Again or Moonin' Low"

Episode 26 (March 5, 1961)

"Bongo Boris or The Hep Rat"/"The Spies of Life or When a Fella Needs a Fiend"

All the TV antennae in Frostbite Falls are missing, bitten off with teeth. Rocky and the sheriff set a trap: a giant TV antenna with instructions for eating. Bullwinkle has first watch. A giant metal mouse knocks out Bullwinkle and eats the antenna. TV antennae begin disappearing all over the country.

Rocky and Bullwinkle set a giant mousetrap outside an abandoned mansion and attempt to bait it with an iron dumbbell, but Bullwinkle drops it and launches Rocky into the building. A giant mouse attacks Rocky, but gets its tail caught in the wall and he runs down.

Rocky and Bullwinkle are captured by the giant mice and taken to the mice's leader, Boris in a mouse suit. Boris plans to take over the country by destroying all the TV antennae so everyone moves away. He then sics the biggest mouse on them, but the mouse runs down.

Boris and Natasha wind up the other mice and release them. Rocky and Bullwinkle decide to stay and fight. They feed the mice caramels, which ruins their bite and renders them useless. Then, a flying saucer lands, and unloads more giant mice. It is their friends the Moon Men, Gidney and Cloyd, who were tricked into bringing 100,000 mice to earth by Mr. Big.

Mr. Big landed on the moon after stealing an ingot of upsidaisium in the previous story arc and appointed himself leader. Rocky, Bullwinkle, Gidney, and Cloyd barricade themselves in a house and Bullwinkle begins playing the ukulele and singing, which entrances the moon mice. Boris, who has lost control, pretends to be Colonel Tomsk Parkoff (a parody of Colonel Tom Parker), and books Bullwinkle into a stadium with all the mice, which he intends to destroy with TNT.

Meanwhile, on the moon, Mr. Big has run out of materials to make more mice. He goes to earth to visit the ones there, but Boris' TNT blows the stadium to the moon. It runs into Mr. Big's saucer, which is destroyed. "Hello, Badenov," he says. "A funny thing happened to me on my way to the earth this evening." Mr. Big is without any moon mice, so he beats up Boris.

FUN FACT: Mr. Big is mentioned but does not appear in the serials "Jet Fuel Formula" and "Missouri Mish-Mash."

GIGGLE RATING: Looks, Zero Giggles. Mr. Big actually resembles Jay Ward. Voice, Four Giggles. Too bad Paul Frees and Daws Butler weren't available.

AVAILABILITY: Retitled *Rocky & Bullwinkle & Friends* (2003) for legal reasons, there are DVD of Season 2 and the complete series.

The Dick Tracy Show (1960)

Dick Tracy was a smart, hard-nosed detective character created by Chester Gould in the eponymous comic strip. Other cartoonists have kept the strip running to this day. Daffy Duck parodied him as "Duck Twacy" in *The Great Piggy Bank Robbery* (1946), and in 1990, Warren Beatty famously made a live action movie version.

In 1960, UPA turned the strip into an animated cartoon series. Every episode would begin with Tracy saying, "OK, Chief, I'll get on it right away," before subbing the case out via his wrist radio to one of his staff, mostly immigrants such as "Go Go" Gomez, basically a human Speedy Gonzales; Hemlock Holmes, an English bulldog in a bobby hat who sounds like Cary Grant; and Jo Jitsu, a bespectacled, bucktoothed pastiche of Oriental detectives like Mr. Moto, although he is not a Peter Lorre-wannabe. Sam Catchem was Tracy's partner in the strip, but here he is a silent partner. Tracy would always sign off the wrist radio call with the non-sequiturs, "Six two and even, over and out." Another bit used in every show was when the protagonist would be in imminent danger from, say, a falling rock or a flying bullet, he would say, "Hold everything," and call Tracy on his wrist radio. When he finished his call, the action would resume. The show is stigmatized today because of its ethnic stereotypes, especially Jo Jitsu and "Go Go" Gomez.

Villains were often named for some congenital deformity, like the most popular villain, Flattop, "the world's most vicious criminal", who sounds but does not look like Peter Lorre; and B.B. Eyes, who sounds but does not look like Edward G. Robinson. The villains usually work in pairs, and Flattop and B.B. Eyes are usually teamed together, although each has occasional solo appearances.

Season 1
Episode 1 (1960)
"Red Hot Riding Hoods"

UPA Productions. Directed by Ray Patterson, Abe Levitow. Written by Homer Brightman. Produced by Glen Heisch, Henry G. Saperstein, Peter DeMet. Cast: Everett Sloane (Dick Tracy), Jerry Hausner (Hemlock Holmes), Mel Blanc (Flattop).

The East Side, West Side Bank is being robbed by B.B. Eyes and Flattop, and Hemlock Holmes and his squad, the Retouchables are put on the case. The Retouchables are named after *The Untouchables* (1959), but are more like the Keystone Cops. A running gag is that the Retouchables take off in the squad car, leaving Hemlock behind. He catches the rear of the car, which stops, sending Holmes through the windshield. "Hey B.B. Eyes," says Flattop, "de police, de police!" B.B. Eyes tells Holmes he has a call from Judy. "Judy, Judy, Judy," says Holmes, imitating Larry Storch imitating Cary Grant. B.B. Eyes hands him a stick of dynamite to talk into, which explodes. "I don't particularly care for policemen," says Flattop, "but this cop's good for laughs." Following a chase, Holmes catches the crooks.

Episode 3 (1960)
"Jewel Fool"

UPA Productions. Directed by Brad Case, Abe Levitow. Written by George Atkins. Produced by Glen Heisch, Henry G. Saperstein, Peter DeMet. Cast: Everett Sloane (Dick Tracy), Benny Rubin (Jo Jitsu), Mel Blanc (Flattop).

Tracy calls Jo Jitsu on his wrist radio. "Flattop has stolen the world's most valuable piece of jewelry, the Singleton Tiara, belonging to the Duchess of Stiffingham. Flattop last seen in vicinity of Madame Torso's Wax Museum in London. Six-two and even. Over and out."

Jitsu correctly deduces that Flattop is going to replace the fake tiara on the wax statue of the Duchess, which is near the statues of Tracy, Jitsu, and Flattop, with the real tiara. "There you are, Duchess, the real thing.

Stunning, isn't it?" Jitsu shows up and Flattop takes the tiara off her head. "I must get rid of that cop. Bon voyage, Duchess," says Flattop, and pushes the statue onto Jitsu.

Flattop sets up a guillotine and puts the tiara in back of it. "One look and he'll lose his head over my lovely tiara." Jitsu fools him by using his wax head. Flattop steals the tiara back, but gets caught.

Episode 13 (1960)
"Phony Pharmers"

UPA Productions. Directed by Ray Patterson, Abe Levitow. Written by Ed Nofzinger, Bob Ogle. Produced by Glen Heisch, Henry G. Saperstein, Peter DeMet. Cast: Everett Sloane (Dick Tracy), Mel Blanc (Flattop), Jerry Hausner (Hemlock Holmes), Howard Morris.

The Able Sable Fur company has been robbed by Flattop and B.B. Eyes. "Watch those curves, Flattop, see?" "You watch them, I'm busy driving. We're out in the sticks, you can relax." They hide the stolen fur truck on a farm. "Flattop, you're gonna be a farmer, see? Now, uh, cover the truck with hay, yeah. Ya get the pitch?" "Very funny, B.B. Eyes."

Holmes goes to the farm. "I think I should eliminate this flatfoot," says Flattop. "Now wait," says B. B. Eyes, "I, uh, got a better idea. Yeah." He sends Holmes and the Retouchables into the hay baler. "I always wanted to run a hay baler," says Flattop. He throws a pitchfork at Holmes. "This is very pleasant work." The pitchfork deflates the bobby hat, another running gag. Flattop and B.B. Eyes cover Holmes and the Retouchables with popcorn and molasses, turning them into Cracker Jack. "That takes care of those cornballs," says Flattop.

Flattop and B.B. Eyes stop to throw some live skunks into the fur truck and are caught by Holmes and the Retouchables.

Episode 17 (1960)
"The Parrot Caper"

UPA Productions. Directed by Clyde Geronimi. Written by Al Bertino, Dick Kinney. Produced by Glen Heisch. Cast: Everett Sloane (Dick Tracy), Benny Rubin (Jo Jitsu), Mel Blanc (B.B. Eyes/Flattop).

B.B. Eyes and Flattop are smuggling parrots across the border, so Jo Jitsu goes to investigate. The border is like a giant elastic, and he walks right underneath. Just on the other side, Flattop is rehearsing the parrots. "OK, now once again from the beginning. 'I was born in New York.'" The second bird refuses to lie, so Flattop grabs him and calls B.B. Eyes. "This bird doesn't read his lines right. He needs another lesson," and giggles insanely. Then he sees Jo Jitsu and tells B.B. Eyes they have to flee across the border. Jitsu goes up on the roof and points a gun at B.B. Eyes through the skylight. Flattop tries to hit him with a bat, but Jitsu flips him through the glass window.

Jitsu goes to the door to arrest them, but they fool him by coming out in drag with baby carriages, which are full of parrots dressed as babies. The second parrot gives up Flattop and B.B. Eyes. "Parrot," says Flattop, "you're a stool pigeon. One side, copper," and pushes past Jitsu, who uses the elastic border as a slingshot to shoot Flattop and B.B. Eyes back to a Mexican jail.

Episode 20 (1960)
"The Snow Monster"

UPA Productions. Directed by Brad Case, Abe Levitow. Written by George Atkins. Produced by Glen Heisch, Henry G. Saperstein, Peter DeMet. Cast: Everett Sloane (Dick Tracy), Benny Rubin (Jo Jitsu), Mel Blanc (Flattop).

Flattop is trying to convert the Abominable Snowman to crime, so Jo Jitsu goes out to Snow Mountain to stop him. The Snowman is not abominable, but rather little and cute. "Now this is a machine gun," says Flattop. "You can learn to destroy with it." The Snowman eats the gun's stock. "No, no, don't waste it." The Snowman fires at Flattop. "No no no, I'm a bad guy, only shoot good guys."

The sound of gunshots brings Jitsu over. Flattop gives the Snowman a bomb. "Now this is a good guy. Remember what we do with good guys?" The Snowman eats the bomb. "You don't seem to understand. I want you to be mean, dirty, and loathsome, like me. But only to good guys." Jitsu wins over the Snowman with a yo-yo. Flattop shoots at Jitsu, who turns the bullet back on Flattop using a pair of chopsticks. The bullet bounces off Flattop's bulletproof vest, but causes an avalanche that buries him.

Episode 27 (1960)
"Flea Ring Circus"

UPA Productions. Directed by Steve Clark. Written by Bob Ogle. Produced by Glen Heisch. Cast: Everett Sloane (Dick Tracy), Mel Blanc (B.B. Eyes/Flattop), Jerry Hausner (Hemlock Holmes).

Someone has kidnapped the World Famous Ferguson's Flying Fleas from the Dingaling Circus, and Hemlock Holmes and the Retouchables are on the case. "I told you we shouldn't have stayed for the show, B.B. Eyes," says Flattop. "Now the place is crawling with police." "Just don't drop that jar, Flattop," says B.B. Eyes, "or we'll be crawling with fleas, see? Don't worry about the police, Flattop, I have a plan."

The plan involves both of them putting on a fat lady's dress. "I'm just running over to mama's with this pepper," says Flattop in a falsetto. Holmes realizes that the fatty has four legs, and recognizes Flattop and chases after him. "I knew it wouldn't work," says Flattop, and ducks into a tent. "They blocked the entrance," he says. "Now what do we do?" B.B. Eyes shoots Holmes out of a cannon. He bounces off a drum and into the high trapeze platform where B.B. Eyes and Flattop are standing, causing Flattop to drop the jar of fleas onto Holmes. Flattop and B.B. Eyes try to escape by trapeze. "Blast you, Flattop, you lost the fleas." Flattop says, "It was either me or the fleas." They fall off into Holmes' net.

Episode 41 (1960)
"Baggage Car Bandits"

UPA Productions. Directed by John Walker. Written by Al Bertino, Dick Kinney. Produced by Glen Heisch. Cast: Everett Sloane (Dick Tracy), Mel Blanc (B.B. Eyes/Flattop), Jerry Hausner (Hemlock Holmes).

Flattop and B.B. Eyes are going to rob the Sunshine Limited, so Hemlock Holmes and the Retouchables go to head them off. The usual car gag is done this time with a helicopter. When they spot the train, Holmes asks for volunteers to bail out and catch the crooks. The Retouchables literally kick him off the helicopter. He knocks into Flattop and B.B. Eyes and falls off the train. "Ta-ta and farewell, flatfoot," says Flattop, but Holmes follows on a handcar. He pulls the railroad switch and sends the train to a siding, and catches Flattop and B.B. Eyes.

Episode 42 (1960)
"Gym Jam"

UPA Productions. Directed by Clyde Geronimi, Abe Levitow. Written by George Atkins. Produced by Glen Heisch, Henry G. Saperstein, Peter DeMet. Cast: Everett Sloane (Dick Tracy), Benny Rubin (Jo Jitsu), Mel Blanc (Flattop).

Flattop has stolen a gold brick from a Federal Reserve Bank. "Such a pity to leave so many beautiful gold bricks back in de vault," he says, "but they're so heavy. And it's so hard to get criminal employees to help you steal dese days. Dey want retirement benefits, sick leave, coffee breaks, and overtime for working nights." He comes upon a gym and decides to build himself up so he won't be such a goldbricker. (Get it?) The gym is where Jo Jitsu works out, and he disguises himself so he can screw with Flattop before making the collar. Flattop discovers the truth, and boards Jitsu up in the Steam Room, then sets the temperature to "Par Boil". Jitsu pretends to run a casino in the Steam Room and tricks Flattop into coming in with the gold bar, then Jitsu sets the temperature to "Hottern Blazes". The heat melts the gold all over Flattop, making Jitsu the first detective to win an Oscar for solving a crime.

Episode 43 (1960)
"Bowling Ball Bandits"

UPA Productions. Directed by Clyde Geronimi. Written by Homer Brightman. Produced by Glen Heisch. Cast: Everett Sloane (Dick Tracy), Mel Blanc (B.B. Eyes/Flattop), Jerry Hausner (Hemlock Holmes).

Flattop and B.B. Eyes have stolen all the bowling balls in the city. "Now anyone who wants to bowl pays our prices," says Flattop, and giggles insanely. Hemlock Holmes and the Retouchables are on the case. Holmes pulls over Flattop's truck. Flattop hits him with an old-school turn signal. "Shove off, B.B. Eyes!"

When they reach the bowling alley, Holmes is there. They dump the balls on him and try to get away through the bowling alley. "It's slippery!"

Holmes hits them with a bowling ball and they are trapped in the pinsetter. "We were framed."

Episode 57 (1960)
"The Elevator Lift"

UPA Productions. Directed by Jerry Hathcock, Abe Levitow. Written by Dick Shaw. Produced by Glen Heisch, Henry G. Saperstein, Peter DeMet. Cast: Everett Sloane (Dick Tracy), Benny Rubin (Jo Jitsu), Mel Blanc (B.B. Eyes/Flattop).

The elevator at the Fleabag Plaza Hotel has been stolen, and Dick Tracy sends Jo Jitsu to investigate. B.B. Eyes and Flattop return on the elevator, then steal it again. On the next trip, Jitsu hides on the elevator and learns Flattop and B.B. Eyes have attached the elevator to a balloon and are using it to transport stolen goods. "De world's largest pile of uncut diamonds! We'll be de kings of de underworld! Nobody can stop us now!" Jitsu tries, but B.B. Eyes knocks him out with a crate of diamonds and drops him out of the balloon. Jitsu bounces off a flagpole and lands on top of the balloon, which B.B. Eyes shoots holes through. Tracy, in a helicopter, rescues Jitsu, but B.B. Eyes and Flattop fall down an industrial smokestack and are arrested.

Episode 78 (1960)
"The Big Blowup"

UPA Productions. Directed by Jerry Hathcock, Abe Levitow. Written by Al Bertino, Dick Kinney. Produced by Glen Heisch, Henry G. Saperstein, Peter DeMet. Cast: Everett Sloane (Dick Tracy), Mel Blanc (B.B. Eyes/Flattop), Paul Frees ("Go Go" Gomez).

Dick Tracy is tasked with finding out who is making firecrackers and how they are being sold. He and Sam (played now and always by a stationary silhouette) will cover the uptown area and he tells "Go Go" Gomez to investigate downtown. He discovers a "Prof. Cabeza Aplaztada" giving violin lessons and realizes the name means "Flattop" in Spanish, so he goes undercover as a violin student. Flattop brains him with a fiddle. "Quick, B.B. Eyes, let's get rid of him!" Gomez asks for one last cigarette, which he uses to light the gunpowder and blow up Flattop and B.B. Eyes, and, not incidentally, himself.

Episode 80 (1960)
"Bettor Come Clean"

UPA Productions. Directed by Paul Fennell, Abe Levitow. Written by David Detiege. Produced by Glen Heisch, Henry G. Saperstein, Peter DeMet. Cast: Everett Sloane (Dick Tracy), Mel Blanc (B.B. Eyes/Flattop), Jerry Hausner (Hemlock Holmes).

B.B. Eyes and Flattop are running a phony betting racket in the back room of a laundromat so Hemlock Holmes and the Retouchables try to take them by surprise. The Retouchables hide in washing machines while Holmes dons a disguise and goes in to see Flattop and B.B. Eyes, who flee and trap Holmes in a washing machine. Flattop starches Holmes and literally hangs him up to dry. "How's this, B.B. Eyes?" The Retouchables get out of their washing machines and arrest Flattop and B.B. Eyes.

Episode 81 (1960)
"The Great Whodunit"

UPA Productions. Directed by Steve Clark, Abe Levitow. Written by Tom Hicks, Bob Ogle. Produced by Glen Heisch, Henry G. Saperstein, Peter DeMet. Cast: Everett Sloane (Dick Tracy), Mel Blanc (B.B. Eyes/Flattop), Paul Frees ("Go Go" Gomez).

B.B. Eyes and Flattop kidnap escape artist The Great Whodunit and take him to his prop warehouse to force him to reveal his secrets. "Boy, once we learn his escape tricks," says Flattop, "they'll never be able to hold us in prison." Gomez go-goes over there and traps them with the Mexican Finger Puzzle.

Episode 82 (1960)
"The Skyscraper Caper"

UPA Productions. Directed by Steve Clark, Abe Levitow. Written by Tom Hicks, Bob Ogle. Produced by Glen Heisch, Henry G. Saperstein, Peter DeMet. Cast: Everett Sloane (Dick Tracy), Mel Blanc (B.B. Eyes/Flattop), Paul Frees ("Go Go" Gomez).

Flattop and B.B. Eyes are stealing change off the desks of employees at the Umpire State Building (I am not making this up), and Dick Tracy sends "Go Go" Gomez to investigate the window washers. Gomez runs right into a safe opened by Flattop. Flattop closes him in and he and B.B. Eyes drop Gomez off their window washing platform. "He asked for it," says Flattop. The safe lands on a board, which launches two paint cans into the air. The paint covers Flattop and B.B. Eyes and they are arrested.

Episode 85 (1960)
"The Copped Copper Caper"

UPA Productions. Directed by John Walker, Abe Levitow. Written by Bob Ogle. Produced by Glen Heisch, Henry G. Saperstein, Peter DeMet. Cast: Everett Sloane (Dick Tracy), Mel Blanc (B.B. Eyes/Flattop), Paul Frees ("Go Go" Gomez).

B.B. Eyes and Flattop have escaped and are headed to the airport. "Go Go" Gomez guards the airport entrance while Dick Tracy goes in and looks around. B.B. Eyes cold-cocks Tracy, ties him up, gags him, and locks him in a trunk. Later, on the plane, Flattop says, "That sure was funny, B.B. Eyes, telling the inspection agent that trunk is full of law books." He giggles insanely. Tracy sends Gomez a message on the wrist radio with Morse Code. An air traffic controller understands the code and radios the pilots, who take evasive maneuvers just as Flattop and B.B. Eyes are about to drop the trunk into the ocean. The plane lands and Flattop and B.B. Eyes are caught.

Episode 92 (1960)
"Gang Town"

UPA Productions. Directed by Steve Clark, Abe Levitow. Written by David Detiege. Produced by Glen Heisch, Henry G. Saperstein, Peter DeMet. Cast: Everett Sloane (Dick Tracy), Mel Blanc (B.B. Eyes/Flattop), Paul Frees ("Go Go" Gomez).

B.B. Eyes and Flattop have taken over an old western ghost town and are changing it to Gang Town, a hideout for criminals on the run. Dick Tracy sends "Go Go" Gomez and follows by helicopter. B.B. Eyes shoots at Gomez, who hides in a barrel. "You are obviously the fastest machine gun in the west, B.B. Eyes!" Tracy arrives and arrests Flattop and B.B. Eyes.

Episode 107 (1960)
"A Case for Alarm"

UPA Productions. Directed by Grant Simmons, Abe Levitow. Written by Al Bertino, Dick Kinney. Produced by Glen Heisch, Henry G. Saperstein, Peter DeMet. Cast: Everett Sloane (Dick Tracy), Mel Blanc (B.B. Eyes/ Flattop), Paul Frees ("Go Go" Gomez).

B.B. Eyes and Flattop are aboard "Go Go" Gomez's ship, seeking to steal the diamond-studded Swiss alarm clock Gomez is guarding. He always sets it for his two o'clock siesta. Dick Tracy plans to land on the helicopter deck before the ship docks. Gomez falls into the water and B.B. Eyes grabs the clock, but Tracy hears the alarm when it goes off. "Without the clock," says Flattop, "they've got nothing on us! Get rid of it!" B.B. Eyes throws it out the porthole and Gomez recovers it. B.B. Eyes and Flattop are arrested.

Episode 116 (1960)
"The Big Seal Steal"

UPA Productions. Directed by John Walker, Abe Levitow. Written by Homer Brightman. Produced by Glen Heisch, Henry G. Saperstein, Peter DeMet. Cast: Everett Sloane (Dick Tracy), Mel Blanc (B.B. Eyes/Flattop), Jerry Hausner (Hemlock Holmes).

B.B. Eyes and Flattop are in Mukluk capturing government-protected seals to corner the sealskin coat market. They have stolen a two-way wrist radio and that somehow lets them eavesdrop on Dick Tracy's communications with Hemlock Holmes. "That was a stroke of genius," says Flattop. "With your ability to imitate Tracy's voice, we can give Hemlock the fits." B.B. Eyes calls Holmes and tells him, in a perfect Everett Sloane voice, to jump off a cliff. "That's funny," Flattop giggles insanely. Tracy hears these communications, but instead of just telling Holmes, Tracy flies up to Mukluk. Meanwhile, B.B. Eyes as Tracy tells Holmes B.B. Eyes and Flattop are disguised as polar bears. When Holmes tries to arrest a polar bear, it chases him off a cliff and he lands on top of B.B. Eyes' igloo and he arrests B.B. Eyes and Flattop.

Episode 118 (1960)
"Choo Choo Boo Boo"

UPA Productions. Directed by John Walker, Abe Levitow. Written by Al Bertino, Dick Kinney. Produced by Glen Heisch, Henry G. Saperstein, Peter DeMet. Cast: Everett Sloane (Dick Tracy), Mel Blanc (B.B. Eyes/ Flattop), Jerry Hausner (Hemlock Holmes).

B.B. Eyes and Flattop have abducted the Retouchables and tied them to a railroad track. "Dey're all ready for de express under duress," Flattop giggles insanely. "Now, all we need is a train." B.B. Eyes hijacks one. Hemlock Holmes arrives on the scene by helicopter. Flattop throws Holmes from the train, but Holmes hits a switch and diverts the train away from the Retouchables onto a siding, where it wrecks.

Episode 120 (1960)
"The Bank Prank"

UPA Productions. Directed by John Walker, Abe Levitow. Written by Cal Howard. Produced by Glen Heisch, Henry G. Saperstein, Peter DeMet. Cast: Everett Sloane (Dick Tracy), Benny Rubin (Jo Jitsu), Mel Blanc (B.B. Eyes/Flattop).

The Last National Bank has not received any night deposits in a week. B.B. Eyes and Flattop have been putting a box in front of the real night deposit slot and taking the cash. "It's time to put our money-maker to work," Flattop giggles insanely. Jo Jitsu asks the bank manager for $20,000 to deposit so he can make a test case. With nothing to do until morning, he goes to an all-night porn theater. (My hand to God.) The next day, the money is missing. That night, he hides in a fire hydrant and catches B.B. Eyes and Flattop with jujitsu.

FUN FACT: Howard Morris would later play Flattop on *The Famous Adventures of Mr. Magoo* (1965) and *Archie's TV Funnies* (1971), but did not imitate Lorre.

GIGGLE RATING: Five Giggles.

AVAILABILITY: All episodes were released by Classic Media on a four-disc DVD Collector's Edition set, *The Dick Tracy Show, The Complete Animated*

Crime Series (2012). An earlier two-volume set can be found on the internet, usually for much less money.

Mister Magoo (1960)
Season 1
Episode 45 (February 13, 1961)
"High Spy Magoo"

UPA Productions. Directed by Paul Fennell. Animated by Bob Bentley, Ed Solomon. Written by George Atkins, Nick George. Produced by Henry G. Saperstein. Cast: Jim Backus (Mister Magoo), Mel Blanc (Voice on Radio), Paul Frees, Jerry Hausner, Daws Butler.

Mister Magoo, a nearsighted man inspired in part by W.C. Fields, started out as a series of theatrical cartoons for United Productions of America. Columbia reluctantly agreed to the first short, a departure from the funny animal cartoons that dominated the market, and it was an instant success.

Magoo's character became more sympathetic in the fifties, and the series ended in 1959. However, it was revived by UPA as a TV series in 1960. Paul Frees narrated the TV series. Frees, like Mel Blanc, was known as "The Man of a Thousand Voices". He started in vaudeville in the 1930s and did voice acting for cartoons, radio, records, and film almost up until his death in 1986. He famously portrayed Peter Lorre in Spike Jones' record of *My Old Flame*.

Agent X-27 is broadcasting to the motherland. He is tall, lean, bald, and has a full beard and mustache, but he sounds like Peter Lorre. "X-27 wishes to report that Agent 26 has disappeared." He is told X-28 will soon be there as a replacement.

Just then, Magoo barges through the door and introduces himself to his "new neighbor", a robot. "Are you X-28?" asks X-27. Magoo says no and gives his home address. X-26 thinks Magoo is a brilliant spy. "Here is the list. With these, we control everything."

Magoo mistakes it for a grocery list, and a military base for the store. He takes a "shopping cart", which is actually filled with nuclear waste, back into the base, causing an evacuation.

With the base now empty, Magoo is free to do his "shopping". He picks up some secret formulas, a nuclear bomb, and a few other sundries. X-27 thinks Magoo is the best spy ever. "Perfect, comrade. Even Special Formula X-6-X." Magoo, who thought he was buying emulsified artichoke juice, not formula, returns the goods to the "store". X-27 follows him, but manages to fall on top of a nuclear missile just before Magoo accidentally launches it. "Well, my country can't be too angry with me. They got first man in space." Magoo sees the nuclear holocaust and says, "By George, what a beautiful full moon."

GIGGLE RATING: Looks, Zero Giggles; Voice, Five Giggles. All the usual suspects (Blanc, Frees, and Butler) are here. It is not known which one played X-27.

AVAILABILITY: On the DVD *Mr. Magoo, The Television Collection, 1960-1977* (2011).

The Yogi Bear Show [Snagglepuss] (1961)
Season 1
Episode 4 (February 20, 1961)
"Fraidy Cat Lion"

Hanna-Barbera Studios. Produced and Directed by Joseph Barbera, William Hanna. Written by Warren Foster, Michael Maltese. Cast: Daws Butler (Snagglepuss/J. Evil Scientist), Jean Vander Pyl (Mrs. J. Evil Scientist), Don Messick (Mouse).

Yogi Bear was an anthropomorphic bear in Jellystone Park who hangs out with Cindy Bear, his sometime love interest; and his pal, Boo-Boo Bear, a cub.

Snagglepuss first appeared on *The Quick Draw McGraw Show* (1959) as Snaggletooth, an orange mountain lion, before he turned pink, changed his name, and landed his own regular segment in thirty-two episodes of *The Yogi Bear Show* (1961). His voice, as performed by Daws Butler, was an imitation of Bert Lahr's.

Mrs. Scientist is preparing Guillotine Stew, and asks Mr. Scientist, "Where's Junior?" Junior is in Mr. Scientist's lab, "playing with some harmless chemicals."

Junior pulls a mouse out of its hole in the baseboard, bombards him with rays and makes him the size of Haystacks Calhoun. He walks behind

Mr. Scientist, who is reading horror comics ("delightfully gruesome," he says with an insane giggle) into the kitchen, where he spooks Mrs. Scientist. Mr. Scientist gets the cat, who leaves upon seeing the mouse.

The doorbell rings (a normal sound this time). It is Snagglepuss, described by Mr. Scientist as "a moldy-looking mountain lion." Snagglepuss is offended, but is in no position to bargain, as he is willing to work for food. "How are you at catching mice?" asks Mr. Scientist. Upon learning there is only one, Snagglepuss goes to Junior's nursery to get it. When he sees the mouse, he utters one of his catchphrases, "Heavens to Murgatroyd!", and then another, "Exit stage left!" The mouse grabs him by the throat and throws him up against the wall. "Exit stage right!" Junior activates a trap door. Snagglepuss falls down and bounces back up, right into the mouse's arms.

The mouse puts Snagglepuss into a box. Junior pulls a lever and Snagglepuss is reduced to the size of a mouse. "Exit stage left!" and through the mouse's hole, where he at least finds a piece of cheese to eat.

GIGGLE RATING: Five Giggles.

AVAILABILITY: On November 15, 2005, Warner Home Video released the complete series on DVD Region 1. A Region 2 DVD was released on January 31, 2011. A Region 4 DVD was released on September 6, 2011.

The Beany and Cecil Show (1962)
Season 1
Episode 6 (February 3, 1962)
"Beany and Cecil Meet the Monstrous Monster"

Bob Clampett Productions, Snowball Studios. Directed by Robert Clampett. Produced by Robert Clampett. Written by Dale Hale, Robert Clampett, Jack Kinney. Cast: Jim MacGeorge (Beany), Irv Shoemaker (Cecil).

Bob Clampett created the puppet show *Time for Beany* (1949), with Stan Freberg and Daws Butler, after leaving Warner Bros. The cartoon premiered Sunday, October 11, 1959 as *Matty's Funday Funnies*. By 1962, it was on Saturdays in prime time, bespeaking its popularity amongst adults. Beany and his Uncle Captain sail the seas on the Leakin' Lena, accompanied by their serpent, Cecil.

A monstrous monster is eating ships, and it's up to Beany and Cecil to destroy him. Cecil consults with his informants: Snapsy Maxie, a lobster; Jack the Knife, a Maurice Chevalier-like sawfish; Louie the Loan Shark; and Staring Herring, a big-eyed hypnotic fish who talks like Peter Lorre.

Cecil locates the monster by the Fog Bank. The monster, who sounds a bit like Ed Wynn and Bert Lahr, tries to eat the Leakin' Lena. The monster hits Cecil on the head with a submarine. Cecil's friends rush to his aid. To the tune of "Ride of the Valkyries", Snapsy Maxie pinches the monster's toe with his claw, Jack stabs him in the butt, and Staring Herring hypnotizes him into believing he is a Mississippi steamboat ("Look into my eyes"), and off he paddles.

GIGGLE RATING: Five Giggles.

AVAILABILITY: On the DVD *Bob Clampett's Beany and Cecil, the Special Edition* (2000).

Bozo The World's Most Famous Clown (1958)
Season 3
Episode 33 (1962)
"Manhunt Stunts"

Larry Harmon Studios. Directed by Paul Fennell, Larry Harmon. Written by Paul Fennell, Larry Harmon, Carl Kohler, Homer Brightman. Produced by Paul Fennell, Larry Harmon. Art Direction by Lou Scheimer. Cast: Larry Harmon (Bozo), Paul Frees (Narrator).

The character of Bozo the Clown was created by Alan W. Livingston and originally played on records by Pinto Colvig. Colvig started appearing on television as Bozo in 1949. In 1956, Larry Harmon bought the rights to the character and franchised the show out to local TV stations. Willard Scott was one of the many local Bozos.

Two years later, Harmon created the cartoon *Bozo The World's Most Famous Clown* (1958). A total of 157 five-minute shorts were produced in 1958, 1959, and 1962. Larry Harmon played Bozo and Paul Frees played the Narrator. As of 2009, this show had been in syndication continuously since its inception.

Bozo's Troubleshooter Computer has been taken from the government by Slippery Bly. Bozo gets his dog, Sniffer (a Droopy sound-alike) on the trail. Fortunately, Sniffer has the other "Computicator" which they use to track Bly.

Bly resembles Peter Lorre and sounds like Paul Frees doing Peter Lorre. "Now that I've got this hot computer, I need a cooling-off place for both of us." He spies a sign for the city dump. "Ooh, how fortunate for me! The city dump! They'll never think of looking in the city dump!" Bozo and Sniffer actually do think of it, but Sniffer's Computicator no longer works because of all the metal in the dump. He has to use his nose. Like Quick Draw McGraw's similarly named dog, Snuffles, Sniffer works for treats–in this case, XYZ-3 Bones. Sniffer's nose leads him right to Bly. "How humiliating. I've been found by a hound."

Bly hides under some tires. Sniffer uses his super snout to move the tires by inhaling. The tires land on top of Sniffer and Bozo. "Won't those two snoopers ever learn?" cries Bly, who hides in a pile of junk. Sniffer moves it with his mighty muzzle and it buries him with everything, including the kitchen sink. "This whole situation," Bly giggles insanely, "is going from bad to better." He takes off.

Sniffer's sniffer is all snuffed out, so Bozo throws him another XYZ-3 Bone, which caroms off a stove pipe and into Bozo's mouth. Bozo smells Bly hiding in a perambulator. "Yes, sir, that's my baby!" he says.

"No sir, don't mean maybe," answers Bly. Bozo inhales and brings the pram to a crashing halt and captures Bly and gets back the computer.

GIGGLE RATING: Five Giggles.

AVAILABILITY: The entire series was released as a four-volume VHS set. "Manhunt Stunts" is on the volume entitled *King Size Surprise* (VHS HI-FI CHE 8041) (Unknown year).

Stingray (1964)

AP Films, Associated Television. Directed by Alan Pattillo, David Elliott, John Kelly, Desmond Saunders. Writing Credits: Gerry Anderson (creator), Sylvia Anderson (creator), Alan Fennell, Dennis Spooner. Produced by Gerry Anderson, Sylvia Anderson. Cast: Don Mason (Captain Troy Tempest), Ray Barrett (Fisher/Titan/Commander Sam Shore), Robert Easton (Lt. George "Phones" Sheridan/Surface Agent X-2-Zero), Lois Maxwell (Lt. Atlanta Shore), David Graham (Marineville Tracking Station/Doc/Admiral Jack Denver/Various Supporting Characters).

"Stand by for action!" (Opening narration.) Following the success of *Supercar* (1961), which took place on land, and *Fireball XL5* (1962), which was set in outer space, producer Gerry Anderson looked for a backdrop for his next show. "One possibility was underwater," he said. Placed in a world approximately one hundred years hence with high-tech weaponry, but also dial phones, analog watches, phonographs, reel-to-reel tape, and personal computers the size of intermodal containers, Stingray is the flagship nuclear submarine of the World Aquanaut Security Patrol (WASP), which is part of the World Security Patrol (WSP). It is based in the inaptonymous land-locked Marineville, connected to the Pacific Ocean via a tunnel leading to an "ocean door".

The first British TV series to be filmed in "colour" (to capital-ize on the lucrative American market), the show used a process called "Supermarionation", a word which is a portmanteau of "super", "mari-onette", and "animation". The puppets had poseable hands (although real hands were sometimes used in closeups), glass eyes, and large inter-changeable fiberglass heads containing internal solenoids allowing them to lip synch dialogue. Each head had a different expression, but the ones most frequently used give the characters a perma-smirk. The show used elaborate (for the time) special effects to simulate the underwater envi-ronment (fairly successfully) and hide the puppets' strings (not so much.) Supermarionation's "bête noire" was character movement, so whenever pos-sible, characters sit or stand still. The paraplegic Commander Shore rides around on a "hoverchair".

The captain of Stingray is manly Troy Tempest, who is based on James Garner. His navigator is the Southern-accented George Lee Sheridan, nick-named "Phones" for the headset he wears constantly. Phones is played by Robert Easton, and the character is based on Sparks, the radio operator Easton portrayed in *Voyage to the Bottom of the Sea* (1961), which also starred Peter

Lorre. It's no surprise that one of the bad guys, Surface Agent X-2-Zero, also voiced by Easton, looks and sounds like Lorre. X-2-Zero lives in a cottage on the island of Lemoy, which is not far from Marineville. He is green-skinned, but dons whiteface and a variety of wigs, fake beards and mustaches, and eyeglasses so he can pass among the Terrainians. This comes in handy when he has to spy on them for his boss, Titan, the archenemy of Stingray. Titan is supposedly based on a young Laurence Olivier and he rules the Aquaphibians, stupid creatures with scaly green skin, in the undersea land of Titanica. Other major characters include Samuel Shore, the gruff but loveable Commander of the WASP base; his daughter, Control Tower Lieutenant Atlanta Shore, interested romantically in Troy, probably based on Lois Maxwell herself; Sub-Lieutenant John Horatio Fisher, who is training to become a sub captain; and Marina, a tail-less mermaid from a "dumb [mute]" race and formerly Titan's slave, who has been likened to Brigitte Bardot or Ursula Andress. Another villain sometimes seen is El Hudat, the obese former dictator of oil-rich Hudatvia. El Hudat is overthrown by his identical brother (the word twin is not uttered), Ali Khali, and then imprisoned after he kidnaps Marina.

Original airdates are from ITV London. The series premiered in the United States in syndication in 1965. Thirty-nine regular episodes were produced.

Season 1
Episode 1 (October 4, 1964)
"Stingray"

Two Aquaphibians in a large mechanical fish launch a torpedo and sink a WSP submarine and WASP is tasked with investigating. Stingray passes Lemoy Island, where Surface Agent X-2-Zero is keeping watch. A beeping noise and a flashing chandelier alert him, and with the touch of a button, the ocean cottage converts to a high-tech communications center and he reports in. "The underwater radar system informs me that the World Aquanaut Security Patrol vessel Stingray has just passed the island, heading in the direction of explosion zone. I will continue to report on progress."

A mechanical fish torpedoes Stingray and Troy and Phones are captured. Troy wakes up in Titan's palace in Titanica and Marina is looking at him. Troy and Phones are sentenced to death and are transported via mechanical fish to Aquatraz along with Marina. Marina unties them and they overpower their Aquaphibian guards and escape on the mechanical fish, towing Stingray behind them. Marina joins WASP.

FUN FACTS: No actual episode title is shown onscreen, but documentation from ITV calls it "Stingray". It is sometimes referred to as "Stingray (The Pilot)" or simply "The Pilot", but it is not technically a pilot since the series format was already approved by Lew Grade, the Andersons' financial backer.

A ninety-nine-minute special episode created in 1963 for Japanese TV executives, "Stingray", comprised this episode along with the episodes "An Echo of Danger", "Raptures of the Deep", and "Emergency Marineville" as well as new footage. This was never aired, however, a condensed twenty-nine-minute reconstruction, which excluded material from "Raptures of the Deep", was created in collaboration with BBC Wales and shown on BBC Four on January 2, 2008.

A compilation film, *The Incredible Voyage of Stingray* (1980), comprised this episode along with the episodes "Plant of Doom", "Count Down", and "The Master Plan".

Episode 7 (November 15, 1964)
"The Man from the Navy"

"I have just observed the testing of a new marine missile by the Terrainians," X-2-Zero tells Titan. "The missile would be an invaluable asset in your war against Troy Tempest and Stingray." There is another test the next day.

Captain Jordon, the Navy sub captain, is an overbearing French jackass and Troy ruins Marina's dinner party because of his disagreements with Jordon. Atlanta cozies up to Jordon.

The next day, Aquaphibians take over the Navy sub and force Jordon to arm the test missile he is shooting at Stingray. Jordon tries to warn the crew in code. This time, Stingray evades the missile and it goes off. Stingray tells Jordon he has one minute to surrender. The Aquaphibians escape and Jordon is arrested. Jordon is found to be innocent of the charges, but still guilty of being an overbearing French jackass, so Troy calls him out and Jordon leaves. Atlanta asks Troy's forgiveness.

Episode 8 (November 22, 1964)
"An Echo of Danger"

X-2-Zero is playing the piano and almost misses a call from Titan. "I'm sorry for de delay." Titan's new plan is to get Troy and Phones replaced with inexperienced aquanauts. "A masterful scheme, Your Excellency," says X-2-Zero, "but how can I get them relieved of duty?" Titan leaves the details up to him.

Disguised as a window washer, X-2-Zero gets the details of Stingray's next mission: protecting a ship transporting oil. He drops a remote-controlled echo transmitter from his own sub and while Stingray is distracted, torpedoes the tube containing the oil. He giggles insanely and switches off the echo transmitter. Phones is accused of hallucinations and relieved of duty.

Then X-2-Zero poses as a psychiatrist and gets Phones to meet him at the cottage on Lemoy Island. "By de time I'm finished with him, he'll be laughed out of de WASPs forever!" He giggles insanely. Meanwhile, Troy has an idea to clear Phones. He and Fisher go out to the spot where Phones heard soundings.

At their meeting, X-2-Zero tells Phones to close his eyes and X-2-Zero converts the cottage to the high-tech communications center. When Phones opens his eyes, he thinks he was hallucinating. X-2-Zero tells him to close his eyes again, and converts everything back to a cottage. Phones is convinced he's crazy, and he tells X-2-Zero Troy's plan, which he now thinks is all in vain.

X-2-Zero intercepts Stingray in his own sub, but Troy gives chase, so X-2-Zero activates the echo transmitter. Troy finds it, and Phones is cleared.

Episode 10 (December 6, 1964)
"Titan Goes Pop"

"And so, Your Majesty, with my great cunning, using all de experience I have gained working as a Surface Agent, I have discovered dat Duke Dexter is coming to Marineville," X-2-Zero tells Titan. "With the secret measures and all the activity I have seen, he is de most important person ever to have visited Marineville." Titan orders that Duke Dexter, the new, fabulous, dynamic singing star, be brought to Titanica.

X-2-Zero dressed as a groupie gets through the tight security at Marineville–a barrier arm gate–by pretending he is an undercover agent from Special Security. This is accepted unquestioningly. X-2-Zero whisks Duke away to Lemoy Island along with Troy and Phones. Phones doesn't recognize the place from Episode 8, and they leave Duke alone with X-2-Zero. X-2-Zero drugs Duke and takes him to Titanica. "My plan worked better den I dared hope." Titan thinks Duke is an ally, and lets him do his show at Marineville, realizing Duke can wreak more havoc than he ever could.

Episode 13 (December 27, 1964)
"Tune of Danger"

A jazz combo comes to Marineville and decides on a whim to visit Marina's undersea city, Pacifica, along with Marina, Phones, and Atlanta. Troy is unable to join them because of a previous engagement. The group's manager is really F-7-2-1, an undercover agent for Titan and he plants a bomb in the double bass, wired to go off when played. "Tempest's turn will come later," says X-2-Zero when apprised of the plot.

Troy overhears F-7-2-1 explain his plan and tries to arrest him, but F-7-2-1 knocks him out and spirits him off to a cabin in the woods, then starts a forest fire. Troy burns his ropes off and escapes. He and Shore get to Pacifica and stop the concert before it's too late.

Episode 15 (January 10, 1965)
"Rescue from the Skies"

Fisher is to take Stingray out to do some target practice. X-2-Zero learns of the plan by hiding himself in a computer crate that he has delivered to Tower Control. "When Lt. Fisher destroys dis target, he'll destroy Stingray as well. Dese explosives will see to that." He giggles insanely.

The booby-trapped target disables Stingray miles away from Marineville. X-2-Zero attaches a sticker bomb to the outside of the sub. Their only hope for rescue is for Troy to fly an Arrowhead jet there, bail out, and get rid of the bomb in time. Which he does.

Episode 22 (February 28, 1965)
"Tom Thumb Tempest"

Waiting in the Stand-By Lounge for a mission, Troy passes out from the heat. He is awoken by the call to launch stations. He and Phones and Marina find themselves on Stingray inside an aquarium. When they get out, they find they have shrunk down and are in Titan's dining room. Now they are still small, but too big to get back into Stingray. They find the plans to Marineville, but hide when X-2-Zero enters with an Aquaphibian butler. "What is de meaning of dis? De table is a mess!" X-2-Zero leaves, and the butler resets the table. After the butler leaves, Troy sets the plans on fire, and escapes to Stingray. Phones says they are too big now, but somehow they get in and make their getaway. Need I add it was all a dream? Or was it?

Episode 23 (March 7, 1965)
"Eastern Eclipse"

"Dis is Eastern Star 2 to Marineville Tower. Approaching from de east. Request landing instructions," says a pilot (guess who). "I have VIP aboard in person of Ali Khali." He is cleared to land, but doesn't intend to. "It doesn't fit in with my plans," he tells Ali. X-2-Zero bails out over Lemoy Island, leaving Ali to crash the open cockpit biplane into the control tower, which, surprisingly, does not collapse into its own footprint.

"De plan is working well. I started a counterrevolution in Ali Khali's kingdom, and he was overthrown," X-2-Zero tells Titan. "I helped him to escape as planned so dat I could finish his claims to de presidency forever." El Hudat will help Titan in his plan for world domination.

X-2-Zero poses as El Hudat's lawyer. "All dat remains is to restore you as president," says X-2-Zero to El Hudat. "Dere was considerable confusion when I arrived here. if it continues, your escape will be simple."

Commander Shore comes in with Ali Khali. X-2-Zero says, "May I suggest dat de two ex-presidents talk things over quietly together? They may be able to solve their differences and agree to rule jointly." Shore agrees and leaves. X-2-Zero knocks Ali Khali out and El Hudat poses as Ali Khali and walks out of jail. Shore discovers the truth too late. El Hudat flees to Hudatvia by mechanical fish. Stingray torpedoes the mechanical fish, then rises to pick up the survivors. Big, fat El Hudat bobs to the surface, and Ali Khali jumps into the water. They fight and knock each other out. Since no one can tell them apart, Shore puts them both into Marineville jail. Hudatvia, leaderless, falls into anarchy. Mission Accomplished!

Episode 25 (March 21, 1965)
"Stand by for Action"

A feature film is shooting at Marineville, and everyone is playing himself except for Troy, who is played by movie star Johnny Swoonara. "Disguised as Mr. Goggleheimer, de film producer, I have free access to Marineville," X-2-Zero tells Titan. "Troy Tempest is as good as dead." Nevertheless, he misses his chance to shoot Troy, and fails to kill him with a falling lighting batten. Troy and Phones follow the escaping Goggleheimer to Lemoy Island, which now fails to ring any bells for either Troy or Phones. They knock on the door of the same cottage, and X-2-Zero fools them by putting on a different costume, even though he uses the same voice. They leave and he giggles insanely.

Although "Goggleheimer" has disappeared, he has left enough money to complete the movie, which has one day of shooting left on Stingray. Troy asks to be left behind. Titan is angry that X-2-Zero has spent millions and the plot has failed. "I will do anything you say to make up for dis bungling of mine." Titan tells him to attack Stingray, which he does. "Stingray is out of control. Without Troy Tempest, dey'll never get out of dere alive." Troy takes the Sea Bug, a dive scooter, out to the crippled Stingray and rescues Johnny Swoonara, Phones, and Marina.

Episode 32 (May 9, 1965)
"Count Down"

Titan orders X-2-Zero to destroy Marineville. "It will take a master plan of cunning deceit," says X-2-Zero. "I must think." He gains access to Marineville by writing to Commander Shore posing as Dr. Sanders, an authority on teaching speech to dumb people. No, not Troy and Phones, although they attend the lecture and talk to "Dr. Sanders" afterwards about helping Marina. At least he doesn't take them to Lemoy Island this time.

He does, however, trick them into recording a few phrases to help him gain access to Marineville by the ocean door. He plans to go in on his sub ten minutes before Stingray is scheduled to return and plant a bomb to destroy Marineville. He giggles insanely.

After placing the bomb, he escapes past the crack guard staff by posing again as Dr. Sanders. Troy and Phones return early and find the sub and the bomb. Troy manages to get both out in time and eject before the explosion.

FUN FACT: In an audio episode, which may or may not be canonical, Marina's muteness (and that of everyone in Pacifica) is revealed to be voluntary.

Episode 34 (May 23, 1965)
"Plant of Doom"

Marina is homesick and Troy and Phones take her to Pacifica to visit her father. X-2-Zero finds out and Titan tells him to deliver a toxic plant to Aphony in advance. "As is the custom in my part of the underwater world, I bring you a rare and fragrant flower. It is a symbol of peace and an omen of good fortune." When the glass cover is removed, the plant sucks all of the oxygen out of the room. "All is well, your instructions have been carried out," X-2-Zero tells Titan. "Marina and de Stingray crew are doomed."

Troy, Phones, and Marina have dinner with Aphony without removing the glass cover from the plant. Marina gives it as a gift to Atlanta, who takes off the cover and almost dies. Marina is suspected of trying to kill Atlanta, but when Marina almost dies from the same cause, everyone realizes she is not guilty.

FUN FACT: This was actually the second episode made, and the action obviously takes place before some of the ones previously broadcast.

Episode 35 (May 30, 1965)
"The Master Plan"

Titan has lost face, and if he is to keep the conquered races in their place, he must recapture Marina and make her his slave again. He sends a mechanical fish after Stingray and Stingray is hit with a torpedo. Stingray destroys the mechanical fish, but he has to leave Stingray to make repairs, and Aquaphibians come after him and shoot him with poison. Only Titan has the antidote, and the ransom he demands is Marina. Commander Shore refuses to negotiate with terrorists, but Marina surrenders voluntarily to Titan, who sends Troy the antidote.

Meanwhile, Titan, who can make the luscious, nubile Marina do anything he wants, has her (wait for it) scrubbing floors. He waits for Troy to rescue her so he can take him prisoner and use Stingray as his royal yacht. "It is a master plan, indeed," says X-2-Zero. Troy and Phones get access to Titanica by piloting a mechanical fish and impersonating Aquaphibians. They kill the Aquaphibian guards and blind Titan with a gas capsule. "I can't see dem!" says X-2-Zero. Aquaphibians follow on another mechanical fish, but they are taken out by Commander Shore, who is piloting Stingray.

Episode 36 (June 6, 1965)
"The Golden Sea"

Titan is watching the test of a device which summons Gargan, a sort of giant sawfish with glowing eyes and a bad attitude. The test is a success.

"Surface Agent X-2-Zero reporting. A strange craft is being taken to the Kendrick Trench," he tells Titan. "It is their plan to collect riches." Titan says the riches of the Trench are his own. "Stingray will deliver supplies in one month from now. The ship carrying the bathyscaphe is leaving at dawn."

Titan decides to wait a month so he can destroy both Stingray and the bathyscaphe. He plants the device on the bathyscaphe, and Gargan attacks and causes serious damage. Troy takes the Sea Bug and moves the device onto Titan's own craft.

GIGGLE RATING: Five Giggles. Robert Easton was also known as "The Man of a Thousand Voices". He did extensive character work in film, radio, and TV, but is perhaps best known as a dialect coach.

AVAILABILITY: On Amazon Prime and several DVD boxed sets.

The Flintstones (1960)

The first prime-time animated cartoon series, and the longest-running until its record was broken by *The Simpsons* (1989), this show was like *The Honeymooners* (1955) set in prehistoric times. Fat blue-collar loudmouth Fred Flintstone lives in Bedrock with his wife Wilma, their daughter Pebbles, and their pet dinosaur, Dino. Their neighbors and best friends are Barney and Betty Rubble, who have a son, Bamm-Bamm, the strongest kid in the world, and a pet kangaroo-dinosaur hybrid, Hoppy. Much of the humor derives from prehistoric iterations of contemporaneous technology.

Season 5
Episode 9 (November 12, 1964)
"The Gruesomes"

Hanna-Barbera Studios. Directed and Produced by William Hanna, Joseph Barbera. Written by Warren Foster. Cast: Alan Reed (Fred), Jean Vander Pyl (Wilma/Pebbles), Mel Blanc (Barney/Dino), Gerry Johnson (Betty), Don Messick (Bamm-Bamm), Naomi Lewis (Creepella Gruesome), Howard Morris (Weirdly Gruesome/Spider/Flower/Head/TV Announcer).

The Gruesomes, who seem to be prehistoric antecedents to the Evil Scientists, are shopping for a haunted house, and they find a broken-down mansion next door to Fred Flintstone's house called Tombstone Manor. "Sounds repulsively attractive," says Weirdly. "Beautifully run-down. I hope the neighbors are nice." He shakes hands with the realtor. "Clammy, isn't it?"

The Gruesomes drive to their new place. "A little unfixing here and there, and it will be a total wreck," says Weirdly. "Waist-high crabgrass. With real crabs. Delightfully wretched place."

Wilma decides to invite the new neighbors over for cactus tea, and Betty brings peanut butter sandwiches. Weirdly comes to the door. "Hello, Mr. Flintstone. I'm Gruesome." Fred replies, "Yeah, you are, sort of. But knowin' it is half the battle." Weirdly says, "I'm your new neighbor, and I came over to borrow a cup of red ants." Fred thinks this is a great joke. "My anteater didn't have lunch," Weirdly explains. Fred sends him home to bring back his wife. "We always manage to get odd neighbors," says Weirdly. He pets Dino. "What a cute, tender animal." Dino sees Weirdly and runs into the house.

"I think we'll get along with our new neighbors, the Flintstones," says Weirdly to Creepella. "They're revoltingly friendly." He introduces her to Wilma. "This is my nauseatingly lovely wife, Creepella."

"Goblin is the kind of boy you don't take to when you first meet him," Weirdly tells Fred and Barney. "But when you get to know him, you really can't stand him." He giggles insanely. Wilma offers to mind Goblin for a while, but her hairdresser calls and she and Betty take their kids and go see him. Fred and Barney are left to babysit. "It's revoltingly nice of you to mind little Goblin for us."

The Gruesomes arrive home in time to save Fred and Barney from Occy, their pet octopus. Fred decides to move, but when he sees Pebbles watching the Gruesomes on TV, he changes his mind. Weirdly and Creepella watch Fred and Barney rehearse their act for TV. "We certainly have some oddball neighbors, Creepella."

Episode 19 (January 22, 1965)
"The Hatrocks and the Gruesomes"

Hanna-Barbera Studios. Produced and Directed by William Hanna, Joseph Barbera. Written by Herb Finn, Alan Dinehart. Cast: Alan Reed (Fred), Jean Vander Pyl (Wilma, Pebbles), Mel Blanc (Barney, Dino), Gerry Johnson (Betty), Don Messick (Bamm-Bamm), Naomi Lewis (Creepella), Howard Morris (Jethro Hatrock/Weirdly Gruesome/Slab/Waiter/Percy).

Fred gets a telegram from hillbilly Jethro Hatrock, and is afraid Hatrock is coming to kill him because of the Flintstone-Hatrock feud. It turns out Jethro comes in peace, he is stopping by with his family on the way to the World's Fair. Just to be polite, Fred says it's too bad they can't stay the night, and Jethro takes him up on it.

The Hatrocks make pests of themselves, but the next day, they get ready to leave. Just to be polite, Fred says it's too bad they can't stay a week, so they do. When they are ready to leave, Fred again asks them to stay just to be polite, and they agree to stay until hog-branding time.

Fred has an idea. He asks Weirdly to invite them over for a barbecue, thinking that will frighten them away, but they don't scare easily. "I'm sorry we didn't make the wrong impression on the Hatrocks," says Weirdly. His wife asks if they're losing their touch. "Oh no, Creepella, we're just as repulsive as ever we were."

The only thing that can drive the Hatrocks away is "Bug music" (see below). "That music is even more gruesome than we are," says Weirdly. Fred, Barney, Wilma, and Betty sing Bug music and pipe it in through the radio and phone. The Hatrocks flee to the Gruesome house. Weirdly, Creepella, Gobby, and Occy are singing Bug music and even wearing Bug wigs. The Hatrocks run back to the Flintstone house and Pebbles, Bamm-Bamm, Dino, and Hoppy are singing Bug music. The Hatrocks flee to the World's Fair, which is showcasing Bug music, so they head back to Arkanstone.

FUN FACT: Like the Evil Scientists, the Gruesomes appeared in comic books.

GIGGLE RATING: Two and a half Giggles. Howard Morris either can't or doesn't do a good imitation. I guess Mel Blanc was unavailable.

AVAILABILITY: On the DVD *The Flintstones, The Complete Fifth Season* (2006).

The Beatles (1965)

King Features Production. Directed by Jack Stokes, Graham Sharpe, Ron Campbell, Jim Hiltz, Ray Leach, John W. Dunn, Bob Godfrey, Tony Gearty, Tom McDonald, Frank Andrina, Barry Helmer, Mike Jones. Written by Al Brodax (creator), Bruce Howard, Heywood Kling, Dennis Marks, Jack Mendelsohn. Executive Producer: Al Brodax. Cast: The Beatles (The Beatles), Paul Frees (George Harrison/John Lennon/Other Voices) (uncredited), Lance Percival (Paul McCartney/Ringo Starr) (uncredited), Jackie Newman (Female Voices) (uncredited).

The Beatles, in their final form—John Lennon, Paul McCartney, George Harrison, and Ringo Starr—were arguably the most successful act, let alone band, of the twentieth century. At the peak of their career, Al Brodax of TVC and King Features were able to get the Beatles and their manager, Brian Epstein, to agree to this Saturday morning cartoon because of the perception that they wouldn't have to do any work. The songs came from their already-recorded catalogue, which at the point went up to and included the album *Revolver*. Their speaking voices were performed by Lance Percival and Paul Frees. They were "Americanized", which caused Epstein to order that the cartoon not be shown in England, but which Brodax believed made the show more popular in the U.S. The premiere scored a fifty-two share, which was hitherto unheard of in daytime TV. The ratings made Brodax consider producing four prime-time animated specials. These never occurred, although he would go on to do the animated Beatles feature film *Yellow Submarine* (1968), without Frees and with Percival playing only minor parts. In the second season, ratings declined opposite CBS' *Space Ghost* (1966), part of their all-star lineup that included *Frankenstein Jr. and the Impossibles* (1966). Frees was in the cast of both of these shows. The fourth season consisted entirely of reruns from the first three seasons, and was shown on Sunday mornings.

Animation was done at TVC in London and was also done in Australia and Canada. As series animator Chris Cuddington recounted, "It took about four weeks to animate each film and I enjoyed it immensely. The characters were easy to draw, and the stories were simple and uncomplicated." Each episode was bookended by plotted segments named after songs. In the middle of each episode was the Sing Along, which consisted of two songs with the lyrics posted onscreen so the kids at home could join in. This was hosted by either John, Paul, or George, with Ringo providing comedy relief, often filling in for the absent Prop Man. There were few of these host segments, so they were heavily rotated. The Sing Alongs frequently use title songs from the week previous or following. George, nicknamed "The Quiet One", lives up to his moniker here, with most of the lines going to the "The Smart One" (John), "The Cute One" (Paul), and "The Funny One" (Ringo). The few sentences George does speak are done in Paul Frees' Peter Lorre imitation.

FUN FACT: In 1970, Paul Frees would record "Hey Jude" in the vocal stylings of Peter Lorre.

Season 1
Episode 1 (September 25, 1965)
"A Hard Day's Night"

At the Transylvania Hilton, the Beatles find it impossible to rehearse the titular song. George is two beats off. "Well, what'd'ja expect with this blinkin' nipper sittin' in m'lap?" Ringo takes them to a haunted castle near a graveyard for peace and quiet. "Ask any of our hundreds of satisfied users," says George. Inside, they see a Frankenstein-type monster (who sounds like Boris Karloff), a werewolf, a ghost, a vampire, a skeleton, and other scary things. "We're surrounded!" says George. They want to hear more music.

Paul hosts the Sing Along: "Not a Second Time"/"Devil in her Heart".

"I Want to Hold Your Hand"

On an ocean cruise, the Beatles hide from their fans in a "diving bell" (actually a bathysphere). "This looks cozy," says George. A marine biologist drops it into the ocean to find a mate for his captive male octopus. "You can't go out there," says George to Ringo. "That's water. You'll drown." A female octopus falls in love with them and they launch into the title song.

Episode 2 (October 2, 1965)
"Do You Want to Know a Secret"

In Ireland, George takes a chamber pot with his picture on it to the doorstep. "If you leave a jug outside the door, a leprechaun will fill it with gold, they say." A female leprechaun leads them to the Land of Leprechauns, and a secret pot of gold. She turns out to be agent Wilhelmina Morris, an agent, who offers the Beatles a piece of the action if they help the band she reps.

John hosts the Sing Along: "A Hard Day's Night"/"I Want to Hold Your Hand".

"If I Fell"

Mad scientist Dr. Dora Florahyde's assistant, Igor (not a Peter Lorre imitation), sent out for a beetle brain, comes back with the brain of the Beatles, John. Paul Frees has no lines as George.

Episode 3 (October 9, 1965)
"Please Mister Postman"

Stuck in the jungle with no money to send a regular telegram, Ringo uses a hollow log to send a Cannibal telegram, but forgets to reverse the charges and the operator asks for ten pounds. George grabs one of his sticks and says, "If she wants ten pounds, I'll give her ten pounds."

John hosts the Sing Along: "If I Fell"/"Do You Want to Know a Secret"

"Devil in Her Heart"

"You know, this Transylvania place ain't half bad once you get used to it, Ringo," says George. "Look at this picnic casket they packed for us." Ringo meets a marriage-minded witch.

Episode 4 (October 16, 1965)
"Not a Second Time"

In the jungle, the Beatles meet some big fans: crocodiles. "I'd say it ends right about here," says George.

Paul hosts the Sing Along: "Baby's in Black"/"Misery".

"Slow Down"

A western town renames itself after Ringo. Paul Frees has no lines as George.

Episode 5 (October 23, 1965)
"Baby's in Black"

The Beatles are in Transylvania again. "This place gives me the creeps," says George. In a secret laboratory, Professor Psycho creates Vampiress, half-girl, half-bat. Paul is rescued from marrying her.

"And now boys and girls, the most exciting part of the show," says George. "The Sing Along, in which you people in the audience join in on the lyrics." He tells Substitute Prop Man Ringo, "I'll tell you what, this next number is loaded with mood, so bring out something appropriate for mood." Ringo brings out a cow. The first song is "I'll Get You". "You kids out there really sang up a storm this time. The only thing was, a couple of you didn't sing as loud as I'd like to hear it," says George. He tells Ringo the next song is a "swingin' ring-a dinger." Ringo drops the Liberty Bell on him. The second song is "Chains".

"Misery"

The Beatles go to the wax museum. They get locked in and attacked by Dracula. Paul Frees has no lines as George.

Episode 6 (October 30, 1965)
"You've Really Got a Hold on Me"

"Some safari. Ten ruddy days in this ruddy African torture bucket and not one sign of big game," says George. A snake falls in love with Ringo.

Paul hosts the Sing Along: "Slow Down"/"Honey Don't".

"Chains"

Ringo imagines he is Captain Bligh and he makes the Beatles walk the plank. "We're sorry old boy. Really. Anything but this," says George.

Episode 7 (November 6, 1965)
"I'll Get You"

Back in Africa, George says, "Peace and quiet, it's wonderful." Mobbed by adoring fans, they commandeer a baggage cart. "Any of you fellas know how to stop this thing?" asks George. Their host is Alan Watermain, the great white hunter. Paul and John pursue a lion, who turns out to be two natives in a lion costume. "You don't suppose John and Paul ran into trouble with that lion, do ye?" asks George. John and Paul dress up like the lion and get shot by Watermain.

"Are you ready out there?" says George. "It's now Sing Along time. And I want every one of you kids out there to join in with us on this next song." He tells Substitute Prop Man Ringo, "This next one is really wild. It comes on like gangbusters." Ringo shoots up the set with a Tommy gun. The first song is "You've Really Got a Hold on Me".

"What I'd like you to do is create an atmosphere that will get the folks watching at home to really sing up a storm," George tells Ringo. Ringo douses him with water, and George flattens Ringo with a right cross. The song is "Any Time at All".

"Honey Don't"

"I can hardly wait to see the rodeo," says George. Ringo rides Honey the bull.

Episode 8 (November 13, 1965)
"Any Time at All"

In a French art museum, the Beatles imagine they are four of the Three Musketeers.

John hosts the Sing Along: "I'll Be Back"/"Little Child".

"Twist & Shout"

In a different French art museum, George admires a "sculpture." "It's called a water fountain," he learns.

Episode 9 (November 20, 1965)
"Little Child"

On the Texas Indian Reservation, the Beatles are ensnared by a young squaw.

John hosts the Sing Along: "Long Tall Sally"/"Twist & Shout".

"I'll Be Back"

Ringo gets a solid gold guitar, which is stolen. "You should have kept up the payments," says George.

Episode 10 (November 27, 1965)
"Long Tall Sally"

The Beatles, lost in the fog, stop at a haunted castle for the night.

George hosts the Sing Along. The introductions are recycled from Episode 5. The songs are "I'll Follow the Sun" and "When I Get Home".

"I'll Cry Instead"

In Japan, George's hand gets autographitis. "Thanks for helping me carry it, Ringo." They mistake a judo dojo for the hand doctor, and George has to fight the champ. "Fight? Let me out of here!"

Episode 11 (December 4, 1965)
"I'll Follow the Sun"

The Beatles' car breaks down. "Maybe we can fix the motor," says George. They are kidnapped by a highwayman and held for ransom.

Paul hosts the Sing Along: "I'll Cry Instead"/"Everybody's Trying to Be My Baby".

"When I Get Home"

The Beatles go to Paris and they hear Quasimodo. "Probably the Hunchback of Notre Dame," says George. Quasimodo opens for them onstage. "We better watch out," says George. "That's real competition."

Episode 12 (December 11, 1965)
"Everybody's Trying to Be My Baby"

The Beatles, lost in Japan, stay the night in a temple and are locked in by natives who mistake them for their ancestors.

George hosts the Sing Along. The intros are recycled from Episode 7. The songs are "I'm a Loser" and "I Wanna Be Your Man".

"I Should Have Known Better"

The Romano City Music Hall is burned to the ground, so the Beatles rehearse in the Coliseum. Paul Frees has no lines as George.

Episode 13 (December 18, 1965)
"I'm a Loser"

In Hollywood, Ringo becomes a stuntman. Paul Frees has no lines as George.

Paul hosts the Sing Along: "No Reply"/"I'm Happy Just to Dance With You".

"I Wanna Be Your Man"

In Rome, George reads the news, "Millions in gold coins stolen from Roman Etruscan Company. Wow, who's going to do what with all that gold?" The thieves have melted down the coins and cast it as a statue of the goddess Musica, which they paint white. The Beatles buy it for the British Museum and the crooks try to get it back.

Episode 14 (December 25, 1965)
"Don't Bother Me"

A criminal and his Odd Job-like henchman try to steal the Beatles' new songs.

John hosts the Sing Along: "It Won't Be Long"/"I Should Have Known Better".

"No Reply"

A Charlie Chan-like detective warns the Beatles about a jewel thief, the master of disguise, Anyface. Anyface disguises himself as Paul.

Episode 15: (January 1, 1966)
"I'm Happy Just to Dance with You"

"A Roman street festival!" says George. Paul gets caught in a bear hug by a dancing bear. "Sing, Paul, sing!" says George.

John hosts the Sing Along: "Don't Bother Me"/"Can't Buy Me Love".

"Mister Moonlight"

The Beatles are adrift in a lifeboat with a stowaway.

Episode 16 (January 8, 1966)
"Can't Buy Me Love"

On a South Seas island, George is finding a coconut particularly tough to crack. "How do those tiny monkeys ever get these bloomin' things open?"

George hosts the Sing Along. The intros are recycled from Episode 5. The songs are "Anna (Go to Him)" and "Mr. Moonlight".

"It Won't Be Long"

In Japan, the Beatles are shrunk by a mad bonsai scientist.

Episode 17 (January 15, 1966)
"Anna"

In Japan again, the Beatles are in a boat. "Let's stop here. I'm getting tired just from watching them row," says George. Paul falls in love with a woman on ghost ship.

Paul hosts the Sing Along: "Matchbox"/"Thank You Girl".

"I Don't Want to Spoil the Party"

Paul, George, and Ringo ditch John at a museum to go to a Greenwich Village party. "Boy, they got all types here," says George. "Poets, painters, even a circus strongman."

Episode 18 (January 22, 1966)
"Matchbox"

In Hawaii, the Beatles buy a trailer and park it on top of a volcano, which is about to erupt. "I think we're going on a trip," says George.

George hosts the Sing Along. The intros are recycled from Episode 7, the songs are "I Don't Want to Spoil the Party" and "Help!"

"Thank You Girl"

The Beatles are getting "fat, fat, fat, fat!" from rich French cuisine, so they are put on a strict weight reducing diet. They even get their money taken away so they can't buy fattening food. They go to a French cooking school and sing for their supper.

Episode 19 (January 29, 1966)
"With Love from Me to You"

At the beach, George reads an ad. "Are you ashamed of your body? Why be a weakling? Have the kind of body women admire." He is not strong enough to tear out the coupon. He is challenged to a surfboard fight by Surf Wolf. George paralyzes him with Instant Starch.

FUN FACT: The actual song title is "From Me to You".

Paul hosts the Sing Along: "Please Mr. Postman"/"I Saw Her Standing There".

"Boys"

"At last, a quiet, deserted beach where we can relax and enjoy California the way it really is," says George. They are interrupted by a contest to find Mr. Hollywood. George wins the trophy. "Unaccustomed as I am to public speaking," he says in his acceptance speech.

Episode 20 (February 5, 1966)
"Dizzy Miss Lizzy"

The Beatles are skating. "Don't let go of me, Ringo!" cries George. As a gag, John and Paul enter George in a skating race. He is paired with a fat little fraulein.

John hosts the Sing Along: "Ticket to Ride"/"From Me to You".

"I Saw Her Standing There"
In Spain, John is challenged to a duel. Paul Frees as George has no lines.

Episode 21 (February 12, 1966)
"What You're Doing"
A Romani woman tries to marry Ringo. "Stop!" says George in drag. "He's engaged to me! Come along, Poopsie." A Romani man takes a fancy to George.

John hosts the Sing Along: "Dizzy Miss Lizzy"/"All My Loving".

"Money"
The Beatles go to Coney Island with their share of the box office receipts sewn into Ringo's pocket. Ringo is pursued by a bespectacled man with a big nose and loses all his money. The man takes off his disguise and reveals himself as George. "I really pulled the wool over your eyes that time."

Episode 22 (February 19, 1966)
"Komm gib mir deine Hand"
In the Alps, the Beatles sing "I Want to Hold Your Hand" in German. They receive a Beatles flag which they are to plant on top of a mountain.

George hosts the Sing Along. The intros are from Episode 5, the songs are "Bad Boy" and "Tell Me Why".

"She Loves You"
On board a ship, the Beatles are spying on a mysterious passenger. "He's got a beautiful lady in there," says George. "She's a prisoner of that madman." The man tries to kill them.

Episode 23 (February 26, 1966)
"Bad Boy"
In the Alps, the Beatles meet a young boy who wants to run away to become a Beatle.

Paul hosts the Sing Along: "Please Please Me"/"Hold Me Tight".

"Tell Me Why"
In Spain, the Beatles meet a donkey who runs like a racehorse when he hears loud music. "You just gave me a great idea," says George. He enters

her in a race. "You blokes just sing good and loud and she'll win in a romp," he says to the Beatles. Ringo is the jockey and wins by a nose.

Episode 24 (March 5, 1966)
"I Feel Fine"

Paul says everything in Hollywood is phony, including leading man Dick Dashing, so Dick challenges Paul to do what Dick does.

George hosts the Sing Along. The intros are recycled from Episode 7. The songs are "What You're Doing" and "There's a Place".

"Hold Me Tight"

George and Ringo are at the Statue of Liberty. "Look at that suspicious-lookin' bloke and notice that package he's holdin' so gingerly." George thinks he is a terrorist with a bomb and chases him to the statue's crown. "Got you now, you bleedin' saboteur!" he says, in an apparent reference to Alfred Hitchcock's 1942 movie of that name. He falls off the statue but is rescued. The "bomb" turns out to be a cream cheese and jelly sandwich.

Episode 25 (March 12, 1966)
"Please Please Me"

In Spain, Ringo knocks out a bull who is scheduled to fight, so John and Paul dress up in a bull costume. Ringo is the matador and George is the picador. "You either have it or you don't."

Paul hosts the Sing Along: "Roll Over Beethoven"/"Rock & Roll Music".

"There's a Place"

The Beatles go to a TV studio and Mr. Marvelous, a trained ape, escapes. Paul Frees plays an Ed Wynn-like stage manager.

Episode 26 (March 19, 1966)
"Roll Over Beethoven"

Paul is Beatlenapped by Beethoven the elephant, so John suggests they play music to get Beethoven to free Paul. "It's worth a try," says George.

John hosts the Sing Along: "I Feel Fine"/"She Loves You".

"Rock & Roll Music"

The Beatles are mistaken for a string quartet. "Imagine," says George. "Us playing in a real Duke's palace."

Season 2

The second season boasted a new theme song, "And Your Bird Can Sing", and new opening credits with dedicated animation as well as scenes from the upcoming season.

Episode 1 (September 10, 1966)
"Eight Days a Week"

Lips Lovely, a Brandoesque romantic lead, can't kiss anymore, so Paul takes over for him.

Paul hosts the Sing Along: "Run for Your Life"/"Girl".

"I'm Looking Through You"

In Egypt, George points to a pyramid and says, "There's a nice shady place to practice for our next show." A mummy who has unwrapped himself steals Ringo's body.

Episode 2 (September 17, 1966)
"Help!"

In Paris, Paul and Ringo try to nab a fashion thief. Paul Frees as George has no lines in this episode.

George hosts the Sing Along. "This song starts off with a bang." Ringo sets off a cannon. The first song is "The Night Before". "This next song is one that really takes off." Ringo builds a plane, which crashes. The second song is "Day Tripper".

"We Can Work It Out"

"Since we've been out here, I've found that practically every great Hollywood star is superstitious," says George. "They go to people who tell them what's in their future, so they can avoid having bad luck." The Lucky Wizard has overheard this, and he tries to fleece them out of money. They capture him in his crystal ball and turn him over to the police.

Episode 3 (September 24, 1966)
"I'm Down"

In French wine country, Ringo spills a batch of wine and the Beatles have to replace it in two hours. "No use whining over spilled wine," says George.

John hosts the Sing Along: "Eight Days a Week"/"Paperback Writer".

"Run for Your Life"

At the Palace of Versailles, Ringo imagines he is helping Marie Antoinette during the French Revolution.

Episode 4 (October 1, 1966)
"Drive My Car"

The Beatles enter a hot rod race.

Paul hosts the Sing Along: "Yesterday"/"We Can Work It Out".

"Tell Me What You See"

In Hollywood, the Beatles meet the Man of a Thousand Faces (played by the Man of a Thousand Voices, Paul Frees). He turns Ringo into a Frankenstein-type monster. Frees imitates Jimmy Durante. Swee'Pea from Popeye has a cameo.

Episode 5 (October 8, 1966)
"I Call Your Name"

In Hollywood, Ringo adopts a frog and names him Bartholomew. The other Beatles make him turn it loose, but Ringo is offered a lot of money for the frog by a film producer, so all the Beatles look for Bartholomew. Bartholomew wears a hat and dances like Michigan J. Frog.

George hosts the Sing Along. The introductions are recycled from Season 2, Episode 2. The songs are "She's a Woman" (original broadcast, replaced with a repeat of "I Feel Fine")/"Wait".

"The Word"

The Beatles are in Egypt to entertain a sheikh's harem. They see the harem girls' faces and their punishment is to be thrown to the crocodiles. They say the password, "Love," and are rescued.

Episode 6 (October 15, 1966)
"All My Loving"
The Beatles go to an Indian Charm School, not knowing it is for charmers of snakes and tigers.

John hosts the Sing Along: "I'm Looking Through You"/"Nowhere Man".

"Day Tripper"
An extraterrestrial takes the Beatles for a ride on her spaceship and drops them off on a planet 23 billion miles away.

Episode 7 (October 22, 1966)
"Nowhere Man"
"There's nothing like a healthy tramp in the woods nearby," says George. They stumble upon a hermit's cave.

Paul hosts the Sing Along: "And I Love Her"/"Michelle".

"Paperback Writer"
The Beatles are asked to write the story of how they met.

Season 3
Episode 1 (September 16, 1967)
"Penny Lane"
The Beatles go to the titular street to foil a robbery.

George hosts the Sing Along: "Good Day Sunshine"/"Rain". The intros are reused from Season 2, Episode 2.

"Strawberry Fields"
"Permission to speak, sir. We've stopped, sir," says limo driver George. "I think, sir." They're in front of an orphanage and decide to visit.

Episode 2 (September 23, 1967)
"And Your Bird Can Sing"
The Beatles are on a birdwatching hike and they spot a green double-breasted tropical worsted.

George hosts the Sing Along: "Penny Lane"/"Eleanor Rigby". Yup, same intros from Season 2, Episode 2 they used last week.

"Got to Get You into My Life"

In India, the Beatles visit Swami Rivers. "We want to escape from our bodies," says George.

Episode 3 (September 30, 1967)
"Good Day Sunshine"

Ringo thinks he's a jinx.

Paul hosts the Sing Along: "Strawberry Fields Forever"/"And Your Bird Can Sing".

"Ticket-to-Ride"

"My hobby's electricity," says George. "Come into my laboratory and you'll see my latest experiment." It's a robot. "Don't be afraid of him. I built him myself." Ringo shakes hands with the robot and destroys it.

Episode 4 (October 7, 1967)
"Taxman"

Ringo dreams he is back in the day of Robin Hood.

George hosts the Sing Along: "Got to Get You into My Life"/"Here, There and Everywhere". That's right, you guessed it.

"Eleanor Rigby"

The kids think Mrs. Rigby is a witch, but she's just lonely and shy.

Episode 5 (October 14, 1967)
"Tomorrow Never Knows"

At Stonehenge, the Beatles fall down a well to the inner world.

John hosts the Sing Along: "She Said She Said"/"Long Tall Sally" (repeat).

"I've Just Seen a Face"

Ringo has lost his voice, so the Beatles take him to a haunted house.

Episode 6 (October 21, 1967)
"Wait"

The Beatles must find the Prince of Kropatkin, and, per George, "bring him back in time to stop her wedding to the wicked prime minister."

George hosts the Sing Along: "Penny Lane" (repeat)/"Eleanor Rigby" (repeat). No comment.

"I'm Only Sleeping"

John dreams he is in King Arthur's court.

GIGGLE RATING: Looks, Zero Giggles; Voice, Four Giggles. Not Frees' best Lorre.

AVAILABILITY: Various DVD editions of the complete series, of dubious legality, are available:
The Beatles Cartoons DVD–Complete (Unknown year)
The Complete Beatles Cartoon Show, Vols. 1-5 (Unknown year)
The Beatles Cartoon Series, Ultimate 3 DVD Box Set (Unknown year)

The Secret Squirrel Show (1965)

Hanna-Barbera Productions. Produced and Directed by Bill Hanna and Joseph Barbera. Story by Tony Benedict, Warren Foster, Dalton Sandifer, and Michael Maltese. Cast: Mel Blanc (Secret Squirrel), Paul Frees (Morocco Mole/QQ/Yellow Pinkie), Don Messick.

Made at the height of the James Bond parody craze, when every spy was Double 0-something and every spymaster had a letter name, Secret Squirrel, Agent 000, is actually more of a crime fighter than a secret agent. Sometimes he even works for the World-Wide Detective Agency, other times he works for the Sneaky Service or the Super Secret Service or the International Super Service. Sometimes he works for more than one in the same episode. Although the title song touts his mastery of disguise, he rarely uses it, and mostly relies on high-tech devices for his crime-fighting. His assistant is the fez-wearing Morocco Mole, played by Paul Frees as a Peter Lorre-type. When Secret enters, he announces himself, and Morocco usually says something like, "Ditto Morocco Mole." Their much put-upon boss, QQ, just wishes they would use the front door. Yellow Pinkie is their archenemy. His name is a parody of Bond villain Goldfinger, but he looks and sounds like Sydney Greenstreet. The score varies between serious stock music from *Jonny Quest* (1964) and lighter fare from H-B comedies.

The characters were introduced on the first prime-time cartoon pre-view, the hour-long *The World of Secret Squirrel and Atom Ant* (1965) on September 12. This show was not available for viewing and very little information seems to exist. It apparently had a live-action segment with Hanna and Barbera getting out of a helicopter, and then episodes from the titular characters. On Saturday mornings, Secret Squirrel shared his show with segments from Squiddly Diddly and Winsome Witch.

Season 1
Episode 1 (October 2, 1965)
"Sub Swiper"

A nuclear sub disappears into thin air at its christening. Secret is told to bring the sub back intact. He finds the sub with a giant magnet. It was disappeared by Captain Ahab, the international sub swiper, who captures them and explains that he plans to blow up the whole world, just for kicks. Secret escapes and throws the bomb into the arms of Ahab, still on the sub. Ahab is captured by Secret, who has to reassemble the sub with Morocco. "The elbow joint's connected to the ankle joint. The ankle joint's connected to the overdrive."

This episode included a brief Secret Squirrel/Morocco Mole interstitial, but no lines are spoken.

Episode 2 (October 9, 1965)
"Masked Granny"

Masked Granny plans to steal the balmy bomb and take over the world. Secret is in charge of guarding it, and he hides it in his lunchbox, but Masked Granny has him under surveillance. Secret delivers the bomb to the Pentagon, but Granny follows him and steals it. Secret and Morocco get it back, but Granny gets knocked on the head in the process. "Gosh, Secret Squirrel, she doesn't sound mean anymore."

Episode 3 (October 16, 1965)
"Scotland Yard Caper"

The Crown Jewels have been stolen and Secret flies to London. He mounts a jewel detector on his rental car. Not surprisingly, it beeps in front of a jewelry store. They stop two blokes from stealing the Crown Jewels and return the sacks to Scotland Yard. The Queen had sent them out for cleaning, and Secret and Morocco are to be imprisoned for theft. They escape the country dressed as dogs. "Little do they know that you're the best disguise man in the business," says Morocco.

Episode 4 (October 23, 1965)
"Robin Hood & His Merry Muggs"

Secret and Morocco are relaxing at home watching *Robin Hood* on TV when they hear a million dollars has been stolen. QQ puts them on the case. Secret gets on the crooks' telepathic wavelength with his Super Secret Sonic Sonar Detector and tails them with his triple reflex super radar finder. They end up at the TV station that broadcasts *Robin Hood*. Morocco looks in the dressing room and sees the three crooks, who are the stars of the show. Robin Hood sounds like Humphrey Bogart. Morocco and Secret pursue the crooks onto the soundstage during a live broadcast. Secret stops them with his Super-Atomic Neutralizer Bazooka. "Smile, Morocco, you're on TV." Morocco giggles insanely.

Episode 5 (October 30, 1965)
"Wolf in Cheap Clothing"

Wiley Wolf is smuggling sheep across the border, and Secret is on the case. Morocco dresses up like Little Red Riding Hood to lure the wolf to Secret's Instant Grandma Cottage (just add water). The wolf captures Morocco and steals his outfit and goes to Grandma's house. The sun dries out Grandma's house and shrinks it, capturing the wolf. "Boy, Secret, you sure are smart."

Episode 6 (November 6, 1965)
"Royal Run Around"

Secret and Morocco are tasked with escorting the visiting young Pasha of Puncha Baggy. The little Pasha ditches them and takes off on his flying carpet. "I like this country. I think I'll buy it." He eludes them at every turn until Secret's moths eat his carpet. Secret and Morocco put him on a plane for home, and somehow they end up with the flying carpet. "What was wrong with the old car, Secret? I liked it better den dis."

Episode 7 (November 13, 1965)
"Yellow Pinkie"

QQ tells Secret to bring in the notorious enemy agent, Yellow Pinkie. His hideout is on an island offshore. Secret uses his Freezer Squeezer to catch Yellow Pinkie, but when he brings him in, Yellow Pinkie pulls off his mask and reveals he is actually QQ. QQ pulls off his mask and is actually Secret Squirrel. Secret pulls off his mask and is actually Yellow Pinkie, who makes his escape. Morocco tries to pull his own head off. "I just wanted to make sure I am ME!" says Morocco, and giggles insanely.

This episode is heavy on exposition and introduces Secret's archenemy Yellow Pinkie, and was likely the pilot. This may have been shown originally in the prime-time special.

Episode 8 (November 20, 1965)
"Five Is a Crowd"

Dr. Dangit makes five copies of his archenemy, Secret Squirrel, and sends them out to commit crimes. They beat up on Morocco. Secret follows them back to Dangit's hideout and records Dangit's secret plan. After the quintuplicate Squirrels steal everything, Dangit will junk them. Secret plays back the tape for the quints and the quints gang up on Dangit. "He wanted to get rid of one Secret Squirrel," says Morocco. "Right, Morocco. And now he's got six of us to worry about!"

Episode 9 (November 27, 1965)
"It Stopped Training"

The Silver Streak Express, the world's most modern train, is about to go on its first journey when it is stolen. Secret and Morocco are put on the case. Morocco finds a gold button, which Secret analyzes to identify the thief, Yellow Pinkie, who lives on Devil's Cake Island.

"Well, if it isn't my old friend, Secret Squirrel," says Yellow Pinkie, who shows them his hobby, a model railroad. The train is the actual Silver Streak Express, shrunk down by Yellow Pinkie's Electronic Micro-Reducing Ray Gun. He shrinks down Secret and Morocco and puts them on trains headed towards each other, but diverts the Silver Streak Express at the last moment. Secret and Morocco shrink him down to miniature size and arrest him. "The warden's got a nice warm cell for you, Pinkie," says Secret. "Yeah, in his desk drawer," says Morocco, who giggles insanely.

Episode 10 (December 4, 1965)
"Wacky Secret Weapon"

Secret and Morocco are guarding a secret weapon. While Morocco bolts the door, Yellow Pinkie comes in through the window. He sprays sleeping gas on them and substitutes a phony paper secret weapon for the real one. When they wake up, Morocco sneezes, and the phony weapon collapses and Secret realizes the real one has been stolen. Secret analyzes the thief's footprints with his Supersonic Audio Picture Speaker and realizes Yellow Pinkie is at the waterfront. Yellow Pinkie has made copies of the secret weapon and is preparing to load them onto a boat. Secret and Morocco hijack the boat and dump all the weapon copies into the ocean. Yellow Pinkie flees with the original secret weapon. Secret turns the weapon onto Yellow Pinkie. While waiting for QQ to arrive, Morocco discovers the secret weapon makes popcorn. "Delicious," he says, and giggles insanely.

Episode 11 (December 11, 1965)
"Cuckoo Clock Cuckoo"

Big Ben has been copped, and Scotland Yard sends for Secret. "Seems to me someone rreeeally big stole that rreeeally big clock, Morocco," says Secret, channeling Ed Sullivan. Ditto Morocco Mole: "And look, there's a rreeeally big footprint!" Secret's Super Electro-Novifier sniffs out the criminal. It smells beanstalk, which points to the giant as the culprit. He has put the clock face into his cuckoo clock. He falls asleep, and Secret and Morocco try to get the clock before the next cuckoo. Morocco wakes up the giant, who agrees to give Big Ben back if Morocco will stay on as the cuckoo.

Episode 12 (December 18, 1965)
"Catty Cornered"

A cat has swallowed a high-explosive capsule that could blow the whole country to bits and Secret and Morocco must get him down from a pole. Secret uses his Instant Dial-a-Meal to produce a fish. The cat is lured down, but he is chased by a dog. Morocco tries to run away. Secret says, "What kind of a hero are you, anyway?" "A live one," says Morocco. "And I'd like to stay dat way." Secret uses the Dial-a-Meal to make a bone to attract the dog. The bone is attached to a jet fighter, which pulls the dog away.

Episode 13 (December 25, 1965)
"Leave Wheel Enough Alone"
A crook has stolen a million dollars in gold from the mint. Secret uses his Reversa-Time Tattle Tape Recorder to find out that Yellow Pinkie committed the robbery and plans to get the money over the border via the Cross-Country Auto Races. Secret and Morocco enter the race with their Instant Speed Fold-a-Car and Secret catches Yellow Pinkie with his Super Magnetic Car Stopper. Yellow Pinkie balks at ordinary handcuffs, so Secret gives him solid gold ones. "Oh, I tell you, that Secret Squirrel, he's all heart," says Morocco, who giggles insanely.

Episode 14 (January 1, 1966)
"Jester Minute"
Yellow Pinkie jumps out of the cake at the King's birthday party and steals his crown. Secret and Morocco follow Yellow Pinkie to Midnight Mountain. With the crown, Yellow Pinkie plans to rule the world and all its gold from the moon. He takes off in a rocket, but Secret uses his Retracting Rocket Reacher to bring him down to earth. Secret brings back the crown and launches it from the cake. It lands on Morocco's head with a loud conk. The King enjoys this and wants to see it over and over again. "Mind if I don't come next year? Something tells me I will need a rest. OUCH!"

Episode 15 (January 8, 1966)
"Not So Idle Idol"
Yellow Pinkie steals the Kredoran gold idol from a cargo plane. Secret stops Yellow Pinkie with his Electro-Freeze Ice Converter. Morocco breaks the idol and has to put it back together. "De toe bone connected to de foot bone. De foot bone connected to de ankle bone. And de ankle bone connected to de leg bone."

FUN FACT: Parodies *The Spy Who Came in from the Cold* (1965), which was then in theaters.

Episode 16 (January 15, 1966)
"Gold Rushed"
Yellow Pinkie steals the Washington Monument and replaces it with a duplicate. Then he takes all the gold in an armored truck from the Graborian Embassy. Secret tracks him with his Radar Truck Determinator to the fake Washington Monument, which is really Rocket XY leaving for Planet Z. Yellow Pinkie is going to build a gold palace and be a dictator. Secret catches him with his Airphibian Car-to-Rocket Converter. Morocco is given the job of putting back the real Washington Monument, which he installs upside-down. "I'm sorry, I thought the pointy end went in first."

Episode 17 (January 22, 1966)
"Double Ex-Double Cross"
Archcriminal Double Ex has sprayed the island of Oki-Doki with petrifying powder from a crop-dusting plane and plans to do Tokyo next. Secret turns the powder back on Double Ex. QQ turns the petrified Double Ex into a coat, hat, and umbrella stand. "It's good to see Double Ex doing an honest job," says Secret. "Yeah, it's de first time he can't be arrested for holding up something," says Morocco, who giggles insanely.

Episode 18
"Capt. Kidd's Not Kidding" (January 29, 1966)
Secret and Morocco are sent to an old galleon to get Capt. Kidd's ghost off it. "Capt. Kidd's ghost" is revealed to be Yellow Pinkie, with a glow from phosphorous. He escapes on his one-man submarine. Secret and Morocco follow in their sub and shoot him with their Periscopic Gun. Yellow Pinkie surrenders. He is put on display at the "Worlds Fair" as Capt. Kidd's ghost. As Morocco and Secret say, "You can't Kidd all of the people all of the time," Morocco giggles insanely.

FUN FACT: Mel Blanc does an homage to his "Mexican" routine.

Episode 19 (February 5, 1966)
"Bold Rush"

Yellow Pinkie steals a gold shipment. Secret, who is on vacation, helps Morocco catch Yellow Pinkie without letting Morocco know. Yellow Pinkie swaps out one of Secret's golf balls with an explosive one. Morocco stops Secret to correct his grip. Yellow Pinkie steps out to correct Morocco's grip, and when he hits the ball, it explodes. Morocco brags that he caught Yellow Pinkie all by himself. "And furthermore, Secret, I want a raise so ha ha ha ha, Secret, old boy."

Episode 20 (February 12, 1966)
"Tusk-Tusk"

Secret and Morocco go to the Maharajah's Royal Stables to find his elephant, Poojie. Morocco finds a peanut, and Secret's Electro-Fortune Cookie Computer reveals Poojie is being held prisoner in the Grand Wazir's Palace. Secret and Morocco gain entrance posing as court jesters. The Grand Wazir charges them on Poojie, but Secret uses his Invisible Elephant Tranquilizer, or Pachyderm Pacifier. Poojie throws off the Grand Wazir and runs away. Morocco tries to lure Poojie back with a peanut, but the Grand Wazir steals it and Poojie jumps out of the tree where he is hiding, right on top of the Grand Wazir. As Secret and Morocco make their way home on a cruise ship, Poojie comes out of Morocco's suitcase. "Can I help it if he likes me?"

FUN FACT: An homage to *Horton Hatches the Egg* (1942) (qv).

Season 2
Episode 1 (September 10, 1966)
"Robot Rout"

Yellow Pinkie uses his Robotizer to turn people into his slaves. They all support him for president. Secret and Morocco go to his secret hideout. Yellow Pinkie robotizes Morocco and orders him to destroy Secret. "Yes, Master." Pinkie tries to use his Robotizer on Secret, but Secret uses his Anti-Robotizer Gun. "All right, Pinkie, you're under arrest." "Yes, Master." Secret derobotizes Morocco. Secret Squirrel becomes the people's choice for president. Yeah, as though a cartoonish, rodent-like TV star with orange hair could ever get elected.

Episode 2 (September 17, 1966)
"The Pink Spy Mobile"

Secret has to stop Yellow Pinkie, who has developed a Spymobile that can destroy the city. Incredibly, it can even make skyscrapers collapse into their own footprints. Secret uses his Awful Spymobile Mangler. Yellow Pinkie then destroys Secret's car. "What do we do now, Secret?" The chase continues on scooter and skateboard.

Episode 3 (September 24, 1966)
"Scuba Duba Duba"

Scuba Duba has stolen an underwater missile and intends to destroy the city unless he is paid one million dollars. In their flying car, Morocco says, "Our readout seems to be picking up a signal in the ocean, Secret." They dive down and find the missile. Secret uses his Sleeper Gun and knocks out Scuba Duba. Secret turns the missile out to sea, but it hits his flying car.

Episode 4 (October 29, 1966)
"Hi-Spy"

QQ arranges a face-to-Squirrel confrontation in Paris with Hi-Spy, the world's foremost master of scientific criminology. After torturing Secret, Hi-Spy reveals he is really QQ. The real Hi-Spy is upstairs waiting for Secret. Secret tortures himself. "Why are you doing dat, Secret Squirrel?" asks Morocco. "If I have to go through all this again, Morocco, I might as well get used to it."

Episode 5 (November 12, 1966)
"Spy in the Sky"

Hi-Spy plans to become King of the World from his satellite. Secret flies up there and defeats him with karate pills. On the way back, Morocco presses the satellite's automatic destruction button and they are forced to orbit the earth for several years. "Don't worry, Secret. I had foresight. I brought a checkerboard along."

Episode 6
"Ship of Spies" (November 28, 1966)

Hi-Spy has an invisible spy ship in the harbor. Secret's job is to find the spy ship and stop Hi-Spy's plans to destroy the city. He and Morocco run into it and climb aboard. "I feel awful silly, climbing up nothing," says Morocco, who giggles insanely. They encounter Hi-Spy, and Secret uses his Revisible Spray Secret Squirrel Water Pistol to make the ship visible. Then he pulls the plug and sinks the boat.

FUN FACT: Daws Butler played Morocco Mole and Yellow Pinkie on the LP *Hanna-Barbera Presents Secret Squirrel and Morocco Mole in Super Spy* (Hanna-Barbera Records Cartoon Series HLP-2042).

GIGGLE RATING: Five Giggles.

AVAILABILITY: On the DVD *The Secret Squirrel Show, The Complete Series* (2015).

The Milton the Monster Show (1965)

Hal Seeger Productions, Siren Entertainment. Directed by Hal Seeger. Written by Jack Mercer, Kin Platt, Heywood Kling. Produced by Hal Seeger. Cast: Bob McFadden (Milton/Heebie/Fearless Fly), Larry Best (Count Kook), Dayton Allen (Professor Weirdo/Flukey Luke).

This show began life during Hal Seeger's production of what was then *The Fearless Fly Show*. Like Atom Ant, whose eponymous cartoon premiered a week before this one, Fearless was a crime-fighting insect. In the first three episodes produced, Fearless Fly's opponent was Professor Weirdo. Except for the color of his clothes, his appearance is identical to the character in Milton the Monster cartoons, and his voice is the same. In Episode 2, Count Kook joined forces with Professor Weirdo. His voice and appearance are the same as in Milton the Monster. In the third episode, animated by Shamus Culhane, sometimes considered the "Milton Pilot", Professor Weirdo homebrews a Frankenstein's monster-type named George, played by Bob McFadden with a big, dumb voice. Count Kook takes George to town, where he scares the residents. This brings him to the attention of Fearless Fly, who realizes he is harmless. Count Kook reports this to Professor Weirdo, who sends a mechanical man and two monsters, the green, furry, one-eyed Jeebie, who sounded like Peter Lorre; and the skull-faced Heebie, to destroy George. Fearless Fly takes them all out.

Culhane redesigned the character and named him Milton. Producer Hal Seeger realized he had a hit on his hands and sold the show to the ABC network. Bob McFadden was an actor who would later voice Franken Berry (qv) and play a character on the TV series *Voyage to the Bottom of the Sea* (1964), based on the movie with Peter Lorre. In an interview, McFadden said, "The producers, the animators, and everyone flipped over the character. No one in the public had seen it yet, but everybody was so crazy about the character and what was happening with it that they decided to change the name of the show from *Fearless Fly* to *Milton the Monster* with Fearless Fly segments."

Seeger understood that Professor Weirdo and Count Kook could no longer be Fearless Fly's antagonists, so Dr. Goo Fee and his assistant, Gung Ho were created. The Fearless Fly segments with Professor Weirdo and Count Kook were inserted into the middle of the season. Bob McFadden played Milton like Jim Nabors' character Gomer Pyle. Milton had a coal-fired head that blew smoke of different colors depending on his mood. In another change, Jeebie now sounded like Heebie formerly did and Heebie sounded like Peter Lorre.

Each episode began with the main title theme for the show, which included Heebie's saying, "Introducing the star of the show, Milton the Monster!" There were three segments per show, one Milton, generally one Fearless, and a wild card—either Penny Penguin, Flukey Luke, Muggy-Doo, Stuffy Durma, or a second Milton. Each Milton segment would begin with the dedicated theme song, which explained he became nice because Professor Weirdo added too much Tincture of Tenderness. At the end of the show, there would be a preview of the following week's episode. Heebie appears in the closing titles, but does not speak. The original run of the series was October 9, 1965 to September 8, 1968.

Season 1
Episode 1
Milton the Monster: "Zelda the Zombie"

After Fearless Fly, there is an interstitial with Heebie to set up the commercial. "You rang, sir?" says Heebie to Dr. Weirdo. There is a second interstitial after Flukey Luke in which Heebie appears but does not speak. In the Milton segment, Professor Weirdo is fighting a war with his rival, Professor Fruitcake. Count Kook suggests arranging a marriage between the families. Professor Fruitcake has just created a girl monster, Zelda the Monster, and it is proposed she marry one of Professor Weirdo's monsters. "I don't want to get married," says Heebie, but when he meets her, he says, "Watch me turn on the charm." Heebie, Jeebie, and Milton sing a song for Zelda. Zelda makes her decision: Count Kook. Count Kook won't marry her, but he will go steady. In the intro to the preview segment, Heebie appears but does not speak.

Episode 2
Milton the Monster: "Boy Meet Ghoul"

In the interstitials, Heebie appears but does not speak. In the Milton segment, Professor Weirdo is trying to get rid of Milton, and thinks he has found the answer in a personal ad from a woman seeking matrimony. Milton goes to the park and meets Miss Peaches, a homely woman with a baritone voice. Miss Peaches has two sisters and she wants them to meet Milton's two brothers. Heebie and Jeebie see the sisters and they flee. The sisters look like Heebie and Jeebie. Miss Peaches cancels the engagement, but the Professor homebrews a wife for Milton. Heebie has no lines in this episode.

Episode 3
Milton the Monster: "Monsters for Hire"

The landlord tries to evict Professor Weirdo for nonpayment of rent, but Heebie and Jeebie scare him off. Professor Weirdo realizes that he needs to raise money, so he tries to hire out his monsters. Milton is the one who gets a job. In his absence, Heebie and Jeebie install a torture rack in his room. "When he comes home from work, he can stretch out and relax," says Heebie. Milton's job is helping the landlord throw out Professor Kook. With the money Milton earns, he rents the house and lets everyone else live with him.

Episode 4
Milton the Monster: "Who Do Voodoo?"

In the interstitial, Heebie says to the carrier bat, "This is a very important message!" In the Milton segment, Professor Fruitcake uses a voodoo doll to extort $100 from Professor Weirdo, who gets ready to die. Heebie helps with the coffin measurements. "Professor Weirdo, it's ready." Professor Weirdo is about to be buried when Professor Fruitcake lowers his demand to $5.

Episode 5
Milton the Monster: "The Pot Thickens"

Professor Weirdo's Aunt Hagatha is coming, and he is afraid she won't give him her monster recipes if she sees Milton, so he sends Milton away to the North Pole. Aunt Hagatha arrives. "Dinner is served," says Heebie. Her secret recipe turns out to be for spaghetti and meatballs.

Episode 6
Milton the Monster: "Medium Undone"

Professor Weirdo sees a ghost, so he tells Count Kook to wake the monsters for a seance. "Why did you wake us up?" says Heebie. "I was getting my beauty rest." At the seance, Heebie says, "This is going to be spooky." Professor Weirdo hears a knocking sound. "Those are my knees," says Heebie, but he's no yellow-belly. "My belly's purple like everyone else's." The ghost appears. It is Dr. Fruitcake, who sells Dr. Weirdo his monster-making secrets for $3. Professor Weirdo gives him a five, and Professor Fruitcake promises to give him change at the graveyard. "I dig graves," says Heebie. "Now I'm getting scared." It turns out to be a trick. Professor Weirdo says he will kill Professor Fruitcake tomorrow.

Episode 7
Milton the Monster: "Monster Mutiny"

An interstitial repurposes the footage from the last episode where Heebie says, "Now I'm getting scared." In this Milton segment, Professor Weirdo brews Vicious Soisse, an antidote for Tincture of Tenderness, but it looks so good, he drinks it himself. He turns into a tyrant, but only until the effects wear off, so he plans to brew a potion ten times stronger. Afraid of what will happen, Count Kook tells Heebie and Jeebie he's revolting. "You think you're revolting," says Heebie. "Look at us." They plan to take over Horror Hill. Count Kook sends Milton to the grocery store for tangerines, but he returns as they are throwing Professor Weirdo into the dungeon. Milton falls in, too, but he knows where the secret door is, and they escape.

Episode 8
Milton the Monster: "Ghoul School"

The first interstitial is repurposed footage from Episode 6, with Heebie saying, "Why did you wake us up? I was getting my beauty rest." In the Milton segment, Milton wants to join the Secret Brotherhood of Monsters and bangs on the door of their cave. Professor Weirdo decides to get Aunt Hagatha come and teach the monsters etiquette. She dresses them in sissified outfits. "Jeeb, you pull my curls once more and I'll clobber you," says Heebie. Heebie and Jeebie tell Milton he can join their club if he gets Aunt Hagatha out of the house. Milton gets her out of the house, but she moves into the cave.

Episode 9
Milton the Monster: "Hector the Protector"

Professor Weirdo puts an ad selling Milton in the *Monster Gazette*. He is bought by Hector the Protector to collect debts. He collects an entire safe full of money at his first stop, but gives it away at his second. Hector returns Milton to Professor Weirdo.

Episode 10
Flukey Luke: "Palace Malice"

Flukey Luke is a cowboy who came east and works as a detective and solves cases by coincidence. His horse is named Pronto, and his faithful Indian companion, Two Feathers, has an Irish accent.

An Alfred Hitchcockian narrator sets the scene. Prince Elmer the End from the country of Louise, who sounds like Bill Thompson as Wally Wimple, comes to America and is welcomed by a James Masonian ambassador. The Prince hopes to get a million-dollar loan, and the ambassador schemes to steal it with a general. They dispatch their assistant, Gumbo, a gigantic man in a fez who sounds like Peter Lorre, to take out the only impediment to their plan, Flukey Luke, with his scimitar. Pronto breaks the scimitar with his horse shoes and Luke and Two Feathers give chase on horseback through the New York City subway system. Gumbo returns to the ambassador and the general. "It was too much for me." Flukey Luke? "No, the subway at the rush hour." Luke and Two Feathers arrive and the general's palace guard chase them. Pronto takes out the palace guard and Luke rescues the Prince.

Milton the Monster: "Horrorbaloo"

Milton and Abercrombie the Zombie attend a meeting of the Secret Brotherhood of Noble and Exalted Monsters in the cave and Abercrombie nominates Milton for president. Heebie nominates himself, and they vote by secret ballot. "It was a close race," says Heebie, "but I win unanimously." Abercrombie and Milton quit to start their own club. Both clubs try to get Fangenstein, a monster biker reminiscent of Marlon Brando, to join. Fangenstein decides to make one big club with himself as president. "All in favor of our kicking out our new president, say aye," says Heebie. Fangenstein kicks them all out and they have to meet in a tumble-down shack.

Episode 11
Milton the Monster: "Goon Platoon"

Milton, Heebie, and Jeebie are drafted into the army as Monster Privates. They screw up at basic training and are sent away during the war games. They mistake the colonel for a monster and capture him. "I bet we win the Monster Medal of Honor." They are sent home, and Professor Weirdo and Count Kook run away.

Episode 12
Milton the Monster: "The Dummy Talks"

Milton uses a shrunken head as a ventriloquist's dummy and it begins to talk on its own. Professor Weirdo gives him a suit of armor as a body. The shrunken head, which is now ambulatory, learns Professor Weirdo's great-great-grandmother shrunk his head and vows to shrink Professor Weirdo's head for revenge. Professor Weirdo pretends to shrink his own head with the help of a reducing glass.

Episode 13
Milton the Monster: "A Pie in the Sky"

Professor Weirdo sends Milton to Professor Fruitcake's house to borrow a cup of hairy knuckle powder, but Abercrombie gives Milton a black eye. Professor Weirdo bakes a pie with a bomb in it and sends it to Professor Fruitcake, but Professor Fruitcake frosts it and sends it back to Professor Weirdo as a cake, and it blows up. Heebie and Jeebie throw Abercrombie down a well, but Professor Fruitcake captures Heebie and Jeebie. Professor Weirdo calls Milton and tells him to come over to Professor Fruitcake's. He does, and frees Abercrombie. Abercrombie beats up everybody but Professor Weirdo, who is punched in the eye by Professor Fruitcake.

Episode 14
Milton the Monster: "Monstrous Escape"

Professor Weirdo has Milton put Heebie and Jeebie in the dungeon, but they escape. They dine and dash at a fancy restaurant. "You don't expect monsters to have money?" Professor Fruitcake catches them and sells them back to Professor Weirdo, who doesn't know they are Heebie and Jeebie.

Episode 15
Milton the Monster: "Abercrombie the Zombie"

Professor Weirdo steals Abercrombie from Professor Fruitcake and then sells Milton to Professor Fruitcake. Professor Fruitcake learns Milton is not a good monster, and gets Professor Weirdo to buy him back. Meanwhile, Heebie has sent Abercrombie home. "We caught him cheating."

Episode 16
Fearless Fly: "Fearless Fly Meets the Monsters" [Milton Pilot]

Professor Weirdo and Count Kook have to choose a monster to destroy Fearless Fly. It's Heebie's day off, the Mechanical Man has to see his dentist, and Jeebie says, in a Peter Lorre voice, "I'm his dentist." Professor Weirdo decides to homebrew a monster, but he adds too much Tincture of Tenderness. However, George the monster is so scary-looking, he makes people panic anyway. Fearless Fly and George end up playing ball together. Professor Weirdo sends all his monsters to destroy Fearless Fly, but he beats them.

Heebie appears in an interstitial using repurposed footage from "Horrorbaloo" but he has no lines.

Milton the Monster: "V for Vampire"

Professor Weirdo screams when he sees a vampire. "For that you woke us up?" says Heebie. Professor Weirdo sets a trap and catches the vampire, who is really Count Kook. He just wanted a good view of the cemetery. Professor Weirdo promises him a coffin with a glass top.

Episode 17
Milton the Monster: "Monster vs. Mobster"

The monsters are playing Jekyll-and-Hyde-go-seek. "I told you we should have hidden inside the grave," says Heebie. Milton witnesses two gangsters burying stolen jewels and they take him for a ride. Heebie sounds the monster alarm. Professor Weirdo, Count Kook, Heebie, and Jeebie take off after the gangsters. The gangsters agree to share the loot with Professor Weirdo, but Milton leads the police to the jewels, and Professor Weirdo is arrested.

Heebie appears in an interstitial. "The Secret Monster Club calls on Milton."

Milton the Monster: "Witch Crafty"

In the second Milton segment, Milton is playing catch with his croc when he sees the annual witches' convention and he tells Professor Weirdo, who sends Heebie and Jeebie out to spy on them. "I hope they don't catch us," says Heebie. They are caught, and turned into frogs. Professor Weirdo has Milton go out in witch drag to get the witches to change Heebie and Jeebie back. Milton wins Witch of the Year award, and he gets one wish. He wishes the frogs be turned back into monsters. The witches realize they've been tricked, and take off after Professor Weirdo, Count Kook, and the monsters. Milton shoots them down with smoke from his head.

Episode 18
Milton the Monster: "Camp Gitchy Gloomy"

Professor Weirdo decides to send the monsters to camp to get some peace and quiet. The monsters have a cookout on Milton's head and share it with the counselor. It's "Spider cider," says Heebie. After more spot gags, the monsters go home. Professor Weirdo still wants peace and quiet, so he puts his head in a vise.

Milton the Monster: "The Hearse Thief"

In the second Milton segment, someone steals Professor Weirdo's hearse, so he forms a posse. Milton finds the hearse in the woods and drives it back, but he gets arrested by Professor Weirdo and is tried at Horror Hill and is imprisoned. In the dungeon, Milton sees someone steal the hearse, so he breaks out and follows. Professor Fruitcake is the culprit. Everybody gets thrown in the dungeon. Heebie and Jeebie get thirty days. "That's only fifteen days apiece," says Heebie.

Episode 19
Milton the Monster: "Boo to You"

Professor Weirdo sends Heebie and Jeebie to the dungeon because he is upset with their table manners. "We'll dress up as ghosts," says Heebie, "and scare Professor Weirdo into being nice to us." Milton sees them and warns Professor Weirdo. Heebie and Jeebie encounter real ghosts, which come to haunt Professor Weirdo. Milton blows smoke at them and they leave.

Milton the Monster: "Kid Stuff"

In the second Milton segment Professor Weirdo decides to adopt an underprivileged child (it is implied he is doing this for the money), so a social worker brings the kid, Herbert, out, but first the social worker has to evaluate the home. Heebie and Jeebie scare him off, but he leaves Herbert behind. Herbert terrorizes the household. "You little monster!" says Heebie. "I'll take care of you!" The social worker returns and collects the child, who takes Milton with him. The agency calls with another adoption for Professor Weirdo. It is Milton.

Episode 20
Milton the Monster: "Horror Scope"

Professor Weirdo's Horror Scope tells him he is under a curse: an evil spirit will try to take his place at Horror Hill. To reverse the curse, he must be buried in a grave for an hour. "Can we go with you?" asks Heebie, but Milton alone buries Professor Weirdo. Milton is knocked out and can't remember where he buried Professor Weirdo. Count Kook writes Professor Weirdo's eulogy and his own acceptance speech as new leader of Horror Hill. Jeebie thinks another hit on the head will help Milton to remember. Unfortunately, Heebie has the same idea and Milton loses the memory he regained. Meanwhile, Count Kook's croc digs up Professor Weirdo, who returns.

Milton the Monster: "The Flying Cup & Saucer"

In the second Milton segment, Monsters from the Moon, or "Moonsters" land at Horror Hill in a flying cup and saucer and knock out Professor Weirdo's monsters. The only thing that can stop them is the "Meansters": Fangenstein and Abercrombie the Zombie. The Moonsters beat up the Meansters. "Watch the monsters beat up the Moonsters," says Heebie, but he and Jeebie also fail. Milton gets the Moonsters to fight each other, then sends them on his way.

Episode 21
Milton the Monster: "Monster-Sitter"

Milton destroys Mike the Mechanical Man and rebuilds him as a computer, which beats up Professor Weirdo and Count Kook. Heebie does not appear in this episode.

Milton the Monster: "The Moon Goons"

In the second Milton segment, Milton falls off the roof, and uses his head as a retro rocket. Professor Weirdo realizes Milton could fly to the moon and study Moonsters. "Good luck, Milton," says Heebie. "Keep a stiff upper head." He falls back to earth, but radios Professor Weirdo that he has reached the moon. A monstrous Boris Karlovian news reader broadcasts the story to the world. As Professor Weirdo is being congratulated, Milton shows up, exposed as a fraud by another reporter.

Episode 22
Milton the Monster: "Think Shrink"

Heebie and Jeebie are trying to get a shrunken head to reveal the whereabouts of the shrunken treasure. "We got ways to make you talk," says Heebie. Fangenstein steals the head. The monsters take off after him. Heebie and Jeebie get the head, but it falls into the water and Milton rescues it. The head reveals the location of the "treasure". It is really shrinking solution, and Heebie, Jeebie, and Fangenstein get their heads shrunk.

Milton the Monster: "Skullgaria Forever!"

In the second Milton segment, a mummy who sounds like Boris Karloff sneaks into the castle and replaces a mummy in a casket. The mummy knocks out Milton and brings him to a Skullgarian spy submarine to brainwash him into stealing the Professor's formulas. Milton accidentally gets unbrainwashed and goes back to the sub and beats up the spies and breaks their compass.

Episode 23
Milton the Monster: "Crumby Mummy"

A lightning storm brings Professor Weirdo's mummy to life. "We'll get him back in the case," says Heebie. The mummy beats up Heebie and Jeebie, so Professor Weirdo sends them away, along with Milton. The mummy chases Professor Weirdo and Count Kook around, so he brings back the monsters to put the mummy back in his case. Heebie and Jeebie again fail, but Milton succeeds.

Milton the Monster: "Fort Fangenstein"

In the second Milton segment, Fangenstein builds a mummy corral, and Milton reports this to Professor Weirdo. "Don't worry, Professor Weirdo," says Heebie, "us monsters are here with you." Professor Weirdo kicks Heebie and Jeebie out, and they join forces with Fangenstein to hijack Professor Weirdo's new mummy. They assault Count Kook and make off with the mummy. Professor Weirdo dresses Milton up as a mummy to entrap Heebie and Jeebie. He falls off Professor Weirdo's hearse, and Heebie and Jeebie steal him. At Fort Fangenstein, Milton's true identity is revealed and Fangenstein shoots at him. Heebie and Jeebie come to Milton's rescue and they all agree to have a showdown in the swamp. Milton wins the showdown, and Professor Weirdo gets back his mummy.

Episode 24
Milton the Monster: "Batnap"

Professor Weirdo's bat, Blackie, seems a lock to beat Professor Fruitcake's bat again and Professor Weirdo will get to keep the trophy. "He flies faster than my uncle," says Heebie. Professor Fruitcake pays off the judge, Fangenstein, to fix the race, but Blackie wins. Professor Fruitcake and Fangenstein steal the trophy, but Milton gets it back and seals them in a tomb.

Episode 25
Milton the Monster: "Dunkin' Treasure"

Milton is playing catch with his croc, who discovers sunken treasure in the moat. Heebie and Jeebie look but find nothing. "I don't think there is any sunken treasure down there," says Heebie. Milton dives down with the croc and brings up the treasure, which goes to the croc.

Milton the Monster: "Monstrous Monster"

In the second Milton segment, the Mayor calls and tells Professor Weirdo he has 24 hours to get his monsters out of town. Professor Weirdo decides to show the Mayor that his monsters are as normal as anyone else. Tidying up, Heebie finds evil spirit solution. "We can't let the Mayor see that," he says, and accidentally breaks the jar. Evil spirit solution gets into Milton's head and turns him into a beast. Milton must be destroyed. A knock on the head turns him back to normal. Or is he?

Episode 26
Milton the Monster: "The Mummy's Thumb"

Milton finds a Mummy's thumb that turns everything it touches into gold. Milton accidentally spills the beans to Fangenstein, who gets Abercrombie the Zombie to help him steal the thumb. They shell the castle. The monsters hold the fort, or "What's left of it," as Heebie says, holding up a bit of crenellation. Milton frees the Mummy, who gets his thumb back before Fangenstein can take it.

GIGGLE RATING: Voice, Five Giggles; Looks, Zero Giggles.

AVAILABILITY: On March 20, 2007, Shout! Factory released the complete series on a four-DVD set. This can be hard to find and pricey if you do. At the time of this writing, it was available for rent on DVD.com.

The King Kong Show (1966)
Season 1
Episode 13 (1967?)
"The Electric Circle"

Rankin/Bass Productions. Produced by William J. Keenan, Arthur Rankin Jr., Jules Bass, Larry Roemer. Cast: Billie Mae Richards (Billy Bond), Carl Banas (Prof. Bond), Bernard Cowan, Susan Conway, John Drainie, Alf Scopp, Paul Soles.

"You know the fame of King Kong/Ten times as big as a man" (lyrics from the theme song).

Anime in Japanese simply means animation, but in English it refers to Japanese or Japanese-style animated TV or film entertainment. This was the first traditionally animated anime series produced in Japan for an American company. From Skull Island (sometimes called Mondo Island), the giant ape and the Bond family go on adventures and save the world from threats.

The General, who sounds like Peter Lorre but is tall and angular, peers through the periscope of a submarine and tells Dr. Luboff they have reached Skull Island precisely on schedule. Luboff plans to establish a ground station and keep a fleet of nuclear missiles constantly threatening the enemies. Meanwhile, Kong rescues Prof. Bond and Billy from the Killer Triceratops.

Bond is brought into Luboff's camp at gunpoint. Luboff asks him if the stories of great beasts on the island are true, and Bond answers, "I have survived." Luboff decides to eliminate him because he knows too much. (Wait, what?) Bond says, "I wouldn't do that," and whistles for Kong, who buries Luboff and the General with a handful of dirt and rescues Bond. "There will be no work for us here unless we liquidate that big gorilla," says Luboff. "That will be difficult," says the General. "Bullets don't stop him. We must grab him."

The General's men kidnap Billy and hold him hostage. They tie him to a post and surround him with stakes that will "come alive with a nuclear voltage" and electrocute Kong when he comes to the rescue. "Clear the area," says the General. Billy warns Kong not to come close. "It's not working," says the General. The Killer Triceratops runs past Kong and is cooked to tri-tips. Kong rescues Bobby. Luboff and the General escape in a lifeboat, but Kong pokes a hole in their submarine. "It's a long row back to the homeland," says the General.

GIGGLE RATING: Looks, Zero Giggles; Voice, Five Giggles. It is not known who plays the General.

AVAILABILITY: On the DVD *King Kong Animated Series Volume 2* (2012).

The Super 6 (1966)
Season 1
Episode 10C (September 17, 1966)
"The Mummy Caper"

DePatie-Freleng Enterprises. Directed by Steven Clark, Hawley Pratt, Norm McCabe, George Singer, Robert McKimson, John Walker. Written by Tony Benedict, Alan Dinehart, Don Jurwich, Walter Black, John Freeman, Lee Mishkin, Homer Brightman, Dale Hale, Jack Miller, Bill Danch, Bill Hamilton, Art Diamond, Cal Howard, Jim Ryan. Produced by David H. DePatie, Friz Freleng. Cast: Daws Butler, Paul Frees, Arte Johnson, Charles Smith, Paul Stewart.

The last executive in charge of Warner Bros. Cartoons, Inc. was David H. DePatie, appointed in 1961, and ordered to shut down the studio in 1962. In 1963, he and Friz Freleng opened Depatie-Freleng Enterprises in the old Warner Bros. Cartoons studio. They outsourced cartoons for three years before bringing production back in-house. Robert McKimson, who took a two year break when Warner Bros. shut down its cartoon division, was hired back.

A parody show with half-dozen odd superheroes under the command of the dyspeptic Superchief. Each show would have a segment from Super Bwoing, then one from the Brothers Matzoriley (not part of the Super 6), and finish with another of the five superheroes.

Elevator Man wore a safari suit and a belt with buttons on the buckle that could make him tiny or gigantic. The show had voiceover narration and a noirish tone. Occasionally, a bad guy would even die.

The Quantex Idol has been stolen in the Mediterranean country of Bulrabia. Elevator Man is sent to get it back. He goes to Addis Addis, a small town near the pyramids where the idol was stolen, and checks into the Addis Addis Hilton. Walking around the streets, a turbaned local throws a knife at him, which he dodges by shrinking. Still small, he hitches a ride on his assailant's turban to the hideout of the bad guys.

At the hideout, Mr. X (who looks and sounds like Sydney Greenstreet) tells Asp (who looks and sounds like Peter Lorre) that he will not pay for the idol until the "stranger" is eliminated. "But you have nothing to worry about, my dear Mr. X," says Asp. "Ahmal the assassin is even now disposing of the American. Ah, he has returned. Well, Ahmal?" Ahmal reports that the American has disappeared, "like the mighty genie of *Aladdin*."

"Bring the stolen jeep around," says Asp. "You will drive us to the home of the mummy. And see that you are not observed. Another mistake will cost you your unworthy life."

Ahmal brings the jeep around, and Elevator Man jumps out of his turban and makes himself regular-sized. Ahmal flees. Elevator Man turns giant to catch him, and Ahmal leaps to his death.

Elevator Man takes the jeep and drives out to the pyramids. "Someone is there," says Asp. "It must be that American. Come, there is a way to trap him." A secret door inside the pyramid opens. Elevator Man goes in, and the door closes behind him. He finds a tiny crack, makes himself small, slips out, and accosts Asp and Mr. X. Asp pulls a gun and Elevator Man becomes giant-sized. The bullets bounce off him. Asp and Mr. X flee with the idol, but Elevator Man catches them.

GIGGLE RATING: Five Giggles. It is not known who plays Asp. Butler? Frees? I assume Frees is Mr. X.

AVAILABILITY: TGG Direct (under license from MGM Home Entertainment) has released the entire series on DVD.

Scooby-Doo Where Are You! (1969)
Season 1
Episode 17 (January 17, 1970)
"That's Snow Ghost"

Hanna-Barbera Studios. Directed by William Hanna, Joseph Barbera, Charles Nichols. Written by Ken Spears, Joe Ruby, Bill Lutz, Howard Swift. Produced by William Hanna, Joseph Barbera, Lew Marshall. Cast: Don Messick (Scooby-Doo), Frank Welker (Freddy), Stefanianna Christopherson (Daphne), Casey Kasem (Shaggy), Nicole Jaffe (Velma), Hal Smith (Mr. Greenway), Vic Perrin (Leech), John Stephenson, Jean Vander Pyl.

Young people and a cowardly dog with a speech impediment roam the country in a van, the Mystery Machine, and investigate supposed paranormal activity. Originally developed as a response to the backlash against violence in superhero cartoons where people die (see above) under the title *W-Who's S-S-Scared?*, it was rejected for being too frightening for children, so several changes were made. The dog became the star, the scary stuff was dialed back, and the comedy was emphasized. The revamped show became the keystone of CBS's 1969-70 Saturday morning lineup and whelped a media franchise.

The gang—Freddy, Daphne, Velma, Shaggy, and Scooby-Doo—pull up to Wolf's End Lodge, a "run-down, creepy" ski resort, in the Mystery Machine, and they can hear real wolves howling. The proprietor, Mr. Greenway, is a fat man with a British accent like Sydney Greenstreet. A small, bug-eyed man named Mr. Leech enters and asks Mr. Greenway, in a Peter Lorre-esque voice, to put his suitcase in a safe place. He pats Scooby-Doo's head and giggles insanely.

Mr. Greenway shows the gang to their rooms and warns them to lock their doors and windows before they go to sleep or the Snow Ghost will get them and turn them into ghosts. Shaggy checks the window and the Snow Ghost is outside it. "Zoinks!" The gang runs away and out the door of the lodge.

Freddy gets a couple of snow cars and follows the Snow Ghost's tracks. They lead to the edge of a chasm. The Snow Ghost is on the other side and he flies past them. The gang follows and sees a cave with a light burning and sends Scooby to investigate. Inside, it looks like a Tibetan temple. Velma rings the gong, and a lama, Fu Lan Chi, comes out. They tell him about the

Snow Ghost, and Fu says it is he the Snow Ghost seeks. When the Snow Ghost was a live yeti, he died pursuing Fu, but his Ghost returned to seek revenge and Fu fled. The Snow Ghost followed.

Back on the snow cars, the gang finds footprints covered in sawdust. They follow them to an old sawmill. They split up and search the place. While Scooby is admiring himself in a mirror, first Velma disappears, then Shaggy. Velma is chained to a log headed toward the saw. Scooby fends off the Snow Ghost and escapes down the flume, with Velma still chained up. The Snow Ghost sends another log after them, with dynamite tied to it. After they land in the water, Scooby uses his tail as a propeller to get away.

Back at the sawmill, the gang finds Shaggy, all white. He falls into a pool of water and it washes off the white stuff. The Snow Ghost throws a barrel at them, and they flee. Freddy, Daphne, and Velma hide among logs, and one turns out to be hollow and filled with jewels.

The Snow Ghost flies after Shaggy and Scooby on their snow car. They pass through some water and are frozen into ice cubes, but they get away. Scooby plans to throw water on the Snow Ghost, but the Ghost surprises him from behind and the water is frozen. The Snow Ghost is about to throw him off a cliff, but Shaggy hits the Snow Ghost with a giant snowball. Scooby and the Snow Ghost roll down the hill and hit the gang and the Snow Ghost's mask falls off. It's Mr. Greenway.

Back at the lodge, Greenway and Leech are tied up. They were the masterminds of one of the largest rings of jewel thieves in the country. Leech would bring the jewels to Greenway in a suitcase, then Greenway would send them down the river and across the border in hollowed-out logs. He assumed the costume of the Snow Ghost to scare people away and simulated flying by using transparent plastic skis. They would have gotten away with it, too, if not for those meddlesome kids.

FUN FACT: The cast includes frequent Peter Lorre impersonators Don Messick, Frank Welker, and Casey Kasem.

GIGGLE RATING: Five Giggles. Vic Perrin also appeared on *Scooby's All-Star Laff-a-Lympics* (1977) and *The New Scooby and Scrappy-Doo Show* (1983) (both qv).

AVAILABILITY: On DVD: *Scooby-Doo's Spookiest Tales* (2001)
Scooby-Doo Where Are You! Seasons 1 and 2 (2004)
Scooby-Doo Where Are You! The Complete Series (2010)

The Pebbles and Bamm-Bamm Show (1971)
Season 1
Episode 16 (1971)
"The Birthday Present"

Hanna-Barbera Productions. Directed and Produced by William Hanna, Joseph Barbera. Written by Neal Barbera, Walter Black, Larz Bourne, Tom Dagenais, Bob Ogle, Larry Rhine, Richard Robbins. Cast: Sally Struthers (Pebbles), Jay North (Bamm-Bamm), Lenny Weinrib (Moonrock Crater, Bronto), Mitzi McCall (Penny), Don Messick (Schleprock, Weirdly Gruesome), Carl Esser (Fabian Fabquartz), Alan Reed (Fred), Jean Vander Pyl (Wilma, Creepella Gruesome), Mel Blanc (Barney, Zonk, Stub), Gay Hartwig (Wiggy Rockstone, Betty, Cindy Curbstone), John Stephenson (Mr. Slate, Noodles).

The first spinoff of *The Flintstones* (1960) (qv), with Pebbles and Bamm-Bamm as teenagers. It has been described as one of the worst moments of the franchise. Morals were beginning to creep into Saturday morning cartoons.

Pebbles buys her mother a compact for her birthday. It is stolen by her tiny pet mammoth, Wooly, who buries it in the yard. Creepella Gruesome comes to the door to borrow some steak tenderizer. When Pebbles discovers the compact is gone, she blames Creepella. With their friends Wiggy (the most annoying voice in all of cartoons), Penny, and Moonrock, she volunteers to babysit Junior so Weirdly and Creepella may attend the Gruesome family reunion.

"It is time to depart," says Weirdly, and the gang searches the Gruesome house with no luck. They decide to go to the reunion, and put on prehistoric Groucho glasses as a disguise. Hilarious antics ensue, but Pebbles learns to judge people more fairly. "You think weird, just like we do," says Weirdly, who giggles insanely.

FUN FACT: The last appearance of Weirdly Gruesome under that name, although the character design would make one more cameo.

GIGGLE RATING: Looks, Five Giggles. Voice, Three Giggles. I guess Mel Blanc was unavailable.

AVAILABILITY: Amazon Prime.

Yogi's Ark Lark (September 16, 1972)

Hanna-Barbera Studios. Directed by William Hanna, Joseph Barbera. Written by Don Christensen, Fred Freiberger, Bob Ogle, Dick Robbins, George Gordon, Clark Haas, Warren Tufts. Produced by William Hanna, Joseph Barbera, Zoran Janjic, Norm Prescott, Iwao Takamoto, Lewis Marshall, Art Scott. Cast: Daws Butler (Yogi Bear/Huckleberry Hound/Wally Gator/Quick Draw McGraw/Snagglepuss/Augie Doggie/Peter Potamus), Don Messick (Boo-Boo Bear/Ranger John Smith/Muttley/Touché Turtle/Atom Ant), John Stephenson (Doggie Daddy), Henry Corden (Paw Rugg), Allan Melvin (Magilla Gorilla), Mel Blanc (Secret Squirrel), Josh Albee, Julie Bennett, Tom Bosley, Walker Edmiston, Virginia Gregg, Jim MacGeorge, Rose Marie, Hal Smith, Jean Vander Pyl, Vincent Van Patten, Lennie Weinrib, Jesse White, Paul Winchell.

A pilot for *Yogi's Gang* (1973) (qv). Morocco Mole only appears in the credits and has no dialogue.

FUN FACT: The cast includes frequent Peter Lorre impersonators Daws Butler, Mel Blanc, and Don Messick as well as frequent Sydney Greenstreet imitators Allan Melvin and Hal Smith.

GIGGLE RATING: Looks, Five Giggles; Voice, N/A.

AVAILABILITY: See *Yogi's Gang* (1973).

Yogi's Gang (1973)

Hanna-Barbera Studios. Directed by Charles A. Nichols. Written by Neal Barbera, Alan Dinehart, Neal Israel, Bill Lutz, R.T. McGee, Jack Mendelsohn, Sloan Nibley, Bob Ogle, Ray Parker, Dick Robbins, Paul West. Executive Producers: Joseph Barbera, William Hanna. Cast: Daws

Butler (Yogi Bear/Huckleberry Hound/Wally Gator/Quick Draw McGraw/ Snagglepuss/Augie Doggie/Peter Potamus), Don Messick (Boo-Boo Bear/ Ranger John Smith/Muttley/Touché Turtle/Squiddly Diddly/Atom Ant), John Stephenson (Doggie Daddy), Henry Corden (Paw Rugg), Allan Melvin (as Alan Melvin) (Magilla Gorilla), Mel Blanc (Secret Squirrel), Josh Albee, Julie Bennett, Tom Bosley, Walker Edmiston, Virginia Gregg, Jim MacGeorge, Rose Marie, Hal Smith, Jean Vander Pyl, Vincent Van Patten, Lennie Weinrib, Jesse White, Paul Winchell.

Yogi's Ark Lark (1972) (qv) served as both pilot and finale for this series, because why not? As in the pilot, Morocco Mole has no dialogue.

Season 1
Episode 1 (September 8, 1973)
"Dr. Bigot"

Episode 2 (September 15, 1973)
"The Greedy Genie"

Episode 3 (September 22, 1973)
"Mr. Prankster"

Episode 4 (September 29, 1973)
"Mr. Fibber"

Episode 5 (October 6, 1973)
"Gossipy Witch"

Episode 6 (October 13, 1973)
"Mr. Sloppy"

Episode 7 (October 20, 1973)
"Mr. Cheater"

Episode 8 (October 27, 1973)
"Mr. Waste"

Episode 9 (November 3, 1973)
"Mr. Vandal"

Episode 10 (November 10, 1973)
"The Sheik of Selfishness"

Episode 11 (November 17, 1973)
"Mr. Smog"

Episode 12 (November 24, 1973)
"Lotta Litter"

Episode 13 (December 1, 1973)
"The Envy Brothers"

Episode 14 (December 8, 1973)
"Captain Swipe"

Episode 15 (December 15, 1973)
"Mr. Hothead"

Episode 16 (December 22, 1973)
"Yogi's Ark Lark Part 1"

Episode 17 (December 29, 1973)
"Yogi's Ark Lark Part 2"

GIGGLE RATING: Looks, Five Giggles; Voice, N/A.

AVAILABILITY: On February 19, 2013, Warner Archive released the series on DVD in NTSC picture format with all region encoding as part of their Hanna-Barbera Classics Collection. This is a Manufacture-on-Demand (MOD) release, available exclusively through Warner's online store, Walmart.com, and Amazon.com. Also available for download via iTunes.

The Secret Lives of Waldo Kitty (1975)

Filmation Associates. Directed by Hal Sutherland. Written by Bill Danch, Jim Ryan. Produced by Lou Scheimer, Norm Prescott. Cast: Howard Morris (Waldo), Jane Webb (Felicia), Allan Melvin (Tyrone).

Lou Scheimer met Hal Sutherland at Larry Harmon Pictures when they were working on *Bozo The World's Most Famous Clown* (1958) (qv). Later, they formed the television production company Filmation Associates with Norm Prescott. The company was so named because they did animation on film. However, in the 1970s, they also began to do live action series, as well as hybrids, which is what this series was. Scheimer wrote, "*Waldo Kitty* [1975] was one of our three [parodic] shows for the fall, as we attempted to break into doing some more humor; clearly, we had gotten over our earlier aversion to [parody], and with the popularity of *Laugh-In* [1968], *Mad* magazine, and other media properties, it seemed the time was right. We wanted to do something that was really for kids, but that older viewers would get some joy out of because they knew what we were making fun of."

Lorna Smith, who was in charge of layout for several Filmation series, claimed she first brought the idea to Scheimer. Although he said he didn't remember the conversation, he gave Smith credit. The idea was "inspired" by the short story *The Secret Life of Walter Mitty* by James Thurber, and Thurber's widow sued, resulting in the live-action segments being deleted from subsequent broadcasts of the show on *Groovie Goolies and Friends* (1977) and title being changed to *The Adventures of Waldo Kitty*. NBC lowered the episode order from sixteen to thirteen, making it more difficult to sell. The dog was blackballed for chasing the cats all over the set. (His testicles showed on camera, so they were painted black.) Scheimer admitted the show was "a mistake on many levels."

Waldo and Felicia are two cats owned by a woman named Maureen. Tyrone is the bullying English bulldog belonging to Mr. Wetzel next door. Every show begins and ends the same way: In the live action opening, Tyrone is harassing Waldo or Felicia, or their friends, a parakeet named Sparrow or Pronto the bunny. Waldo, a "scaredy cat", would dream in animation that he was Cat Man, a superhero; Catzan of the Apes, a Tarzan parody; the Lone Kitty, a Lone Ranger spoof; Robin Cat, a burlesque of

Robin Hood; or Captain Irk in "Cat Trek", a lampoon of *Star Trek* (1966); vanquishing his evil dog foes. Allan Melvin, who played Tyrone, sometimes sounded like Sydney Greenstreet, but he would vary his voice for each villain role. He always had the same henchdogs: a fat shepherd, a thin Walter Brennan-esque hound, and a small cocker spaniel named Peter, who sounded like Lorre. At the end, in another live-action segment, Waldo would trick Tyrone into doing something that would get him into trouble with Mr. Wetzel or Maureen.

Season 1
Episode 1 (September 6, 1975)
"Cat Man"
Tyrone is supervillain the Jester, who makes Peter and the henchdogs giggle insanely every time he rings his bells. The Jester plans to steal all the flea collars so that he can take over the city while everyone is scratching. The Police Commissioner calls in Cat Man and Sparrow, the Bird Wonder. The Jester has also catnapped Lady Felicia, head of Felicia's Flea Collars, Inc.; and Cat Man rescues her and captures the Jester.

Episode 2 (September 13, 1975)
"Catzan of the Apes"
Waldo is Catzan and Felicia is Lady Vain. Tyrone is Sydney Greenalley, a bird poacher. "Aren't these endangered species?" asks Peter. Sydney puts his booty into his boat, the African King, but Catzan catches them and frees the birds. Sydney decides to grab Catzan and sets a trap for him, but Catzan is not fooled. "It was all set to go off at the slightest touch," says Peter. Sydney gives it the slightest touch and is snared. They try "The old branches over the pit in the ground trick," but Catzan avoids it, making Peter cry. Sydney decides to kidnap Lady Vain. "Then, Catzan will be powerless to prevent our pillaging, right?" asks Peter. Catzan frees her and Sydney and his henchdogs flee. Catzan catches them and they are sent to the jungle jailhouse.

Episode 3 (September 20, 1975)
"The Lone Kitty"

Tombstone Tyrone is whipping Pronto and the Lone Kitty rescues him and jails Tyrone and the gang. The sheriff promises as long as he wears his badge, justice will be served. Tyrone steals his badge and breaks out. The school-marm, Miss Felicia, is branding her one-steer herd with a rubber stamp. Tyrone's gang steals the entire herd, but the Lone Kitty is hot on their trail. "It's him!" says Peter. Again, they are jailed, and again, Tyrone lifts the sheriff's badge and they escape. Tyrone tries to rob a prospector, but is captured by the Lone Kitty yet again. Yet again, they steal the sheriff's badge and get out. This time, Tyrone tries to rob the train Injun 99. The Lone Kitty again puts them in jail, which by this time, literally has a revolving door. The Lone Kitty catches them again and this time, puts a star on the sheriff with a rubber stamp, so it can't be stolen.

FUN FACT: The music is a pastiche of the Lone Ranger's theme, "The William Tell Overture".

Episode 4 (September 27, 1975)
"Robin Cat"

King John tasks Tyrone the Sheriff with capturing Robin Cat, who is steal-ing back food the King had stolen. Peter comes up with a plan: "Capture Maid Felicia and then Robin Cat will have to come to save her." While Robin and his merry band are on their way to save her, they run into Peter disguised as the Out-of-Town Crier. "Come one, come all! King John's Annual Jousting Tournament and Barbecue! Takest the freeway to the turn-off at Nottingham Drive. See Tyrone the Sheriff challenge all archers. See the henchdogs bark up the right tree. See the lovely Maid Felicia award the prize. It's pot luck. Bring thine own dip and chips." Robin and his band go to the barbecue. Peter giggles insanely. "They fell for it!" Robin res-cues Maid Felicia and restores Richard the Lionhearted to the throne, and Tyrone and his henchdogs are carted off to jail.

Episode 5 (October 4, 1975)
"Cat Trek"

Waldo is Captain Irk of the Starship Secondprize, delivering kibble to the Dog Star. The ship is attacked by Tyroneus Caneus and the Klickoffs, who want the kibble. "Villains like them," says Peter, "give the rest of us a bad name." Irk decides to board Tyroneus' ship while Mr. Crock (a parody of Mr. Spock) entertains Tyroneus with an Al Jolson imitation. Irk tricks Tyroneus into destroying his own weapon.

Episode 6 (October 11, 1975)
"Cat Man Meets the Poochquin"

Tyrone is Cat Man's archenemy, the Poochquin. "He's a crook," notes Peter, who amends this by saying, "You're okay in our book." Poochquin has kidnapped the Police Commissioner's niece, Felicia. The Commissioner meets with the Chief, who now sounds like Jimmy Durante, unlike in his previous appearance. They call in Cat Man and Sparrow, who speed to the Poochquin's hideout while the Commissioner and the Chief literally fall into the Poochquin's trap. The Poochquin releases Felicia and Peter giggles insanely. Cat Man and Sparrow trick the Poochquin and his henchdogs into getting into a paddy wagon.

Episode 7 (October 18, 1975)
"Catzan or Not Catzan"

Tyrone returns as Sydney Greenalley, who accidentally uncovers a lost jungle city. Catzan enters, and tells them to leave. "Don't argue with him, Sydney," says Peter. "There's no telling what Catzan will do if you irritate him." Sydney dresses Peter up like Catzan and has him stir up trouble with the beasts of the jungle. "I'm sick and tired of swinging around in this hot, miserable costume," Peter says to Sydney, who tells him the plan is working and he won't have to do it much longer.

Lady Vain tells Catzan something is wrong and he runs into Peter dressed as Catzan. Sydney flees in the boat African King and Catzan catches him.

Episode 8 (October 25, 1975)
"The Lone Kitty Rides Again"

Tombstone Tyrone, who, unlike his previous appearance, now sounds like John Wayne, is trying to free Pecos Paul, whom the Jimmy Stewart-like marshal is taking by stagecoach to the jail. Also on the stage is M.S. Kittycat (Felicia). It's up to the Lone Kitty and Pronto to stop Tyrone. "Who was that masked cat?" asks M.S. Kittycat. "No one special," says the Marshal. "You big fibber," say Peter and the henchdogs.

Episode 9 (November 1, 1975)
"Sheriff of Sherwood"

"Robin Cat could learn from us," says Peter. "We take from the poor." King John summons his wizard, Merlin, who sounds like Boris Karloff. Merlin catnaps Maid Felicia to get Robin Cat to come to her rescue. King John pretends to fire Sheriff Tyrone and "hires" Robin in his stead. The henchdogs bump into Robin, causing the stolen goods they have planted on him to fall out. King John imprisons him in the tower. Grizzle John and Friar Duck free him and they frame the real Sheriff and rescue Maid Felicia.

Episode 10 (November 8, 1975)
"Cat Man Meets the Puzzler"

"Hey Puzzler, how come we're knocking over this big city eraser company?" asks Peter. After stealing all the erasers, the Puzzler steals all the dictionaries. "And the city will pay us dearly for their return." The Commissioner calls Cat Man. Peter reads road signs put up by Cat Man, who catches the Puzzler and finds the stolen objects.

Episode 11 (November 15, 1975)
"Dr. Livingstone, I Perfume?"

Sydney wants to find Dr. Stanley Livingstone so he can live off the fat of the land. "From that belly on you," says Peter, "you've been living off it for a long time." Catzan tells them to leave the jungle, then he goes to Dr. Livingstone's pharmacy to get perfume for Lady Vain. Dr. Livingstone sounds like Ed Wynn. When Catzan leaves, Sydney and his henchdogs enter to steal the flower from which the perfume is derived. They take off down the river in the African King and Catzan swims after them and turns them in.

Episode 12 (November 22, 1975)
"Ping or Pongo"

Captain Irk changes course for the Planet Pongo to aid Emperor Ping, who appears to be in distress. Pongo has melted Daliesque watches everywhere. Ping captures the crew and forces Irk to claim a constellation for Pongo. Fortunately, Crock has foreseen this event and created an android double of Irk. The android Irk flies to the constellation by a remote-control device while the real one rescues his crew. "We've got him in the path of our electronic cage," says Peter, and traps Irk, who pulls the plug. "Hey, no fair," says Peter. "We have one trap left: the Inviso-Shield," says Peter. Irk passes through the Inviso-Shield with a portable zipper. He drills through the floor to get to his crew and they call back the Secondprize and escape.

Episode 13 (November 29, 1975)
"Chaw the Bullet"

Felicia the schoolmarm is getting ready for the big land rush. Tombstone Tyrone (no longer channeling John Wayne) plans to take all the land for himself. He takes all the wheels off their wagons, but the Lone Kitty puts them back on. "Tombstone, you know who that masked cat is?" asks Peter. The Lone Kitty foils Tombstone Tyrone. "That's the Lone Kitty," says Peter.

GIGGLE RATING: Looks, Zero Giggles. Nothing special is done to make Peter look like Lorre. Voice, Five Giggles. It is not known who played him. Howard Morris?

AVAILABILITY: In August 1989, United American Video released three of the episodes on VHS.

Scooby's All-Star Laff-A-Lympics (1977)

Hanna-Barbera Studios. Directed by Charles A. Nichols, Ray Patterson, Carl Urbano. Series Writing Credits: Neal Barbera, Tom Dagenais (story). Executive Producers: William Hanna, Joseph Barbera. Cast: Don Messick (Scooby-Doo/Boo-Boo Bear/Pixie/Mumbly/Dastardly Dalton), Casey

Kasem (Shaggy/Mr. Creepley), Frank Welker (Tinker/Dynomutt/Sooey Pig/Magic Rabbit), Scatman Crothers (Hong Kong Phooey), Daws Butler (Scooby-Dum/Yogi Bear/Huckleberry Hound/Hokey Wolf/Snooper/ Blabber/Wally Gator/Quick Draw McGraw/Dirty Dalton/Snagglepuss), Gary Owens (Blue Falcon), Julie McWhirter (Jeannie), Joe Besser (Babu), Mel Blanc (Captain Caveman, Speed Buggy), Marilyn Schreffler (Brenda Chance/Daisy Mayhem), Vernee Watson (Dee Dee Sykes), Laurel Page (Taffy Dare/Mrs. Creepley), John Stephenson (Dread Baron/Great Fondoo/ Doggie Daddy), Bob Holt (Grape Ape/Orful Octopus/Dinky Dalton), Jimmy Weldon (Yakky Doodle), Julie Bennett (Cindy Bear), John Astin, Ted Cassidy, Henry Corden, Stefanianna Christopherson, Micky Dolenz, Joan Gerber, Florence Halop, Pat Harrington, Hettie Lynn Hurtes, Nicole Jaffe, Ann Jillian, Heather North, Vic Perrin, Alan Reed, Mike Road, Ronnie Schell, Hal Smith, Susan Steward, Jean Vander Pyl, Janet Waldo, Bill Woodson.

This show ran concurrently with *The Scooby-Doo Show* (1976), the third iteration of that series, but it is not considered canonical. It aired over three seasons under three different titles, including *Scooby's All-Stars* (1979) and *Scooby's Laff-a-Lympics* (1980). Over 45 Hanna-Barbera stars were divided into three teams: the Yogi Yahooeys, the Scooby-Doobies, and the Really Rottens. Some were established characters, like Yogi, Cindy, and Boo-Boo Bear (qv); Quick Draw McGraw (qv), Huckleberry Hound (qv), Wally Gator (an Ed Wynn-like crocodilian), Hokey Wolf (a lupine con artist), Grape Ape (a giant purple gorilla), Augie Doggie and Doggie Daddy (qv), Pixie and Dixie (twin mice), and Snooper and Blabber (qv) for the Yogis; Dynomutt from his eponymous show with his human companion, Blue Falcon; Speed Buggy from his eponymous show and his human companion, Tinker; Babu from *Jeannie* (1973), Captain Caveman and the Teen Angels from their eponymous show, and Scooby (qv) and his friends for the Scoobys; but except for the gigantic Dinky Dalton and his brothers from *The Huckleberry Hound Show* (1958), most of the other characters in the Really Rottens were invented for this cartoon. Dread Baron is a knockoff of Dick Dastardly, whom Hanna-Barbera wanted to use but couldn't. His Muttley-like sidekick is Mumbly, repurposed from *The Mumbly Cartoon*

Show (1976), where he played a Lt. Columbo-esque detective. The Great Fondoo is a Eurotrash prestidigitator with a Magic Rabbit. Daisy Mayhem is a cutoff-wearing hillbilly and Sooey is her pig. Mr. and Mrs. Creepley are basically spiritual descendants of The Gruesomes from *The Flintstones* (1960) and the Evil Scientists from Snooper and Blabber. Junior is their son, and Orful is their octopus, based on the Gruesomes' pet, Occy. Creepley is short and mustachioed, with blue skin and a somewhat Lorre-esque voice. He is played by Casey Kasem, who did cartoon voices for fifty years, including Shaggy Rogers in various iterations of Scooby-Doo, but who is best known as the radio DJ that hosted *American Top 40* (1970). I guess Mel Blanc, Daws Butler, Don Messick, Vic Perrin, and Frank Welker were all unavailable.

Teams compete in a parody of *Battle of the Network Stars* (1976). Each show would take place successively in two locations. Snagglepuss (qv) and Mildew Wolf (a vocal parody of Paul Lynde) provide the play-by-play. They wear the yellow jackets of the sportscasters at ABC, the network this show was on. Other Hanna-Barbera stars like Barney Rubble and Fred Flintstone (qv) and Jabberjaw (a Curly Howard-like shark) occasionally provide color commentary. The Rottens sometimes win events through, well, rotten means, but they often get caught and are penalized. The other teams apparently cheat, too (the rules are sometimes ambiguous), but nothing happens to them.

Season 1
Episode 1 (September 10, 1977)
"The Swiss Alps and Tokyo, Japan"

In Switzerland, the Great Fondoo, Magic Rabbit, Mr. Creepley, and Orful Octopus comprise the Rottens bobsled team. Dread Baron and Mumbly tie an anchor to the bobsled of Captain Caveman and the Teen Angels for the Scoobys. The sled takes off without them. The Yogis (Wally Gator, Augie Doggie, Quick Draw McGraw, and Grape Ape) launch their sled without incident. The Rottens get a boost from Orful Octopus' tentacles. "Time to stop being rotten and be sneaky," says Creepley. They take a shortcut through a snowbank with a drill. They win the race, but they don't cross the finish line.

In Tokyo, Grape Ape sumo-wrestles the Dalton Brothers, who tickle him. "How terrible," says Creepley. And the winner is–oh, who cares?

[Creepley does not appear in Season 1, Episode 2 "Acapulco and England" except for the stock footage in the opening titles.]

Episode 3 (September 24, 1977)
"Florida and China"

In China, Blue Falcon, with one paddle, is holding his own against Orful Octopus in ping-pong even though Orful has eight paddles. Creepley, giggling insanely, steals Falcon's paddle and Orful wins. The anti-cheat cameras catch the Rottens in the act, and they are penalized.

Episode 4 (October 1, 1977)
"The Sahara Desert and Scotland"

In the Ups and Downs Dune Buggy Race, it's Tinker and Speed Buggy for the Scoobys, Yogi and Boo-Boo for the Yogis, and Mrs. Creepley and Mumbly for the Rottens. Tinker gets stuck on top of a pointy sand dune. He gets off, but Dread and Creepley have put up a flexo-steel net in his way. He goes underneath, but the net catches Yogi. The Rottens win, but they cheated, so they get last place.

Episode 5 (October 8, 1977)
"France and Australia"

In France, it's Grape Ape versus Captain Caveman versus Orful in the Captivating Capture the Flag at the Top of the Eiffel Tower Contest. Creepley pours "Slippery, goopy, greasy grease" down the girders and giggles insanely. Grape Ape wins anyhow.

In Australia, it's Dread versus Doggie Daddy versus Falcon in the Boomerang Throw. Creepley has Horrible Hawk, an actual falcon, try to catch Blue Falcon's boomerang, but it is too fast.

Episode 6 (October 15, 1977)
"Athens, Greece and the Ozarks"

In Athens, the teams must pole vault from an "X" marked on the ground. "Notice the X covers a ten-foot deep hole filled with mush," says Creepley. Scooby sinks into the mush and gets no points. Blue Falcon discovers Creepley's cheating and the Scoobys get second place.

In the Ozarks, Creepley paints a trompe-l'œil tunnel on a rock to derail Blue Falcon and Dynomutt in the Titanically Terrific Teeter-Totter Rail Car (or handcar) Race. "When Blue Falcon tries to teeter-totter through this tunnel, he'll make a big hit." However, Blue Falcon lets Grape Ape and Doggie Daddy go ahead of him, and Grape Ape crashes a hole through the rock.

Episode 7 (October 22, 1977)
"Italy and Kitty Hawk, North Carolina"

Creepley only appears in crowd scenes and has no solo lines.

Episode 8 (October 29, 1977)
"Egypt and Sherwood Forest"

In Egypt, there's a race to the tip of the pyramid. It's Tinker and Speed Buggy versus Yogi and Boo-Boo versus Creepley and Orful. Creepley and Orful use a hoist placed by Mumbly to race up the pyramid. When they get to the hoist, Mumbly sends them up on a jack. The Rottens' cheating is detected, and Dread saws the tip of the pyramid off so no one can win. Tinker catches it with his whip and wins. Creepley and Orful descend ignominiously on the jack.

In Sherwood Forest, there's a footrace in full armor with Shaggy and Scooby versus Grape Ape and Huck versus Dinky and Dirty Dalton. Creepley switches the directional signs "to bog down the competition," and giggles insanely. Dinky unwittingly switches the signs back and gets bogged down himself. "Now he's going to be a good sport in spite of himself."

Episode 9 (November 5, 1977)
"Spain and the Himalayas"
In the Hang the Bell on the Abominable Snowman Contest, it's Grape Ape versus Blue Falcon versus Daisy Mayhem. The race starts and Daisy floats up into the clouds. "All it takes is invisible wire and a cloud-camouflaged pedal chopper," says Creepley, who controls the aforementioned vehicle. He lowers her down, but she balks at belling the yeti. Blue Falcon saves her, but meanwhile, she hangs her bell on the snowman. However, she loses her bonus points for unsportsmanlike behavior.

Episode 10 (November 12, 1977)
"India and Israel"
In the Sand Sail Sledding Contest in Israel, it's Tinker, Speed Buggy, and the Teen Angels for the Scoobys; Hokey Wolf, Wally Gator, and Quick Draw for the Yogis; and Orful and the Creepleys for the Rottens. The Rottens jump out in first place with Orful acting as a fan to blow their sail, but Tinker uses the exhaust from Speed Buggy to blow his sail and beat them.

Episode 11 (November 19, 1977)
"Africa and San Francisco"
In San Francisco, Orful Octopus is roller-skating against Pixie and Dixie for the Yogis, and Babu for the Scoobys. Creepley puts Orful into the sidecar of his motorcycle to cheat and win. "Who says it doesn't pay to be sneaky?" However, they are caught and points are deducted.

Episode 12 (November 26, 1977)
"The Grand Canyon and Ireland"
In Ireland, the Daltons plan to trap the Leprechaun and Creepley plans to steal the Leprechaun's gold. Grape Ape and Falcon team up to foil their plan.

Episode 13 (December 3, 1977)
"Hawaii and Norway"
In the Viking boat race, Creepley uses atomic power. It's not cheating because it's on the high seas. Grape Ape blows on his sail and the Yogis easily win.

Episode 14 (December 10, 1977)
"North Pole and Tahiti"

At the North Pole Grand Prix Igloo-Building Contest, Creepley sabotages Quick Draw's igloo with a blowtorch. Dinky accidentally destroys his igloo and the Yogis win.

In Tahiti, the Rottens are losing the Pedal Boat Pontoon Pedal Boat race so Creepley, in the support boat, releases Orful to start a whirlpool. All the teams are caught in the whirlpool, but Orful lifts the Rottens' boat out. To ensure victory for the Rottens, Fondoo magically creates a bed of kelp which ensnares the Yogis' boat, but the Yogis use it to their advantage and win.

Episode 15 (December 17, 1977)
"The Old West and Holland"

In the Windmill-Riding Contest, Creepley cheats by using Orful's eight legs as the windmill blades. "OK, Orful, let's go into passing gear." They get caught and their score is halved.

Episode 16 (December 24, 1977)
"Quebec and Baghdad"

Creepley and Orful Octopus are in the tree-chopping competition. "Let's wind up a little rotten power." Their tree falls first, but it knocks down the Yogi's tree so the Yogis win.

Season 2
Episode 1 (September 9, 1978)
"Russia and the Caribbean"

Creepley only appears in crowd scenes and has no solo lines.

Episode 2 (September 16, 1978)
"New York and Turkey"

Creepley enters Hansom Carriage Race through Central Park. The Dalton Brothers create a detour over a frozen lake. "After you, Blue Falcon," says Creepley. Blue Falcon spins out on the ice and Creepley takes the lead. The Blue Falcon flies and overtakes Creepley. "He uncheated himself," says Creepley. "I'm through being a nice guy." He tries to put Doggie Daddy into the gorilla cage at the zoo, but ends up there himself. "Hey, knock it off, you big ape." She spanks him and he says, "I'm sorry, mummy."

Episode 3 (September 23, 1978)
"South America and Transylvania"

In Transylvania, Mr. and Mrs. Creepley enter a scavenger hunt. They have to get an autograph from a Frankenstein-type monster who sounds like Boris Karloff and catch a vampire bat.

Episode 4 (September 30, 1978)
"French Riviera and New Zealand"

In the three-way tug of war, Junior Creepley cheats by using a bulldozer, but still isn't winning. "We'll just double our efforts," says Creepley, adding a second bulldozer. "Full speed ahead to victory!" The rope snaps and the Rottens lose. "Remember, kid, it's not how you play the game, it's how dirty you play it."

Episode 5 (October 7, 1978)
"New Orleans and Atlantis"

In the Antique Aircraft Distance Contest, Creepley fills Huckleberry Hound's plane with cement. "I'd like to see this bamboo bomber try to fly." In the dragon race, Creepley gives the other teams the slip "the oil fashioned way" by pouring grease on the track. He giggles insanely.

Episode 6 (October 14, 1978)
"Morocco and Washington, D.C."

In the Rally Race through D.C., Creepley and Junior stop traffic with a parade and the Rottens pull into the lead. The Rottens win the games for the first and only time. In Morocco, there are no references to *Casablanca* (1942) or Morocco Mole.

Episode 7 (October 21, 1978)
"Canada and Poland"

Creepley enters the pole vault standing on the shoulders of his team. "Now we'll show them what really rotten vaulting is." He makes a fifty-foot vault, but everyone falls on top of him. "If this is the top, I'll take the bottom."

Episode 8 (October 28, 1978)
"Siam and the Moon"

Creepley only appears in crowd scenes and has no solo lines. The teams tie for the first and only time.

FUN FACTS: Like the Scientists and the Gruesomes, the Creepleys appeared in comic books.

Peter Lorre claimed he and his friends invented and popularized the slang word "creep", although they spelled it "kreap" and it did not have the same connotations.

GIGGLE RATING: Looks, Five Giggles; Voice, Four Giggles.

AVAILABILITY: On DVD:

Scooby's All Star Laff-A-Lympics, Volume One (2010) Contains Season 1, Episode 1 "The Swiss Alps and Tokyo, Japan"; Season 1, Episode 2 "Acapulco and England"; Season 1, Episode 3 "Florida and China"; Season 1, Episode 4 "The Sahara Desert and Scotland". *Scooby's All Star Laff-A-Lympics, Volume Two* (2010) Contains Season 1, Episode 5 "France and Australia"; Season 1, Episode 6 "Athens, Greece and the Ozarks"; Season 1, Episode 7 "Italy and Kitty Hawk, North Carolina"; Season 1, Episode 8 "Egypt and Sherwood Forest". *Scooby-Doo! Laff-A-Lympics, The Complete First Collection* (2012) Neither complete nor first. Discuss. Contains Season 1, Episode 1 "The Swiss Alps and Tokyo, Japan"; Season 1, Episode 4 "The Sahara Desert and Scotland"; Season 1, Episode 5 "France and Australia"; Season 1, Episode 8 "Egypt and Sherwood Forest"; Season 1, Episode 10 "Spain and the Himalayas"; Season 1, Episode 10 "India and Israel"; Season 1, Episode 11 "Africa and San Francisco"; Season 1, Episode 12 "The Grand Canyon and Ireland"; Season 1, Episode 13 "Hawaii and Norway"; Season 1, Episode 14 "North Pole and Tahiti"; Season 1, Episode 15 "The Old West and Holland"; Season 1, Episode 16 "Quebec and Baghdad".

The second season has not been released.

The New Fred and Barney Show (1979)
Season 2
Episode 2 (September 15, 1979)
"Fred & Barney Meet the Frankenstones"

Hanna-Barbera Productions. Directed by Ray Patterson, Oscar Dufau, George Gordon. Produced by Art Scott, William Hanna, Joseph Barbera. Written by Doug Booth, Andy Heyward, Len Janson, Glenn Leopold, Chuck Menville, Bob Ogle, Ray Parker, Dave Stone, Chip Yaras. Cast: Henry Corden (Fred), Jean Vander Pyl (Wilma, Pebbles), Mel Blanc (Barney), Gay Autterson (Betty), Donald Messick (Bamm-Bamm), John Stephenson (Mr. Slate), Jim MacGeorge, Barney Phillips, Janet Waldo.

Another spinoff of *The Flintstones* (1960) (qv),with Pebbles and Bamm-Bamm as toddlers again. The Frankenstones, another monster family, replaced the Gruesomes as Fred's neighbors on spinoffs. Here, the head of the family, Frank Frankenstone, who looks like Frankenstein's monster and sounds like Boris Karloff, manages a "condorstonium" that Fred and Barney consider moving to. Frank invites them to a party, where the guests include a couple called the Ghoulstones, who very much resemble Weirdly and Creepella Gruesome. Their son, Junior, however, here looks like a fur ball with the legs of a wading bird. "Mr. Ghoulstone" has no lines.

GIGGLE RATING: Looks, Five Giggles; Voice, N/A.

AVAILABILITY: Streaming services.

Drak Pack (1980)

Hanna-Barbera Pty., Ltd. Directed by Chris Cuddington. Written by Doug Booth, Larz Bourne, Glenn Leopold, Cliff Roberts. Executive Producers: Joseph Barbera, William Hanna. Cast: Hans Conried (Dr. Dred), Don Messick (Fly/Toad), William Callaway (Frankie/Howler), Jerry Dexter (Drak Jr.), Chuck McCann (Mummy Man), Julie McWhirter (Vampira), Alan Oppenheimer (Count Dracula).

"From the monsters of the past comes a new generation, dedicated to reversing the evil image of their forefathers. Under the leadership of none other than Count Dracula, known as 'Big D', three teenagers formed a do-gooder group named The Drak Pack. With special powers, they can transform into super, mighty monsters and use their skills against all evildoers, especially the diabolical Dr. Dred and his renegade rascals– Toad, Fly, Mummy Man, and Vampira–a group known as O.G.R.E., the Organization of Generally Rotten Enterprises. It's right versus wrong, good over greed, niceness against naughtiness, that's the dedication of the terrific trio: Frankie, Howler; and Drak Jr.; the Drak Pack!" (Opening narration.)

Hoo boy, where to begin? Drak Jr. sounds like Don Adams' character from *Get Smart* (1965) and, like that inaptonymous spy, he is not the sharpest tooth in the head. Despite his name, he is not the son of Big D, he's the nephew. Or maybe great-grandnephew. Who knows? When the three characters touch hands (aww) and say, "Drak Whack!", he turns into a–what, exactly? He's not a vampire, he doesn't suck blood. He's a teen boy with too much eyeshadow. He can fly, and like Big D, he has the power to turn into a bat or mist. Or a mouse, a seagull, an eagle, a hand drill, or anything else the writers need him to be to get out of a jam.

Frankie is a young Frankenstein's monster. When he does the Drak Whack, he becomes super-strong. He's also super-strong before he does the Drak Whack, so there's that. However, even when they are in dire peril, he can only use his super-strength when he's mad. OK, the Drak Whack does turn his skin green and give him some kind of electrical powers. He's sort of like Milton the Monster (qv) on 'roids. He even has a vague Southern accent.

Howler, who sounds a bit like Curly Howard, is not as well-developed as the other two protagonists. When he does the Drak Whack he gains an ultrasonic howl, super-strong breath (I mean that in a good way), and–well, that's it. Just those two things. By not directly referencing the Big, Bad Wolf when he huffs and puffs, he has the power to avoid lawsuits. The three travel around in an amphibious flying car that is called (wait for it) The Drakster.

Dr. Dred is the standard-issue mad scientist who comes up with schemes to rule the world, like stealing the color from everything. Wait, what? Vampira is the eye candy, a shape-shifting Zsa Zsa (or Eva) Gabor sound-alike who can turn into a dragon, sea monster, cat, lobster, lizard, insect, spider, horse, snake, bird, seemingly anything but a good script. Fly, well, flies. He also walks on walls and eats bat guano. Just kidding about the guano. Mummyman is super-strong and can use his bandages to do anything ropes can. He frequently ties up the Drak Pack, who apparently also contract temporary amnesia, because they forget Drak can just turn into a bat and fly away, Frankie can break free, and Howler can probably blow the ropes away. Toad, and here we finally get to something of interest, is a goggle-eyed amphibian who sounds like Peter Lorre. He is Dred's right-hand minion, but often accidentally helps the Drak Pack. When he does something wrong, Dred swats at him with a "toad-tapper", or he hits himself and says, "Bad toad." They get around in an airship called (wait for it) The Dredgible.

Much of the humor derives from Big D slamming his hand in his coffin, Dred mispronouncing Drak's name, or both Dred and Big D saying, "Kids today!" In almost every episode, Dred calls a meeting with Drak and then tries to kill him. Drak never gets wise to this ploy. Viewers apparently did, however, and the show was canceled after sixteen episodes.

Season 1
Episode 1 (September 6, 1980)
"Color Me Dredful"

"The master is in a very touchy mood today," says Toad, shushing Vampira. Vampira says Dr. Dred has an inferiority complex from being beaten so many times by the Drak Pack (who wouldn't?) Toad literally bumps into Dred and breaks a gargoyle. "I'm sorry master, I didn't mean to interrupt your inferiority complex." Dred says he doesn't need to be more colorful, he needs to make the world less colorful with his Dr. Dred Color Collector, which steals the color from anything the ray hits.

Dred tries it out on a traffic signal and Frankie runs the stoplight and ends up on the steps of the art museum. All the paintings in the museum have been robbed of their color. They are summoned back to headquarters by Big D, who appears on a telescreen. He and all his possessions have had their colors stolen. The Drak Pack is kidnapped and tied up. Toad giggles insanely while stealing all the pink from the world and filling a tank the Drak Pack is in with it. He breaks for lunch, and the Pack breaks out of their ropes. (They were never in danger of drowning because Dred left open the door to the tank, so the pigment only came up to their necks.) "Dr. Dred, there's a beautiful yellow streak down your back," says Toad.

Episode 2 (September 13, 1980)
"Mind Your Manners Dr. Dred"
Dr. Dred plans to steal King Tut-tut's artifacts from the Midtown Museum, which are worth billions, at midnight tonight. "Your criminal computerized mind is calculatingly clever, Dr. Dred," says Toad. Dred ties up the Pack and leaves them at the museum to frame them, because apparently in his world, thieves tying themselves up at the scene of the crime after they get rid of the loot is a thing. The Pack escapes and goes to Ogre Island, a floating dreadnought, and they are again held captive. "A captive audience," Toad giggles insanely. "That's funny, Dr. Dred." Drak escapes and tricks Toad into freeing Frankie and Howler and they flood the island and O.G.R.E. escapes in the Dredgible. "Could you gentlemen use a toad stoolie around the house?" Toad asks the Drak Pack. "I dust, I scrub floors, I wash, I iron, cook, sew, sing, dance."

Episode 3 (September 20, 1980)
"Happy Birthday Dr. Dred"
On his birthday, Dr. Dred is unhappy with the cupcake Toad presents him with. "But I baked it myself!" Toad decides to get him the Pack for his birthday and he tries to catch them with a butterfly net but, oddly, fails. Dred traps them at Pack HQ, which he plans to launch into orbit with missiles. Toad accidentally frees the Pack and also steals all the missiles and sets them up around the dreadnought. Dred shoots himself into orbit.

Episode 4 (September 27, 1980)
"Dredful Weather We're Having"
"Oh, fiendish Dr. Dred," Toad speak-sings, "how could you be so mean for to invent such a terrible machine? Tornadoes smash, hurricanes rage, and lightning hits the scene. There is no place on earth that's safe from Dr. Dred's machine." Now that he can control the weather, Dred plans to blackmail the world. The Pack literally stumbles into Dred's underground hideout and Mummyman ties them up. They escape and turn Dred's ma-

chine on him.

Episode 5 (October 4, 1980)
"The Perilous Plunder of Pirate Park"

"I've been down here so long, I'm turning into a prune," says Toad, who is underwater looking for the sunken treasure of Pirate Park, where, coincidentally, the Pack plans to visit. "According to Dr. Dred's map, I should start drilling here," says Toad, who causes a tidal wave. The Pack goes down the hold after Dr. Dred, who, you guessed it, ties them up. They escape and foil Dred's escape. Toad gets de-pantsed. "Nude toad, nude toad."

Episode 6 (October 11, 1980)
"Night of the Terbites"

Dr. Dred has invented Terbites, lavender egg-shaped creatures who eat anything they are told to. He uses them to eat the bases of monuments, like the Statue of Liberty, which he then steals. Mummyman ties up the Pack (yawn), but they escape and steal back the statue. "Stop, thieves!" says Toad. Frankie steals a Terbite, which eats Dredquarters.

Episode 7 (October 18, 1980)
"Time Out for Dr. Dred"

"It works, Dr. Dred! Your Time Stopper really does stop time!" says Toad. "Oh, Dr. Dred, this proves you are the rottenest, evilest, nastiest, crummiest villain of all time!" Dred uses the ray to hijack a plane from the U.S. Mint with billions of dollars (in coins?) His next target is the Mint itself. The Pack turns the Time Stopper on O.G.R.E., and makes time go backwards. "Good toad, good toad!"

Episode 8 (October 25, 1980)
"Hideout Hotel"

"We're going on vacation," Toad sings, "we're going on vacation!" Dred uses Vampira, Fly, and Mummyman to scare away patrons from a hotel so Dred can turn it into a hideout for criminals. Toad is the bell captain. "I'm so excited, getting to meet all the crummy crooks of the world. My kind of people." What they don't know is Big D is holding a monster convention in the basement and he summons the Pack. They arrive, and Mummyman (all together now) ties them up. They escape, and with Big D and his monsters, drive out the crooks and Dred.

Episode 9 (November 1, 1980)
"Dred Goes Hollywood"

The Pack arrives at a theater for a Big Sneak Preview, which is a movie of the Drak Pack doing mean things that they never really did. It's all part of Dred's plan for world domination or something. "You belong in Hollywood, Dr. Dred," says Toad. "Your scriptwriting is really rotten." The Pack shows up at Dredful Production [sic] and Toad, in disguise, takes them on a tram tour to the Famous Collapsing Bridge, which Fly and Mummyman knock down. The Pack Drak Whacks, and Frankie saves them, but they end up crashing into the water anyway and are eaten by a mechanical shark. Frankie gets mad and busts them out, and they foil Dred's plan. "This is a real horror movie," says Toad.

Episode 10 (November 8, 1980)
"Dred's Photo Finish"

Dred's new invention, the Photo Grabber, can turn anything into a two-dimensional photo. Later, he can reverse the process and change it back. "I can hardly wait to see what will develop," says Toad. "I made a joke. Photograph? Develop? Get it?" Dred plans to use it on the 13th National Bank, but Toad gets the control box mixed up with the camera of a lepidopterist trying to capture a butterfly on film. Dred takes off after the photographer, the Drak Pack takes off after Dred, and the Dredgible takes off after them. The Drak Pack is captured, but this time, Mummyman doesn't tie them up. No, actually he does. They escape by the clever means of unwinding the bandages, but the photographer makes them all even more two-dimensional than they already were. Toad accidentally reconstitutes them and they turn the Photo Grabber into a photo.

Episode 11 (November 15, 1980)

"Dr. Dred Is a Shrinker"

"I never had trains when I was a polliwog, Dr. Dred," says Toad, after Dred shrinks an empty freight train down to HO scale. "May I play with it, huh? May I?" The Drak Pack are shrunk down along with a stolen train and they infiltrate Dredquarters and learn Dred plans to use the trains to steal the gold from Fort Knox. Dred you-know-whats them to the model railroad tracks and then he shrinks himself and O.G.R.E. and they go to Fort Knox. Meanwhile, the Pack escapes and follows them. Drak steals the Micro-Miniaturizer and restores the Pack to normal size. Dred and O.G.R.E. are captured.

Episode 12 (November 22, 1980)
"A Dire Day at Dredfulland"

"Dr. Dred," says Toad, "something's wrong. The scary-go-round isn't going round." Dred is opening an amusement park, and he offers free rides to the Pack. Mummyman ties them up because of course he does and Dred shoots them into outer space. They get back to earth because Howler blows really hard. Seriously. Drak announces they are opening a park next door so Dred destroys Dredfulland.

Episode 13 (November 29, 1980)
"Package Deal"

"They are going on a secret mission," says Toad while spying on the Pack. Big D has asked them to go to Transylvania to pick up a package for him. O.G.R.E. goes to Transylvania and Toad poses as a coachman and picks them up and takes them to their destination, a castle with a graveyard behind it where the package is buried, then leaves. They dig up the package and decide to stay the night. Toad tries to steal the package but he gets Frankie's snack instead. Mummyman pushes the bed they are sharing into the moat, but they do the Drak Whack and escape at the last minute and bring the package back to Big D. It is his teddy bear.

Episode 14 (December 6, 1980)

"Grimmest Book of Records"

Drak meets Dred on a desert isle. "Tell him what we're going to do, Dr. Dred," says Toad. "Tell him. Tell him." Dred is going to set a new Grimmest Book of Records record for the most major international crimes ever committed in a three hour period, and he challenges the Pack to stop him. Drak accepts the challenge. Dred leaves, having destroyed Drak's boat. Drak starts an engine on the palm tree, which turns the island into a helicopter and he flies away. No lie.

The spree starts with Mummyman stealing a clock face from Big Ben. The Pack tracks the clock to Dredquarters by its chime. Mummyman ties them up for the last time. Dred steals a racehorse and replaces him with Frankie. The Pack reunites too late to prevent Dred from committing his third crime, hijacking a super tanker. They follow him back to Dredquarters, where he plans to broadcast to the world. They interrupt the broadcast and keep Dred out of the record books.

Episode 15 (December 13, 1980)
"International Graffiti"

Dred is replacing the faces on all the world's famous sculptures with his own with the Facemaker. He lures the Pack to Egypt, where he puts his face on the Sphinx and gets away. "You're batting zero, Drak," Toad giggles insanely. Dred heads for Mt. Rushmore and the Pack uses the Facemaker against him.

Episode 16 (December 20, 1980)
"It's in the Bag, Dr. Dred"

Dr. Dred invents the world's most powerful vacuum cleaner to uncover the lost desert city of Burbankium. The Pack helps an archaeologist find Burbankium. Drak rearranges the vacuum hose so it inflates the Dredgible, which pops. Dr. Dred tells Toad to clean up the mess. "May I use the vacuum cleaner?" he asks. "Now that's what I call a successful conclusion," says Howler. Yeah.

FUN FACT: Chuck McCann played Peter Lorre on the episode "Trump: The Last Family" of the audio series *Friend or Foe* (2017).

GIGGLE RATING: Five Giggles.

AVAILABILITY: Visual Entertainment released *Drak Pack, The Complete Series* on DVD in Region 1 (Canada only) on February 5, 2008. On September 6, 2011, VEI (distributed by Millennium Entertainment) released the complete series on DVD in the US.

The New Scooby and Scrappy-Doo Show (1983)
Season 1
Episode 12 (December 3, 1983)
"Where's Scooby-Doo?"

Hanna-Barbera Studios. Directed by Oscar Dufau, George Gordon, Carl Urbano, John Walker, Rudy Zamora, Ray Patterson (supervising director). Writing Credits: Charles M. Howell IV (story) (as Charles M. Howell) & Tom Ruegger (story). Executive Producers: Joseph Barbera, William Hanna. Cast: Don Messick (Scooby-Doo/Scrappy-Doo), Casey Kasem (Shaggy Rogers), Heather North (Daphne Blake), Hal Smith (Sidney Gaspar).

The sixth iteration of this show. Scrappy is Scooby's aptonymous little nephew. No one finds it odd that two dogs with reason and a command of the English language investigate paranormal phenomena. Fred and Velma are long gone, but Daphne returns after four years. Shaggy is in every version.

The gang has received free tickets to the Orient Express from their "MYSTERIOUS ADMIRERS", and Scooby has a red suitcase full of Scooby Snacks. A fat man in a fez named Sidney Gaspar; Dr. Natasha, a female physician; Beatrice Whimsey, a sweater-knitting old lady; and a Little Guy with big eyes who talks like Peter Lorre have identical red suitcases. The Little Guy says a Mummy has been chasing him around the world.

Scooby buys a newspaper with the headline "Fuel Formula Stolen By Spy". Someone steals the remaining copies. The Mummy chases Scooby and Shaggy, and they crash into the other passengers and the red suitcases get mixed up. On the train, Scooby goes to find the little old lady whose suitcase he has and he encounters the Mummy.

The Little Guy tells Shaggy, "Excuse me, but I believe your friend the big dog is in great danger," and is snatched by the Mummy. The gang goes searching for Scooby, and they go to Beatrice Whimsey's compartment. She says Scooby returned her suitcase but she had Gaspar's. The Mummy appeared and chased him away. She tells them Gaspar is always in the dining car and they go there. The train is dark while it passes through a tunnel and when the lights come on, Shaggy is holding the Mummy's hand. Shaggy gets away. Daphne and Scrappy, meanwhile, have been snooping in another compartment and found the stolen newspapers, with the headline story ripped out.

The gang finds Gaspar in the dining car, and he tells them that Scooby, in various drag, tried to steal his suitcase, which turned out to actually belong to Dr. Natasha. The gang goes to see Dr. Natasha, who tells them that Scooby, dressed as a physician, tried to steal her suitcase, but it really belonged to the Little Guy. The gang goes off to find him.

The Little Guy pulls Shaggy into his compartment. "You already know all you need to find your friend," he says before being snatched again by the Mummy.

Daphne realizes they haven't yet checked the baggage car, so they go there. Scooby is there, in the Mummy's sarcophagus, and they find the Scooby Snacks. Scooby had been kidnapped by the Little Guy and the Mummy, and Beatrice Whimsey and Dr. Natasha were in cahoots. The four of them all pop out from behind bags. They are members of the Mystery Club, and this was their initiation test. They were the mysterious admirers who sent the tickets, and Gaspar is dressed as the mummy. Daphne realizes Beatrice Whimsey's sweater is knitted in Morse Code, and she is the one who stole the formula. "Beatrice" rips off her mask, and she is a beautiful young woman. She tries to escape with the Scooby Snacks. Scooby foils her by pulling the emergency brake. She would have gotten away with it, too, if not for those meddlesome kids.

GIGGLE RATING: Five Giggles. It is unknown who plays the Little Guy. It doesn't sound like Don Messick or Casey Kasem. It may be Vic Perrin or Frank Welker.

AVAILABILITY: On the DVD *The New Scooby and Scrappy-Doo Show* (Unknown year). Also, the entire first season has been released by Warner Bros. on the iTunes Store and Amazon Prime under the title *Scooby-Doo and Scrappy-Doo, Season 5* (Unknown year).

The Brave Little Toaster (July 10, 1987)

Hyperion Pictures, Kushner-Locke Productions. Directed by Jerry Rees. Written by Joe Ranft, Jerry Rees. Story: Thomas M. Disch, Joe Ranft, Jerry Rees. Animated by Randy Cartwright, Joe Ranft, Rebecca Rees (Animation Directors). Produced by Donald Kushner, Thomas L. Wilhite. Cast: Jon Lovitz (The Radio), Tim Stack (Lampy, Zeke), Timothy E. Day (Blanky/Young Rob), Thurl Ravenscroft (Kirby), Deanna Oliver (Toaster), Phil Hartman (Air Conditioner/Hanging Lamp), Joe Ranft (Elmo St. Peters), Judy Toll (Mish-Mash/Two-Face Sewing Machine), Wayne Kaatz (Rob), Colette Savage (Chris), Mindy Stern (Mother/Two-Face Sewing Machine), Jim Jackman (Plugsy), Randall William Cook (Entertainment Center), Randy Bennett (Computer), Jonathan Benair (Black and White TV), Louis Conti (Spanish Announcer), Beth Anderson, Pat Ericson, Gary Falcone, Roger Freeland, Janis Leibhart, Joe Pizzulo.

Disney bought the rights to the story *The Brave Little Toaster* by Thomas M. Disch in 1982. Disney provided some initial funding, but production was transferred to then-new Hyperion Pictures at a greatly reduced budget. Writer Joe Ranft took classes with the Groundlings improv group in LA, where he met members Phil Hartman and Jon Lovitz. Hartman and Lovitz improvised dialogue which actually wound up in the final film.

At a summer home, old appliances including Toaster, The Radio, Lampy; Blanky, an electric blanket; and Kirby, a vacuum cleaner, await the return of the Master, who was eight years old when they last saw him a decade ago. When the home goes up for sale, they decide to go to the city to find him, à la *The Incredible Journey* (1963). Unbeknownst to them, the Master, Rob, who has graduated high school and is going to college, is on his way to collect them to furnish his new place.

The appliances get stuck in quicksand and are rescued by Elmo St. Peters, who takes them back to his shop, "Parts". "Seems like a nice enough fella," says The Radio.

A Hanging Lamp giggles insanely. "Yes, Mr. St. Peters is quite an amusing fellow, isn't he?" he asks. He notices Lampy's bulb is burned out. "Here, you can have one of mine. Use it in good health. While you still can," and again giggles insanely.

Mr. St. Peters cannibalizes a blender for its motor. "You see?" Hanging

Lamp giggles insanely. "You never quite know what he's going to do! He's so spontaneous."

"How do we escape?" says Lampy. "Did you hear that, boys?" says Hanging Lamp. "He wants to know how to escape!" All the appliances giggle insanely. An old-school gramophone plays funereal organ music. "Sit down for a spell," Hanging Lamp speak-sings in the song "It's a B-Movie". "You don't look so well."

St. Peters comes back looking for radio tubes. Toaster, Blanky, Lampy, and Kirby turn themselves into a makeshift ghost and spook St. Peters with his own reflection. He runs into the wall and knocks himself out. All the appliances make a run for it.

The appliances find the Master's house. He is not there, but they meet their old friend from the cabin, Black and White TV. The rest of the appliances in the home are new and cutting-edge electronics, who are jealous of Rob's fondness for the older appliances, so they kick Toaster, Kirby, Lampy, Blanky, and The Radio out the window into a dumpster for Ernie's Disposal. A truck comes and takes them away. This is seen by Black and White TV, who gets Rob to go there. Rob finds the appliances but is trapped on the conveyor belt leading to the crusher. Toaster throws himself into the gears and stops the crusher. Rob collects all the appliances and takes them home, where he fixes Toaster and takes them all with him to school.

Disney, which owned the television rights, moved up its release date, causing the theatrical distributor, Skouras Pictures, to withdraw. The film premiered on the Disney Channel and then later was released to theaters and home video.

GIGGLE RATING: Five Giggles. Hartman plays both the Lorre-esque Hanging Lamp and the Jack Nicholsonian Air Conditioner. His credits include *The Simpsons* (1989), *Gravedale High* (1990), and *The Ren & Stimpy Show* (1991) (all qv).

AVAILABILITY: The DVD is available from Walt Disney Home Entertainment in the United States and Australia; Divisa Home Video and Aurum Producciones in Spain; and formerly by Prism Leisure Corporation in the UK.

Mighty Mouse The New Adventures (1987)

Ralph Bakshi Animation Productions, Bakshi-Hyde Ventures, Viacom Productions Inc. Directed by Ralph Bakshi, Kent Butterworth, Eddie Fitzgerald, Steven E. (Steve) Gordon, Bob Jaques, John Kricfalusi, David Marshall, Tom Minton, Jim Reardon, John Sparey, Bruce Woodside. Written by Eddie Fitzgerald, Nate Kanfer, Tom Minton, Doug Moench, Rich Moore, Jim Reardon, Andrew Stanton. Produced by Ralph Bakshi and John W. Hyde. Cast: Patrick Pinney (Mighty Mouse/Mike Mouse/Frawley/Bub), Dana Hill (Orphan Scrappy), Rodger Bumpass (Moe), Wendell Washer (Chester P. Chieseler).

Mighty Mouse, the anthropomorphic murine superhero, appeared in 80 theatrical films for Terrytoons between 1942 and 1961. These were broadcast on American television 1955-1967. Filmation revived the character in 1979. In Ralph Bakshi's modern take on Mighty Mouse, his secret identity is Mike, a rodent who works at the factory owned by former damsel in distress Pearl Pureheart. Scrappy is his wisecracking mouse sidekick. The show launched the career of John Kricfalusi, later famous for creating *The Ren & Stimpy Show* (1991) (qv). Bakshi was a mercurial boss with large appetites and disgusting habits, and Kricfalusi would parody him in later years.

Bakshi presented CBS with several pitches, including one with Kricfalusi's characters Ren and Stimpy, but CBS turned them all down before "buying" the rights to Mighty Mouse, which they already owned.

Season 1
Episode 3B (October 3, 1987)
"Scrap Happy"

Scrappy is crying because he is an orphan with no friends. Mighty Mouse flies down and tells him he will be Scrappy's friend. "You mean if I'm ever in a tight spot, you'll come and save the day?" asks Scrappy.

"Of course I will," says Mighty Mouse. "But don't you go calling your super friends just any old time. Make sure you're really in trouble."

Scrappy runs into a gang consisting of three mice: Bub, with heavy lids and a voice like Peter Lorre; Moe, and Frawley. Scrappy asks if he can hang with them. "Certainly not," says Bub. Scrappy starts to leave, and Bub says, "Wait a minute. Let's play a gag on the little hairball. You know the apple tree up at Old Man Weasel's place?" Moe tells Scrappy if he can take an apple from the tree, he's in.

Weasel catches them and sells them to Chester P. Chieseler, who puts them to work in a carnival. "A vulgar situation, indeed," says Bub. Scrappy considers calling Mighty Mouse, but remembers his admonishment and decides to liberate them himself by finding incriminating documents in Chester's trailer. "This should do the trick, Scrappy," says Bub. Chester catches them and puts them on a runaway roller coaster. They are rescued by Mighty Mouse, who punches Chester.

GIGGLE RATING: Five Giggles. Good mouse caricature, good vocal imitation. Patrick Pinney's credits include *Robot Chicken* (2005).

Episode 8B (November 7, 1987)
"Scrappy's Playhouse"

On Cartoon Matinee Day, Bub, Moe, and Frawley sneak into a movie theater, followed by Scrappy. Scrappy gets caught by the usher, but Bub and the gang escape to the projection room. "There must be a million cartoons here," says Bub. Moe splices them all together onto one reel. Scrappy does a running commentary. When the lights come up, the usher chases him. The gang pulls him up onto the balcony and the usher is buried in celluloid, which spills out the front of the theater like *The Blob* (1958).

Old Terrytoon footage was used for the cartoon-within-the-cartoon. This saved money and was a business decision, not a creative one, according to Kricfalusi.

GIGGLE RATING: Looks, Five Giggles; Voice, Four Giggles. Sounds like a different voice actor. Since Patrick Pinney apparently doesn't do anything else in this segment (Mighty Mouse never appears), perhaps he actually was unavailable. It might be Neil Ross, but I have nothing to compare it to. Joe Alaskey apparently worked on this episode, also, but I don't think he voices Bub.

Episode 9B (November 14, 1987)
"It's Scrappy's Birthday"

It's Scrappy's birthday, but it's also the big Cheese Day Celebration down-town. Scrappy half-heartedly goes and sees Bub, Moe, and Frawley riding on each other's shoulders to see over the crowd. "Hey Scrappy," says Bud, "Want to be next? We're taking turns being top dog." Scrappy says no, and joins a gang of hobo clowns until he is rescued from a runaway boxcar by Mighty Mouse, and the mice throw Scrappy a birthday party.

FUN FACT: Kricfalusi left the show after one season.

GIGGLE RATING: Five Giggles. Pinney's back!

Episode 10A (November 21, 1987)
"Aqua-Guppy"

At the Seafood Shanty, a blue cat who sounds like Peter Lorre says, "Yes, give me that big crab over dere. The one with the wooden claw." The man behind the counter obliges. "It's nice to eat this for a change instead of always eating Pearl Pureheart's cat food. " The mention of Pearl Pureheart gets the attention of Captain Acrab, who also wears an eyepatch. "Tell me where she is or you'll be combin' the beaches with your teeth." The cat says she is in Mouseville, and Captain Acrab goes there. Mighty must stop him and rescue Pearl.

GIGGLE RATING: Five Giggles. It is not known who plays the Peter Lorre cat, but it is probably Pinney.

Episode 11B (November 28, 1987)
"Pirates with Dirty Faces"

"At last, Moe, I thought we'd never get there," says Bub. Practicing to be pirates, they dig at the spot marked on Frawley's map, Mrs. Burke's garden, much to the distress of Mrs. Burke. "Avast, it's the evil Sea Hog," says Bub. "Run, Matey!" Mighty stops them and makes them promise to fix the garden, but they have no plans to keep their word. Mighty overhears this.

That night, they are captured by a flying pirate ship captained by a Marlon Brando clone. He makes them clean up the captain's mess. "Why don't you guys have a mutiny?" asks Bub. The crew explains that the captain hasn't slept in 365 years. Frawley suggests throwing him a slumber party. The captain falls asleep and the crew pushes him overboard, then they tie up Bub, Moe, and Frawley. Mighty rescues them and shows them the error of their ways. "We're sorry, Mighty Mouse," says Bub. "Please take us home." It was all a dream. Or was it? On the pirate ship, Mighty takes off his Brando mask.

GIGGLE RATING: Five Giggles.

Season 2
Episode 3B (October 1, 1988)
"Mundane Voyage"

In a scary castle, Pearl Pureheart is being tortured by Cardigan, a mad scientist, to get her recipe for cat food byproducts. She refuses, and we hear the unmistakable whistled strains of "In the Hall of the Mountain King" as a Peter Lorre-type descends from the ceiling as in the Edgar Allan Poe story "The Pit and the Pendulum", giggling insanely. She calls for Mighty Mouse, and he makes Cardigan switch places with Pearl, as the Peter Lorre-type continues to descend. "I can't help myself!" Pearl asks Mighty if they'll ever see Cardigan again. "Quoth the raven, nevermore!"

GIGGLE RATING: Five Giggles. Likely Pinney again.

AVAILABILITY: On January 5, 2010, CBS Home Entertainment (distributed by Paramount) released the complete series on three DVD, uncut and in the original full screen video format.

Teenage Mutant Ninja Turtles (1987)
Season 1
Episode 4 (December 17, 1987)
"Hot Rodding Teenagers from Dimension X"

Wang Film Productions Co., Ltd. Written by David Wise, Patti Howeth. Produced By Kara Vallow, Fred Wolf. Cast: Cam Clarke (Leonardo/Rocksteady), Barry Gordon (Donatello/Bebop), Townsend Coleman (Michelangelo), Rob Paulsen (Raphael/First Clown), Peter Renaday (Splinter/General Traag), Renae Jacobs (April O'Neil), James Avery

(Shredder), Pat Fraley (Krang/Zak/Police Chief/Second Clown), Tress MacNeille (Kala), Thom Pinto (Dask/Lieutenant Granitor).

The titular characters are four anthropomorphic chelonians named after Italian Renaissance artists who live in the sewers, eat pizza, and fight crime. Starting out in comic books, they spawned a media franchise empire comprising toys, food, video games, movies, live action TV shows, and four animated series, of which this was the first.

Krang's Stone Warriors, General Traag and the Peter Lorre sounda-like, Lieutenant Granitor, come to the Technodrome from Dimension X through a portal in pursuit of the Neutrinos, the episode's titular hot-rod-ders. "They refuse to join any army!" says Granitor. The Turtles are after the Neutrinos, too, and catch up with the Neutrinos first. The Turtles vow to protect them against the Stone Warriors, who attack. This attracts the police and National Guard, and the Turtles hide in the sewer.

"We must fight our way through them and find the Neutrinos!" says Granitor. "We must get back to the Technodrome! Those Neutrinos could attack Krang at any moment!" The Neutrinos and the Turtles go to the Technodrome, which is underneath the "Global Trade Center". They open the Dimensional Portal and send the Stone Warriors and the Neutrinos back home.

GIGGLE RATING: Looks, One Giggle. Not much of a resemblance other than perhaps the eyes. Voice, Four Giggles. Thom Pinto's credits include *Harvey Birdman, Attorney at Law* (2000) (qv). Some sources credit Pat Fraley as Granitor. Fraley would later play the Peter Lorre-ish Dyna-Mole in *The Tick* (1994) (qv).

FUN FACTS: Raphael (Rob Paulsen) imitates Edward G. Robinson.

Cam Clarke, another frequent Lorre impersonator, plays Leonardo.

AVAILABILITY: On DVD in the boxed set released on April 20, 2004.

A Pup Named Scooby-Doo (1988)
Season 1
Episode 8 (October 29, 1988)
"Snow Place Like Home"

Hanna-Barbera Productions. Directed by Arthur Davis (as Art Davis), Oscar Dufau, Bob Goe, Don Lusk, Paul Sommer (as Paul Sommers), Ray Patterson (supervising director). Writing Credits: Lane Raichert (story) & Bill Matheny (story) & Laren Bright (story), Mary Jo Ludin (teleplay). Produced by Joseph Barbera, William Hanna, Tom Ruegger. Cast: Don Messick (Scooby-Doo, Newscaster), Casey Kasem (Shaggy Rogers), Christina Lange (Velma Dinkley), Kellie Martin (Daphne Blake), Carl Steven (Freddie Jones), Frank Welker (Spider), B.J. Ward (Mrs. Morganson), Paul Eiding (Mr. Peterson, Mr. Forester, Ice Demon).

The eighth iteration of the Scooby-Doo franchise featured all the major characters as their younger selves, following the "babyfication" trend of the time. Fred and Velma return.

A van pulls up to Snowy Mountain Lodge and the gang hops out. It is an old, spooky place run by two old, spooky people, the green-skinned Morgansons. "You must be de Freddie Jones party, here for the weekend," says Mr. Morganson, who is short and sounds like Peter Lorre.

Mr. Peterson, a developer, arrives and shows them the plans for a mall he wants to build on the site. The Morgansons turn him down. "And dat's final," says Mr. Morganson. Mr. Peterson says they won't be able to give the place away once people find out about the Ice Demon. Mr. Morganson giggles insanely. "It's just an old story. He's saying dat to make us sell."

That night, the Ice Demon chases the gang around. They decide to investigate and meet a ranger, Mr. Forester, who tells them there is a gold mine on the site, which is long tapped out. To prove it, he shows them a map, but there is a piece missing. The gang decides to visit the mine.

The Ice Demon starts an avalanche, but they get to the mine anyway and find the missing piece of the map. The Ice Demon chases them again. They run into Mr. Peterson, who reveals that the Morgansons are about to default on their mortgage. Velma comes up with a plan to catch the Ice Demon. It is Mr. Forester, who learned the geological conditions in the mine were right for diamonds, which he planned to steal. He would have gotten away with it too, if not for those meddlesome kids.

GIGGLE RATING: Five Giggles. It is not known who plays Mr. Morganson. Frank Welker? Other frequent Lorre impersonators in the cast include Don Messick, Casey Kasem, Hamilton Camp, Jim Cummings, and Chuck McCann.

AVAILABILITY: DVD, Amazon Prime, and the iTunes Store.

Count Duckula (1988)

Cosgrove Hall Films. Directed by Chris Randall. Written by Jimmy Hibbert, John Sayle. Produced by Brian Cosgrove, Mark Hall. Cast: David Jason (Count Duckula/Burt/Pierre/Oddbeak/Morris the Strongman), Jack May (Igor), Brian Trueman (Nanny/Pirate Cap'n/The Phantom/Charlie the Clown), Jimmy Hibbert (The Egg/Ruffles/Krool/Mr. Mate/Gaston), Barry Clayton (Narrator).

A spinoff of *Danger Mouse* (1981). Count Duckula is the latest in a long line of dreadful vampires. They can be destroyed by a stake through the heart or exposure to sunlight, but brought back to life by a secret rite that can be performed once a century. As the Vincent Price-esque Narrator states, "The latest incarnation did not run according to plan." Ketchup was added instead of blood, turning the latest Count Duckula into a vegetarian and an unfunny Daffy knockoff. Duckula's castle leaves Transylvania and goes to other cities for no apparent reason. He is always accompanied by his old Nanny and his butler, Igor, who is not a Peter Lorre-wannabe.

Season 1
Episode 21 (February 7, 1989)
"A Fright at the Opera"

The castle is in Paris at the Opera House. Igor literally runs into his old friend, Krool, a short, chubby, Peter Lorre soundalike who is now working for the Phantom of the Opera. The Phantom plans to divanap Elvira, the star, and force her to sing his score. When she hits high C, a bomb he planted in the Opera House will detonate. By mistake, Krool, a self-described "stupid, useless, bungling, idiotic, fatheaded dolt," birdnaps Nanny. The Phantom decides to get her to sing anyway, which she does. She doesn't hit high C, but drives everyone out of the Opera House. As they leave their box, Igor slams the door on Duckula's foot, causing him to hit high C. Duckula, Igor, and Nanny escape just in time.

FUN FACT: The title is a reference to the Marx Brothers movie *A Night at the Opera* (1935).

Season 4
Episode 5 (February 2, 1993)
"Venice a Duck Not a Duck"

The castle is in Venice. Archvillain the Egg has assembled most of the regular villains who have tangled with Duckula in the past, including the Phantom of the Opera and Krool.

An anonymous benefactor has gifted Duckula with a portrait of one of his ancestors wearing the gem the Eye of the Borgias. A piece of parchment on the back appears to be a map leading to the place where the gem is hidden.

The Phantom and Krool await Duckula. When he enters, they will lock him in and trip a trap door, plunging Duckula into the canal. Duckula comes and goes and Krool fails to trip the trap. "I got stuck." The Phantom tries to pull him out from behind a pillar and the trap door is activated, dumping them into the canal. All the other villains are similarly hoist on their own petards.

GIGGLE RATING: Five Giggles. Jimmy Hibbert would go on to play the Peter Lorre-esque Harry Slime in *Avenger Penguins* (1993).

AVAILABILITY: Season 1 has been released on DVD in Regions 1 and 2. Seasons 3 and 4 are not yet released in Region 1 or Region 4. Season 4 was released in Region 2 as *Count Duckula, The Complete Third Series* (2007). The DVD *Count Duckula, The Complete Collection* was released in Region 2 (2008) and Region 4 (2013).

Chip 'n Dale: Rescue Rangers (1989)

Disney Television Animation. Directed by John Kimball, Bob Zamboni, Alan Zaslove. Written by Somtow Sucharitkul, Kevin Hopps, Buzz Dixon, Terry Wise, Dev Ross, Tad Stones, Jymn Magon, Mark Zaslove, Alan Zaslove, Maia Mattise, David Wise, Julia Lewald. Cast: Tress MacNeille (Chip/Gadget/Policewoman/Siamese Twins), Corey Burton (Dale/Zipper/Mole/Snout/Sailor/Lawyer), Jim Cummings (Monterey Jack/Professor Norton Nimnul/Fat Cat/Sergeant Spinelli/Wart/Stan/Blather/Chinese Cat/Fisherman), Peter Cullen (Officer Kirby/Officer Muldoon/Mepps/Police Captain/Sailor), Alan Oppenheimer (Plato/Aldrin Klordane), Rob Paulsen (Detective Donald Drake/Percy/Frenchy).

Chip 'n Dale are cartoon chipmunks created by Walt Disney Studios in 1943. They usually played antagonists of Goofy or Donald Duck, although they had their own shorts.

The original idea for the then-titled *Rescue Rangers* featured two mice, but they were replaced with the established Disney characters at the suggestion of Disney CEO Michael Eisner. The other rangers are Monterey Jack (Monty), a fat Australian mouse who is subject to "cheese attacks" when he smells fermented curd; Zipper, Monty's housefly sidekick; and Gadget Hackwrench, a sexy, brilliant female mouse and inventor. The Rescue Rangers' main enemies are Professor Nimnul, a mad scientist; and Fat Cat, who, sadly, does not sound like Sydney Greenstreet. He has four major henchmen: a lizard named Wart (Jim Cummings), who sounds like Peter Lorre; a skinny cat named Mepps, a rat named Snout, and Mole. A convention of the show is that animals can talk, but people (mostly) can't hear or understand them.

After a preview episode on August 27, 1988, the series premiered on the Disney Channel on March 4, 1989. In September, the second season began with a two-hour movie special, "Rescue Rangers to the Rescue", which was later shown in five parts.

Season 1
Episode 4 (March 19, 1989)
"Flash the Wonder Dog"

Flash the Wonder Dog is Dale's favorite show. Fat Cat dognaps the actor who plays Flash and Fat Cat and his henchmen go around dressed as Flash committing mayhem. Wart vandalizes a billboard. "Finally, I get a chance to express my true artistic nature!" The Rangers rescue Flash, but he has to restore his reputation.

Episode 7 (April 9, 1989)
"Adventures in Squirrelsitting"

Fat Cat has stolen the Maltese Mouse, and the Rangers trash a squirrel's house while pursuing him. They agree to babysit the squirrel's two children, a teen and a toddler, while the squirrel straightens up her place.

Chip 'n Dale dress up like chipmunk chanteuses to infiltrate Fat Cat's casino on top of the cat food factory inside a statue of a cat. They toss their hankies to the audience and Dale catches the eye of Wart, who says, "C'mon, baby, if you want this back, you have to pucker up for Warty-poo." The Rangers get back the Maltese Mouse, and Fat Cat and his henchmen get canned, literally.

Season 2
Episodes 1-5 (September 15-17, 1989, depending on market)
"Rescue Rangers to the Rescue"

This is a prequel to the first season, showing how Chip 'n Dale became Rescue Rangers and met up with the rest of the team.

Fat Cat swipes the Clutchcoin Ruby for archcriminal Aldrin Klordane and frames a retiring police detective, Donald Drake. "Wow, Fat Cat, you got the ruby," says Wart. "They said you couldn't swipe it." Drake's dog, Plato, who is incarcerated along with Drake, advises the aspiring chipmunk crime-fighters on how to proceed. They follow Fat Cat to the docks.

On a ship, they meet Monty and Zipper, but they get thrown overboard by Fat Cat. Fat Cat and the ruby fly to Glacier Bay. To follow them, Monty looks up his old aviator friend, Geegaw Hackwrench. Geegaw is dead, but his daughter, Gadget, gives them Geegaw's old plane and flies it for them. Klordane uses the ruby to try to steal from the Global Gold Reserve, but the newly constituted Rescue Rangers foil him. Klordane is arrested, but Fat Cat remains at large.

Episode 6 (October 3, 1989)
"A Lad in a Lamp"

A crook selling a magic lamp is busted by an undercover cop, but the lamp is stolen by a pelican, who delivers it to Fat Cat. "This must be pretty important to you, Fat Cat," says Wart. Fat Cat stiffs the pelican, who steals back the lamp, but drops it in the harbor. Monty finds the lamp, and rubs it, making a genie appear. The genie tricks Monty into switching places with him. Meanwhile, Wart smells cheese. "The fat one with the lamp must be close by," he says. Mole literally bumps into the lamp. "With this, he can make us all rich," says Wart. "The genie of the lamp will be Fat Cat's slave."

Fat Cat rubs the lamp and Monty pops out. Fat Cat wishes for the Rescue Rangers to appear, and they do. Then he wishes they be turned to dust, but he is out of wishes. He gets Mole to wish them to their doom, but Monty tricks him into wishing the Rangers were set free. Mepps gets the lamp next, and Monty tricks him into wishing for fish, and Fat Cat's headquarters gets flooded. Chip 'n Dale wish none of this had happened. A crook selling a magic lamp is busted by an undercover cop. This time, the pelican doesn't steal it.

Episode 8 (October 9, 1989)
"Battle of the Bulge"

Crooks are stealing jewels from safes in armored helicopters and leaving behind fruit detritus. Meanwhile, Monty has decided to go on a strict diet and exercise regimen and he forces the other Rangers to go along with him. Starving, Chip 'n Dale dive into a box of fruit that is stolen by Fat Cat's henchmen. "This one will do," says Wart. "I'll grab some bananas." Fat Cat has hired Jamaican fruit bats to steal jewels in-flight and pays them in produce. The Rangers follow the bats in the Ranger plane and catch them in the act. Monty, Chip, 'n Dale jump into the bag of loot and ride back to Fat

Cat's hideout in the cat statue. Gadget attaches the helicopter's winch to the cat statue's nostril and pries it open, spilling out everyone and everything. The jewels are recovered by the cops.

Episode 17 (October 20, 1989)
"Robocat"

Ignatz Stanislavsky has built a better mousetrap, a robot cat. It goes haywire, and he throws it out. Gadget decides to take it home and reprogram it with a nonviolent video game cartridge, *Dogs and Cats*, and they name him Tom.

Meanwhile, Fat Cat has his henchmen try to steal a rare tropical fish, Luna. "We tried to nab her at the docks when she came off the boat," says Wart, but they failed. They try to steal the fish from the owner's home, but there is a security system and a large bulldog, Butch. They catnap Tom, and re-reprogram him with a war game cartridge. Tom steals Luna, and Butch goes out looking for them and runs into the Rangers. They arrange to meet at the cat food cannery.

At that moment, Wart is preparing to serve the fish for dinner. "The marinade's almost done, boss." Wart puts her in to soak for a half hour. The Rangers burst in and pour it all down the sink. Then, they eject the video game cartridge that makes Robocat violent and put in the *Dogs and Cats* cartridge. Everyone goes looking for the fish in the sewer, and Tom saves Luna. Luna's owner adopts Tom.

Episode 42 (March 21, 1990)
"When You Fish Upon a Star"

The Rangers go to Canine Island to rescue a mouse from a sinking ship, the Lucitetania, and find out that Fat Cat sank it by mistake. He wanted to sink the Raging Prawn and capture its cargo, the rare fish, the Moby Carp. He captures the Rangers as the Raging Prawn approaches. Gadget learns Fat Cat is using fireflies to pose as stars and mislead sailors onto the reefs of Firefly Island, where they actually are. The Rangers dress up Zipper as a lady firefly to distract the fireflies and the Rangers squirt them with water. Meanwhile, Fat Cat and his henchmen row towards the Raging Prawn when Mepps spies something in the water. "I don't want to hear it," says Fat Cat. They hit a reef. "You don't want to hear it," says Wart. Monty turns them over to the dogs of Canine Island.

Episode 46 (May 1, 1990)
"Gorilla My Dreams"

Kuku the gorilla has lost her playmate, Boots the kitten. The Rangers go to find Boots, leaving Dale behind to play with Kuku. Fat Cat has catnapped Boots to blackmail Kuku into doing his dirty work. The Rangers rescue Boots, but before they can return, Fat Cat chimpmunknaps Dale, thinking he is Boots. Kuku breaks out and agrees to help Fat Cat. "Boss," says Wart, "now that we've got the gorilla, can we dispose of the kitty?" Fat Cat says no and then notices it is actually Dale. Fat Cat is about to kill Dale, but he realizes Kuku has bonded with Dale and Kuku will still do his bidding. Fat Cat sends her to steal gems. The Rangers stumble upon a jewelry store that has just been robbed, and they hitch a ride on a cop car to a burglary in progress. Kuku tells them Fat Cat has Dale.

Meanwhile, back at Fat Cat's hideout, Wart says, "Howzabout you let us play 'Bury the Chipmunk?'" Kuku returns and Fat Cat sends her out on another job. The Rangers break in and rescue Boots, then they find Kuku before she can steal the diamond.

GIGGLE RATING: Looks, Five Giggles; Voice, Two and a half Giggles. I guess Rob Paulsen and Corey Burton were unavailable.

AVAILABILITY: Walt Disney Studios Home Entertainment has released in Region 1 the first 51 episodes of the series. The first volume was released on November 8, 2005 (containing episodes 1-27) and the second on November 14, 2006 (containing Episodes 28-51). No word from Disney regarding the release of a third volume set for Episodes 52-65. In the United Kingdom, Disney released one Region 2 volume, titled *Walt Disney's Chip 'n Dale Rescue Rangers First Collection* (2007). Despite the set being similar to the US version, the DVD contains only the first 20 episodes. Several other similar releases were then made to other countries. A second DVD set of the series was released in the UK, but as a Region 2 version of Volume

2, titled *Walt Disney's Chip 'n Dale Rescue Rangers Season 2* (2012). There are no plans to release the rest of the series, or the seven episodes missing between the first two sets. The complete series is also currently available for purchase in SD and HD on iTunes and Google Play (Volume 2 on Google Play is only available in SD), also released in 2016. It is not available at this writing on Amazon Prime.

Tugs (1989)

Clearwater Features, TVS Television. Directed by Robert D. Cardona, David Mitton, Chris Tulloch. Written by David Mitton (creator), Robert D. Cardona (creator), Tarquin Cardona, Chris Tulloch, Roy Russell, Gloria Tors. Produced by Robert D. Cardona. Cast: Patrick Allen (Captain Star), Simon Nash (Ten Cents), Shaun Prendergast (Sunshine), Nigel Anthony (Warrior), John Baddeley (Top Hat), Sean Barrett (Big Mac), Timothy Bateson (O.J.), Lee Cornes (Grampus), Chris Tulloch (Zorran), Mike Mulloy (Zug), Don Austen (Coast Guard's Messenger), David Mitton (Old Rusty), French Tickner (Owner of The Municipal Garbage Corporation).

"The tugboat, for its size, is the most powerful craft afloat. And the Star tugs are the power behind the docks and waterways that make up the Bigg City Port. This–is *Tugs* [1989]." (Opening narration.)

In the early eighties, before *Thomas the Tank Engine & Friends* (1984) premiered, David Mitton of Clearwater Features, a producer, ran into personal financial difficulties, and, convinced that Thomas would tank, sold his 50% ownership in the series to the other producer, Britt Allcroft, and from that point worked on the series as a contractor and later an employee, not sharing in the huge profits that resulted from the long run and merchandising campaign of the show.

Robert D. Cardona (Mitton's partner at Clearwater) and Mitton decided they wanted to work for themselves and create their own characters and stories. In 1986, one of them (it is unclear which) came up with the idea for *Tugs* (1989). Set in a fictitious location in the 1920s, the show is about the rivalry between two anthropomorphic tugboat fleets, the Star Fleet and the Z-Stacks. The Star Fleet, led by Captain Star, who narrates the series, consists of Ten Cents, Big Mac, O.J., Top Hat, Warrior,

Hercules, and Sunshine. They are the protagonists, vying for contracts with the antagonists, the dodgy Z-Fleet or Zeds, including Zorran, Zebedee, Zak, Zip, and the Peter Lorre-based character Zug. Some sources say Zug was played by Mike Mulloy of *The Benny Hill Show* (1986), others credit theater and radio actor Nigel Anthony, who also played Warrior. The website BehindTheVoiceActors.com has credited both of them. Other running characters include Lillie the Lightship, Grampus the submarine, and Izzy Gomez, a Central American-accented banana boat.

Building on the technology used for *Thomas the Tank Engine & Friends* (1984), live-action tugboat models on moveable chassis, with moveable eyes and heads (but not mouths), were pulled through the water with transparent string and shot at the models' eye level with the Clearwater Periscope lens system.

Production lasted twelve months, and thirteen episodes were made, each running fifteen to twenty minutes. Zug appears in ten, including three non-speaking cameos. Mitton, short on cash again, sold his share of the rights to Castle Communications for an early video release of four episodes. The show eventually aired in the Children's ITV slot on the ITV network in the UK, but the early release of the videotape lessened its asking price and impacted its merchandising unfavorably, and Clearwater was crippled. Mitton and Cardona parted ways. The series has never been shown in the United States, but it remains a cult favorite, especially with Gen X-ers. The footage was reused in *Salty's Lighthouse* (1998), but voices were redubbed, removing Zug's Peter Lorre impression.

Season 1
Episode 1 (April 4, 1989)
"Sunshine"

Sunshine, a switcher, joins the Star Fleet as they win the contract for the ocean liner Duchess. To get the contract from the Star Fleet, Zorran tells Zip to run Big Mac into the mudbanks. "You've done it before to yourself, Zip, so you'll soon catch on," says Zug. The Duchess arrives early. Ten Cents finds Big Mac on the mudbank, and Big Mac tells him to go help bring in the Duchess. Zorran forces Sunshine into the rudder of the Duchess, so the Star Fleet has to accept help from the Z-Stacks. Sunshine goes away in shame, but Izzy has witnessed the whole thing and tells Ten Cent. Sunshine is exonerated and officially welcomed into the fleet.

Episode 2 (April 11, 1989)
"Pirate"

Ten Cents has to deliver parts to Scuttlebutt Pete the dredger, and he runs into the Zeds. "Look what the wind's blown in," says Zug. "Goody Two Screws." Ten Cents just wants to drop off his load, but Zug says, "All work and no play makes Ten Cents a dull tug." That night, the parts are stolen by an eyepatch-wearing tug called Sea Rogue.

"Hey! Where is it?" Zug asks the next morning. "I always said Star Tugs couldn't be relied on." The next morning, Captain Star and Captain Zero call a meeting for both fleets. They plan to set a trap for the thief.

Grampus discovers the thieves at their hideout. Sea Rogue is being forced to steal barges by green-eyed tugs who have captured his uncle. Grampus tells Ten Cent and Sunshine, who go off to find Sea Rogue. Zug and Zip, still thinking Ten Cent is stealing barges, follow him. "I knew he shouldn't be trusted. Come on."

They find the barges. "We're heroes!" The green-eyed tugs chase them off. Grampus frees the old tug, and Ten Cent and Sunshine capture the green-eyed tugs. "Somebody had to flush them out, so we did," says Zug before he backs into a flare.

Episode 3 (April 18, 1989)
"Trapped"

The Stars and Zed Stacks are bringing timber and tanning bark down from the sawmills upriver. Billy Shoepack, an alligator tug, delivers gasoline and dynamite to the lumber camps. Zorran has been waiting for Zug, who is towing a tramp steamer. Zug giggles insanely. "Captain Zero said to take it to the breakers yard on my way." Zorran "helps" by pushing the ship aground, blocking the river and trapping Zug and most of the Stars on the other side. "It wasn't my fault," says Zug to the Star tugs. "Ask Zorran." Ten Cent, downriver, gets a crane. Billy blows the steamer up, and the explosion drives Zorran up on the rocks.

Episode 4 (April 25, 1989)
"Jinxed"

Ten Cent and Sunshine find a derelict tug called Boomer, who begs them to leave him alone because he is a jinx. They tow him in, and accidents happen until he is turned into a houseboat. Zug has a cameo.

Episode 5 (May 2, 1989)
"Quarantine"

O.J. dodges a runaway motorboat and accidentally hits a ferryboat, sinking it. "Dead clumsy if you ask me," says Zug. "We'd have towed her in before she went down, wouldn't we, Zorran?"

Episode 6 (May 9, 1989)
"High Winds"

A bad tramp steamer named Johnny Cuba gets Zebedee to help him with his criminal plans until Zebedee works up the courage to turn him in. Zug has a cameo.

Episode 9
"Warrior" (May 30, 1989)

Izzy Gomez tries to get into the harbor without a tow, which is illegal. "And stupid," says Zug. Izzy runs aground, and Ten Cent selflessly tries to keep him from capsizing. Zug and Zip refuse to help, thinking that they will be able to salvage Izzy for themselves. Clumsy Warrior saves the day.

Episode 11 (June 13, 1989)
"Munitions"

Loading a naval ship leads to a disaster in Bigg City Harbor. Zug has a cameo.

Episode 12 (June 20, 1989)
"Regatta" aka "4th of July"

Grampus is to be used for target practice, and the Star tugs come up with a plan to save him. Ten Cents tells Zorran and Zug he needs their lumber barge. "Yeah, he needs it, all right," says Zug. Zorran threatens to call Captain Star. "He'll sink you!" Zug giggles insanely. The Star tugs leave the barge in Grampus' place and the Navy blows it up. They haul Grampus back into the harbor. "Ten Cents said he'd let us in on it," says Zug. Hercules chases them off. The Navy sells Grampus to Captain Star.

Episode 13 (June 27, 1989)
"Bigg Freeze"

S. S. Vienna can't be towed in unless Lillie Lightship is lit, and she needs fuel. Because the harbor is frozen, Zorran has the only fuel barge, which he is taking to the S. S. Vienna. Ten Cents remembers where there is another emergency light barge and he and Sunshine go to retrieve it. Zug thinks they are trying to get the fuel to the S. S. Vienna instead. "We can't let that happen!" Zip and Zug block the creek where Ten Cents and Sunshine are. A rising tide floats their boats and they make it to Lillie just in time.

GIGGLE RATING: Looks, Five Giggles. Imaginative use of Lorre's eyes. Voice, Four Giggles.

AVAILABILITY: A number of VHS versions of the series were released between 1989 and 1993 in the United Kingdom, Australia, and Japan. Three of these videos contained three fifteen-minute episodes, while two contained two twenty-minute episodes. Not all episodes released include Zug. Those released include:
Episode 1 "Sunshine"/Episode 2 "Pirate"
Episode 3 "Trapped"/Episode 7 "Ghosts"/Episode 6 "High Winds"
Episode 4 "Jinxed"/Episode 5 "Quarantine"/Episode 8 "Up River"
Episode 13 "Bigg Freeze"/Episode 9 "Warrior"/Episode 10 "High Tide"
Episode 11 "Munitions"/Episode 12 "4th of July" aka "Regatta"
A four episode, 65-minute version was released in 1993: Episode 3 "Trapped"/Episode 7 "Ghosts"/Episode 6 "High Winds"/Episode 12 "4th of July" aka "Regatta"

Gravedale High (1990)

Hanna-Barbera Productions, NBC Productions. Directed by Robert Alvarez, Oscar Dufau, Don Lusk, Ray Patterson, Paul Sommer, Carl Urbano. Written by Ernie Contreras, Glenn Leopold, Bruce Reid Schaefer, Paul Dell, Tod Himmel, Bill Matheny, Chris Schoon, Robert Tarlow, Steven Weiss, David Kirschner. Executive Producers: Joseph Barbera, William Hanna. Cast: Rick Moranis (Max Schneider), Shari Belafonte (Blanche), Roger Rose (Vinnie Stoker), Eileen Brennan (Miss Dirge), Georgia Brown (Headmistress Crone), Tim Curry (Mr. Tutner), Barry Gordon (Reggie Moonshroud), Sandra Gould (Miss Webner), Jackie Earle Haley (Gill Waterman), Ricki Lake (Cleofatra), Maurice LaMarche (Sid the Invisible Kid), Brock Peters (Boneyard), Kimmy Robertson (Medusa), Frank Welker (Frankentyke/J.P. Ghastly III), Jonathan Winters (Coach Cadaver).

In 1990, Rick Moranis was hot off appearances in franchise films *Ghostbusters II* (1989) and *Honey, I Shrunk the Kids* (1989) when he got top billing in this show, sometimes known as *Rick Moranis in Gravedale High*. He plays Max Schneider, a human teacher who goes to work at a high school for monsters in Gravedale, a suburb of Midtown consisting mostly of cemeteries. The students are mostly children of famous monsters: J.P. Ghastly III, a wealthy, blue skinned Peter Lorre type; J.P.'s sometime love interest, Blanche, a Southern zombie shopaholic; Sid the Invisible Kid, a budding standup comic and impressionist; Vinnie Stoker, a slacker vampire; Frankentyke, a pint-sized creature assembled in a lab; Reggie Moonshroud, a nerdy werewolf; Gill Waterman, a surfer dude and lagoon creature; Cleofatra, a pudgy mummy; and Duzer, the nickname for Medusa, a snake-haired Gorgon Valley girl. There is also a minor character, a hunchback named Iggy, which is presumably short for Igor, but he is not a Peter Lorre-wannabe. Faculty and staff include Headmistress Crone, who runs the school with an iron fist, literally; Coach Cadaver, a sadistic gym teacher; Mr. Tutner, a mummified principal; and Boneyard, an undertaker-type who does various jobs at the school. A running gag is Clawford, a green cat rapidly going through his nine lives, trying to capture the hunch-backed rat who rings the school bell.

Season 1
Episode 1 (September 8, 1990)
"Long Day's Gurney into Night"

The traditional "introduction" episode is eschewed. At the opening of the series, Schneider has already started his job a few days earlier. The class is asked what they want to be when they grow up. Sid wants to be a standup comedian, playing to an SRO house, but the class hates his jokes. J.P. wants to be the "wealthiest monster in the world." Blanche wants to marry J.P. She gets him a drink and asks him if he wants anything else. "Some bat jerky would be nice."

Sid falls ill and Schneider takes him to the Community Hospital. After school, Schneider tries to get the class to go see him there. "You couldn't even pay me to go," says J.P. Schneider fakes an accident to get them all to take him. "I hope he has a good life insurance policy," J.P. giggles insanely. "If I catch any human germs in here, Mr. Schneider, you're going to hear from my attorney." The doctors tell Sid his tonsils will have to be taken out, and Sid takes off. Schneider and the class try to find him. Sid stumbles into the children's ward, where he finds an appreciative audience. "You did it, Sid," says Schneider. "Standing room only."

Sid imitates Rodney Dangerfield, a clown, Robin Williams, a skeleton, Michael Jackson, Groucho Marx, Snagglepuss (qv), and Sammy Davis Jr.

Episode 2 (September 15, 1990)
"Do the Rad Thing"

Kahuna Bob, a retired surfing star, takes Gill under his wing, and Gill neglects his schoolwork and his friend, Frankentyke. Schneider takes the class to the beach to try to win Gill back. "The place is crawling with humans," says J.P., although later, he says, "This is what I call a beautiful evening. Cold. Damp." Gill returns to school, and so does former dropout Kahuna Bob.

Sid imitates Billy Crystal's Fernando.

Episode 3 (September 22, 1990)
"Cleo's Pen Pal"

Cleo has no VCR, so she sits in class watching Billy Headstone (Phil Hartman), the monster star of her favorite soap, *Trudy and the Beast*. "New money," scoffs J.P. "So bourgeois." She writes him a letter asking him to move the show's time slot, and sends him a picture of Duzer instead of herself. "Love letters," says Blanche. "I could just die." "That would be redundant, Blanche," says J.P. Billy writes back to say he is coming to visit her.

Meanwhile, Schneider asks the class if they want to go someplace fun. "The tar pits?" asks J.P. Schneider has passes to an amusement park. Cleo gets Duzer to stay behind and impersonate her. Duzer takes Billy to the amusement park. Duzer is too wild for the thoughtful, contemplative Billy, and he ends up with the real Cleo. He gives her a VCR so she can tape *Trudy and the Beast*.

Sid imitates Peter Falk as Lt. Columbo.

Episode 4 (September 29, 1990)
"Monster Gumbo"

Every year, Coach Cadaver's class raises more money for the United Monster Fund than any other and wins the Guardian Monster Trophy. Schneider's class is determined to beat them this year. "Don't look at me," says J.P. "I gave at the grave." Blanche spills her Monster Gumbo all over the class. "You'll be getting a cleaning bill for this, Blanche," says J.P. It tastes delicious, however, and the class decides to sell jars of it. "Break it and you bought it," she tells J.P. "I can afford it, bimbo," he replies. Soon, they are selling it as fast as they can make it. "I'm impressed," says J.P.

A waitress who looks like Flo from *Alice* (1976) reports back to her boss, a Paul Prudhomme-like chef at Big Daddy's Gumbo Emporium, that the gumbo is the best she ever tasted. He confirms this for himself and tries to buy Blanche's recipe, but she refuses to sell. Meanwhile, she turns into a tyrant. "I liked her better when she loved to shop," says J.P. The class quits, and Blanche tearfully confesses she just wanted to prove she could sell things as well as buy them. Big Daddy buys the recipe, which puts Schneider's class over the top, and they win the trophy.

Episode 5 (October 6, 1990)
"The Dress Up Mess Up"

The gang is at the mall to buy a birthday gift for Schneider. "Which of these CDs are on sale?" J.P. asks the terrified clerk, who tells him, "Any one you want, man!"

"Let's try Gadgeteria," suggests J.P. "They're bound to have something useless and expensive for Mr. Schneider." He test-drives an Auto-Groomer. "I love the eyebrows, but the lipstick has got to go." Hungry Gill stops at a restaurant, Le Haute Pan, but he can't read the menu.

"It's in French, you heathen," J.P. giggles insanely. "You won't find a pizza in there." They decide to treat Schneider. "I must advise you," says J.P. "This French eatery is tres expensivé." Cleo passes the hat. "This meal better be worth it," mutters J.P.

Duzer borrows the class's money to buy a dress which gets ruined and is not returnable. Duzer tries various jobs at the mall to get back the money, but her snakes get her fired from the first two. At Snakey Pete's, a cowboy-themed restaurant, she makes some money on tips, but not enough to pay back the class.

At Le Haute Pan, Schneider and the class arrive for dinner. J.P. produces a battle-ax. "I'm hungry! I want some snails NOW!" Frankentyke starts a food fight with the next table and they get thrown out. They end up at Snakey Pete's, where Duzer confesses and promises to pay back the money. "With interest, of course," says J.P. Duzer douses him with condiments.

Sid imitates Bert Parks and George Jessel.

Episode 6 (October 13, 1990)
"The Grave Intruder"

Duzer is unimpressed with Headmistress Crone's school paper, the *Gravedale Gazette*, and says she could do better, so Crone gives her the job of editor. Duzer hands out assignments to the class. J.P. is assigned to cover business. "I love giving people the business," he giggles insanely. Duzer changes the name of the paper to *The Grave Intruder* and prints fake news. "It's already a collector's item," says J.P. The class decides to teach her a lesson and write a false story about her love of Frankentyke. "We'll just let your readers decide," says J.P. They get Duzer to make the paper respectable again, but Crone fires her.

Sid imitates Karl Malden and Gene Shalit.

Episode 7 (October 20, 1990)
"Fear of Flying"

Vinnie is helping Reggie with his science project, a flying suit, when Reggie collides with Nardo, one of Coach Cadaver's football players who flies. Nardo challenges Vinnie to a game of "Fly or Splat" after school. They both fly up, then down, and whoever stops last wins, unless he splats.

Reggie develops aviophobia. Schneider takes him to a doctor. "There's a very good monster clinic near the East Side Cemetery," says J.P. A psychiatrist says Vinnie's noodle is scrambled and grounds him.

After school, Vinnie gets his mojo back. "I guess his noodle is finally unscrambled," says J.P. Vinnie wins the challenge.

Sid imitates Howard Cosell.

Episode 8 (October 27, 1990)
"He Ain't Scary, He's My Brother"

Frankentyke's brother, Big Frankie (Phil Hartman, impersonating Jack Nicholson), returns to his alma mater and Frankentyke looks forward to spending time with him, but the girls monopolize all Big Frankie's attention. "He's not even rich," says J.P. "He's just a working stiff." Big Frankie rescues Frankentyke from hoodlums and they spend time together.

Episode 9 (November 3, 1990)
"Frankenjockey"

Hoover, an escaped racehorse, meets Frankentyke and immediately bonds with him because of Frankentyke's horsehair toupée. The horse's owner, Colonel Saddlesore, comes to claim him and Frankentyke overhears the trainer, Liverpool, tell Hoover that after he loses the steeplechase race, he will go to the glue factory. Frankentyke, the only one who has been able to ride Hoover, is hired as the jockey. "I'm gonna teach you to ride her properly," says J.P. Schneider makes Saddlesore promise to retire Hoover if he wins. Liverpool tells Red, the rival horse owner, that he will make sure

Frankentyke doesn't finish the race. They kidnap Frankentyke and lock him away, but the gang finds him in time for the race. Liverpool takes over for Red's jockey and beats Frankentyke, but is disqualified.

Episode 10 (November 10, 1990)
"Save Our School"

There is a student election coming up and Schneider tells the class the results will affect all of their lives. "Most of our lives are already over," says J.P. "I usually sell my vote. I supplement my income that way."

Vinnie runs for president to avoid going to summer school. His opponents are Elephant Boy, who sounds like William F. Buckley Jr.; and Suey, a pig-girl who paraphrases Lloyd Bentsen. Although Vinnie tries to throw the election, he wins anyway but plans to resign.

Meanwhile, unscrupulous developers Marvin and Belle Gardens (think Harry and Leona Helmsley) are trying to buy the school to turn it into a hotel, but Headmistress Crone turns them down. They bribe Inspector Nitpicker, who sounds like Pat Buttram, to get the school closed down for health violations. Gravedale has forty-eight hours to make things right. President Vinnie motivates the students to help. J.P. even gets rid of his leeches. "I was really attached to those little guys." The school gets cleaned up, but Nitpicker finds dust on the roof and condemns the property.

Just as Marvin and Belle are getting ready to tear down the property, Vinnie mobilizes the monsters from the cemetery, and Nitpicker confesses to being bribed. The corpses chase away the Gardens. Vinnie resigns.

Sid imitates John F. Kennedy, George H. W. Bush, Richard Nixon, Ronald Reagan, Ed Sullivan, Walter Cronkite, and Jackie Mason.

Episode 11 (November 17, 1990)
"Night of the Living Dad"

The talent show is coming up, and all the students' parents are coming except Frankentyke's father, who wasn't invited by Frankentyke. Frankentyke confesses to Gill that he is embarrassed that his father is the human who created him. Frankentyke goes to Bud's Body Shop to get parts to build a fake dad, but he drops the jar with the genius brain. Bud, who sounds like Marlon Brando, tells Frankentyke he can't return or exchange the genius brain, but takes pity on him and gives him an agent's brain instead. Frankentyke thinks it is from a secret agent, but it is from a Hollywood agent. "Frankentyke's dad is a real take-charge kind of monster," says J.P.

Marty, the fake dad, gives notes to Vinnie, Gill, Duzer, and Reggie, who are all in Stagefright, a band with Frankentyke. Frankentyke buys the hype that Marty feeds him and begins to think he is too good for the group. Gill accidentally lets the truth about Frankentyke's father slip to Schneider. At the talent show, Sid's mother imitates Eva (or Zsa Zsa) Gabor and Edith Bunker from *All in the Family* (1971). Sid's father imitates Jackie Gleason and Edith's husband, Archie. Marty's obnoxiousness makes the members of Stagefright quit, and Frankentyke goes on as a solo act. Frankentyke's real father, who sounds like Boris Karloff, comes up the aisle and applauds Frankentyke. Marty leaves, and Stagefright reunites onstage.

Sid imitates Elvis Presley.

FUN FACT: "Bud" was Marlon Brando's nickname.

Episode 12 (November 24, 1990)
"Goodbye Gravedale"

J.P. does the intro: "Don't go away. We'll be right back with more *Gravedale High* [1990]. Trust me." He giggles insanely.

The class is watching home movies of their childhood. Schneider suggests they make a class video. "I could direct," J.P. giggles insanely. "My father used to own a monster movie studio, you know."

Schneider receives a letter from Midtown Prep accepting his application for a position. He applied there before he got the job at Gravedale and has no intention of accepting it, but he drops the letter. The students find it and think he is leaving them. The class literally deserts him. "Fade to black," says J.P. The next day, the class walks out again, and he takes the job at Midtown Prep.

Schneider is as disillusioned with his new job as his old class is with their substitute teachers. "And we're accepting no substitutes," says J.P. Reggie goes to talk to Schneider. J.P. goes along. "I'd be a fool to miss this photo opportunity." The principal at Midtown throws Reggie and J.P. out.

The new substitute is Mr. Creepers, who learns that the class found Schneider's letter and thought he was leaving. Mr. Creepers tears his mask off and reveals himself to be Schneider, and he says he will stay because at least they know he's alive. "We won't hold that against you," says J.P.

Episode 13 (December 1, 1990)
"Monster on Trial"

Schneider is teaching Driver Ed. Reggie is driving when Miss Fresno (Ruth Buzzi) cuts him off and he taps her bumper. She says she has whiplash and sues Schneider for $1,000,000. Schneider goes to a lawyer, Z Lasstop, who also sounds like Marlon Brando. Lasstop refuses to take the case, so Schneider decides to defend himself. Miss Fresno shows up in a full body cast and Judge Killjoy finds in her favor, so Schneider has to give her the money. "You know teachers are grossly underpaid," J.P. says to the judge. The class is arrested, but Frankentyke and Reggie make a break for it.

Reggie and Frankentyke see Miss Fresno driving, now out of her cast, and they follow her. She flees, and she crashes into a stationary car and cries whiplash. The car's owner is Judge Killjoy, who realizes she is a fraud and releases Schneider and the students.

Sid imitates James Cagney and Edward G. Robinson.

GIGGLE RATING: Five Giggles.

AVAILABILITY: Never officially released on home video, but available as a bootlegged DVD. Don't do anything I wouldn't do.

Tiny Toon Adventures (1990)
Season 1
Episode 31 (November 5, 1990)
"Sawdust and Toonsil"

Warner Bros. Animation, Amblin Television. Directed by Rich Arons. Written by Gordon Bressack & Charles M. Howell IV. Produced by Tom Ruegger. Cast: Frank Welker (Gogo Dodo/Silas Wonder/Dragon), Charlie Adler (Buster Bunny/Roustabout Minions/Devil), Tress MacNeille (Babs Bunny), Joe Alaskey (Plucky Duck), Susan Blu (Sphinx).

In Warner Bros.' first original animated television series, Plucky Duck, Gogo Dodo, Shirley the Loon, Babs and Buster Bunny (who are not siblings), and others are attending Acme Looniversity to become the next generation of cartoon stars. Tom Ruegger joined Warner Bros. Animation to oversee production.

The Do-Do Bird made his first appearance in the Looney Tune *Porky in Wackyland* (1938). According to writer Paul Dini, the Do-Do is the father of Gogo Dodo.

Babs, Buster, and Plucky return from a fun day in Wackyland with Gogo, but when Gogo sees the train from Silas Wonder's Wonderful Circus of Wonderment, he returns to Wackyland, rolling up the road behind him so no one can follow. Plucky sees the circus as his entree to show biz, and he, Babs, and Buster meet Silas, who sounds like Ronald Reagan. Gogo is watching via telescope, and he goes to rescue his friends.

In the circus tent, two roustabout minions pull back the curtains to reveal Silas' "wonderbeasts": a scrawny Pegasus, a sick dragon, and a sad Sphinx, whom he gets to perform by using his taser-like wand.

Gogo saws his way into the Sphinx' cage and throws the cage on top of Silas. Gogo, the Sphinx, Babs, Buster, and Plucky escape, with the minions in hot pursuit. Gogo explains that Silas kidnapped the wonderbeasts from Wackyland, "and now he wants me. Silas breaks out of his cage. The minions catch Gogo and the Sphinx and they leave on the train with Silas. "Now my collection is complete," says Silas.

Gogo doesn't do well in captivity, but Silas says he'll learn to enjoy it like the others, who are miserable. Gogo morphs into Peter Lorre and says, "If dat's enjoyment, I'll have pain on rye and hold de mayo." Then he turns into Edward G. Robinson and tells the Sphinx, "Now listen up, see? We're bustin' outta here at midnight, see? I swiped a spoon from the mess hall. We're gonna dig our way outta here, ya got it? Myeah." She points out that the cages are made of steel. Gogo realizes if he doesn't tank up on wackiness in Wackyland soon, he'll be a "done dodo."

After discarding their earlier disguises (Babs wears Groucho-like glasses), Buster, Babs, and Plucky pose as a three-headed duckbilled rabbit and pretend to want to join the sideshow. Silas puts them on top of a high platform and makes them jump into a thimble of Jello. They manage to catch a trapeze with their ears on the way down and land in a pool of water. Plucky decides to talk to Silas about his career, and Babs and Buster use the distraction to free Gogo and the others. "They look like they're dying," says Buster. Gogo morphs into George C. Scott as Patton and says, "I want you to 'member, dodos don't die, they just fade away." Buster digs a tunnel to the train tracks, where they commandeer a handcar. They return to rescue Plucky, and Silas chases them with the train. They abandon the handcar and "book it to Wackyland." Silas follows them, taking the train off the tracks. Gogo rolls up the road and Silas plunges off the cliff and goes to Hell, where the Devil says, "Now my collection is complete."

GIGGLE RATING: Five Giggles. Frank Welker's numerous credits include *Aladdin* (1992), *Robot Chicken* (2005), *Duck Dodgers* (2003), *Jackie Chan Adventures* (2000), *The Sylvester & Tweety Mysteries* (1995), *Timon & Pumbaa* (1995), *Animaniacs* (1993), *Yo Yogi* (1995), *The Simpsons* (1989), and various iterations of Scooby-Doo (all qv).

AVAILABILITY: On the DVD *Tiny Toon Adventures, Season 1, Volume 1* (2009).

Episode 61 (February 20, 1991)
"New Character Day"

Warner Bros. Animation, Amblin Television. Written and Directed by Eddie Fitzgerald. Produced by Richard Arons, Sherri Stoner. Cast: Charlie Adler [Charles Adler] (Buster Bunny), Tress MacNeille (Babs Bunny/Hatta Mari), Joe Alaskey (Plucky Duck), Frank Welker (Boxcars/Ticklepuss), Gail Matthius (Shirley the Loon).

In the segment "The Return of Pluck Twacy", Babs and Buster are auditioning new talent for the show. Daffy Duck shows up in Duck Twacy drag. Buster asks, "You sure you're a new character?" "Honest to Warren Beatty," replies Daffy. "I got my demo tape right here." He puts it in the VCR. At Acme Looniversity, Duck Twacy is lecturing the class.

"Duck Twacy is my hero," says Plucky, before he slips on a banana peel thrown by Shirley the Loon and is knocked cold. Plucky dreams he is Pluck Twacy and Shirley hires him to find her runaway aura. The aura is

Hatta Mari from *Plane Daffy* (1944), sans German spy accent. She pretends she has been kidnapped and sends Plucky into a secret room filled with archvillains, including Ticklepuss, Soupy Man, Jack the Zipper, the Boston Dangler, Flatbottom, Wolvertoon, and the Generic Thugs. Flatbottom (whose name parodies Flattop, but who does not sound like Peter Lorre) launches planes off his butt. Ticklepuss tickles Plucky. Hatta Mari activates a trap door, which sends Plucky down a chute onto a tiny train with Boxcars (who does sound like Peter Lorre). "In the Hall of the Mountain King" plays on the soundtrack. "Why did he run away like that?" asks Boxcars. "It makes me want to do terrible, horrible things to him." Boxcars traps Plucky in one of the coaches and giggles insanely. "OK, thumb wrestle," he says. "I win." Their hands fight on top of the speeding train. Plucky pulls the brake cord, throwing Boxcars off the train. Plucky wakes up in the classroom.

FUN FACTS: This is a parody of and homage to *The Great Piggy Bank Robbery* (1946), a Daffy Duck short directed by Robert Clampett. The director of this segment, Eddie Fitzgerald, was a big Clampett fan, and would go on to work on *The Ren & Stimpy Show* (1991) (qv). The cast includes frequent Peter Lorre impersonator Joe Alaskey.

GIGGLE RATING: Five Giggles.

AVAILABILITY: On the DVD *Tiny Toon Adventures, Season 1, Volume 2* (2009).

The Ren & Stimpy Show (1991)

Ren Höek is an "asthma hound Chihuahua" with huge eyes, rotten teeth, and a small body. He often wears a monogrammed fez and sounds like Peter Lorre. His voice in the first two seasons was done by series creator John Kricfalusi, although Billy West, who took over the role in season three, always supplied the character's insane giggles. Although Kricfalusi auditioned Frank Welker, Joe Alaskey, and Patrick Pinney for the role of Ren, West claims Kricfalusi probably always intended to play the part, although this was not initially obvious. West also played Stimpson "Stimpy" J. Cat, a pleasant but dumb fat red cat with a bulbous blue nose. His fur color and nose shape (but not nose color) is based on the "Durante cat" in Robert

Clampett's Looney Tune, *A Gruesome Twosome* (1945), although he is much fatter, and his voice is an imitation of Larry Fine of the Three Stooges. John Kricfalusi created the characters in college for his own amusement, but Ralph Bakshi shopped the show to CBS in the pitch meeting for what eventually became *Mighty Mouse The New Adventures* (1987) (qv). In 1989, Kricfalusi pitched a show called *Your Gang* or *Our Gang* to Nickelodeon's Vanessa Coffey with Ren and Stimpy as supporting characters. Coffey didn't like the show but she liked Ren and Stimpy and gave them their own series, premiering along with *Doug* (1991) and *Rugrats* (1991). This block of "Nicktoons" instantly boosted Nickelodeon's ratings and changed children's TV animation forever.

Continuity is ignored in the series. Their ages vary, sometimes by decades. In different episodes, Ren and Stimpy can be cowboys, spacemen, homeowners, sometimes even house pets. Frequently, one or both will die, only to return the next episode.

Interstitials, few of which feature Ren, include fake commercials for dodgy toys like Log and nauseating breakfast foods like powdered toast, and Stimpy in "Ask Dr. Stupid". Sometimes the final segment is "What'll We Do Till Then?", with Ren suggesting increasingly absurd things to occupy Stimpy's time until the next show.

Supporting characters include their "official owner", George Liquor, American, a man so conservative "that he thinks the Republicans are Commies"; Powdered Toast Man, an incompetent superhero; Mr. and Mrs. Pipe, a white suburban couple; Muddy Mudskipper, a piscine children's show host; Wilbur Cobb, an ancient, senile former cartoon producer; Haggis McHaggis, a stereotypical Scotsman; The Fire Chief, who hates circus midgets; Mr. Horse, whose catch phrase is, "No sir, I don't like it"; Mrs. Buttloaves, a fat, ugly woman in curlers and a pink nightgown; Old Man Hunger, a nudist; the Shaven Yak, the poster child for his eponymous day; and the Baboon, a vicious primate.

Guest stars include frequent Peter Lorre imitators Stan Freberg, Phil Hartman, Frank Gorshin, and Gilbert Gottfried.

The show frequently ran afoul of Standards and Practices at Nickelodeon for its crude humor, which was largely based on bodily emissions, sexual innuendo, and hyper-violence. Due to this and Kricfalusi's lackadaisical attitude towards deadlines, his relationship with Nick grew steadily worse until his contract was terminated after the second season.

Seasons 1 and 2

Spümcø, Games Animation. Directed by Bob Camp, Bong Hee Han, Gregg Vanzo, John Kricfalusi, Kelly Armstrong, Ron Hughart, Chris Reccardi. Written by John Kricfalusi (creator), Bob Camp (creator), Will McRobb, Jim Gomez, Ron Hauge, Vincent Waller, Richard Pursel. Executive Producer: Vanessa Coffey. Produced by John Kricfalusi, Jim Ballantine, Bob Camp, Jim Smith. Cast: John Kricfalusi (Ren), Billy West (Stimpy).

All episodes are given their overall number (order shown).

Season 1
Episode 1 (August 11, 1991)
"Stimpy's Big Day"
Episode 2 (August 11, 1991)
"The Big Shot"

A rare two-parter. Stimpy enters a contest and wins $47,000,000 and a trip to Hollywood with a guest appearance on *The Muddy Mudskipper Show*. He stays in Hollywood eventually getting Muddy's contract. Meanwhile, Ren misses him. Finally, Stimpy admits he misses Ren and returns to him in joyful reunion. However, when Stimpy reveals he has given away all his money, Ren smacks him and says, "YOU FAT, BLOATED EEDIOT!"

Episode 3 (August 18, 1991)
"Robin Höek"

Ren and Stimpy appear in a commercial for Powdered Toast. Then, Ren refuses to read Stimpy a bedtime story. "Read it yourself!" Ren dreams that Stimpy makes up a story about Robin Höek. Stimpy is Maid Moron, trapped in a tower, and Robin has to rescue her. When Ren wakes up, he says, "Thank goodness it was only a dream." Stimpy is next to him dressed as Maid Moron.

In the interstitial, Ren makes the viewers take an oath so they may watch the next cartoon. "I do hereby promise only to watch *The Ren & Stimpy Show* [1991]."

Episode 4 (August 18, 1991)
"Nurse Stimpy"

Ren is very sick so Stimpy must nurse him back to health. This includes Ren taking off his fur and Stimpy giving him a sponge bath, which is witnessed by Mr. Horse, Kirk Douglas, and others. Ren reads about it in the newspaper the next day and has a total relapse. Stimpy nurses him back to health again, but Stimpy becomes ill. "Nurse Ren to the rescue!" Stimpy gulps.

Episode 5 (August 25, 1991)
"Space Madness"

In the year 400,000,000, Commander Höek and Space Cadet Stimpy find themselves on a long journey and Ren is going crazy. "It is not I who am crazy," says Ren, "it is I who am mad." Stimpy has to subdue him. Ren decides to occupy Stimpy by having him guard the Memory Eraser button. Stimpy gives in to temptation and presses the button, erasing Ren and Stimpy from the cartoon and even their logo.

FUN FACT: Ren quotes Kirk Douglas from *Champion* (1949).

Episode 6 (August 25, 1991)
"The Boy Who Cried Rat!"

Ren and Stimpy are strays who come up with a plan to avoid having to eat garbage. Ren will pose as a mouse and Stimpy will pretend to catch him. They choose the Mr. and Mrs. Pipe house, and Mr. Pipe pays Stimpy five bucks, but he expects Stimpy to eat the "mouse", which he does. "I can't stand it!" says Ren. "I'm going mad!" Stimpy coughs Ren up and admits he ate the five bucks. Ren smacks him. "You stupid eediot! You filthy worm! You bloated sack!"

Ren and Stimpy do an interstitial for Shaven Yak Day.

Episode 7 (September 15, 1991)
"Big House Blues"

This was the pilot, originally shown at film festivals. It finally appeared on TV in edited form. An origin story, it explains how a cat and an asthma hound Chihuahua, both homeless, bonded over their mutual hunger. When they are picked up by the pound, they think their troubles are over. Life is a party, they have a square meal a day and a roof over their head. When their new friend gets led away to the gas chamber, they realize they have to escape. Stimpy coughs up hairballs onto Ren and a little girl mistakes him for a poodle and adopts him. Ren insists she take Stimpy, too. The little girl takes them home, where her mother gives Stimpy his "first material possession"–a litter box. Stimpy hugs it to his breast, trapping Ren.

In the unedited pilot, Ren wakes up with Stimpy the first morning in the shelter, and to the tune of "Stranger in Paradise", Ren, still half-asleep, says to Stimpy, "Oh, my darling. My little cucaracha. I kiss your sleep-encrusted eyes. I caress your large, bulbous nose. Let us join lips in one final sweet exchange of saliva."

Episode 8 (September 15, 1991)
"The Littlest Giant"

Ren is dreaming that Stimpy is reading himself a bedtime story. Stimpy is the littlest giant. One of his fellow giants sounds like Curly Howard. "He's barely huge!" The little giant leaves Hugevania and walks through the ocean to an island, where he meets Wee Ren, who is suffering from a drought. The giant's tears fill up the well. Ren offers to do anything for the giant, who asks him over and over if he will really do anything. "Yes, anything, you fat bloated eediot!"

Episode 9 (September 1, 1991)
"Fire Dogs"

Homeless once again, Ren and Stimpy pose as Dalmatians to work at a fire station. The Fire Chief at first takes them for circus midgets, and Stimpy almost blows it by saying he's a cat, but Ren smacks him. "Shut up, you fool!" At the fire, they are squashed by Mrs. Buttloaves' gigantic baby, Mr. Horse, a walrus, and an elephant before rescuing Mrs. Buttloaves herself. For their bravery, they are awarded Golden Fire Hydrant hats, and the dogs can't wait to urinate on them.

Episode 10 (December 29, 1991)
"Marooned"

Commander Höek and Space Cadet Stimpy are marooned on a distant planet with little hope of rescue, so per the space cadet handbook, they scout around. They start hallucinating, and things get worse and worse. Finally, Stimpy consults the handbook and learns they are doomed. "Give me that," says Ren, and beats Stimpy with the book.

Episode 11 (December 29, 1991)
"Untamed World"

Ren and Stimpy are hosting a nature show. Many of the animals resemble Ren or Stimpy. While trying to tag the yak, Stimpy tranquilizes and tags Ren. At the end of the show, Ren says, "Say, Stimpy, what's that on your tongue?" and tags Stimpy and himself.

Episode 12 (February 23, 1992)
"Black Hole"

Commander Höek and Space Cadet Stimpy pass through a black hole. "We're alive!" says Ren. "Alive, I tell you, alive!" Stimpy suggests splitting up, and he divides himself into two Stimpys. Then things get really strange. They have to get to the trans-dimensional gateway by three o'clock, or be trapped forever. They make it, but are thrown off the bus for not having exact change. Ren then realizes he had a whole pocketful of coins.

Episode 13 (February 23, 1992)
"Stimpy's Invention"

Stimpy invents a happy helmet that makes the user ecstatic. Ren says, "You sick little monkey," but the helmet actually works. Ren ends up doing all the chores. Finally, he takes a hammer to the helmet and destroys it. He begins to throttle Stimpy, but realizes he is happy when he is angry and thanks Stimpy. "Happy to be of service?" asks Stimpy. Ren giggles insanely.

Season 2
Episode 14 (August 15, 1992)
"In the Army"

Ren and Stimpy join the army to become tank paratroopers. They constantly screw up and get put on KP by the hard-assed drill instructor. After a long hike and no sleep, Ren finally cracks: "Hey Guido, it's all so clear to me now. I'm the keeper of the keys and you're the lemon merchant. Get it? And he knows it. That's why he's gonna kill us. So we gotta beat it. Before he lets loose the marmosets on us. Don't worry, little missy, I'll save you!" They try to run away, but they are stopped by the DI. They have graduated. In the next scene, they are dropped in a tank out of a plane, presumably to their deaths.

Episode 15 (August 15, 1992)
"Powdered Toast Man"

Powdered Toast Man (Gary Owens) rescues a kitten from an oncoming truck by shooting down a jetliner with his projectile raisin breath and crashing it into the truck, which would have stopped anyway. Powdered Toast Man throws the kitten away, presumably to its death, when he receives another distress call. He goes to see Ren and Stimpy. "We are all out of Powdered Toast," they say, and he gives them some.

Episode 16 (August 22, 1992)
"Ren's Toothache"

Stimpy is brushing his teeth, which Ren considers a waste of time. That night, he gets a toothache. "My tooth. It hurts! Why, Stimpy, why?" The next night, he snores and blows all his teeth, which are now dust, out of his mouth, leaving only nerve endings. The Nerve Ending Fairy, Old Man Hunger, comes, but leaves a hairball instead of money. Stimpy gifts Ren with a gigantic tooth which he has pulled out of his own mouth.

Episode 17 (August 29, 1992)
"Out West"

In the old west, Abner Dimwit and Ewalt Nitwit are ignorant rednecks, a sheriff and deputy. They have run out of people to hang, so they decide to hire villains, Ren and Stimpy, to steal Abner's mount, Mr. Horse, who says,

"I don't like it." Sentenced to hang, Ren says, "Hey Stimpy, I have a little confession to make. At night, while you're asleep, I polish my boots with your tongue." However, Ren is too light to hang and Stimpy has no neck, so Abner and Ewalt hang themselves.

Episode 18 (August 29, 1992)
"Rubber Nipple Salesmen"

Ren and Stimpy are selling rubber nipples door to door. "We'll rule the world!" says Ren. Their first stop is the house of the Fire Chief, who mistakes Ren for a circus midget. Their second stop is Mr. Horse, who doesn't like it. Stimpy begs to talk at the next house. It is the home of Mr. and Mrs. Pipe. Mr. Pipe buys all the rubber nipples, then literally kicks Ren and Stimpy out onto bulls, which they ride off into the sunset.

FUN FACT: The final gag is from a Three Stooges movie, *A Pain in the Pullman* (1936).

Episode 19 (November 7, 1992)
"Svën Höek"

A double episode. Ren anxiously awaits the arrival of his cousin, Svën, as a relief from spending time with the idiotic Stimpy. Svën turns out to be just as dumb and fat as Stimpy, however. The next day, Ren leaves them alone while he goes to work. When he returns home, Svën and Stimpy are playing "Don't Whiz on the Electric Fence". Ren finds his opera records covered in bubble gum; his collection of rare, incurable diseases violated; his dinosaur droppings painted like Easter eggs.

"YOU EEDIOTS!" he screams and confronts Svën and Stimpy. "First I'm gonna tear your lips out. Yeah. That's what I'm gonna do. And then, I'm gonna gouge your eyes out. Yeah. That's what I'm gonna do," he says. "Next, I'm gonna tear your arms out of their sockets. And you wanna know what else? I'm gonna hitcha, and you're gonna fall. Then I'm gonna look down and I'm gonna laugh. But first, FIRST, I gotta take a whiz. You stay right here. Right on this spot. I'll be back." He whizzes on their game, and the house blows up. They awake in Hell.

Episode 20 (November 21, 1992)
"Haunted House"

Stimpy thinks a haunted house would be a great place to kill twelve minutes. "You said it, pal," says Ren. The ghost sounds like Droopy Dog and looks like Elmer Fudd. He tries to scare them, but they unwittingly foil him at every turn. Finally, in desperation, he decides to end it all and takes poison. This turns him into a live African-American man, and he drives away in a car.

Episode 21 (November 21, 1992)
"Mad Dog Höek"

Ren and Stimpy are professional wrestlers, but they have nothing to fear from their massive opponents, the Lout Brothers. "The match is rigged," says Ren. The Lout Brothers proceed to beat Ren and Stimpy to pulps until it's time to throw the fight, at which point the Lout Brothers fall down.

Episode 22 (December 12, 1992)
"Big Baby Scam"

Ren and Stimpy, homeless again, are eating bark. Ren sees two babies and decides he and Stimpy will impersonate them and have an easy life. He gives them fifty bucks to go away.

"You know, Stimpy, this is the best scam yet. We got it made." Their new parents are Mr. and Mrs. Pipe. They are perverts obsessed with defecation, nudity, and physical abuse. Then a policeman shows up with the two babies, blowing Ren and Stimpy's cover. Ren asks for his fifty back, and the babies give him fifty punches in the stomach.

FUN FACT: The original score included "In the Hall of the Mountain King", but Kricfalusi cut this from the DVD.

Episode 23 (December 12, 1992)
"Dog Show"

It's the biggest event of the year, the All-Breed Dog Show, and George Liquor introduces his "prize miniature Great Dane, Champy [Ren]" and his "Cornish Rex Hound", Rex (Stimpy). He subjects them to various forms of abuse in the name of making them champions. The judge is Mr. Horse. "I don't like it," he says of the first entrant, which he feeds to a bulldog. The second entrant begs for his life, but eventually feeds himself to the bulldog. Ren and Stimpy fear the same fate awaits. "It's been a good life," says Ren, but they both make the finals. Stimpy is disqualified for an ingrown dewclaw. Ren tells George Liquor to enter himself, and the Royal American George Hound wins First Prize.

Originally scheduled for September 5, 1992, the episode was held back and finally shown on Nick in censored form.

Episode 24 (January 14, 1993)
"Son of Stimpy"

All about "Stimpy's First Fart", as it was originally titled. Something comes out of Stimpy's butt, it made a sound, and it smelled funny. "You're an eediot," says Ren. Stimpy names the fart Stinky, but it leaves. Stimpy searches the city for him at Christmas time.

At home, Ren is missing Stimpy. Stimpy finally returns. So does Stinky, but he's all grown up now, and he introduces Stimpy to his fiancée, Cora, a rotting fish head. Stimpy joins them in marriage.

Episode 25 (February 13, 1993)
"Monkey See, Monkey Don't!"

Ren and Stimpy, homeless yet again, see zoo animals getting free food. "We could live like kings here! Come, Stimpson, let us see the proprietor of this establishment."

They present themselves as monkeys to the zookeeper and are put in a cage. Being a monkey is harder than it looks, and Ren requests a transfer. When we next see them, Stimpy is a hippo and Ren is an oxpecker cleaning the hippo's teeth.

"I haven't seen such a beautiful bubble
since I was a child." *Hollywood Steps Out* (1941).

Boo Berry Poses Sheet. Monster style guide by Manny Galán and Pat Giles.
Courtesy of Boo Berry and General Mills.

Boo Berry in *Robot Chicken* (2005).
Courtesy Turner.com and Stoopid Buddy Stoodios.

DVD insert from *Monster University TV Special* (2010).
Courtesy Mike Hoffman.

"Bad Brain" from *Monster University TV Special* (2010).
Courtesy Mike Hoffman.

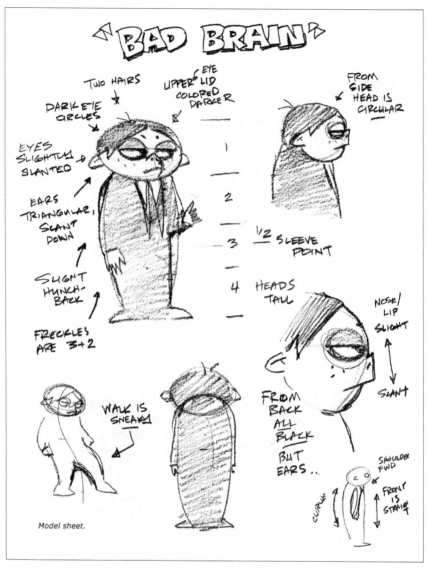

"Bad Brain" model sheet from *Monster University TV Special* (2010).

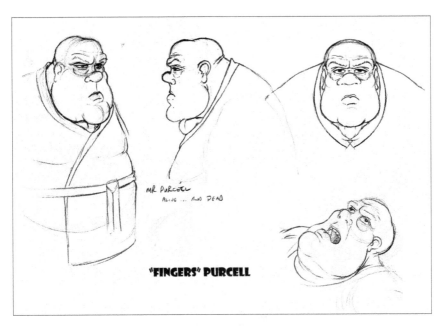

"Fingers" Purcell Model Sheet from *Phil Hartman's Flat TV* "The Monday Night Mystery Theater: The Luther Krupp File" (2019?) by Brian Lemay. Courtesy Paul Hartmann.

"Fingers" Purcell Model Sheet 2 from *Phil Hartman's Flat TV* "The Monday Night Mystery Theater: The Luther Krupp File" (2019?) by Brian Lemay. Courtesy Paul Hartmann.

Chick Hazzard's office from *Phil Hartman's Flat TV* "The Monday Night Mystery Theater: The Luther Krupp File" (2019?) Note black bird in upper right corner. Rav Mudhar modeling, Victoria Jeffrey lighting, Brian Lemay Designs and Art Direction. Courtesy Paul Hartmann.

Early Luther Krupp sketches, *Phil Hartman's Flat TV* "The Monday Night Mystery Theater: The Luther Krupp File" (2019?) by Brian Lemay. Courtesy Paul Hartmann.

Luther Krupp Design Sheet 1, *Phil Hartman's Flat TV* "The Monday Night Mystery Theater: The Luther Krupp File" (2019?) by Brian Lemay. Courtesy Paul Hartmann.

Luther Krupp Design Sheet 2, *Phil Hartman's Flat TV* "The Monday Night Mystery Theater: The Luther Krupp File" (2019?) Courtesy Paul Hartmann.

Luther Krupp Design Sheet 3, *Phil Hartman's Flat TV* "The Monday Night Mystery Theater: The Luther Krupp File" (2019?) by Brian Lemay. Courtesy Paul Hartmann.

Luther Krupp Design Sheet 4, *Phil Hartman's Flat TV* "The Monday Night Mystery Theater: The Luther Krupp File" (2019?) by Brian Lemay. Courtesy Paul Hartmann.

Luther expression sheet, *Phil Hartman's Flat TV* "The Monday Night Mystery Theater: The Luther Krupp File" (2019?) by Brian Lemay. Courtesy Paul Hartmann.

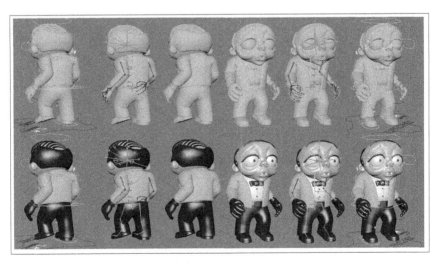

Luther model process, *Phil Hartman's Flat TV* "The Monday Night Mystery Theater: The Luther Krupp File" (2019?) by Brian Lemay. Courtesy Paul Hartmann.

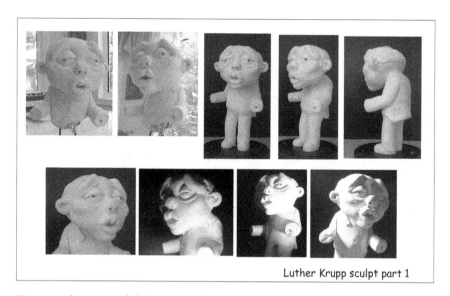

Luther Krupp sculpt part 1

Krupp sculpture 1, *Phil Hartman's Flat TV* "The Monday Night Mystery Theater: The Luther Krupp File" (2019?) by Brian Lemay. Courtesy Paul Hartmann.

Luther Krupp texture guide Photoshop paint-over, *Phil Hartman's Flat TV* "The Monday Night Mystery Theater: The Luther Krupp File" (2019?) by Brian Lemay. Courtesy Paul Hartmann.

Luther Krupp initial 3D model, *Phil Hartman's Flat TV*
"The Monday Night Mystery Theater: The Luther Krupp File" (2019?)
by Brian Lemay. Courtesy Paul Hartmann.

Krupp shaded final, *Phil Hartman's Flat TV* "The Monday Night Mystery Theater: The Luther Krupp File" (2019?) by Brian Lemay. Courtesy Paul Hartmann.

Episode 26 (February 27, 1993)
"Fake Dad"

Ren becomes the Fake Dad for Kowalski, an enormous seven year-old serving a thirty-year sentence for crimes against humanity. While on furlough, he stays with Ren and Stimpy in their trailer. Much to Ren's dismay, Kowalski destroys all the furniture, but Stimpy keeps Ren from beating Kowalski with a spoon. The final straw comes when, on a picnic, Kowalski belches, knocking off Ren's fur. "ALL RIGHT, THAT'S IT! I'VE HAD ALL I CAN STAND FROM YOU, KOWALSKI!" As Kowalski drops his pants, Ren giggles insanely. "It's gonna happen!" When confronted with Kowalski's bare buttocks, Ren says, "Pull 'em up. PLEASE PULL 'EM UP! Pull up your pants." While being taken away in a paddy wagon, Kowalski says, "Goodbye, Daddy!" Ren, in tears, answers, "Goodbye, baby!"

Episode 27 (March 27, 1993)
"The Great Outdoors"

Ren and Stimpy are backpacking through the woods. They go skinny-dipping, only to be joined by Old Man Hunger, who dives in to the tune of "In the Hall of the Mountain King"; and his mother, Mrs. Buttloaves. Stimpy stops Ren from drinking fresh water because, Stimpy says, beavers do their business in it, and imbibing it can cause beaver fever. Stimpy always brings a water cooler along for such occasions. Ren has a cupful, then notices a beaver inside the tank. Ren turns into a beaver, and he beats Stimpy with his tail, to the tune of "In the Hall of the Mountain King". "YOU FAT, BLOATED, STUPID EEDIOT!"

Episode 28 (April 3, 1993)
"The Cat That Laid the Golden Hairball"

Ren learns hairballs will soon be more valuable than gold. He starts a factory to capitalize on Stimpy's output. Stimpy has soon licked off all his hair, and Ren's too. "Stop it! You've rendered me hairless!" Stimpy has to lick the hair from the fat man who works at the factory, but he can't cough up any more hairballs. The fat man crawls inside Stimpy to do an exploratory. Stimpy's hairball gland is broken. It's over.

Episode 29 (April 24, 1993)
"Stimpy's Fan Club"

A double episode. Ren and Stimpy wait for their fan mail. It is all for Stimpy, much to Ren's displeasure. To cheer him up, Stimpy makes Ren president of Stimpy's fan club. His duty is to answer fan mail. Stimpy catches Ren writing an inappropriate reply to a bedwetter, and Ren promises to be kinder. The letters begin to drive him mad and keep him awake at night.

"How easily I could end the farce–with these hands. These dirty hands. And with these hands I hold the fate of millions. They think he's a god. But he's as mortal as we. I know. Just one quick twist, and it's over. Just watch." He stops himself from killing Stimpy. The next morning, he is in the closet, giggling insanely, when the mailman arrives. Ren answers the door in a Stimpy costume and tells the mailman not to bring any more mail for "him." The mailman only has one letter, but it's for Ren. Ren takes it and slams the door. It is a fan letter, and Ren literally rubs it in Stimpy's face. It is from Stimpy. Ren feels like an ass and begins to weep. "No one will ever know," says Stimpy. "You just cry your eyes out." Watching through the window are Mr. Horse, Kirk Douglas, and others.

Episode 30 (May 8, 1993)
"A Visit to Anthony"

A double episode, preceded by the short, "Mr. Horse Returns". Ren interviews Mr. Horse, who likes being home.

In Hollywood, Yugoslavia, Ren and Stimpy get an invitation to visit a fan, Anthony, in America. They swim there, in their Ren and Stimpy costumes. At Anthony's family's house, they destroy Anthony's youthful fantasies by using the bathroom. Anthony's father threatens them and tells them not to do it again. Outside, they are beaten by Victor, the neighborhood bully. Ren tries to administer CPR to Anthony, but Anthony's father comes out at that moment and thinks Ren beat Anthony. He tells them to meet him in the den, where he threatens them further. Stimpy coughs up a hairball onto Ren, which is the funniest thing Anthony's father has ever seen.

Followed by the short "World Crisis with Mr. Horse". He is asked his opinion of the world situation, and, according to his interpreter, Ren, "No sir, he doesn't like it."

Episode 31 (May 23, 1993)
"The Royal Canadian Kilted Yaksmen"

A double episode. Our story takes place thousands of years ago, in 1856. Stimpy volunteers himself and Ren, members of the Royal Canadian Kilted Yaksmen, for a death mission to the great barren wasteland. Ren goes mad. "I can't take it any longer. We are out of food and water. I feel I shall starve. If we keep on going, we will surely die. I tell you, we must turn back!" Stimpy begins to sing the Royal Anthem of the Kilted Yaksmen. Ren joins in. There is a singalong. Follow the bouncing Ren! As the song predicts, they die.

Episode 0 (June 23, 2003)
Ren & Stimpy 'Adult Party Cartoon' [2003] "Man's Best Friend"

Originally scheduled for August 22, 1992, this cartoon was banned by Nickelodeon and not shown until over ten years later on *Ren & Stimpy's 'Adult Party Cartoon'* (2003) (qv). It is discussed here because of its importance in the history of the original show.

George Liquor is admiring Ren and Stimpy through a pet store window, so they "look sharp." It works, and Liquor takes them home in a shopping bag and puts them in a goldfish bowl, after dumping out the fish.

The next morning, Liquor wakes them with "Reveille" and starts them on a rigorous training program. First, he tries to paper-train Ren, who does not move his bowels. Stimpy defecates copiously just looking at the newspaper. Liquor rewards Stimpy with a "treat"–a rubber "lawn cigar". Liquor trains them to misbehave–get on the couch–to teach them discipline, which begets love. He confuses Ren with his mixed signals. When Liquor puts on his dog training bite suit and invites Ren and Stimpy to attack him, Ren does–with an oar to the face. "It's discipline that begets love!" Liquor calls him a true champion. They all dance and have "treats".

Nickelodeon refused to show this cartoon because of violence, tobacco references, and scatological jokes. This was the final straw in their relationship with Kricfalusi, and he was terminated, along with his production company, Spümcø. Nick planned to reanimate the story and show it in the fifth season, but it didn't happen.

GIGGLE RATING: Five Giggles.

Seasons Three, Four, and Five

Games Animation, Bob Camp Productions. Directed by Bob Camp, Bong Hee Han, Gregg Vanzo, Kelly Armstrong, Ron Hughart, Chris Reccardi, Bill Wray, Ken Bruce, Vincent Waller, Mike Kim, Steve Loter, Craig Bartlett, Jim Gomez, Arthur Filloy, Mark Marren, Tom McGrath. Written by Bob Camp, Will McRobb, Jim Gomez, Ron Hauge, Vincent Waller, Richard Pursel, Jim Smith, Vince Calandra, Bill Wray, Mitchell Kriegman, Chris Reccardi, April March, Mike Kim, Steve Mellor, Lynne Naylor, Peter Avanzino, Stephen DeStefano, Billy West, Douglas Petrie. Executive Producer: Vanessa Coffey. Produced by Jim Ballantine. Cast: Billy West (Ren/Stimpy).

Production was moved to Games Animation, which later became Nickelodeon Animation Studio. Kricfalusi was offered a consulting position, but he refused to "sell out." Bob Camp replaced him as director. Billy West refused to quit when Kricfalusi asked him, and he started doing the voiceover for Ren also. West played Ren as a combination of Burl Ives, Kirk Douglas, and a slight "south of the border accent." However, the character remained more or less on model, such as it was, with large eyes, rotten teeth, small body, and occasional fez, so the later seasons can still be considered Lorre Tunes. Interstitials, which don't include Ren, are commercials for disgusting products.

Season 3
Episode 32 (November 20, 1993)
"To Salve and Salve Not!"

A salesman tries to peddle "Salve" to Stimpy. "How dare you take advantage of my blithering idiot?" says Ren, and literally slams the door in his face. The salesman keeps turning up in various forms, including toast. Ren turns him into powdered toast and feeds him to a junkyard dog. Ultimately, Ren finds himself on the toilet with no paper and agrees to buy some Salve. However, Stimpy has already bought it all.

Episode 33 (November 20, 1993)
"A Yard Too Far"

Homeless and hungry yet another time, Ren and Stimpy smell something delicious. Mr. Pipe has cooked up a mess of hog jowls and set them on the windowsill to cool. Ren tells Stimpy to check and see if there is a dog. Stimpy does not see a dog, so Ren goes in and is mauled by a baboon. Finally, Ren distracts the baboon with a lady baboon hand puppet while Stimpy tries to steal the hog jowls. The baboon gets Stimpy to marry him and the puppet. While the baboon is on his honeymoon, Ren and Stimpy finally get to enjoy the hog jowls.

Episode 34 (November 26, 1993)
"Circus Midgets"

Ren and Stimpy have been hitchhiking for three years, and no one has picked them up. Finally, they are picked up by circus midget clowns Schlomo and Momo. "Who were you just laughin' at? Was you laughin' at me and my friend here? Maybe it's me, I'm a little funny in the head, but I think we amuse you. Is that it? We are here for your amusement? Is that why you were laughin' at us?" says Schlomo, like Joe Pesci in *GoodFellas* (1990). "Do we look like clowns?" Stimpy says yes. "We do, don't we?" Schlomo says. Momo knocks Stimpy back into his seat. The clowns force Ren and Stimpy into the act and cram large animals and objects into the tiny car and eventually drive off the road. In the next scene, Ren and Stimpy are hitchhiking again, this time in their clown clothes. They are picked up by the Fire Chief, who hates circus midgets.

FUN FACT: DVD commentary by Ren and Stimpy.

Episode 35 (November 26, 1993)
"No Pants Today"

Stimpy can't find his pants. "Shut up, you fool. You're a cat. You don't have any pants. I'm trying to sleep. So keep quiet," says Ren, who kicks him outdoors. "It's too nice a day to be stupid indoors." Stimpy asks Mrs. Pipe if he can borrow a pair of pants. She agrees until she sees he is a naked cat, and Mr. Pipe drives him away with a hose. Victor, the neighborhood sadist, offers to trade his underwear for a slug in the stomach. Stimpy reluctantly agrees, then Victor's father points out the underwear was a gift from Victor's mother. Victor's father offers his own underwear, which he presumably changes biannually. They tie Stimpy up and throw him out of the car before driving off a cliff. The underwear is stolen by a cow who then butts Stimpy into the Deep Dark Forest. A bear gives Stimpy a squirrel to wear. Back home, Ren dresses them all in matching outfits and they go to the malt shop.

Episode 36 (December 18, 1993)
"Ren's Pecs"

At the beach, a bully kicks cat litter into Ren's face and carries off the two women he was chatting up. "If only I had huge pectoral muscles." Charles Globe appears and tells him how to get large pectoral muscles–pectoplasty, removing fat cells from one part of the body and have them implanted into the chest. Alas, Ren has no fat cells, but Stimpy offers his. After the operation, Ren returns to the beach and beats up the bully with his pecs. He leaves Stimpy and becomes a Hollywood legend.

Episode 37 (December 18, 1993)
"An Abe Divided"

Homeless in Washington, DC, Ren and Stimpy become guards at the Lincoln Memorial. Ren hears a rumor that there is a treasure in Lincoln's head. He and Stimpy cut it off with a two-man saw and Stimpy breaks Lincoln's head. The treasure turns out to be caramel corn. Their efforts to replace the head are unsuccessful, and the next day, their supervisor puts them in place of the head.

Episode 38 (January 8, 1994)
"Stimpy's Cartoon Show"

A double episode. Stimpy is making an animated cartoon like his hero, Wilbur Cobb (Jack Carter), a young, handsome man in an old photo. Ren becomes the producer, while Stimpy does all the actual work. They take their finished work to Wilbur Cobb, who in real life is a demented, decaying wreck. Finally, they watch the cartoon, a disjointed, badly drawn mess. Cobb likes it, and says if they keep it up, one day they will be where he is–in the electric chair.

Episode 39 (February 19, 1994)
"Jimminy Lummox"

Ren is making prank calls, poisoning the water supply with beavers' business, terrorizing baby birds, and torturing flies. Stimpy decides to lend Ren his conscience, Jimminy Lummox (Stan Freberg), who squashes Ren. Without a conscience, Stimpy uses Ren's false teeth to scale fish and washes Ren's collection of used celebrity underwear. Every time Ren hits Stimpy, Jimminy hits Ren, but Jimminy's conscience, Tinkergaloot, hits Jimminy.

Episode 40 (February 19, 1994)
"Bass Masters"

Ren and Stimpy are doing a fishing show when Wilbur Cobb jumps the prison fence and into their boat, pretending he's an Indian guide. Ren has no luck, while Stimpy catches all the fish. Finally, a foul-mouthed bass offers to show Ren how to catch fish if Ren will switch places. Ren does, and he ends up a trophy on the foul-mouthed bass' wall.

Episode 41 (March 12, 1994)
"Road Apples"

Ren and Stimpy are wandering in the desert until they find a road and are picked up by an RV with Mr. and Mrs. Pipe and Wilbur Cobb. Mr. Pipe tortures them relentlessly. That night, when everyone is asleep, the RV drives off the road into a lake. Mr. Pipe throws Ren and Stimpy out to do their business. "We don't want anyone wetting the bed now, do we?" asks Mrs. Pipe, who throws Cobb on top of them. "The joke's on them," roars Cobb. "I already wet the bed."

Episode 42 (April 2, 1994)
"Ren's Retirement"

A double episode. Ren is in the prime of his life until Stimpy reminds him it is his tenth birthday, which is seventy in dog years. Ren starts acting old and decrepit. He decides to be fitted for a coffin, and chooses the Eternal Grand Deluxe 3000, with central air, cable TV, Jacuzzi, stereo hi-fi–the works. Stimpy wants to be buried alive with Ren, and Ren reluctantly agrees. A worm who sounds like Fred Flintstone eats them.

Episode 43 (April 9, 1994)
"Jerry the Bellybutton Elf"

Although Ren warns him not to, Stimpy plays with his own bellybutton. To the tune of "In the Hall of the Mountain King", he even adds baking soda and vinegar to create a bellybutton volcano. Jerry the Bellybutton Elf (Gilbert Gottfried) invites Stimpy to climb inside. The next day, Ren finds only Stimpy's bellybutton, but he can hear noises coming from it. Jerry has Stimpy doing lint-related chores. Soon Mr. Horse, Kowalski, the Ghost, Powdered Toast Man, and Muddy Mudskipper and his wife, Cindy, are all listening to the bellybutton. Jerry morphs into a giant crazy pork chop. A full-blown party is underway at Ren's, with the babies, Wilbur Cobb, the Cow, Mrs. Buttloaves, the Fire Chief, and others in attendance. Stimpy comes crawling out of his own bellybutton, calling for Ren. Stimpy gets pulled back into the bellybutton, along with Ren. Cindy eats all the clam dip, and the party breaks up. So Cindy eats the bellybutton.

Episode 44 (April 30, 1994)
"Hard Times for Haggis"

A double episode. Haggis MacHaggis' TV show is canceled forever and re-placed by *The All-New Ren & Stimpy Show*. In fact, Ren and Stimpy dominate every channel and even move into Haggis' house. Haggis (Alan Young) is liter-ally kicked out into the street. There, he runs into the Fire Chief, who mistakes him for a circus midget. Haggis is on the brink of suicide when he hears about Rent-A-Thug, and he hires two thugs. Ren and Stimpy and the production staff are tied up and Haggis puts on his own show, *The Ben and Stumpy Show*, with puppets voiced by the thugs. The program is a huge hit. The thugs get a contract, and Ren, Stimpy, and Haggis are literally kicked out.

Episode 45 (June 4, 1994)
"Eat My Cookies"

Ren and Stimpy think they are in boot camp, but they are actually in the Barrette Beret Girl Scouts, with a sadistic troop leader (Rosie O'Donnell) who makes them sell cookies, which they eat instead. They fill the empty boxes with cacti and sell them all to one person. The other girls cheat Ren out of all the money at poker. Stimpy goes to earn his snipe-hunting merit badge, and although Ren tells him it is a scam, Stimpy catches one and earns the badge. Ren earns all the merit badges and learns the Barrette Beret Girls' secrets: they are all men.

Episode 46 (June 4, 1994)
"Ren's Bitter Half"

Stimpy is a genetic engineer who has made himself an extra buttock with the "XB-49 Gene-Splicing Formulae [sic]". Ren shakes up the Formulae and it explodes all over him. He splits into his two sides, his Evil Side and his Indifferent Side. Stimpy is overjoyed that he has two best friends. Evil Ren splits into Evil Ren and Hideously Evil Ren. They marry each other.

FUN FACT: At one point, Ren looks like the Beautiful Girl of the Month from *Mad* magazine.

Episode 47 (July 30, 1994)
"Lair of the Lummox"

A double episode and another edition of *Untamed World*. Ren and Stimpy go to Ignoramia to find the elusive Lummox. They befriend one, and he brings them into his lair and they bond over televised sports and dietary fat. Another male Lummox shows up, ready to mate. A Lummox cow appears and selects the second male Lummox to mate with. The first Lummox becomes enraged and challenges the second Lummox to a belching contest. The first Lummox wins, and the female claims her champion. Back at the studio, Ren and Stimpy are claimed by male Lummoxes.

Season 4
Episode 48 (October 1, 1994)
"Hermit Ren"

A double episode. Ren returns from a bad day at work to Stimpy playing "Kumbaya" on the accordion and a charred dinner, which burns Ren's mouth. Stimpy tries to put out the fire with long-expired milk. "I just wanna be alone!" He becomes a professional hermit with a private cave.

The Hermits' Union rep tells him the most important rule, no friends.

"Ah, alone at last. No more annoyances, just peace and solitude," says Ren as the soundtrack plays "In the Hall of the Mountain King". "But best of all– NO STIMPY!" He finds a mummified bug man, someone he can talk to who won't talk back. Meanwhile, Stimpy creates a Ren out of his bodily secretions.

Years later, Ren is hungry and hallucinating. He makes a Stimpy out of guano and tries to play cards with his own feelings. The union rep busts him for having companionship and imaginary friends, and kicks him out of the Hermits' Union. He returns home, Guano Stimpy on his back, to find Stimpy playing with Bodily Secretion Ren. Ren calls Stimpy out for finding another Chihuahua in his absence, but Stimpy points to Ren's back.

Episode 49 (October 8, 1994)
"House of Next Tuesday"

Ren and Stimpy move into the futuristic House of Next Tuesday for a ten-day free trial. Stimpy loves the TV of next Tuesday, which "puts you in the picture." It puts Ren in a cooking show as a lobster. After they have mishaps in the bathroom and bedroom, they decide to use the time machine to go back to before they came. It turns out Ren is still watching the TV of next Tuesday and none of their other experiences afterward really happened.

Episode 50 (October 8, 1994)
"A Friend in Your Face!"

Stimpy has a parasite in his head, Chuchu, which he feeds and calls a friend. The parasite's cousin, Looney Bratweiler, moves into Ren's head and starts a compost heap. Ren doesn't understand the stench and the voices in his head and begins to go mad. Looney sets Ren's head on fire. The Fire Chief puts it out and declares Ren's head condemned. Looney moves out. Ren doesn't want his head torn down, so Stimpy renovates his head, building a luxury high-rise for parasites, which he christens with champagne.

Episode 51 (October 15, 1994)
"Blazing Entrails"

Stimpy is crazy and sounds like Mister Magoo (qv). Ren takes Stimpy to Dr. Brainchild (Bill Mumy) to fix Stimpy's brain. Dr. Brainchild inflates Stimpy to make him gigantic and sends Ren inside Stimpy's body. Ren finds the problem–Stimpy's ignorant gland has gotten ahold of his brain. Then Stimpy deflates, trapping Ren.

Episode 52 (October 15, 1994)
"Lumber Jerks"

Ren and Stimpy are paperboys, whose customer, lumberjack Pierre LaJacques, owes them $1200 and change. LaJacques suggests they become lumberjacks and real men, like his wife. At lumberjack school, they learn to watch out for the spiny tree lobster. After graduation, they go looking for a tree, but have trouble finding one. When they finally do, they meet up with the spiny tree lobster, who sounds like Moe Howard. Trying to escape, Ren makes a noise like Curly Howard. The lobster tries to show Ren the error of his ways, but Ren runs the tree over with a steamroller. The lobster kisses Ren, then takes off his mask. It is Pierre. Pierre explains they don't saw down trees, they blow them up. Afterwards, they relax with a wolverine whirlpool.

Episode 53 (November 5, 1994)
"Prehistoric Stimpy"

Ren and Stimpy are at the natural history museum, where Wilbur Cobb is the guide. Cobb tells them all about dinosaurs. At the end, it turns out he is not a guide, but just a bone polisher.

Episode 54 (November 5, 1994)
"Farm Hands"

All Abner and Ewalt's younguns are gone, and they have no one to do the chores, like cleaning the outhouse. They order dehydrated younguns from a comic book and get Ren and Stimpy. Ren goes mad. Then a tornado wipes out the farm.

Episode 55 (November 12, 1994)
"Magical Golden Singing Cheeses"

Long ago, in a little village in the Kingdom of Fie, Renwaldo and Stimpleton, sons of the dirt smith, kept house together. They haven't eaten since the last crusade, so Renwaldo tells Stimpleton to trade the family chigger for some food. Stimpleton searches hither and yon and finally finds the man-eating village idiot. The idiot eats the chigger, but has no food to trade, only magical singing cheeses. Stimpleton must first best him in a battle of witlessness, or be eaten himself. Stimpleton wins easily, and returns home to Renwaldo, who tells him to bury the cheeses because they are unripe.

Stimpleton accidentally digs up a giant ogre, who asks him about the cheeses. Stimpleton says they are actually shoes, and the giant puts them on. When it is time for Stimpleton to get the cheese, the ogre agrees to give them up for Stimpleton's spleen. The cheeses turn back into milk curd princesses, and Stimpleton and Renwaldo starve to death.

Episode 56 (November 12, 1994)
"A Hard Day's Luck"

One of three episodes in which neither Ren nor Stimpy appear.

Episode 57 (November 19, 1994)
"I Love Chicken"

The credits parody those of *I Love Lucy* (1951). Ren brings a chicken carcass home from the grocery store, and Stimpy falls in love and marries it. He even gives the chicken its own monogrammed fez. Ren keeps trying to eat the chicken, and eventually succeeds, much to Stimpy's dismay. Six months later, Ren apologizes and tells Stimpy to unpack the groceries. Stimpy falls in love with a goat head and gets engaged.

Episode 58 (November 19, 1994)
"Powdered Toast Man vs. Waffle Woman"

The second episode in which neither Ren nor Stimpy appear.

Episode 59 (December 3, 1994)
"It's a Dog's Life"

At the State Pound, Ren and Stimpy are already in the gas chamber when they are rescued by Granny. At their new luxurious digs, Ren meets his "roomie", a freeze-dried dog. Stimpy has his paws bandaged to keep him from scratching the furniture and Ren gets a hemo'donut to prevent his rubbing his butt on the rug. They are fed inedible food, neutered, and forced to sleep outdoors in a pet cemetery. They make a break for it, but are stopped by a cop and returned, just in time to see Granny wheeled out in her coffin. Ren and Stimpy are freeze-dried along with her.

Episode 60 (December 3, 1994)
"Egg Yölkeo"

A parody of *Pinocchio* (1940). Renwaldo, Ye Egg Smithee, is crafting a son out of egg yolks, but it falls apart. That night, a chicken carcass in a dress flies in and makes Egg Yölkeo, as he is called, into a real boy. A piece of bacon and a slice of toast kidnap Egg Yölkeo. Colonel Scrambolio, a Tom Parker-type, turns Egg Yölkeo into an Elvis-type. Ren finds Egg Yölkeo in Vegas and rescues him, but Stimpy eats Egg Yölkeo.

Episode 61 (January 7, 1995)
"Double Header"

Ren and Stimpy are hit by a bus and a doctor, who resembles Otto Scratchansniff (qv) sews them together. Ren has to take Stimpy with him to his job at the nuclear missile factory, where Stimpy causes a nuclear holocaust. Ren is fired and they get a job as Siamese geeks at a freak show, where they are hit by a meteorite. This time, all that is left of Ren is his head, which the doctor sews to Stimpy's butt.

Episode 62 (January 7, 1995)
"The Scotsman in Space"

Commander Höek and Space Cadet Stimpy encounter Haggis MacHaggis and bring him onto their ship. He dies when they serve him overcooked eggs and when Ren dusts off his wallet, a genie appears and grants him three wishes. Ren wishes for beautiful women to bring him all the money in the world. Stimpy wishes that no one ever has need of material possessions again and Ren's money disappears. He wishes to be where it's always sunny and no one grows old. Ren and Stimpy fly into the sun.

FUN FACT: Stimpy serves haggis "from the Shamus Culhane recipe."

Episode 63 (January 14, 1995)
"Pixie King"

Stimpy is in the outhouse and can't finish unless Ren reads him a story from a book. In the story, Ren and Stimpy are lowly worker elves who yearn to be pixies. When Ren learns the Pixie King is on his way out, he schemes to ascend the throne. To become king, he steals some of the sleeping giant's eye crust. At last, Stimpy comes out of the outhouse and Ren uses the book's pages as toilet paper.

FUN FACT: This is the last episode where Ren giggles insanely.

Episode 64 (January 14, 1995)
"Aloha Höek"

Ren and Stimpy wash up on an island and move into a giant fish (actually whale) carcass. When Stimpy complains, Ren banishes him to the jungle. In the jungle, Stimpy runs into Marlon Brando (Dom DeLuise), who takes him in and throws him a luau. Twelve years later, a crab family returns to the carcass and find Ren in their house. The father, who sounds like Moe Howard, tells Ren to walk the fly. Ren uses the fly to try to escape (to the tune of "Ride of the Valkyries"), but the fly crashes in the ocean and brings Ren, who is apparently dead, back to Stimpy. Ren is alive, and he and Stimpy are actually spies who rendezvous with their submarine.

Episode 65 (January 21, 1995)
"Insomniac Ren"

Ren has a 6:00 AM tee time the next day and is trying to get some sleep. Stimpy keeps making noise, and finally offers to get Ren some milk. However, in the refrigerator are only roaches, including one that sounds like Moe Howard. (All grown male arthropods apparently are leaders of the Three Stooges.) Stimpy tries a bedtime story and a lullaby. In the morning, the other members of Ren's foursome, Haggis MacHaggis, Mr. Horse, and Muddy Mudskipper show up and Ren offers five bucks to anyone who can knock him out.

FUN FACT: Stimpy imitates two other Stooges, Curly Howard and Joe Besser, for a total of four of the Three Stooges in one episode.

Episode 66 (January 21, 1995)
"My Shiny Friend"

Stimpy is obsessed with TV. Ren finally buries the television set, but Stimpy continues to watch TV with a gopher, so Stimpy smashes the TV to bits. Stimpy begins making frequent trips to the bathroom, where he has hidden a TV in the toilet tank. He overdoses on TV. "We'll have to put you somewhere where you can't hurt yourself any longer." He locks Stimpy in the basement for a year after which Stimpy is no longer addicted to TV, he's a degenerate gambler.

FUN FACT: At one point, Moe and Curly Howard are on TV.

Episode 67 (February 11, 1995)
"Cheese Rush Days"

Ren and Stimpy go west. A happy prospector somewhat reminiscent of Walter Huston in *The Treasure of the Sierra Madre* (1948) shows them all his bleu cheese jewelry and tells them there is plenty more where that came from. They wander through the desert and stumble upon the bleu cheese mountain. They strike a vein of cheese, and Ren makes off with the loot after bricking Stimpy in the mine. The old prospector tunnels in and tells Stimpy he is sitting on a fortune. Ren goes to the bank, where the teller (a Frank Nelson sound-alike) tells him it's fool's cheese and literally kicks him out. He is run over by a car containing Stimpy and the old prospector.

Episode 68 (February 11, 1995)
"Wiener Barons"

Ren and Stimpy are hoboes who go to Canada and strike it rich with wieners. The development of synthetic wieners causes their stock to become worthless. Ren has a vision: it will rain baked beans for forty days and forty nights, and he and Stimpy must build an ark out of wieners and float out of Canada.

Episode 69 (March 4, 1995)
"Galoot Wranglers"

Around the campfire, Wild Will Hickcobb tells Ren and Stimpy how the West was really won: with Galoots, who closely resemble Lummoxes. "And if'n what I told you ain't the bare naked truth, then may I drop dead right here on this spot," and he does.

Episode 70 (March 4, 1995)
"Ren Needs Help!"

Stimpy breaks Ren's glass coffee table that formerly belonged to Danny Thomas, so Ren throws himself into the In-Stink-Er-Ator. Stimpy sends him to the Shady Brain Farm. The doctor is a sloth who sounds like James Mason, and the patients are Muddy Mudskipper, Yak, and the Fire Chief, who says the president is fake: "They put him in a fake suit, and he makes speeches on the moon." Ren incites all the other inmates to escape, but he is carried away by orderlies and put in a fake suit. "Five seconds until your national address, Mr. President." Ren says, "My fellow Americans, the bombing begins in five minutes," from the moon.

Episode 71 (March 18, 1995)
"Ol' Blue Nose"

Ren and Stimpy are in the bus terminal. Stimpy is watching *The Louie Lungbubble Show*, a parody of Ed Sullivan's *Toast of the Town* (1948), on a coin-operated TV and spends all their money, so Ren smacks him in the nose. Stimpy begins singing like Frank Sinatra ("Snotra"). Stimpy starts behaving like a big star, too. Then he reaches the top: *The Louie Lungbubble Show*.

Backstage, Ren smacks him in the nose, and the nose leaves. With a pickle nose, Stimpy cannot sing any longer, and he and Ren are literally kicked to the street, while the nose, Snotty, signs a contract with Louie. "You'll be bigger than Sid Sneezer." Ren and Stimpy are living in a trailer when Stimpy's nose returns.

Episode 72 (March 18, 1995)
"Stupid Sidekick Union"

Ren and Stimpy are shooting an episode of their show when the Stupid Sidekick Union calls a strike. "What are you gonna do?" says Ren. "Go work for Handle-Barbarian?" Stimpy leaves and says he's not coming back until Ren signs the new contract. Ren calls the Scab Sidekick Union and tries out various second bananas, none of whom work out. Stimpy tries to trick Ren into signing the contract, but Ren, thinking he's outsmarting Stimpy, signs "George Washington." The trade papers report that the Father of Our Country has endorsed the contract, and the Stupid Sidekicks go back to work after receiving their biggest concessions ever. The title card now reads *The Stimpy & Ren Show*.

FUN FACT: DVD commentary by Ren and Stimpy.

Episode 73 (April 1, 1995)
"Superstitious Stimpy"

It's Tuesday, Marge 17, the unluckiest day of the year, according to Stimpy. Ren makes fun of his superstitions until Stimpy realizes Ren is the unlucky beast born on Tuesday, Marge 17. Stimpy tries to change Ren's luck forever, but Ren is struck by lightning, twice. So Stimpy gives him his lucky leper's foot, just as the leper rides a pig through the door. "Golly," says Stimpy. "Smited by a leper. Ren is so lucky."

FUN FACT: While Stimpy is chanting mostly nonsense words, he mentions pioneer animator Ub Iwerks.

Episode 74 (April 1, 1995)
"Travelogue"

Ren and Stimpy, hosts of a travel show, visit Acromeglia and lose their heads.

FUN FACT: Stimpy imitates Popeye.

Season 5
Episode 75 (June 3, 1995)
"Space Dogged"

Renovich and Stimpski are Soviet cosmonauts in 1954. Although every other rocket has blown up, theirs launches successfully, but they have to scramble to keep it from crashing, throwing everything but the Matisse into the furnace which propels the ship. They become first in space, but are out of fuel, so they try to siphon gas from an American space capsule. Stimpski accidentally hooks up the hose to the American septic tank, and they suck in a capitalist pig (Phil Hartman) who talks like John Wayne. "You'll never take me alive. Remember the Alamo," he says, before jumping into the furnace. His lard gives them a head start in the space race, but the capitalist pig who remains in the American rocket passes them. Stimpski takes off his socks and Renovich throws them into the furnace. They win, but they land outside the White House. The U.S. government pretends they are American astronauts and gives them a ticker-tape parade to celebrate being first in space. The American ship crashes and burns in the U.S.S.R., and the burnt pig gets a parade celebrating being number two.

Episode 76 (June 3, 1995)
"Feud for Sale"

The third episode in which Ren and Stimpy do not appear.

Episode 77 (July 1, 1995)
"Hair of the Cat"

Ren is allergic to something, but he doesn't know what. Finally, he realizes he is allergic to cat hair. He solves this problem by putting Stimpy in a pickle jar.

FUN FACT: Stimpy imitates Jerry Lewis.

Episode 78 (July 1, 1995)
"City Hicks"

Ren and Stimpy are dust farmers who believe in Dusty Claus. Their crop is ruined by a rainstorm. They ride sheep into the city, where they have trouble keeping a job. Finally, Dusty Claus appears to take them to the dust mine, where they will toil and slave for the rest of their life.

Episode 79 (October 7, 1995)
"Stimpy's Pet"

A German attack circus clown (Phil Hartman), who sounds like Jack Nicholson, is abandoned on Ren and Stimpy's doorstep. Stimpy takes him in and names him Sid. After Sid attacks Ren for speaking Slavic, Ren flushes him down the toilet. Sid returns and has clown puppies, but Ren carelessly speaks German and the puppies attack.

Episode 80 (October 7, 1995)
"Ren's Brain"

Stimpy is a freelance brain surgeon who needs a perfect brain to experiment on, and he selects Ren's. He puts it in a tank, but the next morning, it crawls out and goes to work. Stimpy puts a telephone in Ren's head where his brain used to be. Stimpy is delighted to have brainless Ren as a playmate. Ren's brain comes home from work and is enraged to find them together. Stimpy tries to sedate Ren's brain, which blows up the world. Ren's brain flies into space, saying, "You EEDIOTS!" This line was voiced by John Kricfalusi, and was taken from the episode "Svën Höek".

Episode 81 (October 28, 1995)
"Bellhops"

Ren and Stimpy are bellhops who always respect the privacy of their guests. There are reporters lurking about, and Mr. Noggin, a Howard Hughes-type recluse, in the penthouse is not to be photographed or disturbed in any way. While taking out the garbage, Stimpy is offered a million dollars for a photo of Mr. Noggin, which he refuses. Ren agrees to do it for five bucks, and sneaks into the penthouse. Mr. Noggin is, well, just a noggin. To prevent Ren from taking a picture, he jumps out the window with Mr. Noggin and they land on top of Mrs. Buttloaves. She and Mr. Noggin fall in love and get married. Mr. Noggin gives Ren a million bucks, but the hotel manager steals it.

Episode 82 (October 28, 1995)
"Dog Tags"

Stimpy begs Ren to take him to the dog lodge, and Ren reluctantly agrees. To Ren's dismay, he is barred from entering, and Stimpy becomes top dog. Stimpy says he only wanted to hang out with Ren. For fraternal companionship, they hang out at a cat bar, with Ren dressed as a kitty.

FUN FACT: The password to the lodge is "Weatherwax", the name of Lassie's trainer.

Episode 83 (November 4, 1995)
"I Was a Teenage Stimpy"

Stimpy hits puberty. He gets zits, loses his baby teeth, sprouts chest hair, and goes through a growth spurt. He talks incessantly on the phone, spends all his time with his delinquent friends, and steals Ren's "corn" magazines from his underwear drawer. Stimpy goes into the pupa stage and emerges as a full-grown man. Ren thinks now Stimpy will take care of him, but Stimpy leaves home.

Episode 84 (November 4, 1995)
"Who's Stupid Now?"

Ren and Stimpy's producer has them switch roles. In order to gain weight, Ren has to drink shakes made from Stimpy's fat and Stimpy becomes slim. The audience rejects fat Ren, and so does Stimpy. Ren quits, throwing Stimpy and the producer at a wall. The audience now loves him.

Episode 85 (November 11, 1995)
"School Mates"

Ren's frat brother, Chuck, visits and bonds with Stimpy, leaving Ren alone and sad. To cheer him up, Stimpy dresses up as a cat so Ren can chase him.

Episode 86 (November 11, 1995)
"Dinner Party"

Ren Höek, Master of Etiquette, tells how to throw a dinner party.

Episode 87 (November 18, 1995)
"Big Flakes"

Ren and Stimpy visit Ren's parents' cabin in the winter and get snowed in. By July 4, both of them have gone mad. Meanwhile, outside, it is bright and sunny, but the mountain of snow on the cabin has yet to melt.

FUN FACT: DVD commentary by Ren and Stimpy.

Episode 88 (November 18, 1995)
"Pen Pals"

Ren tries to break into prison to get free room and board after his house is towed away. He is put away for life after accidentally freeing all the other prisoners.

Episode 89 (December 9, 1995)
"Terminal Stimpy"

Stimpy has two of his nine lives left. Ren doesn't want Stimpy to die, because then Ren will have to do all the chores. Ren sends Stimpy down to light the furnace. Stimpy causes a gas leak, but is killed by frozen sewage from a passing jetliner. With one life left, he becomes ultra-cautious. Finally, he accepts his fate. To celebrate the first day of their eventual demise, Ren gets a cupcake and tries to light the candle on top, blowing up the house because of the leaking gas.

FUN FACTS: "The Five Stages to Acceptance" is read by a Alfred Hitchcockian narrator. St. Peter does a Jack Benny imitation.

Episode 90 (December 9, 1995)
"Reverend Jack"

Ren and Stimpy drive a meat truck for Reverend Jack Cheese (Frank Gorshin), putting on shows for children. The Reverend goes mad and has them drive into the desert. They are stopped by the meat patrol, which revokes the

Reverend's meat confectioner license. The Reverend escapes on the back of a beef carcass. Forty-one years later, Ren and Stimpy are doing meat shows for kids when the Reverend returns, heckling them and throwing rocks.

Episode 91 (December 16, 1995)
"A Scooter for Yaksmas"

A double episode, the last episode of the original Nickelodeon run. Stimpy works at Cobbco, making fudge pop sticks. Yaksmas is coming and Stimpy hopes Stinky Whizzleteats will bring him "Johnny Future's Jet Scooter" from the bike shop window. He leaves Ren a series of not-so-subtle hints, but Ren gives him fudge pop sticks. Stimpy goes to visit the scooter in the window and ends up accidentally stealing it. He manages to escape the police, and the next day he returns home to find Ren badmouthing him to TV reporters. He disguises himself and goes to visit Stinky Whizzleteats. Finally, he arrives at the West Pole, but he wrecks his scooter. Upon entering Stinky's room, he finds Stinky and the Yak passed out, and a wrapped gift from Ren: the scooter! Ren didn't neglect to buy it, Stinky forgot to deliver it. Stimpy escapes on his new scooter, one step ahead of the cops.

Episode 92 (October 20, 1996)
"Sammy and Me"

Stimpy receives in the mail a kit to transform into his idol, Sammy Mantis (Tommy Davidson), an insectile Sammy Davis Jr. Stimpy sings Sammy's theme song, "The Mantis Man". ("The Mantis Man can when he bites down on your skull and sucks out all your brains.") Ren belittles him, and Stimpy goes to find Sammy. Sammy is having a party at his house with Joey Beetle, Dean Mayfly, Liberoachy, and Peter Locust (apparently a parody of Lawford, not Lorre). Sammy sucks out Stimpy's brains.

FUN FACTS: Episodes 92 and 93 premiered on MTV.
Stimpy imitates Sammy as Jerry Lewis. Also, Joey Beetle is a parody of Jerry Lewis. Offscreen, Dean Mayfly tells him to "Shut up."

Episode 93 (October 20, 1996)
"The Last Temptation"

Ren chokes to death on lumpy oatmeal and goes to heaven, where Wilbur Cobb is the gardener and Mr. Pipe is God. Ren comes back to life and divests himself of all his most valued worldly possessions, including celebrity toupées from William Shattered, Burt, and Bazoo the Clone. He confesses to Stimpy he has embezzled a million dollars from him and returns the money. Stimpy goes on a spending spree while Ren lives an ascetic life. When Stimpy begins choking to death, Ren must decide whether to save him or let him die and inherit all his possessions. With help from Cobb, Ren rescues Stimpy and gets to spend the next fifty years with him. Cobb confiscates all the worldly goods that Stimpy bought.

GIGGLE RATING: Looks, Five Giggles; Voice, Four Giggles, except for "Ren's Brain", Five Giggles.

AVAILABILITY: Time-Life released several episodes on the DVD *The Best of Ren & Stimpy* (2003). Paramount Home Entertainment released a three-disc box set, *The Ren & Stimpy Show Uncut, The First and Second Season* (2004). These were not uncut, but the set includes the banned episode "Man's Best Friend" as a bonus feature. *The Ren & Stimpy Show, Seasons Three and a Half-ish* (2005) contained all of season three and the first half of season four up to "It's a Dog's Life/Egg Yölkeo". *The Ren & Stimpy Show, Season Five and Some More of Four* (2005) completed the DVD release of the Nickelodeon series on September 20. Like the previous DVDs, some scenes were removed in these releases. Paramount released *The Ren & Stimpy Show Uncut: The Almost Complete Collection* (2018), a nine-disc set that combines the individual season discs into a single package, on February 6, 2018. The original series was released as a nine-disc set, *Die Ren & Stimpy Show, Die Komplette Serie Limitiert und Uncut* (2013) by Turbine Steel.

Yo Yogi (1991)

Hanna-Barbera Studios. Directed by Don Lusk, Joanna Romersa, Jay Sarbry, Paul Sommer, Carl Urbano, Ray Patterson. Written by Sean Roche, Earl Kress, Gordon Bressack, David Ehrman, Charles M. Howell IV, Bob

Kushell, Steve Smith, Sindy McKay. Executive Producers: Joseph Barbera, William Hanna. Cast: Greg Burson (Yogi Bear/Snagglepuss), Don Messick (Boo-Boo Bear/Muttley), Lewis Arquette (Bombastic Bobby), Greg Berg (Huckleberry Hound), Rob Paulsen (Dick "Dickie" Dastardly/Waiter), Kath Soucie (Cindy Bear), John Stephenson (Doggie Daddy), Patric Zimmerman (Augie Doggie), Neil Ross (Morocco Mole).

A non-canonical prequel to the Yogi Bear franchise, with some characters, like Yogi, Snagglepuss, and Huckleberry Hound as teens working for the Lost and Found (L.A.F.) Squad at Jellystone Mall. Other characters are already fully grown, like Doggie Daddy, but Augie Doggie and Boo-Boo seem to be the same age as they were in their original shows. This program did not do well in the ratings, and at this writing, seems to have killed any attempt at reviving Yogi cartoons on TV. It also was the beginning of the end for Saturday morning network animation blocks. Neil Ross is credited with playing a young Morocco Mole in nine episodes, but he seems to have been cut out of the final product. His credits include *Harvey Birdman: Attorney at Law* (2000) and *Animaniacs* (1993) (both qv). Also in the cast are frequent Peter Lorre impersonators Don Messick, Rob Paulsen, Frank Welker, and Pat Fraley, along with frequent Sydney Greenstreet impersonators Allan Melvin and Hal Smith.

Season 1
Episode 1 (September 14, 1991)
"Hats Off to Yogi"

Episode 2 (September 21, 1991)
"Mellow Fellow"

Episode 3 (September 28, 1991)
"The Big Snoop"

Episode 4 (October 5, 1991)
"Huck's Doggone Day"

Episode 5 (October 5, 1991)
"Grindhog Day"

Episode 6 (October 12, 1991)
"Fashion Smashin'!"

Episode 12 (November 16, 1991)
"Yo, Yogi (Pilot)"

Episode 13 (November 23, 1991)
"Jellystone Jam"

Episode 16 (December 13, 1991)
"Super Duper Snag"

GIGGLE RATING: Unknown. It would be interesting to see Morocco as a teen.

AVAILABILITY: An early 1990s VHS release of the show came with 3D glasses. There are no plans for a complete series set release from either Warner Home Video or Warner Archive, but it is available on Amazon and iTunes as part of the Hanna-Barbera Diamond Collection.

2 Stupid Dogs [Super Secret Secret Squirrel] (1993)
Hanna-Barbera Studios. Directed by Larry Huber, Donovan Cook. Written by Mark Saraceni, Roberts Gannaway, Paul Rudish, Lane Raichert, Richard Pursel. Produced by Donovan Cook, Larry Huber, Buzz Potamkin. Cast: Jess Harnell (Secret Squirrel), Jim Cummings (Morocco Mole), Tony Jay (Chief), Kimmy Robertson (Penny).

Martin "Dr. Toon" Goodman of *ANIMATIONWorld Magazine* described this show as one of two "clones" of *The Ren & Stimpy Show* (1991) (qv), the other one being *The Shnookums & Meat Funny Cartoon Show* (1995). *2 Stupid Dogs* (1993), with its toilet jokes and adult humor, was a new direction for Hanna-Barbera, which insisted on a "backup" segment from its catalogue. Producer Cook chose Secret Squirrel, one of his favorite shows. The show premiered simultaneously on TBS and in syndication.

In the new version, Secret and Morocco Mole are redesigned. Morocco wears sunglasses, so we rarely see his eyes. He is voiced here by Jim Cummings, and he sounds less like Peter Lorre. Secret was always supposedly a master of disguise, although we did not see much evidence of that in the first series. Here, he uses makeup, masks, and costumes frequently. He continues to use high tech gadgets. Most characters are now anthropomorphic animals, including Chief (formerly QQ), who is a Cape buffalo. A new character, a female squirrel named Penny, is a parody of Miss Moneypenny from the James Bond series and somewhat of a love interest for Secret. Secret operates out of different buildings on different episodes, but all of them are helpfully marked with signage like "Top Secret Headquarters". The Hanna-Barbera building at 3400 Cahuenga Boulevard (now an LA Fitness center) is used as HQ at least once.

Season 1
Episode 1 (September 5, 1993)
"Goldflipper"

In his volcanic island lair, Goldflipper (Jim Cummings as a pinnipedian version of Yellow Pinkie with the Sydney Greenstreet aspect dialed way down) has created the ultimate evil machine: the Molar Acoustic Synchro-Bicuspid Dental Magnetic Electro-Plaque Conductive Positivizer, which lets him steal the gold in people's teeth. At Top Secret Headquarters, Chief calls in Secret, and Morocco's front tooth is stolen, which causes him to have difficulty with "s" sounds. This iteration of Secret lacks the Sylvesterish lisp that Mel Blanc gave him, and Secret cruelly mocks Morocco's new speech impediment. "Thay," asks Morocco, "are you making fun of me?" Secret sprays his car with Orthodontic Gold Replicator, which gives anything the property of a gold tooth. The Positivizer brings them right to Goldflipper's island.

Inside the lair, Goldflipper swims amongst his gold like an otarine Scrooge McDuck when the doorbell rings. It is Secret and Morocco dressed as Squirrel Scouts selling golden cookies. While Goldflipper goes to get his money, Secret and Morocco destroy his laboratory. Goldflipper's guards tie them up, and Morocco says, "Oh, thwell, that'th jutht thwell," says Morocco. "Firtht I lothe my spethial tooth and then I have to come to this thtupid island." Goldflipper laughs hysterically at Morocco's lisp. "What'th tho funny, fattho?" Still laughing, Goldfinger accidentally pulls the lever that makes the volcano erupt. He and his henchmen flee. Secret blasts the ropes apart and he and Morocco escape in their car with all the gold teeth, which they keep.

Episode 2 (September 12, 1993)
"Greg"

As Morocco says, "Bon bons are going bye-bye," and Chief, who is upset about the loss of his Crunchy Munchy, calls in Secret Squirrel, who finds sugar ants are stealing all the candy. He sprays Morocco with a candy coating, and the ants soon take him. Secret tracks Morocco to an abandoned factory made out of an aluminum-gingerbread alloy where a gingerbread man named Greg (Charlie Adler) is melting down all the candy into a giant creature that will eat kids for a change. The giant attacks Secret and Morocco, who simply eat him and get fat. The ants eat Greg, and Secret sprays them with candy coating and serves them to Chief as Crunchy Munchy.

Episode 3 (September 19, 1993)
"Quark"

Someone is destroying landmarks like the Space Needle, the United Nations Secretariat Building, and Disney World. Chief calls Secret to the Secret Service headquarters. Secret determines the next building to be destroyed will be the Secret Service headquarters, and so it is. The culprit is Quark (Roger Rose), a subatomic Sammy Davis Jr.-wannabe who literally gets inside Secret's head and drives him crazy, which leads Chief to put Secret in the Psycho Wing of the County Jail. Quark ultimately plans to build an amphitheater in Canada to showcase his talents. Morocco busts Secret out of jail: "Secret, I knew you weren't crazy! You're only crazy about catching criminals!" Secret shrinks himself down to subatomic size and leads Quark into the dictionary, where he proves that quarks don't exist. Back at the Secret Service (temporary) HQ, before he returns to normal size, Secret gets inside Chief's head and has him make all kinds of concessions.

Episode 4 (September 26, 1993)
"Queen Bea"

At the Metro Pollen Depository, Penny calls Secret Squirrel to report a honey "sticky-up." The bee bandits flee when they see Secret, but he stops them with flypaper. One of the bees knocks him out and he wakes up in the hive of Queen Bea (B.J. Ward), who wants Secret to marry her. He refuses because she is evil, but she threatens to drown Morocco in a jar of honey. "It's so sticky," he says. Secret reluctantly agrees, and she frees Morocco. Bea takes Secret upstairs to drink her love nectar and Penny breaks in and fights Bea. Meanwhile, Morocco, still covered with honey, is trying to get there. "I'm still coming, Secret!" Bea distracts Penny by saying, "Hey look, it's Fred Flintstone!" and is about to finish Penny off. Secret comes out of the spell of the love nectar and saves Penny. "I got here as fast as I could," says Morocco.

Episode 5 (October 3, 1993)
"Hot Rodney"

At the annual Charity Challenge 500, it's super-speedster Hot Rodney, a rooster, versus Super Secret Secret Squirrel, who wins every year. In the stands, Chief doesn't notice that Morocco Mole, sitting next to him, is kidnapped. When the race gets underway, Rodney says, "Hey, look over there, it's Fred Flintstone!" and gets into first place. Rodney has wrapped Morocco in a dynamite belt and placed him on top of the Big City Tower, about a hundred miles off-course. Secret rescues Morocco, and is ready to concede the race when Morocco says. "Now, that's not the super-secret agent I know talking. You never give up, Secret!" Secret agrees, and they get back into the race and pass Rodney.

As they approach the finish line, Rodney is gaining on them, so Morocco tries to make the car go faster by jettisoning unnecessary parts. Unfortunately, he throws away the engine, and Rodney passes them and wins. "Oopsy," says Morocco. Secret presents Rodney with a "victory belt", which is really the dynamite and blows up Rodney and his car.

Episode 6 (October 10, 1993)
"Egg"

Aboard a Super Secret Airways jetliner, Chief sends for Morocco Mole. Government regulations state that every super secret service agent must be given an assignment at least once in his career. All Morocco has to do is hold onto a rare and important egg for three seconds and give it back to Chief. "What makes it so rare and important, anyways?" asks Morocco. The egg supposedly has an ancient Egyptian curse on it. Morocco drops the egg after two seconds and opens the plane door to let it out so it won't "get all smashéd." Secret appears and literally kicks Morocco out of the plane. Secret jumps out after Morocco and catches the egg. They lack parachutes, so Secret deploys his Instant Haystack Grenade, and they make a soft land-ing–on a road, where Secret is hit by a truck. Morocco finds him at a truck stop and Secret tries to keep the egg. "Oh, no, Secret, it wouldn't be fair for you to do all the work, says Morocco. "This is my assignment." Secret agrees and Morocco drops the egg again. Secret gets the egg back, but is hit by another truck. Morocco finds him at the truck stop and says, "Should I carry the egg this time?" Secret attaches the egg to Morocco's hand with paste, duct tape, clamps, chains, a giant lock, and a blowtorch. Morocco drops the egg anyway, and it rolls into a minefield. Secret gets it back us-ing his Antigravity Galoshes, but Morocco follows him and sets off a mine. They blow up and land on the wing of Chief's plane. Chief lets them in and Morocco maintains control of the egg for three seconds. Chief takes the egg back and is hit by a truck. Morocco catches the egg. "You don't suppose the egg is really curséd, do you?" Secret says no, tapping on the egg lightly and causing it to release an asp, who plans to rule the world. "Oopsy," says Morocco. The asp hops out the door and presumably plunges to its death.

Episode 7 (October 17, 1993)
"Chameleon"

It's a Gala Opening at the Art Museum ("See it before it's stolen"), where most of the paintings are missing, and Chief is director of security for the evening. The museum director (Maurice LaMarche), an owl who sounds like Orson Welles, unveils the museum's "most famous and nearly last piece of art." It, too, has been stolen. Chief tells Secret to "recover the pilfered paintings and apprehend this artful villain." Secret tracks the thief's footprints to under a mobile, which snatches him and Morocco up like crane jaws and carries them up to a secret room in the museum. "Look Secret, it's all the stolen artworks." The culprit is the Chameleon (Roddy McDowall). Secret frees them and the Chameleon flees. Secret traps him in a room with modern art, which the Chameleon loathes, and while the Chameleon is morphing into different abstracts, Secret flattens him with a canvas, then donates the resulting artwork to the museum, calling it "Still Life Without Parole".

Episode 8 (October 24, 1993)
"Agent Penny"

The title card is a parody of the title card for *Charlie's Angels* (1976). At Secret Service Headquarters, Covert Gardens, Chief fires Secret in a cost-cutting move. Penny is promoted to top agent and Morocco replaces her. "I'll be your best executive assistant ever, Chief, and I'll start by reorganizing these files." He puts Goldflipper under "C" for "Criminal." Penny is similarly incompetent in her new job and Secret is bored in retirement. He also tires his friends, Snooper and Blabber (qv), with his old war stories.

Morocco's reorganization ends in disaster, and Chief fires him and also Penny. Then he hires Penny to replace Morocco. He looks for a new spy in the Yellow Pages under "Secret Agents" and Secret Squirrel pops up, in the flesh. "Ooh. Ooh. Ooh. Can–can I be his assistant?" asks Morocco. "Huh? Can I? Can I?" Chief hires them back, but they have to do windows.

Episode 9 (October 31, 1993)
"Scirocco Mole"

On the game show *Platonic Partners*, Secret flashes back to the first time he met Morocco. In Morocco, Secret arrests archcriminal Scirocco Mole (Jess Harnell), who turns out to actually be Scirocco's twin brother Morocco. Scirocco squashes them both with an elephant and proceeds with his plan to steal the Royal Family Jewels. Secret escapes and pursues Scirocco. "Wait for me!" says Morocco. They catch Scirocco in the act of stealing the jewels with a vacuum cleaner.

"It's Secret Squirrel!" cries Scirocco. "And me, Morocco Mole," says

Morocco in the earliest usage of a version of his catchphrase. Secret wrests control of the vacuum from Scirocco, but he sucks the clothes off both twins and is unable to tell them apart.

Each brother tries to prove that he is Morocco by being the biggest bungler. Secret says, "Think fast!" and throws them identical vases. "Think what?" says Morocco, and drops the vase. Scirocco reveals himself by catching the other vase. He uses a rocket in his turban to escape. "Because you saved my life, I swore I'd be your faithful companion forever," says Morocco. "But whatever happened to Scirocco?" The game show host traps them in a cage, then rips off his mask and reveals himself to be Scirocco Mole. "Think fast," says Morocco, and throws Scirocco a bomb. Scirocco catches it, and it blows him through the roof of the studio. In fact, Morocco has a whole box of bombs, and he "even lit them so they'd be ready." The bombs explode, sending Morocco and Secret into the sky, where Secret arrests Scirocco.

Episode 10 (November 7, 1993)
"Platypus"

Outside the Secret Service Solar Energy Station in the Australian Outback, the Platypus (Roger Rose) has tapped into the grid to power his Body Part Descrambling Ray, designed to make him look normal. Secret, Morocco, and Chief burst in to arrest him for stealing electricity. They step in front of his invention, and it shuffles all their bodily bits. Each of them has his own face. Morocco has Secret's hat and lower body and Chief's torso. Secret has Chief's horns and legs and Morocco's sunglasses and torso. Chief has Morocco's fez and legs and Secret's torso. "Look at me," says Morocco. "For once, I am bigger than all of you. I am all-powerful. I am omeni-potent!" The Platypus escapes with his machine, and they attempt to catch him. "I got the platypus, Chief!" says Morocco, but it's really Secret. "Oopsy."

Secret's plan is to disguise the booth for Super Secret Headquarters and Tourist Information as a Platypus Beauty Makeover shop. The price is one descrambler. Platypus agrees, but he'll only pay if he's satisfied. He's not satisfied, but the mirror is held by a female platypus. They fall in love and he gives Secret and Morocco the descrambler, which they attempt to use, but it just rescrambles them worse each time.

Episode 11 (November 14, 1993)
"Doctor O"

Chief is on his way to the Little Buffalo's Room when Doctor O, a possum, launches a satellite which blocks the sun with giant jazz hands. Secret and Morocco go to his lair with lights, which are destroyed. "Too bad you don't have nocturnal vision, like me," says Morocco, taking off his sunglasses to reveal his eyeballs. Secret uses him as his seeing eye mole. Dr. O's bat henchmen beat Secret with balloons. "Yay, Secret, he's our man!" says Morocco. "Swing to your left, swing to your right, stand up, sit down, fight, fight, fight!" Secret locates Dr. O by sound and they struggle for control of the satellite. Secret gets an idea. The lightbulb over his head blinds Dr. O, and Secret, now able to see, defeats him. Chief is finally able to see his way to the Little Buffalo's Room, but now Morocco is in there. "Do you want the seat up or down?" he asks Chief.

Episode 12 (November 21, 1993)
"One Ton"

In China, Secret must stop One Ton (Yoshio Be), a rogue panda, without hurting the endangered bear. "Maybe he's just misunderstooded," says Morocco. Finally, Secret tricks him into beating himself up and takes him into custody for endangering an endangered species. He is placed in a zoo with a sign that says, "See the Socially Maladjusted Endangered Species." "Oh Secret," says Morocco, "you're so good. And gentle, too."

"Let's Make a Right Price" [2 Stupid Dogs (1993)]

The titular characters appear on Let's Make a Right Price, the "Really Really Easy" game show where there's "no math" required. Little Dog, the marginally smarter one, tries to throw the game so he can get the booby prize, a lifetime supply of Granma's Joybone Dog Biscuits, but he keeps winning. Finally, he loses, but because he cheated, he doesn't get the dog biscuits, he gets a new car.

Morocco and Secret have cameo appearances in a commercial on the show within the show. A Rodney Dangerfield-esque dog has them tied up and threatens them. "What's he gonna do, Secret?" asks Morocco. Secret produces a box of treats from his hat. "Granma's Joybone Doggie Treats!" cries Morocco. Secret throws the box, the dog chases it and comes to a bad end.

Episode 13 (November 28, 1993)
"Voo Doo Goat"

Chief is missing his pipe, and he can't say if the pipe's disappearance has anything to do with him flying around. Secret takes out his Super Sniffer-Outer Helmet. "I want to do it!" says Morocco. "I want to do it!" Voo Doo Goat has stolen the pipe to complete his Voo Doo Doll of Chief which will help him accomplish his evil plans. When Secret Squirrel finds him, Voo Doo Goat brutalizes the doll, which has real-life consequences on Chief back home. Secret is not impressed, so Voo Doo Goat produces a doll of Secret. Voo Doo Goat throws away the Chief doll and Morocco picks it up. "Chief? A dolly!"

Secret buys a Voo Doo Goat Voo Doo Doll from a Voo Doo Doll Vending machine. They commit mayhem on each other's dolls, while Morocco "plays" with the Chief doll in a toy taxi. "Up in the sky, flying high!" Chief and a real taxi crash through the roof. "Oopsy." Once Voo Doo Goat is in custody, Morocco controls him through the doll. "Walky, walky, walky! Time to do de splits."

Season 2
Episode 11 (May 1, 1995)
"Cartoon Canines" [2 Stupid Dogs (1993)]

The titular characters impersonate Ren and Stimpy at cartoon boot camp. "Ren" does not speak.

GIGGLE RATING: Looks, Five Giggles. Voice, Three Giggles. I guess Jess Harnell was unavailable.

AVAILABILITY: Season 1 is available on the DVD 2 Stupid Dogs/Secret Squirrel Show, Volume One (2018).

Animaniacs (1993)
Season 1
Episode 1 (September 13, 1993)
"De-Zanitized"

Warner Bros. Television Animation, Amblin Entertainment. Directed by Rusty Mills, Dave Marshall. Written by Paul Rugg. Produced by Rich Arons, Rusty Miller, Peter Hastings, Sherri Stoner. Executive Producer: Steven Spielberg. Senior Producer: Tom Ruegger. Cast: Jess Harnell (Wakko), Rob Paulsen (Yakko/Dr. Scratchansniff), Tress MacNeille (Dot/Hello Nurse), Frank Welker (Ralph the Guard/Thaddeus Plotz).

The replacement for *Tiny Toon Adventures* (1990) (qv) at Warner Bros. Television, this show was created by Tom Ruegger and first aired on Fox Kids and ran from 1993-1998.

An opening *Newsreel of the Stars* explains the premise: the Warner siblings, Yakko, Wakko, and Dot Warner, were toon stars who were locked in the Warner Bros. water tower in the 1930s and escaped in the present day. Ralph the Guard is supposed to keep them under control, while Hello Nurse provides eye candy. Other characters include Minerva Mink, a sexy gold-digger; and the show's Executive Producer, Steven Spielberg, who in 1994 would found DreamWorks Pictures with Jeffrey Katzenberg and David Geffen.

Dr. Otto Scratchansniff is the studio psychiatrist, charged with the job of watching Yakko, Wakko, and Dot. He speaks with an Austrian accent. He is not a caricature of Peter Lorre, but in his office, he has a picture on the wall of himself and Peter Lorre, as Lorre is depicted in *Hollywood Steps Out* (1941), along with the Maltese Falcon.

GIGGLE RATING: Looks, Five Giggles. Voice, N/A.

AVAILABILITY: On the DVD *Animaniacs, Volume 1* (2006).

Season 3
Episode 8 (November 4, 1995)
"This Pun For Hire"

Warner Bros. Television Animation, Amblin Entertainment. Directed by Audu Paden. Written by Gordon Bressack, Charles M. Howell IV, Peter Hastings, Tom Ruegger. Produced by Rich Arons, Rusty Miller, Peter Hastings, Sherri Stoner, Steven Spielberg, Tom Ruegger. Cast: Jess Harnell (Wakko), Rob Paulsen (Yakko/Dr. Otto Scratchansniff), Tress MacNeille (Dot), Frank Welker (Ralph the Guard).

Narrated by Yakko in noir-fashion. He's a private eye, and Wakko and Dot are his operatives. Suddenly, "she" walks in. "She" is Bette Midler. "Not her," says Yakko. Hello Nurse walks in. "I've been followed." Yakko says, "There's a shocker." When she answers a question correctly, Plucky Duck (qv) flies down like Duckie from *You Bet Your Life* (1949) and she wins a date with Wakko.

She holds up a picture of her boss, Dr. Otto Scratchansniff, with a statue of a bird. Scratchansniff has disappeared. She last saw him at the Mambo Room at the Tropicombo Club. "The band had a big dumb guy playing drums. And everyone was dancing under a pole. Then, the doctor vanished."

Yakko says, "Now let me get this straight. He muttered some mumbo-jumbo during the combo samba in the Mambo at the Tropicombo. Then there was a jumbo dumbo playing the limbo on the bongos and then he was gone?"

"That is absolutely correct!" she exclaims. The duck flies down again and she wins another date with Wakko.

The Warners go to the Mambo Room. There, they meet the drummer, played by Ralph the Guard, reading his Sydney Greenstreet-esque lines from a script, badly, but still better than some of the Greenstreet imitations we've heard so far. At least it's funny. "By Gad, sir, I'm a guy who likes talking to guy who likes to talk to a guy what plays the bongos. I like to talk."

"Have you seen this guy?" asks Yakko, holding up a picture of Scratchansniff.

"I don't like to talk about that," says Ralph, who triggers a trap door. The Warners, along with the bongos, fall down a chute. When they reach the basement, the bird statue falls out of the drums.

A voice says, "I'll take that." It is Minerva Mink. Ralph grabs the bird. "Hold it, by Gad sir, de bird is mine." Dr. Scratchansniff steals it. "Ja! Und now it's mine," he says. "The statue is mine! It's mine! Mine, do you hear?"

"I gotta tell ya," says Yakko. "That is the worst Peter Lorre I've ever heard."

"I don't care," says Scratchansniff. "In five minutes, I will sell this statue for millions."

"You mean I'll sell it," says Hello Nurse, and takes the statue.

"Wait a minute, you weren't lookin' for him after all," says Yakko. "You were lookin' for that statue."

"That is absolutely correct," says Hello Nurse. She wins another date with Wakko.

Scratchansniff breaks the statue and takes something from within. "Zis microfilm contains all ze best ideas for making ze funny cartoons." He giggles insanely. "Ooh, zose guys upstairs will pay me millions for zis." He takes it upstairs and offers it to Steven Spielberg, Jeffrey Katzenberg, and David Geffen for their new studio.

"We don't want 'em," says Spielberg. "We have our own, you know, brilliant ideas."

"Who are those guys?" asks Dot.

Yakko replies, "The stuff that DreamWorks are made of."

GIGGLE RATING: Zero Giggles. Scratchansniff looks and sounds nothing like Lorre, but that's the whole point. Rob Paulsen is perfectly capable of doing a fine Lorre if he wants to, as he does in *The Tick* (1994) and *Timon & Pumbaa* (1995) (qv). Fellow Lorre impersonators Frank Welker and Jess Harnell are in the cast.

AVAILABILITY: On the DVD *Animaniacs, Volume 4* (2007).

Avenger Penguins (1993)

Cosgrove Hall Films. Directed by Jean Scott. Written by Jimmy Hibbert, Malcolm McGookin, Roger Stennett, Phil Jackson. Produced by Ben Turner. Cast: Michael McShane (Caractacus P. Doom/Marlon/Barracuda Stink), Jimmy Hibbert (Bluey/Harry Slime/Bella/Brown Badly Drawn Brother/ Poodle Stink/Googerplex), Rob Rackstraw (Rocky/Doc/Cecil Stink/Irv/

Quantum Mechanic), Lorelei King (Sweetheart Fairy Angel/Europhia/Miss Carbaretta Gasoline).

Originally titled *Hell's Penguins* but renamed to avoid offending snow-flakes from the American religious right-wing, this British series was about the three titular motorcycle-riding flightless seabirds: Marlon, the leader (whose name is pronounced by everybody as mar-lawn); Rocky, the not-so-bright muscle; and Bluey, the eccentric genius. Marlon's catch phrase is, "Penguins! Bike up!" They live above Irv's Garage. The show bore a striking but coincidental similarity to *Biker Mice from Mars* (1993). Every week, the Avenger Penguins would foil mad scientist Caractacus P. Doom's latest plot to take over the world with his Monstertron. Doom is, broadly, a parody of Orson Welles, and his assistant is a Peter Lorre sound-alike, the bug-eyed amphibian Harry Slime (Jimmy Hibbert), whose name parodies that of Orson Welles' character in *The Third Man* (1949). The Stink Brothers are a rival bike gang made up of dogs. Bella is the proprietor of Slush City, the ice cream parlor where the Penguins hang out. This was the last Cosgrove Hall production that used hand-painted animation cels. It ran mostly on Children's ITV.

The first season is entertaining and it comes to a satisfying conclusion. Then the show jumps the shark, with the second season ignoring the end of the first one and carrying on as it never happened. It feels padded, with episodes parodying *Star Trek* (1966), Westerns, James Bond, Sherlock Holmes, musicals, and that hoariest of all TV show cliches, *A Christmas Carol*. They even have an episode that turns out to be a dream. Or is it? Lorelei King plays two different characters in back-to-back episodes with the same distinctive laugh.

Season 1
Episode 1 (September 22, 1993)
"The President Is a Fish"
"I wish I had told Mr. Doom that I can't stand heights," says Slime. Too late, as Doom has put up his Doom Tower in Big City by drilling up from under the earth's surface. Doom unveils his animatronic robot of the President of the United Republics of the World, a Ronald Reagan lookalike and sounda-like. Marlon and Rocky are riding their bikes and literally crash through

the door and destroy the "president". "Get them!" says Slime to his bot. Another bot kidnaps the real president and he is tied up with Marlon and Rocky. The animatron goes on TV pretending to be the real president and announces all taxes should be sent to Doom. Marlon, Rocky, and the real president are to be turned into minuscule zombie fish. Rocky calls Bluey for help. Bluey reverses the effects of the machine and they all escape. Doom and Slime are thrown into Big City Jail.

Episode 2 (September 29, 1993)
"The Hog Jamboree"

In the Monstertron, Doom combines Slime's DNA with a motorcycle and a clown car to make a bike for Marlon to compete in the Hog Jamboree. Then, Doom launches a Marlon-seeking missile. Bluey reprograms the missile's guidance system to return to Doom Tower and explode. After the race, the Stink Brothers surround the Slimecycle. "Come on, guys," says Slime, "it's only a race. There's always next year. Let's do a deal." The Stink Brothers decide to use him for spare parts.

Episode 3 (October 6, 1993)
"Quantum Mechanic"

Doom steals Bluey's brain and uses it with the Monstertron to bring to life Quantum Mechanic, Bluey's favorite cartoon superhero. Doom gets Quantum Mechanic to try to kill Marlon and Rocky, telling him that they are standing in the way of Doom's plans for an animal hospital. Marlon and Rocky sneak into Doom Tower to get Bluey's brain back. Doom catches them, but Quantum Mechanic returns, having learned from Bella that Doom is lying, and he saves the day. Marlon steals the brains of Doom and Slime. "A penny for your thoughts, Mr. Doom," says Slime.

Episode 4 (October 13, 1993)
"Big City, Little City"

With his Shrinking Ray, Doom plans to make the population of Big City small and the tiny antimatter monsters he makes in his Monstertron large in his first step to world domination. The second step involves sending Slime to a satellite to turn the ray on the entire earth. The Penguins are sent instead by mistake. Doom decides to destroy the satellite. "What about the Shrinking Ray? Won't it be destroyed along with the penguins?" says Slime. "What about world domination?" Doom says he'll think about that tomorrow. The Penguins reverse the Shrinking Ray and get away in the Escape Pod. The satellite crashes into Doom Tower.

Episode 5 (October 20, 1993)
"Computer Chaos"

Slime discusses what he'd do to the Penguins. "First I'd like to pluck their feathers off," says Slime, giggling insanely, "and then, um, and then, rub them up and down with a cheese grater for two hours each and then dip them in river slime and then give them Chinese rubs and then squish them!" Doom kidnaps Marlon and Rocky. Once he squishes them, he will become King of the World. Bluey bursts in at the last moment and saves them.

Episode 6 (October 27, 1993)
"I Married an Android!"

"This is the place," says Slime, giggling insanely. "The Penguins' lair. I shall affect an entrance. But how? A little jump. Nothing that Harry Slime can't handle, even carrying a top-secret Brain Molecule-Altering Headset. Did I say that? No, I didn't. It isn't, it isn't! It really isn't a headset to be put on Marlon while he sleeps that will change his entire personality and stop him leading the Penguins in their war against Mr. Doom! No! It isn't. It's a um, a um, a–I'll let you know when I think of a really good fib." He jumps and misses. He climbs the stairs. "This is more like it. Sleeping penguins. My target for tonight. Silent, like a ninja warrior. I must walk as silent as the wind and tread as soft as a falling feather." He trips. Finally, he puts the headphones on Marlon. "Mission accomplished!" He falls down the steps. "With one bound, Harry Slime was," he coughs, "free."

"So, I dived out of the tenth floor of the building and did seven perfect somersaults before making a perfect landing below," he tells Doom. "If you want style, you want Slime!" Doom uses the Monstertron to make a beautiful android to marry Marlon and take him away from the others. She does, and Doom becomes King of the World.

Rocky and Bluey go to visit the domesticated Marlon in the suburbs. The android comes home and turns into a flying bot who tries to kill the Penguins. The bot crashes into Doom Tower. Marlon loses his headset and goes back to normal.

Episode 7 (November 3, 1993)
"CatPig: Cat of Iron"

Doom unveils his new tank-like weapon that will spell the doom of the Penguins and asks Slime for his opinion. "It is, um, uh, wonderful. A work of uh, uh, sheer genius. Soon, soon, the world will be in your power! The whole world! All will bow down before the magnificence of Caracatacatacatus P. Doom!" Slime giggles insanely. Doom orders him into the cockpit to track down the Penguins. The Penguins are watching Irv's nephew from the farm, a porker who fancies he is a superhero called "CatPig". Slime captures the Penguins and brings them back to Doom Tower, but they are rescued at the last moment by the Cat of Iron.

Episode 8 (November 10, 1993)
"Nightmare at Tea Time . . ."

Doom invents a machine that puts people to sleep and dream whatever he wants them to dream. "But boss, you promised we'd talk about my wages today on account of the fact that I've never had any and what with the cost of living and inflation–" Doom knocks Slime and the penguins out and watches their dreams.

Bluey dreams about being on the Starship Boobyprize. Marlon dreams about racing with Cecil Stink. Rocky dreams about playing the guitar in concert. Slime dreams about being a swashbuckling hero. Doom turns their dreams into nightmares. The Penguins get Slime to sleepwalk and turn off the machine, which is then used on Doom.

Episode 9 (November 17, 1993)
"Starstruck"

The Penguins go to Hollywood to work on a movie with Rocky's crush, Dolores Devine, but it's all a plot by Doom. "In my impenetrable disguise, I assume the identity of Harry von Slime, director," says Slime. "We hire the idiot penguins as stuntmen, but sadly . . . the stunts go wrong."

On the set, Dolores' manager, Susan, is berating the Woody Allen-esque writer for not making the changes she wanted and he quits. The Penguins roll up just as an alien, who is also smitten with Dolores, walks onto the lot. The alien overhears Doom's plan and warns the Penguins. The Penguins and the alien bike off with Doom in pursuit. Doom blows up the bridge they are about to cross, and they fall off, but the alien makes their bikes fly in an homage to *E.T. the Extra-Terrestrial* (1982). Doom goes off the bridge and Susan feeds Slime to a monster because Dolores has never been paid.

Episode 10 (November 24, 1993)
"The Labyrinth of Doom"

Doom has invented a Ruby Laser World Dominator and Coffee Percolator but he needs the Eye of Mars gem to make it work. He hires Carbaretta Gasoline, the meanest, fastest lady on two wheels, to enter the Labyrinth of Doom, a motorcycle challenge, against the Penguins and the Stink Brothers, where the jewel is first prize. "First, get me that little old ruby," says Doom. "Then, come up and see me sometime, sugar." He promises to crown her queen. Slime is to help her win at any cost. "Harry Slime here, sir. Ready, willing, and able. Slime's the name, sabotage is my game."

The race comes down to Rocky and Carbaretta and Carbaretta wins. Slime pulls a lever and opens a trap door under Rocky, who grabs the lip of the floor to avoid plunging one thousand feet. "Well, well, well, well, well, what have we here? A dingle-dangling Rocky penguin! All dressed up with no place to go," says Slime, who giggles insanely. "EXCEPT DOWN, THAT IS! And the woman of my dreams victorious! A real winner. With a little help from her friends. Or, to be more precise, me." Rocky asks for a hand and Slime kicks one of Rocky's hands away. Doom asks Carbaretta to marry him. Slime raises a mallet to hit away Rocky's other hand. Carbaretta hits Slime with a rocket and knocks him into the pit. Carbaretta suggests the Penguins share the ruby.

Episode 11 (December 1, 1993)
"The Wild, Wild, Wild, Wild West"

Slime steals a transanium crystal that enables time travel for Doom. "Thank you, Mr. Doom. Your pleasure is my reward. Yech! I can't believe I said that." Doom holds Slime's stuffed bear, Benny, hostage and sends Slime back to 1860 to stake gold claims and the Penguins follow. Slime goes into a saloon and runs into doppelgangers of himself (Snake Belly), Doom (Beauregard T. Doom), and the Stink Brothers, who take his maps. Slime tells them the Penguins have come here to steal their claim.

Rocky and Bluey go to a gun store and buy pistols. They run into Beauregard, Snake Belly, and their gang who challenge them to a gunfight. Bluey outshoots them all, but runs out of bullets. The Penguins escape by buckboard wagon, followed by Beauregard and his gang. The penguins fall through the time portal on top of Caractacus, who is knocked senseless.

Back in 1860, Slime says, "Mr. Doom, can I come back now?" He giggles insanely. "I suppose not. Oh well, the show ain't over till the fat lady sings." Then the fat lady sings.

Episode 12 (December 8, 1993)
"A Winters Tale"

It's a cold winter in Big City. Doom is outraged because Slime has brought in a birthday card, so he fires him and turns him out on the street. "How could Mr. Doom throw me out on such a miserable day? I've been so faithful to him." Slime looks through a window and sees a couple and their children eating. "Look at the happy family enjoying the warmth of their home? And look at slimy little me! Outside! Here! Out in the cold! There's nowhere to go and nothing to do on my–BIRTHDAY! Why have I wasted my time on that Mr. Doom? If only I could somehow mend the error of my ways." He gets stuck to a lamppost.

Doom, posing as Phil Anthropy, tricks Irv into signing away the garage, making Irv and the Penguins homeless unless they can come up with a million dollars by midnight.

"This is it then," says Slime. "I'm going to spend eternity frozen to a lamppost! Oh, how I wish I'd been a good person." The Sweetheart Fairy Angel, Godmother of Goodness and All Things Fluffy and Nice (who sounds like Judy Holliday) appears to him. She puts him on the straight and narrow path and they fly away.

Bella and the Slush City patrons give money to Irv to help save the garage. Even the Stink Brothers kick in. Meanwhile, the Sweetheart Fairy Angel grants Slime three wishes. His first wish is to get a lost kitten home. They fly over the garage, where Irv is still a thousand short. Slime uses his second wish to get a grand for Irv and save the garage. His third wish is to send Doom to the planet Mars with his "filthy contraptions." The Penguins throw a party to celebrate.

Episode 13 (December 15, 1993)
"The Revenge of Doom"

One year later, the Fairy's spell has run out and Doom returns to earth, immune to the Fairy. Slime and the Fairy are a couple. Doom comes to Slush City to collect Slime. He literally throws down the gauntlet and challenges the Penguins to keep Slime. The challenges are rigged, including a motorcycle race with Marlon, and Doom wins back Slime. "I am going outside," says Slime to the Fairy. "I may be a little while. Farewell, my lovely. Of all the fairies in all the world, I had to bump into you. And you stole my heart. I'll always remember." Doom snatches Slime away in his sidecar.

Irv tells Marlon that his bike was sabotaged by Doom. This renders the challenge invalid, and they follow after Doom. Doom takes a key from Slime and he ejects the sidecar, leaving Slime behind. "It wasn't me he wanted. It was," Slime giggles insanely, "the key." It is the key to the Mad Annihilation Device, which gives its holder the power to rule the world. The Penguins go to Doom Tower, but Doom has blocked anyone from entering.

Inside Doom Tower, the M.A.D. has two keyholes, red and blue. If the wrong one is used, the machine will blow up. Doom calls Slime, and Slime tells him to use the red keyhole. Doom thinks he is lying, and uses the blue one, so Doom Tower flies to Mars. "I'll explain it to you over a salmon milkshake," says Slime to the Fairy.

Season 2
Episode 1 (September 16, 1994)
"The 23rd Century"

In 2295, the great-great-great grandsons of the original Avenger Penguins, Marlon VI, Rocky VI, and Bluey VI, are being honored by President Huxley at Mega City Bowl, as Lucidious Q. Doom watches on her telescreen from the Doom Star. Her flunky is named Harriet Slime. She speaks with a slightly higher voice and wears a fez-like hat with three balls on it instead of tassels. With the old Monstertron and the new Temporal Freeze Subquantum Cryo X-Ray-type Nozzle, Ms. Doom plans to freeze the new Penguins in the space-time continuum and achieve world domination. "Hard to believe, I know," says Harriet to the camera, "but take her to a dance and she's an utter wallflower."

Lucidious freezes the Penguins, and tells Huxley, who is a woman of color (only took three hundred more years), to resign in twelve hours or all Mega Big City will be frozen. Huxley transports the original Penguins through time to save the day and launches them on a rocket ship to the Doom Star. The crew of the ship includes parodies of Chekhov, Spock, and Scotty from *Star Trek* (1966). From the Doom Star, Lucidious launches Harriet in a fighter to shoot down the Penguins.

"By the time I'm finished with the Starship Innertube, it's going to need a puncture repair kit," says Harriet, giggling insanely. "Finally, I get to do a job properly. Miss Doom will be so pleased with me. Maybe I'll even get paid for a change. I could afford to get my legs waxed and everything. I could be beautiful. All I have to do is hit that spaceship!" Marlon engages the ship's Cloak of Invisibility and Harriet bounces off of it. Marlon and Rocky beam down to the spaceship along with a red-shirt, who almost immediately disappears down a trap door. Doom sends Marlon and Rocky down another trap door and plans to shoot them into the sun. Harriet accidentally flies the fighter into the barrel of the gun and Bluey beams Marlon and Rocky back to the ship just before the Doom Star blows up.

Episode 2 (September 23, 1994)
"Mommy's Boy"

We are back in Big City in the 20th century, and so is Doom (this is never explained). He wants to destroy the Penguins, but they broke all his weapons. "What we need is an infiltrator," says Slime (it is not explained why he is back with Doom, either). "Someone on the inside, a penguin of our own in their gang who could lead them to their downfall and—Mr. Doom, why are you looking at me like that?"

Doom dresses Slime as Dave the Penguin and he coincidentally arrives at Irv's Garage right after Rocky has left to go shopping with his Mommy. The Stink Brothers knock Rocky's parcels out of his hand, and Mommy cleans the Stink Brothers' clocks.

The President (really Doom) goes on TV and announces that his dog is missing. Without the dog, he can't continue and the world may fall into Doom's hands. "We could always look at the local dog pound," says "Dave". He leads them to Doom Tower. Bella figures out it's a trap and Rocky goes to rescue them, with his mother following. She beats up Doom and forces him into the Monstertron, which turns him into a whelk.

Episode 3 (September 30, 1994)
"Who's Afraid of the Big, Bad Penguin?"

The Penguins wreck their bikes and send Rocky out with the last of their money to buy spare parts, but instead, he purchases a remote-controlled combination folding piano, cat basket, and marshmallow toaster. Meanwhile, Doom replaces Slime with Miss Demeanor, a blue-skinned new-style business dynamo. She sends Slime to the Monstertron and turns him into a pedal bin. She decides to rule the world herself, without Doom. She turns Doom's Hypnotic Psyche Sapper on him, but when he mentions Penguins, she loses her composure and drops the Sapper into Slime, the pedal bin, who reveals her plan to Doom. "I may be a waste paper bin, Mr. Doom, but I can still talk. And believe me, you need to listen to me." Doom changes him back to a toad, but Miss Demeanor has programmed the robots to throw out Doom.

Slime says, "I just might have an idea, Mr. Doom. There are some old monster bots in the basement that she won't have reprogrammed." Doom kidnaps Bella and all her patrons and holds them hostage. When the Penguins arrive, Doom gets them to harass Miss Demeanor. They have no effect, because it turns out she is really afraid of pelicans. Doom turns her into one and then sets Fido, the titanium Rottweiler, on the Penguins. Rocky throws him the remote-controlled combination folding piano, cat basket, and marshmallow toaster. Fido eats it and gets destroyed when Rocky activates it. "Uh oh," says Slime, "I think Fido is getting a little overheated." Doom Tower blows up again. The grateful patrons buy the Penguins new bikes. Actually, children's trikes.

Episode 4 (October 7, 1994)
"Surprise Fate"

Slime is watching is favorite show, *Surprise Fate*, a dating game show with a Dame Edna Everage-like hostess. Doom helps Annabelle the Animal, who likes to eat anything black and white, escape from jail. He sends Slime to Irv's Garage with a telegram to invite the Penguins onto the show. "Hooray, hooray, it's your lucky day; because, uh, lucky because luck has come your lucky way." The bachelorette calls herself Sharon, but she is really Annabelle the Animal. She picks Marlon, and they go off to a hotel.

"Good evening and welcome to Dream Motel," says Slime, disguised as a bellhop, "where your every tiny need is attended to with curtness." He shows them to their rooms, and Doom sends him up to the roof to fix the TV antenna. Rocky and Bluey realize that "Sharon" is really Annabelle, and they go to rescue Marlon. Just as Annabelle is about to eat the Penguins, Slime falls down the chimney, covering Doom with black soot and making him more appetizing to Annabelle than the Penguins, who escape.

Episode 5 (October 14, 1994)
"High Doom"

Doc, an ancient patron at Slush City, recalls his days in the Wild West with Beauregard Doom, Snake Belly, the proto-Stink Brothers, and Sheriff Zeke Penguin and his two deputies, Big Jethro and Clink Westwood. Slime does not appear in this episode.

Episode 6 (October 21, 1994)
"The Jewel in the Crown"

The Penguins go to the Club Oasis to hear Dolores Devine sing. Doom is there, too, buying a diamond from the Kung Prawn Brothers. Doom calls Slime, who drills in through the floor in the Mole-a-thon, which is programmed to take Doom to the ancient land of Shangri-lalalalalalalalala, where he will place the diamond into the ancient crown and achieve world domination. He freezes Marlon and Bluey, but Rocky escapes with Dolores and the diamond in the Mole-a-thon with Slime, who tries to turn it around. "I can't, the controls won't respond!" Slime decides to find the crown and achieve world domination himself, but he and Rocky get trapped. Dolores finds the crown just as Doom arrives by bus. He places the jewel in the crown and the King, who sounds like George Sanders, appears and recognizes Dolores from her movies. He turns Doom into a mollusk and frees Rocky and Slime.

Episode 7 (October 28, 1994)
"A Christmas Carol"

"Honestly Santa, I've been ever so good," says Slime, "in a sort of bad sort of way, and I don't want much, in fact, this year, just for a change, anything would be nice. Anything at all. Even just one present. Is that so much trouble?" On Christmas Eve, the Penguins are trying unsuccessfully to put the fairy on top of the tree. Doom shuts off all the electricity and heat in Big City. He keeps his generator going with Slime riding a stationary bike. Then he goes to bed. Meanwhile, the fairy comes to life as the Sweetheart Fairy Angel of All Things Fluffy and Nice. She turns the Penguins into Dickensian ghosts to haunt Doom. Rocky, the Ghost of Christmas Past, shows Doom as a child dropping an anvil on young Slime. Marlon is the Ghost of Christmas Present, dropping him off in the blacked-out downtown of Big City. Bluey is the Ghost of Christmas Future, showing him space with no stars because Doom turned them out. Bluey drops him into a black hole. Doom wakes up and turns on the lights. The fairy is on top of the Christmas tree. Doom drops two anvils on Slime.

Episode 8 (November 4, 1994)
"Fishfinger"

The President from Season 1, Episode 1 calls in the Penguins. Top spy Miss Leatherclad-Fullerain has been kidnapped by Zigmund Fishfinger (Doom) and his slimy sidekick Bobajob (Slime), and the Penguins have to save her. Rocky impersonates a molecule expert to infiltrate Fishfinger's hideout in the Austrian Alps. Marlon and Bluey stowaway in his suitcase. "It's just that, uh, I seem to have, um, misplaced, momentarily you understand, just momentarily," Bobajob giggles insanely, "the key card."

Marlon and Bluey have the key card and they go into a room with a shark in it, like Peter Lorre's laboratory in *Voyage to the Bottom of the Sea* (1961). In the next room, they find Miss Leatherclad-Fullerain. "Caught you redhanded," says Bobajob. Jawbones, a parody of Richard Kiel from the Bond movies, grabs Marlon and Bluey and suspends them over the shark tank. Rocky tries to rescue her, but he, too, is caught, and escapes by helicopter beany and inflatable snow rabbit with Bobajob and Jawbones are in hot pursuit. The penguins steal a plane from a pilot who is reminiscent of Terry-Thomas in *Those Magnificent Men in Their Flying Machines or How I Flew from London to Paris in 25 hours 11 minutes* (1965). They crash-land in Fishfinger's lair, shoot him with his own ray, and make him jump in the shark tank. It was all a dream. Or was it?

Episode 9 (November 11, 1994)
"Disgusting or What?"

Marlon watches his hero, Valentine Lovescones, in a swashbuckling desert movie, and buys Lovescones' cologne, which stinks. Meanwhile, Doom has invented a Disgusterscope which scans for filth and bodily fluids. "Would you like me to describe it in glorious Technicolor detail?" asks Slime. He empties its tanks into the Monstertron. The resulting monster shows up at Irv's Garage and rips the roof off. The Penguins go to Doom Tower and demand restitution. Doom says he has lost control of the monster and they all have to flee. Marlon goes into the Monstertron and makes himself gigantic and sprays the monster with cologne, which defeats him.

Episode 10 (November 18, 1994)
"Rock 'n' Roll Penguins"

Doom gave Rocky a clockwork beak pruner in exchange for the Penguins' bikes and they are bored. They imagine they are rock musicians in concert. Doom tells Slime to fit them with remote-controlled explosive devices, but Slime can't remember whether or not he did it. Doom sings a Barry White-type song. He wears an Elvis-type jump suit in front of an electronic sign that reads "EVILS".

"Oh Benny, I feel so depressed," says Slime to his bear. "Nobody loves me. Why can't I meet a nice girl? Someone I could call my very own. Someone–you know what? This sounds like a cue for a song." He sings a song to his Slime-Girl.

Dolores Devine arrives at Slush City and sings a duet with Rocky. Slime, disguised as a messenger, returns the bikes. The penguins celebrate with a song about haddock milkshakes and they bike up. Doom pushes the plunger for the bombs and blows up Doom Tower.

Episode 11 (November 25, 1994)
"Computer of Doom!"

Bluey is addicted to video games. Meanwhile, Doom develops a computer virus to take over the world. It works and he no longer needs Slime. "I've got nowhere to go, Mr. Doom," says Slime. "Nobody likes me because I work for you and nobody will give me a job or be my friend or say, 'Hi, Harry, how's it going?' I'll be all alone on the mean streets of a world that doesn't care." Bluey invents a Quark Neutrino Digitizer to get the Penguins into the computer network. The Monstertron's alarm reports the intrusion to Doom. "Somehow I feel I've seen this movie before," says Slime. Bluey plugs a program of his own into the system and Doom and Slime are put back into jail.

Episode 12 (December 2, 1994)
"Sherlock's Penguins"

The Prime Minister of the United Kingdom brings the Penguins across the pond because Doom's cousin, Professor Moriarty has introduced an anger serum to London's water supply. "So, the famous Avenger Penguins from

Big City, U.S.A." says Snipes, Moriarty's henchman who looks and sounds like Slime. "Just wait till the boss hears about this." The Penguins hail a hansom cab, which is driven by Snipes. "What are you talking about, you fat feathered fool? Get in and belt up while I overcharge you. And no spitting." They arrive at their destination, 221-A Baker Street. "A measly twenty quid! Call that a tip? Next time, get the bus, fatso!"

At their rooms, they meet the housekeeper, Mrs. Pontoon, who eavesdrops on them. Snipes leads them to Moriarty's hideout in a drainage tunnel, then captures them in a trap. Just when things look hopeless, Mrs. Pontoon arrives and shoots Moriarty and Snipes with darts and saves the Penguins. She is really Miss Leatherclad-Fullerain from MI6 and she has shot them with Moriarty's own anger serum, which makes him pleasant. Moriarty calls Scotland Yard and turns himself in, and so does Snipes.

Episode 13 (December 9, 1994)
"Beauties and the Beasts"

"I want a raise," says Slime. Right now, Doom isn't paying him anything, so Doom promises Slime a 200% raise if Slime gets rid of the Penguins for good, but if he fails, he gets fed to the octopus. The Penguins are rehearsing for their rock concert when Harry breaks through the wall in a manned robot and grabs Marlon. "Pardon me if I don't wait for an encore, guys, but I'm splitting up the band. Starting with the bass player." Bluey hits him with cymbals and the Penguins get away.

Doom decides to create a monster in the Monstertron and he ends up creating two hideously ugly, grotesquely obese women, Raquel 1 and Raquel 2. They turn into Julia Roberts and Marilyn Monroe. He sends them to Slush City to kill the Penguins with his Atomic Warhead Fountain Pen ("one featherlight touch to the nib is all it needs.")

Marlon and Rocky are sitting at the counter when the Raquels come on to them. They ask Marlon and Rocky to autograph their napkins, then they leave. Marlon and Rocky follow them out, saying their pens don't work. The Raquels invite them to Millennium Park, and they accept and bike up. Bluey sees the Raquels shape shift back to their ugly selves. He finds Marlon and Rocky and tells them the Raquels are working for Doom.

The Penguins bike on. The Raquels try to follow, but Bluey has stolen the spark plug from their bike. Raquel 1 blows both Raquels up with the atomic warhead. Slime returns to Doom Tower in the manned robot and throws Doom to the octopus.

GIGGLE RATING: Five Giggles.

AVAILABILITY: In the United Kingdom, the entire series was released on DVD in March 2006 by Delta Media PLC.

Mega Man (1994)

Capcom Entertainment. Directed by Walt Kubiak, Katsumi Minokuchi. Written by Michael Maurer, Richard Merwin, Jeffrey Scott, Kairabo Jihaka, Matt Uitz, Gary Greenfield, Mark Jones, Keiji Inafune, Akira Kitamura, Martin Pasko, Evelyn Gabai, Doug Molitor, Michael O'Mahony. Executive Producer, Producer: John Ledford. Cast: Ian James Corlett (Mega Man/ Rush/Snake Man/Bobby's father/Chef Bot), Scott McNeil (Dr. Wily/Proto Man/Eddie/Drill Man/Brainwashed Adults), Jim Byrnes (Dr. Thomas Light/Quick Man/Actor/Admiral Hayley/Air Man), Terry Klassen (Cut Man/Bomb Man/Computer/Elec Man/Astronaut 2), Robyn Ross (Roll/ Bree Ricotta/Cheer Bots/Evelyn Ray/Female Bystanders), Garry Chalk (Guts Man/Bright Man/Mayor/Dark Man/Ring Man).

Based on a video game franchise, which it follows somewhat closely, this is another entry in the popular genre "Mad Scientist Tries to Take Over World", set in the year 200X, where we now have flying cars but still have fax machines, Polaroid cameras, and phone booths. The place seems to be New York City, or maybe Washington, DC; or the west coast. As outlined in the first episode, which has the shockingly obvious and unironic title "The Beginning", Dr. Wily and Dr. Light were roboticist colleagues developing industrial bots, Robot Masters, to help mankind until Wily steals the proto- types and uses them in his quest for world domination, so Dr. Light builds Mega Man (aka "Rock") to defeat him. Unlike, say, *Avenger Penguins* (1993) (qv), this show is played as seriously as a Strindbergean tragedy, and one is to take the increasingly ludicrous premises and wild coincidences at face value. The robots blast each other with their plasma cannons, and they get knocked around, but it's all in good fun and rarely do any of them sustain serious damage, except for some of the one-off baddies. Even when Mega Man is literally blown to bits, Dr. Light puts him together again. Mega Man sometimes runs out of juice, but one knows that he will get his power cans delivered in the nick of time. Consequently, one never feels anything is at stake, and one does not care. Mega can co-opt the other robots' powers by touching their arms. Wily never corrects this feature. Everybody knows where Dr. Wily's hideout, whose exterior is prominently decorated in Early Evil Lair with a priapic tower, is, but the police never think about just dropping a bomb on it, like they did with MOVE. Conversely, every week, Dr. Wily commits a 9/11-level crime, but nobody ever considers ratcheting up security a notch, they all just carry on with a couple of rent-a-cops. Wily energetically and tiresomely masticates the backgrounds. Ironically, the actor who voices Wily, Scott McNeil, also takes the part of Proto Man, and with that character, he hits the sweet spot between playing straight and justifiably kidding the material. Proto Man is Mega's brother, who vacillates between trying to kill Mega and luring him to the dark side. Cut Man is one of the first Robot Masters. He was originally supposed to be a logging robot, although on his head is not a saw or axe, but shears, which he wields as a weapon. Cut Man has bulging eyes and an insane giggle and talks like Peter Lorre. Terry Klassen, who plays Cut Man, also voiced the role of Zak in *Salty's Lighthouse* (1998) (qv). Cut Man hangs out with Guts Man, who is super-strong, and it is tempting to think this is an homage to Sydney Greenstreet's character Kasper Gutman in *The Maltese Falcon* (1941), but this is probably unintentional. Guts Man is large, but otherwise bears no physical resemblance to Greenstreet and there is no attempt to imitate Greenstreet's voice. Guts Man is also more slow-witted than Gutman. However, some of the characters do pronounce the name "guts-mⱭn" instead of "guts-man". Other Robot Masters enter and leave, often without any fanfare.

Dr. Light is incredibly intelligent, preternaturally good, and really boring. Whatever invention Wily comes up with, we know Light will make something to counter it. Ho-hum. He also builds Mega's sister, Roll, as a household robot (seriously, Capcom?) and instead of a plasma cannon, she has a number of household appliances in her arm, including a vacuum, which really sucks. Mega cannot fly, however, his robo-dog, Rush, can, so Mega gets around by dog-surfing through the air. At one point, Rush shows us that he can morph into numerous iterations, most of which are not that different from the original, and few of which are ever seen again.

The show was syndicated and lasted two seasons. A third season was canceled, reportedly because the tie-in merch from toy-partner Bandai did not meet expectations.

Season 1
Episode 1 (September 11, 1994)
"The Beginning"
Dr. Wily's robots, including Cut Man, attack "Kennedy International Airport" in Wily's bid to control the city. Cut Man slices wings off planes. Mega Man is called in. He flies away on top of Rush, and Roll follows. "Cut Man, let's crush her," says Guts Man. "With pleasure," says Cut Man. He derails a monorail and Guts Man throws it at Roll. Mega pushes her out of the way, but he runs out of power and is crushed. Rush takes Mega back to the lab to be fixed and then they return to the airport. Mega touches Cut Man's arm. "No! Now you've got my weapon!" Mega Man beats the bad guys.

Episode 2 (September 18, 1994)
"Electric Nightmare"
Bright Man, who sounds a little like Ed Wynn, takes out the power company guards so Wily can control the power grid. Mega Man tries to stop them. "I'm going to make paper dolls out of you!" says Cut Man. "Cutting you to pieces is going to be sheer delight." Dr. Light invents something to foil Wily.

Episode 3 (September 25, 1994)
"Mega-Pinocchio"
Cut Man tries to kidnap a scientist but Mega rescues him. "Well, if it isn't that Goody Two-Circuits, Mega Man." The scientist is really one of Wily's robots, and Wily reprograms Mega to think he's a real boy. Wily's robots invade the Capitol, the White House, and, oddly, the Lincoln Memorial. "Let's cut to the chase," says Cut Man. Dr. Light invents something to foil Wily.

Episode 4 (October 2, 1994)
"The Big Shake"

Mega tries to rescue people from an earthquake caused by Wily. "That Mega fool fell into our trap," says Cut Man. Guts Man plants a micro-transmitter on Mega so Wily can follow his movements. Mega foils his plan.

Episode 5 (October 9, 1994)
"Robosaur Park"

Dr. Light has designed robotic dinosaurs for Robosaur Park and Dr. Wily reprograms them to make them vicious. "What do you say we take the bus?" Cut Man asks his dinosaur mount, who eats the bus. Wily has a retro-virus that turns robots into cave-bots that he can control. "Maybe you can get a job selling energy peanuts in the park," Cut Man says to Mega. Dr. Light, of course, has an antidote.

Episode 6 (October 16, 1994)
"The Mega Man in the Moon"

Wily hijacks the space shuttle and kidnaps the crew. The shuttle is to transport the lens of the new sun-focusing super laser from the space station to the moon's surface. Wily plans to use it for world domination. Mega catches up to the shuttle with his rocket pack. Guts Man is playing cards with Cut Man. "You said to 'cut the cards'," giggles Cut Man insanely. Mega reflects the laser back on Wily. "I'm cutting out of here," says Cut Man.

Episode 7 (October 23, 1994)
"20,000 Leaks Under the Sea"

Mega tries to stop Wily's invasion of an underwater mining operation. "You're fish bait, Mega Man!" says Cut Man. "I'm going to slice you into silicon!" Mega Man beats them, and as a reward, Dr. Light receives a new laboratory. It turns out to be a trap by Wily. The lab sprouts legs like an AT-AT Walker and strolls into the sea. The gang escapes and foils Wily's plan.

Episode 8 (October 30, 1994)
"Incredible Shrinking Mega Man"

Cut Man and Guts Man break into "Smithsonian Park" to steal jewels. Mega tries to stop them. "I'll slice and dice him!" says Cut Man. Using the jewels, Guts Man shrinks Mega down with a ray gun. Wily uses the ray to shrink down cities and sell them to art collectors. Tiny Mega and Rush get locked in the glove compartment of Cut Man's van. "Open it nice and slow, so I can give 'em haircuts–from the neck up," Cut Man giggles insanely. Mega and Rush escape. Dr. Light invents something–oh, you know.

Episode 9 (November 6, 1994)
"Bot Transfer"

Mega, Roll, Rush, and Dr. Light are on a plane to the International Science Conference in Geneva when Cut Man and Guts Man try to hijack it. "I'll cut you down to size," says Cut Man. Mega and Roll foil them. Wily plans to kidnap all the scientists at the conference, but he is foiled by Mega Man.

Episode 10 (November 13, 1994)
"Ice Age"

Ice Man and Air Man steal super-freeze technology from Zero Refrigeration to help Wily start a new Ice Age. Dr. Light turns Ice Man against Wily, and Ice Man attacks with his ice bots. "I've always enjoyed ice sculpture," says Cut Man before an Ice Bot throws him headfirst into a car.

Episode 11 (November 20, 1994)
"Cold Steel"

Wily uses mind-control music to make people into human robots. Mega Man flies up to the top of Wily's transmitter. "It's time to clip your wings, Mega Man," says Cut Man. Mega Man blows up the tower.

Episode 12 (November 27, 1994)
"Future Shock"

Dr. Light invents a time machine and Wily's bots try to steal it. Mega Man attempts to stop them. "I'll cut him down to size," says Cut Man. Proto Man tries to destroy the time machine, but Mega shoves Dr. Light into it and sets it for one minute into the future. The time machine returns but it is empty. Mega takes the time machine to look for Dr. Light thirty years in the future. Dr. Wily now controls the city and his robots are new and improved. "Let's see how you do against Kung Fu Cut Man!" The chubby and now ninetyish Dr. Light can still run, climb down a cliff, and leap into the ocean from a great height. Mega takes the time machine back to the present.

Episode 13 (December 4, 1994)
"The Strange Island of Dr. Wily"

"I wonder how long these guys have been here," says Cut Man. Wily has unearthed stone creatures buried by a volcanic eruption on a South Pacific island. "Remote control rocks," says Cut Man. Wily thinks they can be an indestructible army, but it's difficult to see why, since a plasma cannon turns them into gravel. Dr. Light, Mega, Roll, and Rush go to investigate, but the bots turn on Wily. Mega rescues him and his bots and they all have to work together to get off the island safely. Wily double-crosses Mega, but Mega wins in the end.

Season 2
Episode 1 (September 10, 1995)
"Showdown at Red Gulch"

When a radioactive meteorite lands near Red Gulch, an Old West reenactment town, scientists converge on the site. Wily kidnaps them all and presses them into service mining fragments. (Doesn't he have bots who do that?) Mega, Dr. Light, Rush, and Roll arrive late to the party because they apparently drove the whole way. Bits of the meteorite give Wily's bots new powers and they derail a gold train. "Looks like this is our stop," says Cut Man, giggling insanely. Dr. Light gets a piece of the rock. To lure Wily's bots, Mega and Roll walk through town loudly announcing their plans, making the re-enactors look like Barrymores.

"Show us your big, bad meteor," says Cut Man. Mega uses it to short-circuit the power in Wily's bots by bouncing the ray off a chamber pot. I'm not making this up.

Episode 2 (September 17, 1995)
"Terror of the Seven Seas"

Wily hijacks naval ships and joins them into one big ship, which he uses to plunder the world's shipping lanes. Roll gets onto Wily's ship and hacks into the computer, but is discovered by Cut Man. "Better cut that out, Circuit Skirt, or I'll cut you down to size." Mega foils Wily's plan.

Episode 3 (September 24, 1995)
"Mega Dreams"

Wily's new invention gives the mayor nightmares that Cut Man is his mommy. "Prove you're a good boy. Go to City Hall and get your secret passcode out of the vault. Then fax it to me." The mayor sleep-drives to city hall in his pajamas. How it got in his pajamas, I'll never know. Then, Wily gives the police chief a nightmare that he is kidnapped by Cut Man and Guts Man. "Never a cop around when you need one, eh, Chief?" Cut Man giggles insanely. "What we want is information. Special information. The name of the head of security at the Space Research Center." Wily intends to use this information as part of his plan for world domination. Dr. Wily is able to copy the dream machine and use it against Wily. At least he doesn't invent something.

Episode 4 (October 1, 1995)
"Robo-Spider"

Wily develops a giant spiderbot, which does whatever a spiderbot does to help him take over the world. Mega disguises himself as Guts Man. "Wait a second. If you're Guts Man, then who's that Guts Man?" Dr. Light invents something.

Episode 5 (October 8, 1995)
"Master of Disaster"

Wily gets a golden chest and frees an ancient Mesopotamian spirit, Lotos, who helps him become Emperor of New York City. He can't destroy Mega, though, and Wily's bots try to. "I'll cut you to ribbons, Mega Man!" says Cut Man. Mega beats all the bots and Lotos, too. "You never really appreciate your freedom until it's gone," says Dr. Light. Rudy Giuliani resumes his term as mayor.

Episode 6 (October 15, 1995)
"Night of the Living Monster Bots" (October 15, 1995)

Inspector Hedley (Scott McNeil doing a really bad Sean Connery imitation) tells Dr. Light a mummy has terrorized Hampton Village. It's really a bot, and Wily's making a movie as part of his quest for world domination, blah blah blah. He has also made a Dracu-bot, which does a really bad Bela Lugosi. "Three shears for Mega Man!" says Cut Man.

Episode 7 (October 22, 1995)
"Curse of the Lion Men"

A comet awakens some lion creatures, who have the heads of lions and the bodies of men and wear jockeys. Wily tries to get the lion creatures on his side (guess why), but the head lion wants to rule the world himself. The lion creatures can turn men into lions that wear ball caps. Dr. Light invents something to reverse the curse, but he is kidnapped by Guts Man and Cut Man, who giggles insanely. Wily and Dr. Light are turned into lion creatures and the head lion puts the bots under his command, including Roll, who bosses around Cut Man and Guts Man. "She's worse than Wily, and that's pretty bad." Mega gets Dr. Light's invention and turns everybody back.

Episode 8 (October 29, 1995)
"The Day the Moon Fell"

Wily, whom Cut Man calls "The Master of Disaster", pulls the moon out of its orbit with his Gravitron. Mega Man breaks into his lab. "Hold him still, so I can slice and dice him," says Cut Man. Mega steals a part from the Gravitron that Dr. Light needs for his invention to put the moon back.

Episode 9 (November 5, 1995)
"Campus Commandos"

Dr. Light builds a college for bots. Wily's bots break into the cafeteria and Cut Man puts "Mind control chips in the dessert. Those bots will never know what hit them." Wily steals Dr. Light's antigravity machine so he can raise City Hall. Mega foils his plan.

Episode 10 (November 12, 1995)
"Brain Bots"

Dr. Light invents Brain Bot, a genius robot with a supercomputer brain. Wily gets his bots to steal him as part of his plan for (all together now) world domination. "Maybe he's not so smart after all," says Cut Man. Mega gets Brain Bot back.

Episode 11 (November 19, 1995)
"Bro Bots"

Mitchell Deacon is the best candidate for governor in years. Cut Man and Guts Man literally crash the parade. "Hey Deacon, I'm going to make you one sore loser," says Cut Man. Mega goes after them with help from Proto Man, and Dr. Light provisionally makes Proto Man part of the team. However, he is really still working for Wily and plants a scrambler chip on Mega. When Bright Man attacks, Proto Man "saves the day" and Deacon makes Proto Man head of security at the election night rally. Mega sees that Proto let Cut Man and Guts Man into the rally. "You're a politician, Deacon. You should be used to–CUTBACKS!" Cut Man giggles insanely. Wily replaces Deacon with a bot. Mega foils his plan.

Episode 12 (November 26, 1995)
"Bad Day at Peril Park"

At Fun World amusement park, Wily is turning humans into bots. Mega tries to destroy his brain wave transmitter. "I'm going to cut you down to size, Mega Man!" says Cut Man. Mega foils his plan.

Episode 13 (December 3, 1995)
"Mega X"

Vile and Spark Mandrill, bots from the future, help Wily by attacking Dr. Light's new plasma power plant to steal his lightanium rods. Mega Man X arrives from the future to save Mega's titanium behind. "I think our future friend needs a little old-fashioned help," says Cut Man. Wily floods the plant and steals the rods. Mega and Mega X foil his plan.

Episode 14 (January 19, 1996)
"Crime of the Century"

Wily invents a gizmo that turns toys into criminals. A doll rips Guts Man's head off. "Gutsy never looked so good," Cut Man giggles insanely. "I love it! They do all the work, and we get all the credit!" Dr. Light invents something and Mega foils Wily's plan.

GIGGLE RATING: Five Giggles.

AVAILABILITY: Discotek Media released the entire series on DVD September 30, 2014.

The Tick (1994)
Season 1
Episode 2 (September 17, 1994)
"The Tick vs. Chairface Chippendale"

Akom, Graz Entertainment, Sunbow Productions. Written by Ben Edlund, Richard Liebmann-Smith. Executive Producer: C. J. Kettler. Cast: Townsend Coleman (The Tick), Micky Dolenz (Arthur), Rob Paulsen (The Forehead/The-Guy-That-Looks-Just-Like-Peter-Lorre), Kay Lenz (American Maid), Hamilton Camp (Professor Chromedome), Pat Fraley (Zipperneck/Dyna-Mole), Jess Harnell (Sewer Urchin), Tony Jay (Chairface Chippendale), Kevin Schon (Jack Tuber: The Man of a Thousand Faces/The Crease).

The Tick began as an independent comic book series by college student Ben Edlund. Kiscom, a toy licensing and design company, wanted to merchandise the character, but major networks and studios were reluctant. At last, animation company Sunbow Entertainment brought in writer Richard Liebmann-Smith to work on the script with Edlund. Their first effort was rejected by FOX, which gave them five days to fix it. FOX liked the second version. The Tick tried out at the National Super Institute, and was assigned to The City, where he is joined by a sidekick, Arthur. Other superheroes appear, like American Maid.

The Tick and Arthur come upon a robbery in progress, but they also ruin American Maid's plan to follow the crooks back to their hideout. Arthur finds an invitation on one of the unconscious crooks with the address of the archvillain Chairface Chippendale. They plan to sneak into the party as caterers.

At the party, all the supervillains, who, like the bad guys in Dick Tracy (qv), are mostly named for their congenital deformities, are there. The-Guy-That-Looks-Just-Like-Peter-Lorre comes in with a gift. "Happy Birthday, Chairface! I hope you like it. He's Dean, my best henchman. He has de strongest hands in da criminal vorld." He giggles insanely.

The Tick offers him "one of these crab things. They're great!" The-Guy-That-Looks-Just-Like-Peter-Lorre says, "You are paid to serve, oaf, not critique!" "Oh, I think you'll like these," says The Tick, and shoves a bunch of them down The-Guy-That-Looks-Just-Like-Peter-Lorre's throat. American Maid reveals herself, and all the superheroes are tied up. Chairface Chippendale reveals his evil plot to write his name on the moon. The heroes escape and foil him.

FUN FACTS: Some anonymous internet commenters claim Pat Fraley as Dyna-Mole is also imitating Peter Lorre. He has one line as he decorates for the party: "I still think there's too much green." The cast also includes frequent Lorre impersonators Jess Harnell and Hamilton Camp.

GIGGLE RATING: Five Giggles.

AVAILABILITY: Buena Vista Home Entertainment released the first season on DVD as *The Tick vs. Season One* (2006).

Creepy Crawlers (1994)
Saban Entertainment, Saban International, Abrams/Gentile Entertainment, Hahn Shin Corporation, Toyman Inc., Métropole Production. Directed by Peter Kingston, Jean-Luc Ayak. Written by Steve Cuden, Jean Cheville. Produced by Bruno Bianchi, Sam Ewing, Joel Andryc, Eric S. Rollman. Cast: Steve Bulen (Professor Googengrime), Cam Clarke (as Jimmy Flinders) (Spooky Goopy/Commantis), Jonny K. Lamb (T-3), Melody Lee (as Melodee Lee) (Sammy Reynolds), Tony Pope (as Anthony Mozdy) (Hocus Locust/Tom Lockjaw), Jan Rabson (as Stanley Gurd Jr.) (Volt Jolt/Top Hat), Joey Camen (Chris Carter), Art Kimbro (Sting Ring).

Creepy Crawlers was a toy first made by Mattel in 1964, building on previous technology used in the Thingmaker and Vac-U-Maker. Plastigoop is poured into die-cast metal molds of, well, creepy crawly things like spiders and insects and heated to about 390 degrees Fahrenheit to form jiggly replicas which can be removed when they cool. The product was discontinued in the seventies because of safety concerns. In 1978, a safer version was introduced, but the reformulated Plastigoop did not work as well, and the revival did not last long.

In 1992, New York-based ToyMax brought back the Creepy Crawlers brand. The original Plastigoop made a return, but it was used in a Magic Maker which used a lightbulb for heat and could not be opened until the mold had cooled down. The TV cartoon series tie-in was perhaps inevitable, and *Creepy Crawlers* debuted in first-run syndication in fall 1994. It, in turn, launched its own line of toys.

Professor Googengrime is a wizard with a mystical monocle who owns a magic shop that employs "normal kid" Chris Carter. Chris has built a "Magic Maker", which looks like the one from ToyMax. Googengrime fires him, but keeps the Magic Maker. That night is the Magical Millennial Moment, when the stars align and Googengrime will prove himself to be the greatest magician in the world. Although he is capable of actual magic, Googengrime's stage show for some reason consists of hacky tricks. Light reflects off Googengrime's monocle and hits the Magic Maker just as Chris is trying to get it back. Bugs who crawled inside are have their DNA combined with goop and magic tricks to morph into the Goop-Mandos: Hocus Locust, whose ropes have many uses and who does celebrity impersonations, some of which are even identifiable; Volt Jolt, a Hispanic lightning bug who has electrical powers; and T-3, based on a tick and super-strong, with his own miniature sidekick, T-Flea.

Googengrime steals back the box and Chris flees, followed by the Goop-Mandos, who make themselves at home in his house. Chris has an older brother, Todd, who like most young people still living with their parents, owns a custom-made dune buggy worth six figures, which the Goop-Mandos frequently commandeer and transform into the Goozooka "Crawler Cruiser" assault vehicle by adding goop. Later, the Goop-mandos break into the magic shop and accidentally create a new "brother", Sting

Ring, from a wasp and some rings. Other "good" characters include Colonel Ka-boom, a no-nonsense officer who sometimes seems to be the only first responder in a city that is being destroyed by monsters; and Tom Lockjaw, a parody of newscaster Tom Brokaw.

Googengrime's evil lair, a magic shop, is located downtown, clearly marked, and has no security, yet is never raided by the cops. It is also destroyed regularly and then rebuilt by the following week. In some episodes, there are tenants living upstairs. The apartment situation in town must be dire if people are living in a building that could be leveled at any time, or perhaps they have rent control.

Googengrime uses the Magic Maker to create a henchman, Spooky Goopy (Cam Clarke), a green skeleton with handcuffs for claws, a lock for a torso, and a voice like Peter Lorre's. Cam Clarke is a voice actor whose credits include the *Quest for Glory* video game franchise (qv) and Ygor in *Monster High: Frights, Camera, Action* (2014) (qv). Googengrime's henchman has a henchhat, a talking topper, which Spooky Goopy wears on his head and is the best part of the show. As in *Drak Pack* (1980), the good monsters fight the bad monsters created by an evil genius to rule the world. There is a character who lassos things, a good guy who shoots electricity, and a henchman who sounds like Peter Lorre, but this is no *Drak Pack* (1980).

Season 1
Episode 1 (October 4, 1994)
"The Night of the Creepy Crawlers"

Googengrime uses the Magic Machine to make his own "Crime Grimes", including a giant Shockaroach, and goes on a crime spree. "This is going to be a fun night," says Spooky Goopy, giggling insanely. "I can feel it in my bones." Chris and the Goop-Mandos try to stop him, but they run out of goop power ("Looks like you just blew a fuse," Spooky Goopy giggles insanely to Volt Jolt) and have to turn upside down to recharge. Hocus fills the football stadium with goop soup, which for some reason shrinks Shockaroach, but not before he destroys the magic shop. Googengrime says he has no insurance, but it gets rebuilt anyhow. Chris picks up the tiny Shockaroach and keeps him in a jar in his room, as he does with all subsequent shrunken Crime Grimes. Hocus imitates Jane Hathaway from *The Beverly Hillbillies* (1962).

Episode 2 (October 11, 1994)
"Sugar Frosted Crawlers"

Googengrime floods the market with a breakfast cereal that has a living prize inside. Unseen by this author.

Episode 3 (October 18, 1994)
"Who's Afraid of Bees?"

Googengrime puts a bee into the Magic Maker and names him Rumblebee. Spooky Goopy trains Rumblebee: "This is Chris Carter. We don't like him. A lot. We want you to grab him and bring him here." Rumblebee instead snatches Samantha Reynolds, a cute, spunky girl who has just moved next door to Chris. Googengrime schemes to burglarize the bank Sammy's father runs. The Goop-mandos foil the bank job and rescue Sammy. Hocus imitates Beavis and Butthead, John Wayne, Columbo, Sean Connery, and Paul Hogan.

Episode 4 (October 25, 1994)
"Chris Explains It All"

A recap of the first three episodes. Unseen by this author.

Episode 5 (November 1, 1994)
"Power Play"

Googengrime uses the Magic Maker to homebrew a Shockaroach and tries to take over the world. Unseen by this author.

Episode 6 (November 15, 1994)
"Vanishing Act"

Chris and Sammy go to Razzle and Dazzle's magic show. Razzle and Dazzle are really Googengrime and Spooky Goopy, and they capture Chris and Sammy. Chris tells Googengrime to let Sammy go, but Googengrime counters that that would make him a chauvinist. "Very good master," Spooky giggles insanely. "And it would probably be even funnier if I knew the meaning of the word 'chauvinist.'" It would be funnier still if the writers knew it. "Why can't we begin the show now, master?" says Spooky. "I've been good." The Goop-mandos arrive and save Chris and Sammy. Hocus imitates Foghorn Leghorn, Snagglepuss, Woody Allen, Ed Wynn, Jack Nicholson, and Scotty from *Star Trek* (1966).

Episode 7 (November 22, 1994)
"One Creepy Brother"

Spooky rounds up arachnids and Googengrime creates a Spider Patrol with the Magic Maker. Todd comes to Googengrime's store to buy a trick to impress Sammy. "Master," says Spooky, "A customer is upstairs in the shop. I think I've seen him somewhere before." Googengrime recognizes Todd and hypnotizes him into becoming leader of the Spider Patrol. Chris and Sammy shrink the spiders and rescue Todd. Volt zaps Todd with electricity and he remembers nothing. Hocus imitates Curly Howard and W.C. Fields.

Episode 8 (December 6, 1994)
"I Was a Teenage Crawler"

Chris mutates into a grasshopper. Unseen by this author.

Episode 9 (December 27, 1994)
"Mauler Amuck"

Spooky creates an uncontrollable monster called 2-Ugly, which can separate its head from its body. Unseen by this author.

Episode 10 (January 24, 1995)
"The Glob"

Googengrime creates a Blob-like creature that eats all forms of entertainment. He spares this cartoon for obvious reasons. Unseen by this author.

Episode 11 (January 31, 1995)
"All The Way to China"

The new Super Squirminator tunnels to the earth's core, and Sammy's brother Nick falls down the hole. Unseen by this author.

Episode 12 (February 7, 1995)
"Double Trouble"

Houdini's trunk is on display at the county museum. Googengrime makes a double of 2-Ugly called 2-Ugly-2. "Say," asks Spooky, "does that guy look familiar to you?" With 2-Ugly-2's help, Googengrime steals Houdini's trunk, but the Goop-mandos get it back. Hocus imitates Arte Johnson's German soldier from *Rowan & Martin's Laugh-In* (1968), Dorothy from *The Wizard of Oz* (1939), and John Houseman.

Episode 13 (February 14, 1995)
"Attack of the Fifty Foot Googengrime"

Googengrime wants to steal the lens from a giant telescope, but he and Spooky fail. "I'm sorry, Master," says Spooky. "I'll do much better next time." He causes goop to spill on Googengrime, who fires him. "I'm going to show Googie who's really boss," says Spooky. The goop causes Googengrime to grow to a height of fifty feet, but he loses his monocle. He decides to steal the lens and use it as a monocle, and the Goop-mandos go to stop him. They tie him up with cable.

Spooky tries to create his own Crime Grimes and ends up being attacked. "I guess being the boss isn't as easy as it looks," he says. "I miss Googie. Maybe Regis and Kathie Lee can cheer me up." He sees Colonel Ka-boom on TV taking Googie off to Langley and rescues him, but the Goop-mandos give chase. Spooky blasts the lens with the monocle, giving it the monocle's mystic power, just as the Goop-mandos catch up with them at a carnival. They trick Spooky into shooting Googie with the ray from the monocle, returning him to normal size.

Episode 14 (February 21, 1995)
"Return of the Crime Grimes"

Spooky drops a dime on the Goop-mandos to Colonel Ka-boom, using an old lady's voice. "It's horrible. They've invaded the kitchen. Infested the pantry. Inhaled the air freshener." Colonel Ka-boom searches Chris' house for Goop-mandos while 2-Ugly-2 frees the Crime Grimes Chris has collected. Ka-boom arrests Chris.

The Goop-mandos leave Chris rotting in jail and go after the Crime Grimes, who are full-sized again and win the battle. Googengrime takes over as the city's mayor. "It thrills me to the bone," says Spooky.

The Goop-mandos bust Chris out of jail and bust into Googie's lair. The Crime Grimes attack, trampling Spooky. "Luckily, I've got medical insurance," he says. The Goop-mandos shrink the Crime Grimes back down and Googie's shop is destroyed, again. Chris gets his Magic Maker back, but he gives it and the Crime Grimes to Colonel Ka-boom, who turns out to actually be Googie. "Shake, rattle, and roll," says Spooky, "I'm with you to the end, Master!" Hocus imitates Robin Leach and Arnold Schwarzenegger.

Season 2
Episode 15 (September 16, 1995)
"Dawn of the Super Goop"
Googengrime gets a new weapon and tries to take over the world. Unseen by this author.

Episode 16 (September 23, 1995)
"Deja Goop"
Googengrime dabbles in voodoo and tries to you-know-what. Unseen by this author.

Episode 17 (September 30, 1995)
"A Real Numb Skrull"
Googengrime builds a better monster and tries to blah blah blah. Unseen by this author.

Episode 18 (November 4, 1995)
"Camp Nightmare"
Googengrime, apparently on summer vaco from world domination, shakes down kids at camp. Unseen by this author.

Episode 19 (November 11, 1995)
"Bugzilla"
Googengrime makes a giant bug. Guess what happens next. Unseen by this author.

Episode 20 (January 6, 1996)
"T-4-2"

Googengrime accidentally creates T-3's little brother, cleverly named T-4, and tries to–I can't. Unseen by this author.

Episode 21 (January 13, 1996)
"Cold Snap"

Googengrime unleashes his cold-weather monster "Ice Scream" on the city, and Chris counters with the Goop-Mando "Fire Eyes". Oh, snap. Unseen by this author.

Episode 22 (January 20, 1996)
"Revenge of the Mutant Stink Bugs"

Googengrime creates the titular insects, but doesn't try to take over the world. Oh, wait, yes he does. Unseen by this author.

Episode 23 (March 30, 1996)
"The Incredible Shrinking Creepy Crawlers"

Synopsis unknown, but I bet it has to do with world domination. Unseen by this author.

GIGGLE RATING: Looks, Zero Giggles (although the character design is cool); Voice, Five Giggles.

AVAILABILITY: The first season has been released on VHS except for Episodes 2, 4, 5, 8, 9, 10, and 11. Rather a lot, really. No DVD release is planned.

The Sylvester & Tweety Mysteries (1995)
Season 1
Episode 9 (November 25, 1995)
"The Maltese Canary"

Warner Bros. Television Animation. Directed by James T. Walker. Produced by James T. Walker, Tom Minton, Mike Gerard, Jean MacCurdy, Fay Whitemountain. Written by Alicia Marie Schudt. Cast: June Foray (Granny), Joe Alaskey (Sylvester/Tweety/Announcer), Frank Welker

(Hector), Jeff Bennett (Fog Dog), Tress MacNeille (Woman), Maurice LaMarche (Sam Spade).

In the first Sylvester-Tweety cartoons in thirty years, Granny is now a globe-trotting sleuth, but Sylvester is still trying to eat Tweety and Hector the bulldog is still beating him up for it.

In San Francisco, Sam Spade needs to take time off to go to the Venezuelan Tiddlywinks Competition. Granny volunteers to fill in while he is gone.

Granny and her pets arrive at Spade's office. Spade's secretary looks more like Dorothy Malone than Lee Patrick. Mind you, I'm not complaining. Sylvester knocks Tweety out the window and Granny tells Sylvester to bring Tweety back. A woman arrives and kisses Granny before she realizes Granny isn't Spade. She looks more like Lauren Bacall than Mary Astor. Okay, now I'm complaining a little. She says her name is "Miss Smith", and she has lost a valuable knickknack. She mistakes a picture of Tweety for the knickknack. Joel Ferret, a Peter Lorre look-and-sound-alike, arrives at the office also looking for Spade and the same knickknack.

Sylvester comes back, having eaten Tweety. Joel and "Miss Smith" (this is the last time we will use those annoying quotation marks) make him cough Tweety up. "That bird is worthless," says Mr. Greenstreak, the "Dough Guy". Miss Smith pokes his fat potbelly, and he giggles like the Pillsbury mascot, who was originally played by Paul Frees. "It's the jewels underneath that ugly yellow paint that I'm after," he says. "All I have to do is scrape." He pulls a sword. He grabs Tweety, who bites him and gets away. Greenstreak pursues him, but he is too fat to fit through the doorway. As Joel and Miss Smith look for Tweety, Granny sends Sylvester after him.

While Granny entertains Joel and Miss Smith with pictures of herself with Charles de Gaulle and Boutros Boutros-Ghali, Dorothy Malone tries to free Greenstreak with the Jaws of Dough, and Tweety leads Sylvester to the Golden Gate Bridge. Sylvester falls off and washes up on the beach at Alcatraz, where Burt Lancaster, as the Birdman, tells him, "No cats allowed." Sylvester catches Tweety, but Hector beats him up. Sylvester returns Tweety to Granny, and Greenstreak tells the legend of the Maltese Canary. In 1539, the King of Malta received a jeweled canary statue to replace the one eaten by his tuxedo cat. Pirates steal the statue in the 1800s and it is thrown overboard by another tuxedo cat. It is missing until the 1950s, when it turns up as the duck on *You Bet Your Life* (1949). Yet another tuxedo cat tries to grab it and receives a concussion. It has been lost since the show was canceled.

Tweety flies out the window and Joel and Miss Smith see a sign for Mike's Maltese Canary Store—a reference to longtime Warner Bros. writer Michael Maltese (qv)—which is having a sale. They run in, and are arrested. Meanwhile, Dorothy Malone is still trying to free Greenstreak, so Spade has to return through his window. He won the championship again. Greenstreak is pulled out with a crane. Granny makes room on the shelf for Spade's trophy and finds the Maltese Canary. "This is the stuff dweams are made of," says Tweety. Greenstreak breaks free and goes through the wall. accidentally follows him. "Somebody had to take the fall, tweetheart," says Tweety.

GIGGLE RATING: Five Giggles. It is not known who plays Ferret. Alaskey, Welker, and LaMarche are all likely suspects. LaMarche is probably Greenstreak. Perhaps he does the hat trick as Bogie, Greenstreet, and Lorre, as in the cartoon below.

AVAILABILITY: On the DVD *The Sylvester and Tweety Mysteries, The Complete First Season* (2008).

Duckman: Private Dick/Family Man (1994)
Season 3
Episode 1 (January 6, 1996)
"Noir Gang"

Klasky Csupo, Reno & Osborn Productions. Directed by Raymie Muzquiz. Written By Eva Almos, Ed Scharlach. Produced by Sherry Gunther, Everett Peck, Gabor Csupo, Arlene Klasky, Jeff Reno, Ron Osborn, Larry Lefrancis. Cast: Jason Alexander (Eric Duckman), Gregg Berger (Cornfed Pig), Bebe Neuwirth (Tamara Le Boinque), Carl Reiner (Salacious Priest), Maurice LaMarche (Peter Lorre caricature/Sydney Greenstreet caricature/Humphrey Bogart caricature).

Duckman: Private Dick/Family Man (1994), based on the comic book by Everett Peck, was the second animated series by Klasky Csupo, after *The Simpsons* (1989) (qv). Eric T. Duckman is a family man and private dick who fails in both departments. His partner is Cornfed (Corny) Pig.

This episode is in black and white with a noirish voiceover. Corny walks into a confessional booth and tells the priest he has betrayed his partner. It all started when a dame named Tamara Le Boinque (who wears her hair like Veronica Lake) walked into their office and said someone was trying to kill her. They go to the speakeasy where she works, Drooligans.

While the orchestra plays "As Time Goes By", Duckman and Corny accost Peter Lorre caricature, a small man with big eyes, bad teeth, and a machine gun. "Hey, you." The man says, in a middle-European accent, "I didn't do it! It wasn't me! I didn't strangle de German for de letters of transit! I didn't stab the albino and hide de knife in de hooker's G-string! I'm innocent! Innocent!"

"Save it for the late show, creepola," says Duckman. "I was just looking for the men's can." Corny suggests they ask him about Tamara. "Tamara?", asks the little man. "That woman makes me crazy! And when I find her, I'm going to chop her into little pieces and throw her into a stew and feed her to a pack of rabid dogs!" and he giggles insanely. "But you're probably talking about a different Tamara."

Duckman heads over to the tubby guy sitting under a fan. The Sydney Greenstreet caricature doesn't let Duckman get a word in edgewise before leaving to make another trip to the salad bar.

Then Tamara takes the stage. "Of all the drool joints in all the world, she has to bring her act into this one," says Humphrey Bogart caricature. Duckman interrogates Bogie, but the lights go out, and Bogie caricature is killed.

Corny goes to see Tamara, but Duckman is already there as a decoy in her bed. Corny tries to leave, but Duckman brings him back and tells Corny he wants to marry Tamara.

Corny has a dream that he and Tamara are having sex like Jack Nicholson and Jessica Lange in *The Postman Always Rings Twice* (1981). It turns into a nightmare with Duckman wearing a suicide vest. Corny confesses to Duckman he has spent the night and that they are in love.

At the office, Tamara calls Duckman and they go off to meet her grandfather. She tells him he has to make her grandfather laugh. Corny learns her "grandfather" is actually her ancient husband and laughter could be fatal. Tamara tries to run off with Corny, but he sends her up the river.

Corny gives Duckman a pair of Tamara's panties. "What's this?" "The stuff dreams are made of, Duckman. The stuff that dreams are made of."

GIGGLE RATING: Five Giggles.

AVAILABILITY: On DVD: *Duckman, The Complete Series* (2018) *Duckman Season 3 & 4* (2009)

Timon & Pumbaa (1995)
Season 3
Episode 6 (October 7, 1996)
"Catch Me if You Kenya"

Walt Disney Television Animation. Directed by Tony Craig, Roberts Gannaway. Written by Roberts Gannaway. Produced by Chris Bartleman, Blair Peters, Patsy Cameron, Tedd Anasti, Chris Henderson. Cast: Rob Paulsen (Peter-Lorre Husband), Ernie Sabella (Pumbaa), Kevin Schon (Timon).

The Lion King (1994) is the highest-grossing traditionally animated film of all time. A leonine *Hamlet,* it sired a media franchise empire comprising sequels, a remake, video games, stage adaptations, and two animated series, of which this was the first. The show focuses on the meerkat-warthog comedy duo. Unlike the film, the series sometimes shows humans.

Pumbaa, the warthog, meets a butterfly and promises he won't let anything bad happen to it. Timon, the meerkat, comes along, hungry for a butterfly, so Pumbaa hides it under his hat. Timon finds it and catches it, and is in turn caught in Peter-Lorre Husband's butterfly net. Peter-Lorre Husband throws Timon up Pumbaa's nose and puts the butterfly in a jar for his collection. "I'm very happy," he says, and giggles insanely. He goes back to his gated compound with a sign on the entrance that says, "Beware of Tiger!" "Settle down, pussycat," he says. "It's only me." He goes up to his treehouse in an elevator.

Timon and Pumbaa follow him, Pumbaa to rescue the butterfly, Timon to eat it. They try different ways to get over or through the fence, and usually end up getting mauled by the tiger. Finally, Pumbaa buys a bag of magic flying pixie dust. Disgusted, Timon throws it over the wall, and the tiger floats away.

Timon and Pumbaa get into the compound and up into the treehouse, where they see Peter-Lorre Husband putting the butterfly under glass. Pumbaa butts him out of the treehouse. "We are not under any circumstances gonna barbecue these butterflies," he says to Pumbaa. "Well, if you didn't come up here to eat 'em," asks Timon, "THEN WHAT DID YOU COME UP HERE TO DO?" Pumbaa lets them go, and the butterflies are free.

GIGGLE RATING: Five Giggles.

AVAILABILITY: This episode has never been released to home video.

The Simpsons (1989)

The Simpsons began life as animated segments created by Matt Groening on *The Tracey Ullman Show* (1987) on FOX. In 1989, it spun off on its own and it has been running ever since, becoming the longest running scripted prime time series, animated or live action. Fat, dumb Homer is the head of a dysfunctional family that includes his wife, Marge; their children: bad boy Bart, smart Lisa, and baby Maggie; and Homer's father Abe, Grampa Simpson. Ralph Wiggum and Milhouse are schoolmates of Lisa and Bart. The show frequently comments on pop culture and society. The media franchise includes a feature film and video games.

Season 10
Episode 8 (December 6, 1998)
"Homer Simpson in 'Kidney Trouble'"

Gracie Films, Film Roman. Directed by Mike B. Anderson. Written by John Swartzwelder. Produced by Bill Oakley, Josh Weinstein, Mike Scully. Cast: Dan Castellaneta (Homer Simpson/Grampa Simpson/Krusty the Klown/Frenchman), Julie Kavner (Marge Simpson), Nancy Cartwright (Bart Simpson), Yeardley Smith (Lisa Simpson), Hank Azaria (Moe Szyslak/Guide/Cowboy/Carl), Karl Wiedergott (Tux Guy).

Grampa Simpson will die without a kidney from Homer. Homer runs away and signs on to Captain McAllister's Ship of Lost Souls. Captain McAllister is based on Robert Newton. Homer meets the other passengers and says, "Hey, who are you guys?" The heavy-lidded Tux Guy giggles insanely. "Who are we? No one. Where are we sailing? Nowhere. Do we even exist? Who knows?" All share their tales of woe. Tux Guy says, "When Mr. Binkley saw what I had done, I was banned from the car wash forever." Homer confesses he refused to give his own father one of his kidneys, and the others literally throw him off the ship.

"The Ship of Lost Souls" sequence was pitched by former staff writer George Meyer, who also pitched the idea for episode. "You don't see it coming at least," he said, "I don't know if it was totally successful."

GIGGLE RATING: Five Giggles. Karl Wiedergott worked almost exclusively on The Simpsons franchise from 2005-2010, playing characters including Huckleberry Hound (qv) and Tricks the Trix Rabbit (qv). Dan Castellaneta is sometimes credited as Tux Guy. AVAILABILITY: On the DVD *The Simpsons, The Complete Tenth Season* (Various); also on Amazon Prime, iTunes, and the FXNOW app.

Season 27
Episode 17 (April 3, 2016)
"The Burns Cage"

Gracie Films, Film Roman. Directed by Rob Oliver. Written by Rob LaZebnik. Produced by Bill Oakley, Josh Weinstein, Al Jean. Cast: Dan Castellaneta (Homer Simpson/Grampa Simpson), Julie Kavner (Marge Simpson), Nancy Cartwright (Bart Simpson/Nelson Muntz/Ralph Wiggum), Yeardley Smith (Lisa Simpson), Hank Azaria (Chief Wiggum/Cletus Spuckler/Moe Szyslak/Comic Book Guy/Guy in Flash Mob), Harry Shearer (Principal Skinner/Kent Brockman), Pamela Hayden (Milhouse Van Houten).

Springfield Elementary School is holding auditions for the school play, *Casablanca*. ("YOU MUST REMEMBER THIS: BRING TWO PENCILS AND A SNACK.") Lisa blows everyone away with her audition for Ilsa. Milhouse, who has a crush on Lisa, auditions for the role of Rick to get close to her. He gets the role, but Jack Deforest, a young Humphrey Bogart, steals the role away at the last moment. Milhouse is named understudy. Bart reminds him if anything happens to Jack, Milhouse will play the role.

Jack is stealing the show in rehearsal. Ralph Wiggum, who plays Ugarte, literally bumps into him. "You despise me, don't you?" Ralph asks.

"If I gave you any thought, I probably would," replies Jack. Ralph goes inside his "trailer" (locker). Bart hires three kids to beat up Jack, but Jack takes them all out. However, Principal Skinner kicks Jack out of the play for fighting and Milhouse gets the role anyway.

Milhouse is terrible and Lisa complains to her mother. "Whenever I'm dealing with someone who isn't doing a great job, what I do is treat them like they're perfect," says Marge. "If they sense you believe in them, they'll get better."

At opening night, Lisa tells Milhouse, "You're going to be great." He replies, "I already am, because you just told me so." He is great, and at the end of the performance, he takes off his Milhouse mask and reveals he is Jack.

GIGGLE RATING: Five Giggles for execution and degree of difficulty: a woman playing a boy playing Peter Lorre. Nancy Cartwright is in the cast of the upcoming Untitled Ren & Stimpy Short (2019 or 2020).

AVAILABILITY: Amazon Prime, iTunes, FXNOW app.

Yu-Gi-Oh! Duel Monsters (2000)

Nihon Ad Systems (NAS), Studio Gallop. Directed by Hiroyuki Kakudo, Kunihisa Sugishima. Written by Kazuki Takahashi, Matthew Drdek, Lloyd Goldfine, Arthur 'Sam' Murakami, Roger Slifer, Paul Taylor, Junki Takegami, Shin Yoshida, Ken'ichi Kanemaki, Yasuyuki Suzuki. Executive Producer: Tom Kenney. Cast: Dan Green (Yami Yugi), Amy Birnbaum (Téa Gardner), Eric Stuart (Seto Kaiba), Wayne Grayson (Joey Wheeler), Ted Lewis (Bakura), Gregory Abbey (Tristan Taylor), Madeleine Blaustein (Solomon Muto), Darren Dunstan (Maximillion Pegasus), Tara Sands (Mokuba Kaiba), Lisa Ortiz (Serenity Wheeler), Megan Hollingshead (Mai Valentine), Michael Sinterniklaas (Mahad), Marc Thompson (Duke Devlin), Sam Riegel (Para), Richard Will (Gozaburo Kaiba), David Wills (Nezbitt), James Carter Cathcart (Weevil Underwood).

Yu-Gi-Oh is a franchise comprising comic books, animated cartoons, card games, and video games. Yu-Gi-Oh literally means "The Game King", and the first iteration of the story, called *Yu-Gi-Oh!*, was in manga, comics created in Japan (or in Japanese) and conforming to the late nineteenth century style of that country, which has many antecedents. A boy, Yugi, solves the ancient Millennium Puzzle, which awakens a gambling spirit in his body called Pharaoh, aka Yami Yugi, who solves his problems with games. Unofficially, Yugi beat Kaiba, the champion duelist, with his Exodia cards. The Duel Monsters game was a fictitious one made up for the manga, but after the success of the anime versions, a real card game was introduced as a merchandising tie-in. The first anime adaptation, called *Yu-Gi-Oh!* (1998), ran for twenty-seven episodes and was only seen in Japan. The second adaptation, called *Yu-Gi-Oh! Duel Monsters* (2000) ran for 224 episodes and is available subtitled or in two English dubs. Because the first series has never been seen outside Japan, the English dubs (Singapore and North American) are known just as *Yu-Gi-Oh!* (2000), bedeviling generations of researchers yet unborn. I will call it by its full title to avoid more confusion. The North American dub, which is the one that mostly concerns us here, was seen in the U.S. on Kids WB. Weevil Underwood wears eyeglasses with large round yellow frames which make his eyes look bigger, or seem to. He specializes in insect cards and is a great strategist. James Carter Cathcart, who would go on to play Weevil Underwood in the video game *Yu-Gi-Oh! Capsule Monster Coliseum* (2004), gives the character a Peter Lorre voice. The show is done in limited animation that makes *Creepy Crawlers* (1994) look like *Fantasia* (1940).

In the program guide below, the episode number is the overall number in the series. The numeral following in parentheses is the number in the season. The first title is the English dub title, the second is the original translated title. Multi-episode story arcs have their own titles, which are written on a separate line in quotation marks. Air dates are for the North American version.

Season 1
"Duelist Kingdom"
Episode 2 (2) (October 6, 2001)
"The Gauntlet Is Thrown"/"The Trap of Illusionist No Face"

Weevil Underwood is playing against Rex Raptor, who uses his dinosaur cards to overwhelm his opponents. Raptor plays his two-headed Rex. "And all I have is this weak little bug," Weevil giggles insanely. "You've attacked your way into my trap. But then, how could your tiny dinosaur brain know when an enemy attacks, my vortex activates?" He upgrades his insect to give him armor and a laser cannon. Weevil wins and is presented with the trophy by Maximillion Pegasus, the president of Industrial Illusions and the creator of Duel Monsters. Pegasus invites Weevil to compete in a tournament he is hosting at Duelist Kingdom.

Episode 3 (3) (October 13, 2001)
"Journey to the Duelist Kingdom"/"The Lost Exodia"
On the ship to Duelist Kingdom, Weevil says, "To tell you the truth, winning the last championship didn't feel like that much of an achievement. I guess I can't really call myself the champion until I defeat the duelist who beat Kaiba." Weevil tells Yugi there are new rules on the island that require more strategy. He asks to see Yugi's Exodia cards and throws them overboard. "Say goodbye to Exodia!" He giggles insanely. "Now there's no one who can challenge me!" Yugi's friend Joey Wheeler jumps into the ocean and gets the cards back.

Episode 4 (4) (October 20, 2001)
"Into the Hornet's Nest"/"The Insector Combination"
Episode 5 (5) (October 20, 2001)
"The Ultimate Great Moth"/"The Ultimate Perfect Appearance– Great Moth"
[NB: Episodes 4 and 5 released as one part.]
On the island, Weevil runs away from Yugi instead of dueling with him and Yugi chases him. "'Welcome,' said the spider to the fly. You flew right into my trap. Again!" He giggles insanely and a giant arena rises from the ground. "Once you're gone, everyone else's chips will be easy pickings." Weevil is cheating, he has stolen the rules. Yugi sets a trap for him. "You haven't won. I have plenty of tricks up my sleeve," says Weevil. He plays the titular moth. Yugi beats him. Weevil cries, "But I'm the regional champion!"

Episode 8 (8) (November 17, 2001)
"Everything's Relative"/"The Stolen Blue-Eyes White Dragon"

Weevil is sent off the island. "They may be shipping me out, but I'm still Weevil Underwood, bug duelist extraordinaire!"

Season 2
"Battle City"
Episode 56 (7) (January 11, 2003)
"Yugi vs. the Rare Hunter, Part 1"/"Clash! Battle City Begins"

Weevil giggles insanely. "Next time we duel, you won't be so lucky!"

Episode 63 (14) (February 15, 2003)
"Playing with a Parasite, Part 1"/"The Trap of Revenge—Rampage! Paraside"
Episode 64 (15) (February 22, 2003)
"Playing with a Parasite, Part 2"/"The Steel Knight—Gearfried"

A two-part episode. A young boy steals Joey's duel disc and says it was because his own deck was stolen by Weevil, who is by the fountain. Joey goes over there, but it is a trap. The boy has put a parasite card in Joey's deck. "Looking for someone?" Weevil asks Joey. They duel. Weevil plays the moth card again. Joey wins.

Season 4
"Waking the Dragons"
Episode 155 (11) (November 6, 2004)
"The Challenge"/"Target: Nameless Pharaoh"

"I'm the smart one and you're just the goofy sidekick," says Weevil to Rex. They are searching the dump and they don't find any rare cards, but they do find a tandem bike.

Episode 158 (14) (November 13, 2004)
"Fate of the Pharaoh–Part 3"/"The Darkness Within Yugi–Timaeus Disappears"

Weevil and Rex see Yugi get defeated taken by Rafael. "Are you thinking what I'm thinking?" asks Weevil. They go to join Rafael.

Episode 159 (15) (November 20, 2004)
"Trial by Stone"/"A Taken Soul"

"He's getting away!" says Weevil. They drive their tandem bike off a cliff and grab the rope ladder of Rafael's helicopter. They arrive at the hideout of the supervillain Master Dartz. "Yugi and his friends have been making fools of us for years," Weevil tells Dartz. He promises to help Dartz if he will share his power. Dartz gives them cards and wants them to deliver the souls of the Pharaoh and Joey.

Episode 160 (16) (November 20, 2004)
"On the Wrong Track–Part 1"/"The Runaway Train Duel"

Yami Yugi is trapped on a runaway train by Weevil, who giggles insanely. "I want a rematch with the king of games." They duel.

Episode 161 (17) (November 27, 2004)
"On the Wrong Track–Part 2"/"Power-Up Deck! Haga & Ryuzaki"

"Looks like the end of the line for you," Weevil giggles insanely. Nevertheless, they tease this duel out two more episodes.

Episode 162 (18) (November 27, 2004)
"On the Wrong Track–Part 3"/"Timaiosu Hatsudō Sezu"

"This train's been rerouted," Weevil giggles insanely. "Next stop, Loserville." Weevil loses and the train derails.

Season 5
"Grand Championship"
Episode 189 (5) (September 10, 2005)
"Child's Play"/"Hot Battle! Rebecca vs. Vivian"

"Name the last time one of my ideas didn't work!" says Weevil to Rex. They steal the hooded robe of a duelist, Fortune Salim, and impersonate him, Weevil riding on Rex's shoulders. They fall and are discovered but are allowed to play anyway. They lose in one round.

"Dawn of the Duel"
Episode 199 (27)
"Tomb of the Nameless Pharaoh"/"Ultimate Game" (October 15, 2005)

"This is it, Rex," says Weevil. "The Egyptian God Cards will finally be in the hands of someone who deserves them." They actually steal the Millennium items. They flee to an alley, where they are robbed by Yami Bakura, who uses the items to send Weevil and Rex to the Shadow Realm.

Episode 219 (47) (May 6, 2006)
"In the Name of the Pharaoh!"/"In the Name of the Pharaoh!!"

Weevil's deck blows away. "That wasn't so bad," he says.

FUN FACT: Weevil appears in Episode 224 (52), "The Final Duel, Part 4"/"The Story That Concludes in Light" only in the original Japanese-language extended version.

GIGGLE RATING: Five Giggles. In the Singapore dub, Brian Zimmerman also gets Five Giggles.

AVAILABILITY: Dubbed versions not commercially available.

Jackie Chan Adventures (2000)
Season 2
Episode 29 (March 2, 2002)
"Enter the Cat"

Adelaide Productions, Sony Pictures Television. Directed by Michael Chang. Writing Credits (in alphabetical order): John Rogers (creator), Dean Stefan. Produced by Dean Stefan, Michael Goguen, Jackie Chan, Willie Chan, Brian Gersh, Solon So, Duane Capizzi, Richard Raynis, Jeff Kline, Jane Wu Soriano. Cast: Jackie Chan (Himself), James Sie (Jackie Chan) (voice), Sab Shimono (Uncle), Stacie Chan (Jade), Adam Baldwin (Finn), Howard Hoffman (voice), Maurice LaMarche (Cardiff Zendo), Danny Mann (voice), Julian Sands (Valmont).

An animated series following the adventures of a fictionalized version of Hong Kong action film star Jackie Chan, this ran for five seasons on The WB and was also shown on Cartoon Network. Chan is an amateur archaeologist who travels the world with his "niece", Jade, and battles with the evil Valmont. Jackie's uncle, Uncle, back home, provides phone support. The real Jackie Chan appears in the credits and briefly at the end of each episode, but he does not voice his eponymous character.

Jackie and Jade find the priceless statue of the Cat of Khartoum, which is stolen from them by Valmont, who is scratched by the sculpture in the process. Jackie and Jade go to the cafe owned by Cardiff Zendo, the largest collector of art objects in Tangiers. A small man in a fez listens in on the Chans' conversation. Uncle tells Jackie that anyone who gets scratched by the Cat of Khartoum will turn into a cat. The antidote, says Uncle, is "within."

"Excuse me, but there's a phone call for you, m'sieur," says Fez Guy to Jackie. "You may take it in the back." He giggles insanely. In the back, Jackie meets Cardiff Zendo, a fat man in a white suit and a Panama hat. Zendo opens his display case and shows one of his treasures, a black bird. He says the collection will soon be joined by the Cat of Khartoum. "But a little birdie tells me you are after the statue as well," says Zendo. Fez Guy giggles insanely. Zendo correctly surmises that Valmont has kept the statue for himself, and tells Jade to steal it from Valmont in exchange for freedom. She succeeds and brings the statue to Zendo, but she gets scratched. Valmont, now a cat, arrives to steal the statue back from Zendo. Jade, also now a cat, fights him off. Zendo gives the statue to Jackie, who smashes it, releasing the antidote within, and changing Valmont and Jade back to human form. Jackie kicks Valmont, who lands on top of Fez Guy. "Ow, please get off. I bruise easily."

GIGGLE RATING: Five Giggles. It is not known who plays Fez Guy (Maurice LaMarche?), or even what the character's actual name is.

AVAILABILITY: Various DVD issues are out of print. Available on streaming services such as Amazon, iTunes, and Netflix.

Ren & Stimpy 'Adult Party Cartoon' (2003)

Carbunkle Cartoons, Panacea Entertainment, Spike TV, Spümcø. Directed by John Kricfalusi, Vincent Waller, Kelly Armstrong, Bob Jaques. Written by Michael Kerr, John Kricfalusi (creator), Richard Pursel, Vincent Waller,

Jeff Amey, Bob Camp. Produced by Kelly Armstrong, Jessica Beirne, Bob Jaques, Tae Soo Kim, John Kricfalusi. Cast: John Kricfalusi (Ren), Eric Bauza (Stimpy).

An "extreme" reboot of the 1993 hit. Viacom hired John Kricfalusi to do an adult version for Spike TV, the replacement for TNN, as part of their animation block, which included *Gary the Rat* (2003), *Stripperella* (2003), and digitally remastered "Classic" episodes of *The Ren & Stimpy Show* (1991). Kricfalusi returned as the voice of Ren, but Eric Bauza was hired to play Stimpy, replacing Billy West. West thought the show was a terrible idea and he said that the script he was sent, "Onward and Upward", was "an advertisement for NAMBLA." Also, Kricfalusi had demanded West quit the first series when Kricfalusi got fired so Nickelodeon would be forced to hire them both back. West, who describes himself as a journeyman actor, refused because he needed the job and did not want to be blacklisted if the gambit failed. He said:

> Genius is the twin brother of madness—both live in a world created by their own EGO. When I go to work for someone I NEVER bring my personal problems to the arena. The creators of most of the shows I've done don't seem to do that either. John K. wasn't a little bit difficult to work with. He was darn near impossible to work with. His abuse of actors including myself is legendary and was not so much about the search for perfection—it was about borderline sadism and control. His whole fixation with hell dads and boys and torture and punishment . . . well, I've made millions and millions of people laugh but I don't get what's funny about endless repetitions of that crap that he dotes on. There's a difference between cries for help and comedy.

The show was poorly received and ended the Ren & Stimpy revival, dashing hopes at the time for a theatrical movie. The last three episodes were never shown, and three or four other episodes plus two fake commercials were never fully produced. BCDB says one of the episodes, "Life Sucks", was finished and shown August 21, 2003, but it was not viewed by this author. There is an animatic of the episode and a few short scenes on YouTube.

Episode 1 (June 26, 2003)
"Onward and Upward"

Some fans of the original show thought that Ren and Stimpy were in a gay relationship. In this series, their homosexuality is made explicit. They are living in the mouth of a homeless person. Stimpy needs loving, but Ren says, "I'm sorry, Stimpy, but I'm just too damn tired tonight. I just gotta get some sleep. Bugger off, okay?" Stimpy is insistent, so Ren tricks him into kissing the ass of a rat he finds in the homeless person's mouth. "Eediot," Ren says.

Ren's attempt to sleep is foiled because the homeless man snores and his uvula tickles Ren's butt. Ren thinks it is Stimpy's tongue, but Stimpy assures him, "You're the pitcher, I'm the catcher," which he has written multiple times on the blackboard.

In the homeless man's stomach, beer, sausage, sugar, an egg, an apple core, a rat, a chicken foot, and a sock ferment and cause a belch that rips the fur off Ren and Stimpy. "I can't stand this anymore!" screams Ren. "I hate being poor!" Fortunately, Stimpy has some money squirreled away, Papillon-style, quite literally in a squirrel. With the five bucks, they can move uptown. They follow the ancient custom of giving their old house a kick in the ball sack when they move and the homeless man sheds a single tear.

Their new home is a shiny, brass spittoon, and Ren feels they have to be refined gentlemen even as the patrons of the dodgy bar use the spittoon for its intended purpose. "We're living the high life now, buddy!" says Ren. I'll spare you the details. When the "vermin" are discovered in the spittoon, the bartender throws them out on the street and they move back into the homeless man, this time in his butt.

Episode 2 (July 3, 2003)
"Ren Seeks Help"

Ren has gone too far with his words and Stimpy is disconsolate. His tears flood the bedroom. "I know I'm insane," says Ren. "I know I can't control my violent urges. But this time, I'll do something about it. I'll seek help!"

Ren trudges through the city, deserted but for denizens of the street, until he comes to a building with a sign outside that says, "HELP". He goes to the office of Dr. Mr. Horse, Professional. "I'M NOT CRAZY OR

ANYTHING," Ren says, eyes bulging out of their sockets. He tells Dr. Mr. Horse about his childhood. He started young, torturing arthropods before graduating to vertebrates, especially one particular frog. He was about to finish off the frog, but he realizes if he keeps the frog alive, he can inflict more pain on it. Dr. Mr. Horse slips a gun out of his desk drawer in case he needs it.

One day, Ren comes home from work and his minister father sits him down for a talk. Ren's mother is sobbing on the couch. "Son, did you mangle this poor frog?" The frog now has a cast, a peg leg, a crutch, a neck brace, and an IV drip. Ren's mother gives Ren a chainsaw to kill the frog. While she is distracted making out with her husband, Ren puts the still-living frog in the garbage. "Have a wonderful life!" he says. "That was the last I ever heard of that frog."

The conversation turns to Stimpy and Ren tells Dr. Mr. Horse what he did to Stimpy. "What do you think is wrong with me?" asks Ren. Dr. Mr. Horse tells him he's "fucking crazy!" "What kind of psychologist are you?" asks Ren. "I'm a horse!" says Dr. Mr. Horse, who proceeds to "beat the hell out of" Ren. Ren gains the upper hand and pistol-whips Dr. Mr. Horse. Two white-coated men arrive and Ren bites the hand off one.

They take him to the funny farm. The frog shows up at the office and drags himself across the floor. He takes the gun and puts it in his mouth and fires. A bang flag pops out and skewers the back of his head, but he survives.

Episode 3 (July 17, 2003)
"Fire Dogs 2 (Part 1)"

This episode begins with a parody of the credits for *The Honeymooners* (1955). It's *Ralph's Playhouse*, written and directed by Ralph Bakshi. The opening is live action and in black and white. Ralph is a fat slob, his wife is a slim wiseacre. John Kricfalusi calls and tells him that "Fire Dogs 2" is late so tonight they'll show the original "Fire Dogs" cartoon, and then Bakshi will introduce the first half of the all-new "Fire Dogs" starring Bakshi. His wife is upset with him because he has signed away all his rights in perpetuity so she plants in his mind an image of him having sex with her mother. While he is throwing up, she introduces the cartoon, "Fire Dogs" (qv).

After the cartoon, Bakshi is still throwing up. He stops and introduces

"Fire Dogs 2", "maybe the greatest cartoon ever." Then he goes back to puking.

"Fire Dogs 2" takes up where the first one left off. The Fire Chief morphs into the hairy, obese Bakshi, who calls Ren and Stimpy "Tommy" and "Eddie". Bakshi invites them to buy him a pizza, but first he has to stop by his bathroom. Bakshi's apartment is disgusting, with rotting garbage, cigarette butts, feces, and stale beer everywhere.

Bakshi invites Ren and Stimpy into the bathroom while he performs his toilette. He lathers up and shaves with a straight razor, but it doesn't make a dent in his stubble. "You'll be assistant underlings at the station," promises Bakshi. "When we work the next fire, I'll let you choose which people live or die." Ren giggles insanely. "He dies. He dies."

Bakshi does a live action outro and announces "Fire Dogs, Part 2" for next week "if John Kricfalusi gets it here."

Episode 3 (July 24, 2003)
"Fire Dogs 2 (Part 2)"

The title cards announce "*The Eddie & Tommy Show*, Starring RALPH BAKSHI, The World's GREATEST CARTOONIST". The first ten minutes are repeated from Part 1. Then, Bakshi is driving Ren and Stimpy in his car to the pizza place. "We're gonna have parties!" says Bakshi. "Loose women!" Ren says, "At last! HUMAN women!"

After Bakshi has sex with a prostitute, he falls asleep with Ren and Stimpy. He has a nightmare about circus midgets, and tries to kill Ren and Stimpy with a fire axe before falling back into a coma.

The next morning, Ren and Stimpy are wrecks after a night of no sleep, but Bakshi feels great. He drains a beer bottle containing a cigarette butt and then gets weepy. "Promise me you'll take care of me until the day I die," he says. Ren and Stimpy, terrified, say yes. "I love you guys," says Bakshi. "You're fired."

Episode 4
"Naked Beach Frenzy"

Ren and Stimpy are at the beach. "Now for some serious babe-watching," says Ren, but all the babes just "want to pet the pussy." Ren pretends he is a cat so he can fondle the women, but he is mistaken for "a hideous sand crab." A lifeguard, whose body is mostly covered with hair, takes off his swimsuit and whips the "crustacean."

"No more women," says Ren, until he sees women practicing mouth-to-mouth resuscitation. He pretends to be drowning, so they rescue him and the lifeguard performs mouth-to-mouth.

Ren and Stimpy pose as ladies' room attendants. Ren goes into the shower and lathers up one of the women. Stimpy is Shampoo Master, dispensing shampoo from a pump on his crotch. "May I have your autograph?" asks a woman. "Soitenly," says Stimpy, imitating Curly Howard. Ren shaves the first woman, dressed as a window washer and using high rise pulleys.

"Are you the suntan oil dispensers?" asks a woman. "You're just what I need. My friend is burning up on the beach! I need someone to rub suntan oil all over my friend!"

"I'll be right there," says Stimpy, but Ren takes away his oil. "This is my job!" The woman carries Ren to her "friend," who is the lifeguard. Ren gets stuck in the lifeguard's butt, and Stimpy rescues him with a plunger.

The lifeguard recognizes Stimpy. "You made me kiss you!" he says, and chases Ren and Stimpy into the ocean, where they ride away on dolphins.

Episode 5
"Altruists"

Ren is beating Stimpy on the head with a claw hammer when he hears a young woman in a hole crying. She has been evicted, her husband is dead, and her child was born without a head. "We'll help you out, won't we, Stimpy?" asks Ren. "We're altruists," says Stimpy. Ren gives him a right hook to the jaw. "Shut up, eediot!" he hisses. "She doesn't need to know we are godless heathens." He turns back to the woman. "Me and my eediot here will solve all your problems."

The newly minted altruists, Ren armed with a blackjack, decide to burglarize a house with a sign on the fence, "DANGER ANGRY DUCK ON PREMISES". Stimpy tries to go over the fence. "Hey eediot," says Ren, pulling him back. "What the hell were you thinking? Can't you read that sign?"

"What are you gonna do, Ren?" asks Stimpy. Ren replies, "I'm gonna try to refrain from killing you!"

The Angry Duck is in a wading pool outside. Stimpy, costumed as a sexy duck, distracts him. The Angry Duck kisses Stimpy and squeezes his butt so hard Stimpy lays eggs, which hatch into cat-duck hybrids. Ren knocks out the Angry Duck with the blackjack. It raises a lump, and they climb the lump to a window and crack a safe. The two children in the house recognize them. Their parents are Mr. and Mrs. Pipe, who are watching the burglary on live TV. Ren and Stimpy slide down the Angry Duck's lump just as he is waking up, so Stimpy kicks him in the head.

Ren and Stimpy bring their ill-gotten gains back to the woman in the hole. They decide to build her a new house. They steal a lumber truck and cut down the last forty trees of their kind from a wildlife refuge. "Hey dumbass," Ren says to Stimpy, "how does it feel to do good deeds?" To put up the shingles, Stimpy turns into an Italian roofer with a mustache and his fur riding low to expose the crack of his butt. The headless boy is his assistant, "Blue Eyes".

At last, the house is finished and furnished with stolen goods. Just as Ren and Stimpy are leaving, an Irish-accented cop comes to the door looking for two thieves, and arrests Ren and Stimpy. The woman pleads for clemency for Ren and Stimpy and asks for a head for her boy. The cop is a widower and his child has a head but no body, so he joins the two boys together into one. He lets Ren and Stimpy go and courts the woman.

Episode 6
"Stimpy's Pregnant"

The announcer at the beginning reads the scroll, which says, "In this history making teleplay, it is our delight and pleasure to introduce Stimpy J. Kadogan in his groundbreaking role as a woman."

Ren and Stimpy are living in a treehouse over an outhouse, which comes in handy because when Stimpy has to vomit, she can do it right through the hole in the floor into the hole in the privy. Stimpy tells Ren she is pregnant. "We haven't had a job in six years," says Ren. "What are we gonna raise him on? Kitty litter?" Stimpy persuades him to "keep the little bastard."

During the pregnancy, Ren takes it easy while Stimpy shovels coal, mows the lawn, moves the piano, and makes a beer run by canoe down a wild river lined with warlike Indians.

Stimpy whips up a disgusting recipe to satisfy her cravings. Ren forces her head into the bowl. He turns to the camera. "Is there anyone out there in the TV audience that wants to marry an eediot?"

Finally, Stimpy's water breaks. Ren takes off to the hospital without her and has to turn around. After picking her up, he is pulled over by a pig on a motorcycle–an actual porker. He offers them an escort to the hospital, but traffic is heavy, so he starts shooting motorists to get them out of the way. He hands Ren a shotgun. "Here, Mac," he says, "I'm gonna need your help."

Ren tells Stimpy to take the wheel and starts blasting away at the drivers. "Make way for new life!" he cries. They get to the hospital, the pig still firing his pistol. "Make way for life!" he says.

In the delivery room, the nurse is a sheep and the doctor is Mr. Horse. Ren hits Stimpy. "I swear, I didn't see the sign." Mr. Horse realizes from looking at the X-ray that Stimpy is not pregnant, just constipated, but he decides to go through with the "delivery" anyway, for the sakes of Ren and Stimpy. "Is it a boy or a girl?" asks Ren.

"What would you like?" asks Mr. Horse. "A boy?" say Ren and Stimpy tentatively. Mr. Horse makes some minor adjustments to the "baby".

"Congratulations, it's a goddamn boy." They name him "Little Ricky." "Didn't I tell you, Ren?" says Stimpy. "He looks just like you." "Yeah," says Ren. "But he smells just like you." The title card at the end says *The I Love Stimpy Show* in the manner of *I Love Lucy* (1951).

GIGGLE RATING: Five Giggles.

AVAILABILITY: On a two-DVD set, *Ren & Stimpy, The Lost Episodes* (2006).

Duck Dodgers (2003)
Season 1
Episode 5 (September 20, 2003)
"I'm Going to Get You Fat Sucka"

Warner Bros. Animation. Directed by Spike Brandt, Tony Cervone. Written by Spike Brandt & Tony Cervone and Paul Dini & Tom Minton. Cast (in credits order): Joe Alaskey (Duck Dodgers), Bob Bergen (The Eager Young Space Cadet), Jeff Bennett (Count Muerte) (as Jeff Glen Bennett), Edward Asner (Guard Captain), Grey DeLisle (Vampire Bride #1/Vampire

Bride #3), Tasia Valenza (Vampire Bride #2), Michael Dorn (Krag the Klunkin), Kevin Michael Richardson (Cat Head Murphy/Slygoe) (as Kevin Richardson), Dee Bradley Baker (Rookie Guard).

Based on the original theatrical short *Duck Dodgers in the 24 1/2th Century* (1953), itself a parody of the serials *Buck Rogers* (1939) and Flash Gordon. Daffy Duck is Dodgers, Porky Pig is the Eager Young Space Cadet, and there are lots of other Looney Tunes references thrown in for good measure.

Dodgers lands on a scary planet to become earth's ambassador. They are welcomed by Count Muerte, a fat-sucking vampire. The Count is far more interested in the Eager Young Space Cadet and his BMI. Healthy food is like kryptonite to The Count, who hypnotizes Dodgers into luring the Cadet to him. The hypnotized Dodgers becomes like Renfield from *Dracula* (1931), but with a Peter Lorre voice.

Dodgers tells the Cadet to sit in a comfy chair and "DON'T MOVE!" Three Vampire Brides appear. "The master so pleased will be," says Dodgers. Just then, the Cadet walks out of the room. Dodgers asks the Brides, "Why did you not detain him for de master?" "He's such a nice guy," one replies. "We mostly get the crazy bug-eating types," says another. Dodgers eats a bug.

The Count comes in. "Daddy," asks the Brides, "are we going to go hungry tonight?" The Count throws them Dodgers, and the Brides chew on him. The Count flies away.

Dodgers hooks up a liposuction vacuum to a spiked coffin disguised as a bed. "Not this plan shall fail the master." The Cadet keeps putting off going to bed until Dodgers jumps into the coffin himself. The Cadet gets him a pillow. The Count chases the Cadet through the castle and eats a statue of the Cadet made of healthy food and dies. This breaks the spell he had over Dodgers.

FUN FACT: Onetime Lorre impersonator Bob Bergen is in the cast.

GIGGLE RATING: Five Giggles. Alaskey is brilliant as Daffy as Dodgers as Peter Lorre as Renfield. The animators give Daffy large eyes so he looks Lorre-esque.

AVAILABILITY: On the DVD *Duck Dodgers Season 1, Dark Side of the Duck* (2013).

Robot Chicken (2005)
Season 1
Episode 8 (April 3, 2005)
"The Deep End"

Shadow Machine Films, Sony Pictures Digital Entertainment Inc., Stoopid Monkey, Williams Street. Directed by Seth Green. Written by Seth Green, Matthew Senreich, Mike Fasolo, Pat McCallum, Douglas Goldstein, Tom Root. Produced by Alexander Bulkley, Corey Campodonico, Douglas Goldstein, Tom Root, Eric Blyler, Stephanie Meurer, Jeanine Rohn, Keith Crofford, Seth Green. Cast: Seth Green (Franken Berry), Dan Milano (Boo Berry), Seth MacFarlane (Count Chocula), Ryan Seacrest (Himself), Abraham Benrubi, Michael Benyaer.

An American stop-motion animation sketch comedy series based on the comic strip *Twisted ToyFare Theater*. A parody of a broad range of pop culture, it was rejected by Comedy Central, *MadTV* (1995), *Saturday Night Live* (1975), and Cartoon Network before finding a home on CN's Adult Swim.

Franken Berry, the frosted fruit flavored cereal with strawberry flavored marshmallows; and Count Chocula, the frosted chocolate flavored cereal with chocolate flavored marshmallows, were the first of the so-called "Monster Cereals" in 1971. They were followed in December 1972 by Boo Berry, allegedly the first blueberry flavored cereal. In the commercials (qv), Boo Berry was originally voiced by Eugene Weingand (qv), who vaguely looked and sounded like Peter Lorre and called himself "Peter Lorre Jr."

In a sketch on this episode, Ryan Seacrest hosts *Zombie Idol*, with reanimated corpses of dead rockers. The judges are Count Chocula, Franken Berry, and Boo Berry ("I hope our contestants just have fun and be themselves.")

The first performer is the late Bob Marley. "Marmalade," says Boo Berry. Backstage, a little boy from the Make-a-Wish Foundation cracks his head open, starting a zombie feeding frenzy. Cop Ving Rhames blows the zombies' heads off.

GIGGLE RATING: Five Giggles.

AVAILABILITY: On the DVD *Robot Chicken, Season 1* (2006) and Amazon Prime.

Harvey Birdman, Attorney at Law (2002)
Season 3
Episode 4 (August 14, 2005)
"Birdgirl of Guantanamole"

Hanna-Barbera Studios. Directed by Richard Ferguson-Hull. Written by Erik Richter, Michael Ouweleen. Produced by John Cawley, Khaki Jones, Michael Ouweleen, Erik Richter, Linda Simensky, Matthew Charde, Melissa Warrenburg. Cast: Gary Cole (Harvey Birdman/Judge Hiram Mightor/Stan Freezoid), Stephen Colbert (Myron Reducto/Phil Ken Sebben), John Michael Higgins (Mentok the Mindtaker), Thomas Allen (Peanut), Paget Brewster (Birdgirl), Maurice LaMarche (Fred Flintstone, Morocco Mole), Peter MacNicol (X The Eliminator), Bill Farmer (Secret Squirrel), Steve Landesberg.

Birdman first appeared on *Birdman and the Galaxy Trio* (1967), created by Alex Toth, who also created *Space Ghost* (1966), as a superhero who worked for Inter-Nation Security (INS). He had a teenaged sidekick, Birdboy; an eyepatch-wearing contact from INS, Falcon 7; archenemies Reducto and Mentok; and a nemesis-turned-ally, Birdgirl. His real name was Ray Randall, but when he appeared years later on *Space Ghost Coast to Coast* (1994), he was renamed "Harvey".

In this show, he represented Hanna-Barbera cartoon stars such as Secret Squirrel (qv) (on a charge of flashing), Scooby-Doo (qv), and others in criminal, civil, and copyright law cases against prosecutor Myron Reducto. His assistant is Birdboy, his eyepatch-wearing partner is Phil Ken Sebben (say it out loud) and their firm is Sebben and Sebben. The James Bond-style credits roll over a Tom Jones-type song.

Fez, Morocco. As the call to morning prayers sounds, soldiers run past Snagglepuss (qv) and surround a mole hole. They flip through their Most-Wanted playing cards, past Hanna-Barbera's Mr. T and Haji from *Jonny Quest* (1964) to the Ace of Clubs–their now-prisoner, Morocco Mole.

Back at Sebben and Sebben, it's Take Phil's Daughter to Work Day, and he brings Judy Sebben, who is really Birdgirl, and leaves her with Birdman and Birdboy. When Secret Squirrel shows up, Harvey thinks he has been arrested again for flashing. Secret, who now wears boxers, explains that his friend Morocco has been held as an enemy combatant for two years at Gitmole. Secret says Morocco was crossing the border after vacationing at Sandals in Algeria.

Judy changes into her Birdgirl outfit. Neither Harvey nor Phil recognize her, and Phil hits on his own daughter. Later, Birdman drops her off in front of Phil's home, but he remains clueless.

At Morocco's trial, Birdman shows slides of Morocco being tortured, Abu Ghraib style–kept on a dog leash along with Doggie Daddy, forced to be the mole in Smack a Mole; and stacked in a cartoon pyramid with Apache Chief from *Superfriends* (1973), Snagglepuss, Shazzan, and Haji.

Prosecutor Reducto asks to see Morocco's uniform. Anyone not in a uniform is not protected under the Geneva Convention. As the camera pans across the gallery, we see George W. Bush in a uniform. Reducto points out that Morocco has been supplied with a Koran, a string of prayer beads, and a skull cap. "Which would be great if he were Muslim," says Birdman, but he's not, he's a Shriner, third degree, clown unit, hence the fez. Reducto shows a chart linking Morocco to Saddam Hussein, Jon Stewart, Michael Moore, the Dixie Chicks, Iran, and North Korea. Birdman is unable to cross-examine, so Birdgirl steps in. She produces CIA documents that prove Morocco is linked to those entities because he is a mole, in the espionage sense, placed there by the U.S. government. Judge Mentok dismisses the case immediately, providing Morocco steers clear of Mentok's yard.

Birdgirl is made a member of the Bird-team. The last shot parodies *Batman & Robin* (1997), with Birdman wearing exaggerated rubber nipples like George Clooney in that movie.

GIGGLE RATING: Five Giggles.

AVAILABILITY: On the DVD *Harvey Birdman, Attorney at Law, Volume Two* (2006).

T.U.F.F. Puppy (2010)

Billionfold, Nickelodeon Animation Studios. Directed by Michelle Bryan, Ken Bruce, John McIntyre, Gary Conrad, Kevin Petrilak, Butch Hartman. Written by Butch Hartman (creator), William Schifrin, Ray DeLaurentis, Kevin Sullivan, Joanna Lewis, Kristine Songco, Scott Fellows, Whitney

Wetta, Kevin Arrieta, Samantha Berger. Executive Producer: Butch Hartman. Cast: Grey DeLisle (Kitty Katswell), Daran Norris (Chameleon/Chief/Meerkat), Jerry Trainor (Dudley Puppy), Jeff Bennett (Keswick), Maddie Taylor (Snaptrap/Quacky), Rob Paulsen (Birdbrain).

Butch Hartman pitched this show to Nickelodeon as "*Get Smart* [1965] with a dog." T.U.F.F. (Turbo Undercover Fighting Force) is a super secret spy agency, and like most of those, it fights crime in a large city, in this case, Petropolis, where all the characters are anthropomorphic animals. Dudley Puppy blunders into the headquarters of D.O.O.M. (Diabolical Order of Mayhem) one day and accidentally captures a group of villains, so he is made an agent. He is the "perfect combination of every breed of dog known to man", dogged but not all that bright. Eric Bauza was originally cast in the role, but he was replaced by Jerry Trainor. Dudley's partner is Kitty Katswell, a supremely competent feline agent whose kryptonite is cat toys. Their boss is Chief Herbert Dumbrowski, a gruff but loveable flea. T.U.F.F.'s analogue to Q of the British Secret Service is named Keswick, which is also the name of his species. He is an alien from Keswickia who has gills, a pouch, and webbed feet and lays eggs. His inventions rarely work out as they are supposed to. Agent Jumbo is an elephant who is afraid of mice.

The villains naturally all seek world domination and generally announce their plans in advance to T.U.F.F. The leader of D.O.O.M. is Verminious Snaptrap, a venal but dumb rat whose voice is an imitation of Ed Wynn. His henchmen, all smarter than he is, include Larry, his shrewish brother-in-law; Ollie, a British-accented possum; and Francisco, an alligator. Bird Brain is the smartest of the villains, despite his name and his species, which is a blue-bottomed booby. He is surrounded by stupid henchmen: Owl, Bat, Duck, Fly, Ewe; and Zippy, a hummingbird. Quacky the Duck, who sounds like Bobcat Goldthwait, is originally a children's show host seen on "Kid Stuff" (Season 1, Episode 12A), who later turns bad. The Chameleon, who generally works alone, but not by choice, is a high-tech villain with a molecular transformation suit which allows him to turn into almost anything. He is a real lizard, able to walk on walls. Running gags include the Chameleon trying to put on glasses but nothing works with his bulging eyes. In another, he stops whatever he is doing to zap a bug with his sticky tongue. A third is that when he is pretending to be from another land, he says random words in that country's language. He is played with a Peter Lorre voice by Daran Norris, who has over 400 voice acting credits and at this writing, has been cast as the lead in Jason Priestley's upcoming biopic, *Starring Phil Hartman*. Other villains are mostly one-offs. The title song is a pastiche of 1960s secret agent-show themes. There were generally two segments to each half-hour episode, but not always.

NB: Episodes were shown out of production order. Some episodes were shown on Nickelodeon in Australia, New Zealand, and Latin America before they were shown in the U.S.

Season 1
Episode 1B (October 2, 2010)
"Doom-Mates"

The Chameleon, whom Kitty had put in prison, escapes. "I'm coming for you, Kitty!" Dudley is assigned to protect her. Dudley takes her to the T.U.F.F. mobile, which is really the Chameleon. They escape to Kitty's home in the real T.U.F.F. mobile, where Dudley opens a window and lets in the Chameleon. "Kitty Katswell, feel my wrath!" The Chameleon captures Kitty with his sticky tongue and Dudley punches him, sending the Chameleon and Kitty out the window. When she gets back in, Dudley thinks she is the Chameleon and blasts her. She ejects Dudley from her house, but lets him back in when he pleads for another chance. "Dudley" really is the Chameleon, who catches Kitty with his tongue and takes her to his top-secret hideout. He puts her under a glass dome with a Cat Atomic Bomb which is programmed to blow up nine times, once for each of her lives. "And I get to watch, from two angles!" Dudley tunnels into the Chameleon's lair, which looks like a rock, and inadvertently blows up the Chameleon with his own bomb. "I will now defeat you by turning into a pile of smoldering goo."

Episode 3A (November 6, 2010)
"Snapnapped" (cameo)

Keswick invents a machine that makes doughnuts out of thin air and can capture a baker's dozen of villains. The agents of T.U.F.F. are unimpressed because it doesn't make jelly doughnuts. Feeling underappreciated by T.U.F.F., he is kidnapped by Snaptrap and agrees to work for D.O.O.M. Keswick suggests inviting all the villains to the newly remodeled D.O.O.M. headquarters to see his new Doomsday Machine. This is really a ploy to round up a baker's dozen of villains, including the Chameleon, who has no lines.

Episode 4B (October 9, 2010)
"Puppy Love"

"Free at last," says the newly released Chameleon. "And now to exact my revenge on T.U.F.F. for putting me in prison!" All he needs to do is get into T.U.F.F. headquarters and press the self-destruct button. He learns T.U.F.F. needs a secretary, so he poses as Fifi Oui Oui, French poodle secretary. "I'll need a convincing French accent." "She" does not change her voice at all. "Sacre bleu, croissant, Eiffel Tower. Perfect!" Dudley falls in love with her. "Bon Jovi! I look forward to destroying you–uh, I mean, working with you. Notre Dame, Jacques Cousteau." He takes her on a tour of T.U.F.F., showing her the self-destruct button. Fifi later returns to press the button, but before she can escape, she literally runs into Dudley, who asks her to marry him. Just so she can get away, she says yes, but Dudley spills wine on her while toasting, and shorts out the molecular transformation suit. Revealed as the Chameleon, he tells Dudley and Kitty that he has pressed the self-destruct button. They escape, but the chameleon, who has turned himself into a salad dressing bottle, is left behind when the building blows, sending him right back to prison.

Episode 5 (October 23, 2010)
"Toast of T.U.F.F." (cameo)

Keswick fixes the toaster in the break room and gives it artificial intelligence. Renamed RITA, it turns into a crime-fighting machine. The Chameleon is about to unleash his mealworm gas on Petropolis but RITA turns it on him. "I must resist the urge to eat myself. Well, maybe just a nibble." She turns into a giant robot who tries to control all of Petropolis and Dudley and Kitty must stop her.

"Share-a-Lair"

Agents Rodentsky and Weaselman, respectively of T.U.F.F. and D.O.O.M., get the agencies to destroy each other's headquarters several times. They are forced by Bunny, a leporine female real estate agent to share the only building in town. Bunny turns out to be the Chameleon, who also played Rodentsky and Weaselman. "Since you wouldn't annihilate each other, I'll have to do the job myself." Dudley tricks him into turning into Rodentsky and the Chameleon is stomped by the musphobic T.U.F.F. Agent Jumbo.

Episode 6B (November 27, 2010)
"Internal Affairs"

A double episode. General Warthog has been kidnapped by the Chameleon. "I will use his identity to gain access to the Petropolis Military Base and redirect tonight's missile test to fire at T.U.F.F." Kitty is at the movies with Keswick, so the Chief has to rescue the general with Dudley, who has accidentally shrunk himself to the size of a flea. Both are eaten by the Chameleon. "That's going to go right to my hips." Dudley calls Kitty and Keswick tells him to disconnect the wires from the Chameleon's brain to his transformation suit, which turns him back into the Chameleon, but he escapes. Dudley and the Chief jump out of the Chameleon's nose and tie him up with his own tongue.

Episode 7B (November 27, 2010)
"The Doomies" (cameo)

Dudley and Kitty go undercover as villains Dr. Rabies and Madame Catastrophe at an awards ceremony for evildoers. Bird Brain is captured by T.U.F.F. before he can end all life on the planet. The Chameleon plans to rob all the money from the citizens of Petropolis, one quarter at a time, by posing as a parking meter. "This may take awhile." He, too, is arrested by T.U.F.F. The last nominee is Snaptrap, who has mounted his Bad Hair Ray on top of the theater to give everyone in Petropolis a rat's nest of unmanageable hair. Dudley and Kitty divert the ray so it gives bad hair to the villains, who are all captured.

Episode 8B (February 12, 2011)
"Snap Dad" (cameo)

Dudley sees Snaptrap in the house of his mom, Peg, and thinks he's attacking her, but they're on a date. Snaptrap says he's gone straight and the Chief hires him at T.U.F.F. Snaptrap goes back to D.O.O.M and breaks up with Peg, who has a new boyfriend–the Chameleon. "Can I get a glass of milk to wash down these crickets?"

Episode 9B (February 26, 2011)
"The Wrong Stuff" (cameo)

Kitty's former partner, Jack Rabbit, returns to T.U.F.F. on a visit and catches the Chameleon masquerading as a vending machine. "Bravo, Jack Rabbit! You got me again! Since I know resisting you is futile, I will now escort myself to prison, the big house, slammer, hoosegow." However, Jack Rabbit has turned evil and it's up to Dudley and Kitty to stop him.

Episode 11B (April 9, 2011)
"Mind Trap" (cameo)

Keswick's new high-tech device allows anyone who wears it to read minds. The Chief thinks it's bad for morale and throws it in the dumpster, where Snaptrap finds it and uses it to get the combinations to people's safes and rob them. It also allows him to know when Dudley and Kitty are coming so he can evade them. Meanwhile, the Chief is named one of *Fleaple* magazine's Ten Most Eligible Hostages, so Snaptrap kidnaps him for ransom, but he is rescued by T.U.F.F. Keswick invents goggles that allow the wearer to see others' underpants. Kitty throws them in the dumpster where they are found by the Chameleon, who tries them on. "Why do I even bother?"

Episode 12B (August 13, 2011)
"Super Duper Crime Busters" (cameo)

The agents of T.U.F.F. are on a reality show, *Super Duper Crime Busters*. On a monitor, Dudley sees the Chameleon in a grocery store, so he and Kitty get over there to arrest him. "What is it with you people? I'm just doing my grocery shopping." Dudley charges him with having fifteen items in the express lane, but the Chameleon points out a dozen eggs counts as one item, and a judge upholds him.

Episode 13 (March 31, 2012)
"Mission: Really Big Mission"

A double episode. Dudley loses a laser, and Snaptrap plans to recover the three pieces so he can heat up the corn belt and pop all the corn. He gets the Chameleon to help. "I also do celebrity impersonations at the Chuckle Hut every other Friday night." He turns into the Easter Bunny, Toucan Sam; and Po, the Kung Fu Panda. Snaptrap has him turn into everyday household objects. Snaptrap recovers the first two pieces, but Kitty gets the last one. However, the Chameleon pretends to be Keswick and takes it from her. Dudley foils Snaptrap's plan and Snaptrap and the Chameleon have to share a cell.

Episode 14 (August 13, 2011)
"Frisky Business" (cameo)

Peg goes on a trip and leaves Dudley home alone for the first time. He parodies *Risky Business* (1983). The Chameleon turns himself into a winning lottery ticket, but the Pat Buttram-like grocery clerk points out there's no one to claim the prize. "I didn't think this through," says the Chameleon, who steals a hot dog and some sunglasses, which, of course, don't fit. Dudley and Kitty arrive and the Chameleon turns himself into a rocket and blasts through the roof, a chunk of which hits Kitty. Dudley admits he's a mess without his mom.

"Hot Dog"

A sudden heat wave hits Petropolis. The source is the Chameleon's house. Kitty calls him and gets his answering machine, which is really he. "I'm using a giant magnifying glass to superheat Petropolis to 151 degrees!" Everyone will die except cold-blooded lizards. Kitty sets off to catch him, but he grabs her blaster with his tongue, knocks her out, and ties her to a spit. "And now, Kitty Katswell, you will cook along with the rest of Petropolis, only faster and more evenly." Before he can light the grill, Dudley arrives and stops him and reverses the heat wave. "There goes my heating bill," says the Chameleon.

Episode 16A (November 26, 2011)
"Doom and Gloom"

Kitty says that criminals who tell T.U.F.F. where and when they will commit their crimes are boobs. From a cell, the Chameleon says, "Hellooo? These boobs have ears." Snaptrap's gang leaves him and Larry forms G.L.O.O.M., which doesn't tell T.U.F.F. its plans. T.U.F.F. gets Snaptrap to rat out Larry (get it?)

Episode 18 (October 10, 2011)
"The Curse of King Mutt"

Dudley and Kitty spend a night at the museum to protect its King Mutt Exhibit. Dudley buries King Mutt's bone, which, according to the curse, will cause King Mutt to arise from his grave and destroy the thief. Meanwhile, Bird Brain attempts to enter through the museum through the air vent to steal the bone, and he encounters Snaptrap, who just likes museum air vents. They fall out and land on top of an Elizabethan bench, which is really the Chameleon. "We could even form a special villains' club. We will plot hideous crimes and talk about our feelings over International Coffees." Bird Brain nixes that idea, and they go to get the bone.

The Chameleon turns into a windup mouse and distracts Kitty. "That should keep her busy for awhile." Snaptrap inadvertently wraps himself in toilet paper and decides he will pose as the mummy to scare Dudley into revealing the whereabouts of the bone, but Dudley can't remember. Bird Brain does a turn as the mummy, but he fails, too. The Chameleon says, "Like I always say, if you want to scare someone by pretending to be an ancient mystical being, you have to do it yourself," and he morphs into the mummy. He succeeds in scaring Snaptrap, who throws water on him and shorts out his suit, so he has to wrap himself in toilet paper, too. Dudley finds the bone, and the Chameleon runs off with it. Dudley and Kitty dress up as the mummy and scare the crooks into giving back the bone and capture them. "I hope we get the same cell. Then, we really get to bond!"

"Bored of Education"

It is Career Day at the school, and Kitty has bored the class and teacher to sleep. The last guest is the Chameleon, "Petropolis' most engaging and most whimsical supervillain." He tells the kids how great it is to be a supervillain and gives each kid a transformation suit. They rob the Party Store and the Pointless Gadgets Store. Dudley and Kitty burst in on the Chameleon's birthday party and the kids tie them up. The kids open the Chameleon's presents and he changes them into bugs. "You were my friends until you touched my stuff. Now you're my supper." Dudley and Kitty escape and get the Chameleon and change the kids back.

Episode 19B (September 17, 2011)
"Lucky Duck" (cameo)

"It is I, the Chameleon! Whoops, I said that already. Oh, let me check my cards. Pumpkin latte, did that. Let me just cut to the chase. I am going to blow up Pluto! A-haha-haha! The laugh was an ad-lib." The T.U.F.F. agents are more interested in watching *The Quacky the Duck Show* and change the channel on the monitor. Quacky tricks Dudley into kidnapping the network president who has canceled his show. Kitty figures it out and captures Quacky and his accomplice, the Sharing Moose. The next day, the Chameleon appears on the video monitor and says, "It is I, the Chameleon! Since my Pluto plan failed to impress, I'm now going to blow up the Sun! Ten, nine–" Dudley changes the channel to *The Quacky the Duck Show*, live from prison.

Episode 20 (October 10, 2011)
"Guard Dog"

The Chameleon says he saw Snaptrap blow up a combination gourmet cheese and camera shop called "Say Cheese", so Dudley and Kitty are escorting him to Petsburg to testify. "Oh, Agent Puppy, I'm so excited about our train ride together! We'll sing songs and play travel games. People don't normally want to hang out with me. Probably because I'm not that outgoing and I usually try to poison them." He cuffs himself to Dudley and jumps into his arms. "I feel safer already. We'll have to use the restroom together, so I hope you don't have a bashful bladder." While Kitty is distracted by the

Cat Car, filled with scratching posts, fish, caged birds, catnip, toy mice, and a laser pointer, Snaptrap boards the train and blasts Dudley's gun from his hand. Snaptrap is about to blast the Chameleon, who turns into a bigger blaster and jumps into Dudley's hands. Dudley blasts Snaptrap. "We are quite the team!" says the Chameleon. Snaptrap has an alibi for the day that Say Cheese was blown up, and the Chameleon confesses that he did it and framed Snaptrap. The Chief tells Dudley and Kitty to escort everyone back to Petropolis. Kitty takes this shift. "Another train ride with a special friend! Agent Katswell, you can help me clean the bugs out of my headgear!"

FUN FACT: When the Chameleon gets ready for bed, he looks like the Beautiful Girl of the Month from *Mad* magazine.

"Dog Save the Queen"
Dudley and Kitty are sent to London to help B.U.F.F. (British Undercover Fighting Force) capture the Chameleon, who is trying to steal the Crown Jewels, which the Queen is wearing to the Royal Ball. "With my ability to disguise myself as anything, you'll never find me!" Dudley spits out his hot tea onto a clock, shorting out the Chameleon's molecular transformation suit and exposing him. "Pip pip, cheerio, London broil!" He turns into a double decker bus and flees.

The Chameleon gets into the palace and Dudley follows. The Chameleon turns himself into Kitty, who is dressed as a flying Mary Poppins. "Nine lives, ten claws, I like tuna." He knocks out Dudley.

At the ball, the Chameleon turns into Lord of the Flies. "Tallyho, English muffin, fish and chips!" He can't remove the crown from the Queen's head, so he takes her. He turns into a British taxi and spirits her away. Kitty and Dudley fly after them by bumbershoot. Dudley opens a drawbridge and foils the Chameleon's escape. They rescue the Queen and the Chameleon ends up in a hot tea factory. "Foiled again by my archenemy, the hot beverage!"

Episode 21 (December 10, 2011)
"A Doomed Christmas"

A double episode. Snaptrap, Bird Brain, and the Chameleon are in Petropolis Prison on Christmas Eve. Snaptrap doesn't know what Christmas is all about. "Christmas is when a guy named Santa Claus delivers presents all over the world on a sleigh pulled by flying reindeer," the Chameleon explains. "Christmas is hard for all of us bad guys. Every year, I listen to carolers pass by my door. I make them spiced apple cider, but they never drink it! Which is lucky for them because I use poison instead of apples." Snaptrap suggests they shake Santa down for all the presents they never received, and the three break out of prison. The Chameleon turns into Santa Claus and carries Bird Brain and Snaptrap in his bag into T.U.F.F. headquarters, where Dudley takes them to the North Pole transport tube. "I'll be on my way now! Mistletoe, sugar plums, candy cane!" They take over Santa's workshop and T.U.F.F. has to save Christmas. The Chameleon turns into a flying sleigh and Bird Brain and Snaptrap try to escape on him but Dudley catches them.

Episode 23A (May 6, 2012)
"Dudley Do-Wrong"

Dudley answers the phone at T.U.F.F. "It is I, the Chameleon! And I am about to do something incredibly diabolical!" Bird Brain calls and Dudley puts the Chameleon on hold. When Dudley puts Bird Brain on hold and picks up the Chameleon's call, the Chameleon is singing "Camptown Races". "I am going to transform into Petropolis' beloved mayor, Teddy Bear! I will rule the city with an iron fist! Actually, more of a stuffed, fuzzy fist."

Dudley and Kitty go to the mayor's office and Dudley beats him up. Meanwhile, Kitty sees the Chameleon outside parking his car. The real mayor closes down T.U.F.F. and has Dudley and Kitty thrown out. The Chameleon turns into the mayor and locks the real mayor in his own cabinet. "It is I, Teddy Bear, your beloved mayor! Super-cuddly, as far as you know," says the Chameleon on television. "Now that those reckless T.U.F.F. agents are gone, let's celebrate with a parade in my honor! Yay, me!" Dudley reveals to the Chameleon that T.U.F.F. is still working together so the Chameleon calls T.U.F.F. temporary headquarters in Dudley's bedroom. "It is I, Miss Petropolis, the city's beloved beauty queen. The Chameleon has taken me hostage and is impersonating me at the Miss Northern Hemisphere Beauty Pageant!"

Dudley and Kitty go to the pageant, where Dudley beats up the real Miss Petropolis before Kitty sees the Chameleon in the back of the house. The Chameleon turns into the mayor and declares Dudley and Kitty Public Enemies #1 and #2. Dudley giggles at #2. The Chameleon promises to tear down T.U.F.F. headquarters and throw all agents in jail forever. Dudley and Kitty escape. The Chameleon puts the real mayor in T.U.F.F. headquarters before the crane arrives with the wrecking ball. The agents of T.U.F.F. arrive to watch the demolition and Dudley remembers he left his "World's Greatest Secret Agent" mug inside. He runs in to get it and sees the real mayor and saves him, exposing the Chameleon. Bird Brain remains on hold.

Episode 24A (May 5, 2012)
"Top Dog" (cameo)
Dudley's new flea collar poisons the Chief, and Dudley is named temporary chief. Fortunately, Snaptrap, Bird Brain, and the Chameleon are at an evil softball tournament in Petsburg. In Petropolis, Meerkat, who sounds like Paul Lynde, calls to order the first meeting of the Fiendish League of Potential Perpetrators, or F.L.O.P.P., including Escape Goat, who sounds like Pee Wee Herman.

Episode 25 (April 21, 2012)
"Monkey Business"
The Chameleon is mentioned in a shot of Bird Brain's Facebeak page.

"Diary of a Mad Cat"
Dudley and Kitty lose on the game show *Do You Know Your Partner?* The team of Snaptrap and Larry tie with the team of the Chief and Keswick to win a trip to Maui. Trying to find out more about his partner by reading her diary, Dudley accidentally emails it to everyone in Petropolis. The villains use the information in it against her. The Chameleon has transformed himself into a bug hotel, the Camil-E-Inn, and is planning on eating all the

guests. "Yoo-hoo, bugs! I have a vacancy in my stomach! You'll check in, but you'll never check out! Garden view, bellhop, Hotel California." Dudley and Kitty go over there, but the Chameleon turns into Kitty's mother and tortures her with personal details. Kitty leaves, angrily running over Dudley. "Time to open a new hotel by the beach! I'm craving sand flies!" Snaptrap tells Kitty that Bird Brain and the Chameleon got the security codes for the Petropolis military base from her diary and are stealing a weather cannon to make it snow on Maui. Kitty uses the diaries of Bird Brain and the Chameleon against them.

Episode 26A (May 12, 2012)
"Lie Like a Dog"

A double episode. To avoid Spackle and Grout Day at T.U.F.F., Dudley pretends he has an appointment with his dentist, Dr. Fineberg, but instead goes to a ballgame in a rainbow wig and sunglasses. There, he foils D.O.O.M.'s plan to steal wallets, but he can't take credit for it. The next day is Eat Your Vegetables and Clean Behind Your Ears Day, so he fakes another appointment with Dr. Fineberg and goes to the beach in sunglasses and rainbow wig. A beach umbrella is really the Chameleon. "Now for my evil plan. I will turn into a shark, scare everyone away, and steal their stuff! Wait, I can't get my transformation suit wet, so I will have to be a sand shark! Haha! It's clever." He can't breathe on land, so Dudley throws him into the water. The suit shorts out and the burned Chameleon begins to drown, so Dudley rescues him. He is again named a hero, but unable to claim the rewards. The next day is Advanced Calculus day, so Dudley pretends to see Dr. Fineberg again and goes to play cards with dogs. He finally gets caught in his lies, and he actually has to go to the dentist.

Season 2
Episode 2B (May 13, 2012)
"Dog Tired" (cameo)

Snaptrap wants to be Petropolis' supervillain, but every time he tries to commit a crime, Dudley stops him. He watches the Evil Shopping Channel. "It is I, the Chameleon, international supervillain and underpaid cable TV schlock peddler. Our featured evil item today is a nifty gadget called the

Dream Destroyer," which allows one to mess with one's enemy's dreams and render him incapacitated. Snaptrap gives Dudley dreams so good he doesn't want to wake up and Kitty, Keswick, and the Chief have to stop Snaptrap.

Episode 3B (August 6, 2013)
"Time Waits for No Mutt"

Dudley reappears after twelve months while Snaptrap, Bird Brain, and the Chameleon has been on a year-long rampage. The Chief tells Dudley that if he is late again, he's fired. The Chameleon, disguised as a fly, overhears this, and he plots with Snaptrap and Bird Brain to make Dudley tardy the next day. They break into his house to steal his fifty alarm clocks. His watch alarm wakes him up, however, and he goes to work. The Chameleon tries to distract him by shape-shifting. "I am a delicious meatball. Mussolini, cappuccino, Italian Stallion." Dudley runs him over, breaking his molecular transformation suit. They lure Dudley to a fake T.U.F.F. headquarters and launch him into space. Dudley doesn't recognize the walking meatball. "You stooge, I am the Chameleon, and you are late for work." He points to a clock that says, "7:59 AM". Dudley captures all the bad guys and makes it to work on time in the T.U.F.F. Mobile.

Episode 5A (October 13, 2012)
"Bark to the Future"

Mayor Teddy Bear awards a lifetime supply of pizza to the Citizen of the Year, a young chipmunk who helped elderly squirrels store nuts for the winter. Dudley and Kitty deliver the pizza by train, but the Chameleon steals it. "Lifetime supply of pizza and I made a kid cry!" he giggles insanely. "Talk about win-win! Now all I need to do is steal a lifetime supply of paper plates!" Meanwhile, Keswick has bought a lifetime supply of paper plates for T.U.F.F. The Chameleon goes there and transforms into a trash can. The Chief orders Keswick to be locked in a vault and not be let out until he develops a device that can see the Chameleon no matter what he turns into. Dudley is tasked with locking Keswick in and coming up with a code. Kitty tells him he can't use "bacon". He slams Keswick's hand in the door and won't let him out.

To get Dudley to reveal the code, the Chameleon breaks into Dudley's house and transforms himself into Dudley from the future. "Flying cars, laser beams, Soylent Green." Dudley can only remember the code is not bacon, and the Chameleon thinks that is the actual code, which gets him literally kicked out of T.U.F.F. headquarters. Keswick finally manages to modify his own glasses into a Chameleon-seeing device and he is let out of the vault. Dudley puts them on and sees that Future Dudley is really the Chameleon. Kitty blasts him, and he reveals the whereabouts of the pizza train.

Episode 7B (October 27, 2013)
"Agent of the Year"

Dudley and Kitty compete to see who can make the most arrests in 24 hours and win the trophy for Agent of the Year. They arrest everyone in Petropolis and are tied so they arrest each other. The Chameleon returns from vacation. "Go over the falls in a barrel, they said. It'll be fun, they said. You won't break your neck in two places, they said." Since T.U.F.F. is in jail, he decides to blow up Petropolis Falls and flood the city. Dudley and Kitty break out and disarm the bomb. Dudley sends the Chameleon over the falls in a barrel. Dudley and Kitty share the trophy but Dudley tricks her into giving it away. Snaptrap autographs the Chameleon's full body cast.

Episode 10 (October 27, 2012)
"Happy Howl-O-Ween"

A double episode. On Halloween, Snaptrap announces that he, Bird Brain, and the Chameleon are stealing all the candy. "Hijacking Halloween is my most diabolical plan ever," says the Chameleon, who has turned himself into Snaptrap. The real Snaptrap activates the candy magnet. "There's nothing like ruining a beloved children's holiday with your buddies." If Dudley and Kitty don't find the candy by sundown, the mayor will cancel Halloween. Meanwhile, the Chameleon has another plan. "We have the city's remaining toilet paper. You can only get it back if I get—wait for it—one million friends on Facebeak!" Snaptrap demands ten million dollars or he'll destroy all the TP and candy. Dudley and Kitty capture the bad guys and disarm the bomb. The Chief accidentally friends the Chameleon on Facebeak. "Happy Halloween!"

Episode 11 (February 14, 2014)
"'Til Doom Do Us Part"

A double episode. "It is I, the Chameleon. Could someone let me in? There's no doorknob on your new evil door." Snaptrap lets him into the newly re-modeled D.O.O.M. headquarters with the Evil Door Opener. Snaptrap's plan is to steal wedding presents. "I love the plan! As always, I am honored to bask in the shadow of your genius." To catch Snaptrap, The Chief stages a wedding with Dudley and Kitty as the bride and groom, although they are fighting like, well, cats and dogs. "Snaptrap, check out Agent Puppy and Katswell's wedding registry. They're asking for an invisibility cloak, laser scopes, an antimatter cannon–"

Dudley and Kitty make up when the ceremony approaches. D.O.O.M. and the Chameleon hide inside the cake until they know it's not a trap. When they kiss, the bad guys make their move. Kitty captures D.O.O.M. with her garter. The Chameleon turns into a car and tries to escape, but Dudley throws the bouquet and the Chameleon tries to catch it. "Yay, I'm getting fake-married next!" He runs into a wall.

Episode 15 (June 6, 2013)
"Subliminal Criminal"

Dudley is arresting innocent people, so he takes Keswick's serum, Crime-Etapp to understand the criminal mind. "Hello, it is I, the Chameleon! I'm going to steal all the Hawaiian-style potato chips I can steal from the Mini-Mart!" He has transformed into a little old lady, but Dudley is able to recognize and expose him because he now understands how the criminal mind works. However, a side effect of the serum is sleep crime solving.

"Acting T.U.F.F."

Dudley's movie star hero, Woodchuck Norris, comes to T.U.F.F. to research a role. "It is I, the Chameleon, calling with my latest diabolical plan! Is that Woodchuck Norris, star of *The Chuckinator*? Sometimes, I turn into you to get a good table at restaurants. Anyhoo, I'm going to blow up the Petropolis Day Parade because it goes down my street and the spectators are ruining my lawn. Also, the clowns in the tiny car are freaking me out."

Dudley succeeds in stopping the Chameleon, but he blows up the parade himself, so Kitty technically can't arrest the Chameleon. "Get off my lawn!" he says. Woodchuck tells Dudley to stay away from him and leaves with Kitty. Snaptrap kidnaps him and Kitty gets Dudley to help rescue him.

Episode 16B (April 26, 2014)
"Tattle Tale" (cameo)

To get Dudley into trouble, F.L.O.P.P. sends Wanna Bee to spy on him so they can tattle. They catch him napping, making snow from lunch meat, and letting the Chameleon out of jail to play board games. "I won fifteen dollars at the beauty pageant!" Dudley is sentenced to T.U.F.F. detention, where he learns geometry. When F.L.O.P.P. sets off an Earthquake Generator, Dudley uses geometry to destroy it.

Episode 17A (April 19, 2014)
"Crime Takes a Holiday"

Dudley and Kitty are making deposits at the bank when the Chameleon arrives. "Now to commit my most ingenious crime to date!" He giggles insanely as he transforms. "It is I, the Easter Bunny! Hippety hop! Chocolate eggs, Easter Island!" He tries to rob the bank, and Kitty arrests him, under protest from Dudley. Kitty puts him in jail with Snaptrap and Bird Brain, who let him into their crime club, but Dudley lets him escape. "Jelly beans, Easter egg, Carrot Top!" Bird Brain and Snaptrap realize if they dress up like holiday icons, Dudley will set them free, too. Bird Brain puts on Santa drag and Dudley lets him out. Snaptrap uses found items to costume himself as Toilet Breath Terry, who brings air freshener and TP on Toilet Day, so he, too, receives a Get Out of Jail Free card. The Chameleon and Bird Brain go on a crime spree as the Easter Bunny and Santa and they decide to steal the money from Dudley's sock drawer. Dudley spills refreshments on the Chameleon and his molecular transformation suit shorts out, exposing him. Dudley arrests him and Bird Brain.

Episode 19B (August 7, 2013)
"Legal Beagle"

Dudley's ignorance of the law causes a riot, so Keswick develops a Law Zenge for him to take and he absorbs the entire Petropolis *Book of Law*, including all the archaic, silly statutes written by town father Daniel Looney. After busting the Chief, Keswick, and Kitty for minor offenses (their jail time is one minute), he arrests Bird Brain for eating Chinese food within thirty feet of a manhole and the Chameleon for turning into a manhole within thirty feet of someone eating Chinese food. "Serves me right. Why would somebody who can transform into anything in the world turn into a manhole cover? I'm pathetic."

Bird Brain reads *The Book of Law* and learns it is legal for a bird, a rat, and a chameleon to break out of jail as long as they call in and tell T.U.F.F. their diabolical plan. The plan is to blow up T.U.F.F. headquarters, which is legal. Only a direct descendant of Daniel Looney can undo a law. Fortunately, his crazy great-great-grandson lives under the T.U.F.F. stairwell. He signs the order overturning the law with a French fry and Dudley tricks the bad guys into eating Chinese food over a manhole and arrests them.

Episode 22 (May 3, 2014)
"Dancin' Machine"

Kitty wants to be Dudley's partner in the *Dance, Dance, Blast the Ants* video game competition at Petropolis Mall, so she takes dance lessons from Snaptrap. Meanwhile, the Chameleon is in jail for impersonating a game at the Petropolis Arcade. He took quarters, but didn't give out any prize tickets. "I would have gotten away with it, too, if it wasn't for that teenage assistant manager, Toby Finkel. He thinks he's so cool with his so-called authority to ban me from the arcade forever." The Chameleon successfully auditions to be Dudley's dance partner. To get the Chameleon out of jail, Dudley dresses him up in drag. "Call me 'Denise.' She's my favorite character from *The Young and the Feckless*. She's the scrappy ingenue who doesn't always make the best choices, but you just can't help rooting for her." He promises to return to jail after the competition. They are declared the winners by Toby Finkel, and the Chameleon takes off his wig and reveals himself. He locks Dudley in a closet and rigs a bomb to the machine, set to go off if Toby misses a step in the game. Toby points out this is a two-person game. "Oh, right, I didn't think this through." He joins Toby. Dudley gets out and replaces Toby, who is exhausted. Meanwhile, Kitty has graduated from dance school, and she replaces the fatigued Chameleon and later dances both parts while Dudley disarms the bomb.

"The Good, the Bad, and the Quacky"

Quacky hosts *Good Vs. Evil*, which he assures the audience is a legitimate TV show and not a plot to have his enemies destroy each other on live TV. It's Dudley, Kitty, Keswick, and the Chief against Bird Brain, Snaptrap, and the Chameleon. "I am thrilled to be a part of Team Evil." Quacky's attempts to get Good and Evil to destroy each other blow up in his face, sometimes literally. T.U.F.F. and the bad guys have to work together to get through the final challenge, The Gauntlet.

Episode 23A (August 9, 2013)
"Sheep Dog"

The Chameleon is disguising himself as a ram, Ricardo Muttonban, and conning old lady sheep out of their money. "This is my best plan yet! Soon, I'll have more money than I currently have! Plus, the old lady sheep seem to really enjoy the Latin charms of Ricardo Muttonban. Right up until I take all of their money, that is! With this disguise, it's so easy to pull the wool over their eyes!" He giggles insanely. "That was clever and it rhymed! Clever wordplay is the hallmark of comedy!" Dudley goes undercover as Donna, a sheep, and holds a lavish cotillion on the T.U.F.F. yacht to draw out the Chameleon.

"Allow me to introduce myself, Donna. I'm Ricardo Muttonban. Guacamole, Cinco de Mayo, Ricky Martin!" The Chameleon steals Donna's money dress, but Dudley has placed a bomb in it, which blows up. Dudley lets the old lady sheep deal with the Chameleon.

Episode 25A (May 17, 2014)
"Match Me If You Can"

Efficiency is declining at T.U.F.F., so all the agents have to take compatibility tests to match them up with their best partner. Dudley is paired with the Chief and Kitty is paired with Keswick. The Chameleon is holding up a bull in a china shop by transforming himself into a dishwasher. "Load it up." Dudley and the Chief try to stop the robbery with disastrous results. "That was pathetic, and that's coming from a supervillain who's stealing plates!" Team Katswick similarly fails to prevent Bird Brain from kidnapping the Petropolis Philharmonic. Snaptrap steals "pisketti" from Petropolis Pasta Factory and kidnaps Dudley, the Chief, and Team Katswick. It turns out the three crimes are related, per the Chameleon, to, "Our bi-monthly villains' dinner at D.O.O.M.! Normally, we do pizza and paper plates but we decided to class things up." Kitty and Dudley work together to escape and the four agents crash the dinner and catch the bad guys.

Season 3
Episode 1 (March 14, 2015)
"Barking Bad"

Dudley poses as a pizza delivery guy to get Bird Brain's De-Good-Ifyer, which sucks the good out of people. "So we lost the De-Good-Ifyer and fell ten stories," says the Chameleon. "Let's not let that minor setback ruin the rest of our day." The De-Good-Ifyer slips out of Dudley's hands and sucks the good out of Kitty, Keswick, and the Chief, who terrorize Petropolis as the Heinous Association of Villains, Outlaws, and Criminals (H.A.V.O.C.) Dudley tries to stop them, and enlists the help of Bird Brain, Snaptrap, and the Chameleon. He pretends to be bad to get into H.A.V.O.C. Keswick plans to turn the De-Good-Ifyer on Petropolis. Dudley turns the De-Good-Ifyer on them and Re-Good-Inates them.

"Smarty Pants"

Keswick gets Dudley to wear Smarty Pants, which turn Dudley into a genius. Snaptrap, Bird Brain, and the Chameleon are selling weapons to children hidden in stuffed animals called "Stickemuppets." Dudley catches them with his invention, The Indestructi-Bubble. "That's un-bubble-lievable," says the Chameleon. "Only a genius could invent something like that."

Incarcerated, the Chameleon receives a package. "I used my one phone call to order toys to play with while we're in prison," he says. "Check it out! They're called 'Meanie Babies'. They're full of joy, love, and two pounds of pressurized military-grade explosives." Bird Brain points out this is a ripoff of Stickemuppets. They break out of jail, steal the Indestructi-Bubble, and kidnap Kitty, Keswick, and the Chief and tie them to a bomb while they go to destroy the toy factory. Smart Dudley refuses to rescue them because they are highly trained agents who can take care of themselves and he has to stop the bad guys. Kitty gets the old Dudley back by asking him an imponderable question and shorting out his Smarty pants. He rescues them, and destroys the Indestructi-Bubble with the Indestructi-Bubble Burster.

Episode 8 (July 26, 2014)
"T.U.F.F. Break Up"

A two-part episode (as opposed to a double episode). The government cuts T.U.F.F.'s funding and takes all their stuff. Keswick gets intel that Bird Brain, Snaptrap, and the Chameleon are going to do something evil at the Petropolis Pumas' football game, so Dudley and Kitty go over there. Bird Brain plans to replace all the mustard at the stadium with mind-controlling condiment. Snaptrap and the Chameleon are dressed as cheerleaders. "Rah-rah, pom poms, dating the quarterback!" Dudley and Kitty stop them before it's too late, but they incur the wrath of Petropolis by messing up the football game and they gather at T.U.F.F. with pitchforks. Feeling unappreciated, Dudley, Kitty, and Keswick quit and get new jobs. A new supervillain, the Overbear, kidnaps the Chief and demands Bird Brain's mayonnaise as ransom. T.U.F.F. gets the mayonnaise and rescues the Chief. The mayonnaise is actually a mind-controlling condiment called Obey-O-Nnaise. Overbear dumps it into the Petropolis Egg Salad Reserve, just ahead of the Petropolis Egg Salad Festival. Everyone in Petropolis will eat it and become Overbear's slave. Dudley and Kitty foil his plot and win back the love of the people of Petropolis and their government funding.

Season Unknown
Episode Unknown (July 20, 2013)
"Mission Gone Bad"

Unseen by this author. It is unknown what part the Chameleon plays in this episode, if any.

GIGGLE RATING: Five Giggles. One hopes that Daran Norris will continue to favor us with his Peter Lorre.

AVAILABILITY: On DVD: *T.U.F.F. Puppy, Season One* (2014)
T.U.F.F. Puppy, Season Two (2015)

The Cleveland Show (2009)
Season 2
Episode 19 (April 10, 2011)
"Ship'rect"

Persons Unknown Productions, Happy Jack Productions, Fuzzy Door Productions, 20th Century Fox Television. Directed by Ken Wong. Created by Seth MacFarlane & Richard Appel & Mike Henry. Written by Teri Schaffer, Raynelle Swilling. Produced by Kara Vallow, Brandi Young, Courtney Lilly, Aaron Miller, Seth MacFarlane, Mike Henry, Richard Appel, Kirker Butler. Cast: Mike Henry (Cleveland Brown/Rallo Tubbs/Additional Voices), Sanaa Lathan (Donna Tubbs), Kevin Michael Richardson (Cleveland Brown Jr./Lester Krinklesac/Additional Voices), Reagan Gomez-Preston (Roberta Tubbs), Seth MacFarlane (Tim the Bear), Richard Appel (Husband), Aseem Batra (Kendra Krinklesac), Daryl Hall (Cleveland's Angel), Ed Hochuli (Minister), John Oates (Cleveland's Devil), Jason Sudeikis (Holt Richter/Terry Kimple/Kid/Larry), Alec Sulkin (Angus), Al Thompson (Walt), John Viener (Gordy).

Originally one of the drinking buddies of Peter Griffin, along with Glen Quagmire and Joe Swanson, on the sitcom *Family Guy* (1999), Cleveland Brown got his own spinoff as an African-American man who moves back to his hometown of Stoolbend, Virginia with his blended family. He has many wacky friends and neighbors, including a talking bear who wears a shirt and tie. After four seasons, the show was canceled and the Browns went back to Quahog, Rhode Island and rejoined the cast of *Family Guy* (1999).

Cleveland's hangout, The Broken Stool, is holding the Stoolbobber Regatta (Boat Race) for a year's worth of free beer. Cleveland is captain of the team with his buddies, but when he meets his idol, NFL star Barry Shadwell, he defects to Shadwell's team. One of the other teams is the Really Rottens from *Scooby's All-Star Laff-A-Lympics* (1977) (qv), including Mr. Creepley, who has no lines.

GIGGLE RATING: Looks, Five Giggles; Voice N/A.

AVAILABILITY: On the DVD *The Cleveland Show, Season Two* (2011).

Mighty Magiswords (2016)

Directed by Ken Mitchroney. Writing Credits: Kyle A. Carrozza (creator), Richard Pursel, The Great Luke Ski, Zoe Moss, Drew Green, John Berry, Clay Lindvall, Krystal Ureta, Mr. Lawrence, Gabe del Valle, Mike Pelensky. Executive Producers: Kyle A. Carrozza, Tramm Wigzell. Cast: Kyle A. Carrozza (Prohyas Warrior/Announcer/Slug Burger Clerk/Grup the Dragon/Tree-J/Nohyas/Piggy/Zombie Pumpkin Magisword/Robopiggeh/Oinkus Oinkus Magisword/Attractive Voice Magisword/Snowmanpire/Old Man Oldman/Underground Handbeast/Goomer/Franklo/Attacktus), Eric Bauza (Hoppus/Phil/King Rexxtopher), Grey DeLisle (Vambre Warrior/Zange/Mysterious Hooded Woman), Judy Tenuta (Queen Porcina), Mr. Lawrence, Luke Sienkowski, "Weird Al" Yankovic, Hal Lublin, Townsend Coleman.

Created as a series of web shorts, this American Flash animated fantasy-comedy television series was Cartoon Network Video's first online original program in 2015 (qv), and it was picked up as a full-length show and premiered September 29, 2016 on Cartoon Network (CN). It was tied in to a video game, *MagiMobile* (2016) (qv). The second season premiered on April 30, 2018 along with a new mobile game, *Surely You Quest* (2018) (qv). The first twenty episodes were shown on CN, and the remaining ones were released on the Cartoon Network App, with no indication of when they will be shown on CN, if ever. The series has been canceled.

The protagonists, goofy Prohyas and his supremely competent, British-accented sister, Vambre, are Adventure Academy graduates and Warriors for Hire who go around the world collecting Magiswords, magic swords which they use to fight evildoers. These shrink for easy transportation and storage. Some swords are sentient beings, like Zombie Pumpkin Magisword, known by Prohyas as "ZP" and by Vambre as "Zed P". One of his powers is to eat smaller pumpkins and spit the "seeds of the undead" at plants. First introduced in the web short "Zombie Reasonable" (2015), set in Transylberia, he is a nervous stammerer who rarely speaks in full sentences. According to creator and voice actor Carrozza, "What I had to do to make it cute and appealing is throw Peter Lorre into it." Other voice actors making guest appearances include frequent Peter Lorre impersonators Maurice LaMarche, Rob Paulsen, Billy West, Jess Harnell, Gilbert Gottfried, and Jim Cummings.

Supporting characters include Omnibus, a wizard; Grup, an overweight dragon; The Mysterious Hooded Woman (MHW); Füd, a rare food enthusiast; Dolphin Magisword, another sentient being; Witchy Simone; Ralphio, the magisword dealer; Hoppus, a rabbit; Cattus, a fellow Adventure Academy alumnus; Professor Cyrus, the teacher of the Warriors for Hire; Old Man Oldman, a villain; and Robopiggeh, a swinish automaton.

Season 1
Episode 1 (September 5, 2016)
"Mushroom Menace"

ZP appears in the title card. Prohyas, Vambre, and ZP are back in Transylberia. "It's good to see old friends," he says. An ice posy knocks Vambre down and ZP neutralizes it with seeds of the undead. He is rewarded with various pumpkin seeds, which make him different shapes and colors.

MHW tasks Prohyas and Vambre with protecting her house from the giant Smashroom stomping around her property. Prohyas and Vambre, along with ZP, arrive at MHW's house, which is a giant pumpkin. The Smashroom appears and ZP is at first powerless against it. Vambre tries to hold off Smashroom while Prohyas tries to figure out what is wrong with ZP. "I've got planterly powers. Smashroom's a fungus." Prohyas feeds ZP a giant pumpkin seed from MHW's house which makes ZP huge. "You think you can kick his giant patoot now?" asks Prohyas.

"Yeah, bro."

Episode 3 (September 29, 2016)
"Squirrelled Domination"

Füd hires the Warriors to get some rare golden acorns, but Dolphin Magisword falls ill. "Prognosis: not good," says ZP. Prohyas stays behind to take care of Dolphin, so Vambre must go alone and face her fear of squirrels.

Prohyas and ZP act out a story for Dolphin called *Slappy the Magic Elephant Shrew Saves a Ragamuffin*. Jim Bob the Ragamuffin loses a leg. "Perhaps Jim Bob could use a doctor," says ZP.

Episode 7 (October 27, 2016)
"Flirty Phantom"

Prohyas, Vambre, and ZP are searching for treasure when they land by a spooky house. "You shouldn't go in there," says ZP. Prohyas, in a trance, does anyway. They meet a ghost, Penny Plasm, who is infatuated with Prohyas. She throws Vambre out of the house and puts up a force field around it. The Door, who sounds like Frank Nelson, mocks Vambre.

Penny tells Prohyas that he has to cross over to the other side for them to be together. This is a deal breaker for Prohyas, who runs away. "Exit stage right!", he says, but he can't break through the force field, either. ZP shoots seeds of the undead at Penny, making her temporarily powerless. He sings the song "There Once Was a Woodchuck".

Episode 11 (November 9, 2016)
"Potion in the Ocean"

The title card is Vambre as the Little Mermaid. Witchy Simone needs Eye of Newt for a recipe but she is fresh out. She hires the Warriors to go undersea to get one, but insists on going along. However, Man Fish the Fish Man won't let any further harm befall the sea newt, who has already lost one eye. ZP has zombie regenerative powers, so they pluck his eyes out and give them to the newt.

Episode 13 (November 11, 2016)
"Gotta Get Grup to Get Down"

Grup is going to write and sing a song for the talent contest the next day, and he hires Prohyas to accompany him on the Accordion Magisword. The competition is lame, but Grup's song is horrible, and the second verse is the same as the first, so Prohyas joins in with his revisions, and ZP sings backup. "I can do dat." Dolphin takes a solo, and when some squirrels escape their cages, Vambre screams along. Grup wins.

Episode 17 (November 17, 2016)
"Little Sword of Horrors"

Ralphio sells Prohyas a magisword seed that turns into a Carnivorous Plant Magisword that eats everything. ZP is mentioned.

Episode 19 (December 1, 2016)
"Gut Feelings"

Someone stole all of Hoppus' vegetable magiswords and ZP is on the case. "I'm ready to roll." The culprit turns out to be Prohyas' sentient stomach (Gilbert Gottfried).

Episode 47 (December 9, 2017)
"Taming of the Swords"

Vambre is cleaning ZP. "I'm effective," he purrs. She and Prohyas decide to "housebreak" Carnivorous Plant and another problematic magisword, Taunting Jester.

Season 2
Episode 19 (May 24, 2018)
"Helping Cattus Help"

The Warriors attempt to bring back a mythical animal for Omnibus, but they cannot penetrate the door to his lair, so they ask their old friend Cattus for help. Cattus can teleport, but he doesn't know how to do it. They try to relax him into it with a song. ZP again sings the bass line.

Episode 24
"The Pecking Order" (August 24, 2018)

At Warriors for Hire headquarters, Prohyas, Vambre, Grup, and ZP are playing *Who's Going to Walk Through the Front Door?* It is Professor Cyrus. ZP guesses correctly, so he gets to eat all the pumpkins.

Episode 36
"Ghosthaste" (August 24, 2018)

A ghost magisword is being guarded by a pumpkin in a hat. ZP eats the pumpkin and steals his hat. When Vambre picks up the magisword, she can see ghosts but Prohyas can't. ZP warns against it. The ghosts try to lure her over to the other side. ZP says, "You can see ghosts if you wear my eyeballs on your eyes." Prohyas defeats the ghost and locks away the sword.

FUN FACT: The title card is a parody of the Scooby-Doo franchise (qv) with Vambre as Daphne, Prohyas as Shaggy, Penny as Velma, Zombie Pumpkin Magisword as Fred, and Grup as Scooby-Doo. Concurrently, Grey Griffin (Vambre) and Kate Micucci (Penny) were actually playing Daphne and Velma in *Be Cool, Scooby-Doo* (2015).

GIGGLE RATING: Looks, Four Giggles. ZP has enormous eyes, but the resemblance ends there. Voice, Four Giggles. Not a full metal Peter Lorre imitation, but it isn't supposed to be. Carozza is perfectly capable of doing a fine Peter Lorre, and did so on his podcast.

AVAILABILITY: Amazon Prime. Some episodes available on the Cartoon Network App.

Family Guy (1999)
Season 16
Episode 11 (January 14, 2018)
"Dog Bites Bear"

Fox Television Animation, Fuzzy Door Productions. Directed by John Holmquist, Dominic Bianchi (supervising director), James Purdum (supervising director). Writing Credits: Seth MacFarlane (created by), Seth MacFarlane (developed by) & David Zuckerman (developed by), Cherry

Chevapravatdumrong (written by). Cast: Cast: Seth MacFarlane (Peter Griffin/Brian Griffin/Stewie Griffin/Glen Quagmire), Alex Borstein (Lois Griffin/Barbara Pewterschmidt), Mila Kunis (Meg Griffin), Seth Green (Chris Griffin), Mike Henry (Cleveland Brown), Patrick Warburton (Joe Swanson).

Family Guy (1999), which debuted on FOX after Super Bowl XXXIII, is about Peter Griffin, a fat, ignorant Irish Catholic living in Quahog, Rhode Island with his wife, Lois; their kids, Meg, Chris, and baby Stewie; and their anthropomorphic dog, Brian.

Peter meets his hero, Boo Berry (qv), actually an employee in a Boo Berry costume who doesn't make the slightest attempt to imitate Peter Lorre. "You're not the one threatening me on Facebook, are you?" he asks Peter.

"Hey, you know what I always loved about your cereal?" asks Peter. "It tasted like blueberries. Oh my God, boo berries! And you, and you're a ghost!" After shaking Boo Berry's hand, Peter refuses to wash his, despite the entreaties of Lois and his friends Glen Quagmire, Cleveland Brown, and Joe Swanson. Soon his hand is an ecosystem all its own, teeming with microflora and fauna.

Glen, Joe, and Cleveland conspire with Lois to wash Peter's hand. The men show up at Peter's house with Cleveland dressed as Count Chocula (qv). "For the record, I would have preferred to dress as Franken Berry." Lois opens the door for Cleveland, who completely takes Peter in with his imitation, which is a mashup of cereal mascot catchphrases: "Silly rabbit, Count Chocula tastes grrrrrreat!" Peter moves to shake the "Count's" hand, and Cleveland traps Peter's hand in a golf ball scrubber. The miraculous tiny civilization that has sprung up is destroyed by the brushes' bristles.

GIGGLE RATING: Looks, Five Giggles; Voice, Zero Giggles. He sounds nothing like Peter Lorre or Boo Berry, but that's the joke. It is not known who plays him.

AVAILABILITY: Amazon Prime.

SpongeBob SquarePants (1999)
Season 12
Episode 13 (July 12, 2019)
"SpongeBob's Big Birthday Blowout"

United Plankton Pictures, Nickelodeon Animation Studios. Directed by Jonas Morganstein. Writing Credits: Andrew Goodman (animation writer) and Luke Brookshier (animation writer) & Kaz (animation writer), Mr. Lawrence (written by), Kaz (written by). Produced by Jennie Monica Hammond, Marc Ceccarelli, Vincent Waller, Donna Castricone. Cast: Tom Kenny (SpongeBob/Patchy the Pirate/Old Man Walker/Gary/French Narrator/SpongeBob's Dad/Peter Lorre Fish/Grubby Grouper/PA System/ JimBob), Bill Fagerbakke (Patrick Star/Bus Passenger/Passenger/Patron #1), Rodger Bumpass (Squidward/Bus Passenger/Announcer/Yellow Fish/ Manward), Clancy Brown (Mr. Krabs/Unhappy Guy/Party Guest #2/Mr. Slabs/Manager), Carolyn Lawrence (Sandy/Bus Passenger/Little Girl/Carol), Mr. Lawrence (Plankton/Potty/Rube/Larry/Fred/Charleston/Robber).

Marine biologist Stephen Hillenburg originated many of the ideas for this show in 1989 in an unpublished educational comic book titled *The Intertidal Zone*. The title character is an enthusiastic if not too bright fungus who lives in a pineapple in the fictitious undersea city of Bikini Bottom. Other characters include his BFF, a starfish named Patrick; Sandy Cheeks, a Texan squirrel and karate expert who wears a diving suit to breathe underwater; Plankton, a small, green copepod; and Larry the Lobster, a lifeguard. The show is the highest-rated Nickelodeon series ever, the most-distributed property of MTV, and a multi-billion dollar media franchise. Hillenburg died in 2018, and this episode is an homage to him and a celebration of the show's twentieth anniversary and is a hybrid of animation and live-action footage.

It's SpongeBob's birthday and his friends and neighbors have planned a surprise party for him, but first, Patrick has to get him out of the house so the others can decorate. Patrick takes SpongeBob on a tour bus to Surface Land after Plankton steals SpongeBob's keys. On the tour, Patrick and SpongeBob see some "amazing" sights.

Back at SpongeBob's, Larry the Lobster says, "Yo, Dude, is this the line for SpongeBob's party?" A green Peter Lorre fish with heavy lids and rotten teeth turns around and says, "Oh, yes. I brought birthday cake." He holds up what is basically an empty plate, and a few crumbs fall off. "It's gone," Larry points out. "Oh no," says Peter Lorre Fish, rubbing his fat little potbelly. "It's still here." He giggles insanely.

At the party, Sandy Cheeks tries to prevent guests from saying, "Surprise!" prematurely and eating cake. She makes those who do partake cough it back up. She tells Peter Lorre Fish not to sit on a table. "Oh, I'm just having fun," he protests. "And I brought cake." He presents a three-tiered one, which he eats in a single gulp. His body assumes the shape of the cake, and the table collapses under his vast weight. He coughs up the cake. Two fish eat it and projectile vomit it onto Sandy's tail, which she just had done. This makes her hotter than a billy goat in a pepper patch, and she karate chops the cake. Peter Lorre Fish emerges and groans, "Surprise." Sandy punches him in the face. The revelers start dancing, and destroy the house.

SpongeBob returns to find his home leveled and all the partygoers exhausted from dancing. They wake up briefly to mutter, "Surprise." SpongeBob calls it the best birthday he's ever had.

FUN FACT: Larry calls Peter Lorre Fish "Slappy". This is probably not his real name, since the characters do not seem to know each other. Larry is likely referencing the ventriloquist dummy character in the Goosebumps franchise, to whom Peter Lorre Fish is dressed similarly.

GIGGLE RATING: Five Giggles. Excellent character design and voice. Tom Kenny's numerous credits include *Frankenweenie* (2012) and *Tamagotchi Video Adventures* (1997).

AVAILABILITY: Unavailable at press time. Check the usual suspects.

Chapter 3:

Commercial Lorre Tunes

NB: TITLES IN BRACKETS ARE made up by the author. Titles without brackets are actual commercial titles.

Dairy Council
"[Milk]" (Unknown year)

A Peter Lorre imitator sells milk. Unseen by this author, believed to be animated.

GIGGLE RATING: Unknown.

AVAILABILITY: Unknown.

Arab Termite and Pest Control
"[Bugs]" (Unknown year)

A Peter Lorre imitator reads off Arab's hit list of bugs. Unseen by this author, believed to be animated.

GIGGLE RATING: Unknown.

AVAILABILITY: Unknown.

American Lung Association
"Half a Dirty Dozen" (Unknown year)

Peter Lorre, Sydney Greenstreet, Humphrey Bogart, Boris Karloff, Jimmy Cagney, and Edward G. Robinson were in the "It's a Matter of Life and Breath" campaign playing "Half a Dirty Dozen", six bad habits. Lorre was cigarettes, and the Fat Man was overeating. In one commercial, Greenstreet complains that his doctor has put him on a strict diet: mustard, ketchup, and pepper. Lorre giggles insanely. "Yes, but he went back for seconds!" In another spot, believed to be part of this series, Lorre helps a mad doctor build a girl out of healthy foods. Unseen by this author.

GIGGLE RATING: Unknown.

AVAILABILITY: Unknown.

Rice Krispies
["Snap, Crackle, and Pop Meet J. Evil Scientist"] (1960s)

Rice Krispies is a breakfast cereal from Kellogg's made from crisped rice, which has very thin walls that collapse when milk is added, making the sounds "snap, crackle, and pop". It was invented in 1927 and released to the public in 1928. The characters Snap, Crackle, and Pop first appeared on a radio commercial and were drawn as gnomes in bakers' hats by artist Vernon Grant in 1933, first in ads and posters, and then on cereal boxes. They received a major makeover in 1949. In 1955, they made their TV commercial debut. Hanna-Barbera characters were heavily used to promote Kellogg's cereals, and J. Evil Scientist appeared in a TV commercial with Snap, Crackle, and Pop. Not seen by this author and no further information is available.

GIGGLE RATING: Unknown.

AVAILABILITY: Unknown. Kellogg's was unable to locate this in their archives.

Monster Cereals (1971-Present)

As we have seen previously, Bob McFadden originated the role of Franken Berry, which was later played by Robb Pruitt. Count Chocula was first voiced by Jim Dukas and later by Larry Kenney. Boo Berry joined the first two Monster Cereals in 1972. However, imitations of Peter Lorre were also used in commercials for Count Chocula, Franken Berry, and Yummy Mummy, the frosted fruit flavored cereal with vanilla flavored marshmallows. The latter was a replacement for Fruit Brute, a frosted fruit flavored cereal with lime flavored marshmallows and a werewolf mascot, although Yummy Mummy was never considered by General Mills to be one of the Monster Cereals.

Boo Berry dressed a little like Peter Lorre as Toady in *Rope of Sand* (1949), with a hat and a bow tie. He also had a chain around his waist with a bowl and spoon attached to one end and a box of cereal on the other. Boo Berry was originally played by Eugene Weingand, a real estate salesman who attended the Loretta Young Acting School and sometimes performed in small theaters. Weingand was allegedly born April 1, 1934, in Karlsruhe, Germany. His mother was unmarried and he was raised by foster parents, who adopted him. In 1954, he immigrated to the United States. He claimed that people called him Peter Lorre because of their vague resemblance, so he started calling himself Peter Lorie Jr. In July 1963, he tried to make the change legal. Although he stated publicly acting was only a hobby, he privately admitted the change was a publicity stunt. The real Peter Lorre objected, and his attorney Robert Shutan deposed Weingand on September 10:

A Well, I want to have my name changed to Peter Lorie, so I don't want to have no confusion of any kind that people might take me for a sixty-five year old man, so I figure well, I'll tell them I'm Junior. What's wrong with that?

Q I see, you figure that the best way to avoid confusion so that nobody will think that you're related to Peter Lorre, or are Peter Lorre, is to call yourself Peter Lorie Jr.?
A Perhaps.

Q Did it occur to you that there might be less confusion if you introduced yourself as Eugene Weingand?
A Perhaps.

On October 3, 1963, The Superior Court of Los Angeles County considered Weingand's petition. Judge Burnett Wolfson questioned him:

Q Anyone ever call you Bob Hope?
A Not yet.

Q Jack Benny?

Q No.

Q Danny Thomas?
A No.

Q George Jessel?
A No . . .

Q The only reason you want your name changed is because people call you Peter Lorie?
A That's one of them, yes.

Q What's the other reason?
A Because my name is too hard to pronounce.

Q What's hard to pronounce about Eugene Weingand?
A (No response.)

Judge Wolfson, saying Weingand just wanted "to cash in on the repu-tation established over a period of years by Peter Lorre," denied the petition and permanently restrained him from using the name "Peter Lorie", spelled in any fashion, without the real Peter Lorre's written consent. After Lorre's death, Weingand won on appeal and the permanent injunction was lifted. He began passing himself off as "Peter Lorre Jr.", although he stopped short of legally changing his name. He won a few small parts in movies, includ-ing Alfred Hitchcock's *Torn Curtain* (1966), until Peter's brother Andrew Lorre put a stop to Weingand's use of the Lorre name. His last IMDb credit is from 1975, but he hosted a horror movie show on an Austin, Texas television station in 1976-77. He died in 1986. Anonymous internet commenters say Paul Frees voiced Boo Berry for a time. More recently, he has been played by Chris Phillips. Phillips replaced Billy West as Boomer Bledsoe and Roger Klotz on *Disney's Doug* (1996).

"[The First Boo Berry Commercial]" (1972?)

Count Chocula and open the Dutch doors to their castle. "Hello, my name is Boo. Let me finish. Boo Berry. My ghostly good blueberry cereal, Boo Berry," he giggles insanely, "is part of this complete breakfast." A bowl of

Boo Berry is shown with a glass of orange juice, two slices of toast with butter, and a pitcher of milk.

"[Franken Berry-Count Chocula-Boo Berry]" (Unknown year)

Franken Berry sends Boo Berry away on a deflating float. He reappears on a waterspout, touting the merits of blueberry flavored marshmallows compared to those flavored with strawberry or chocolate, frightening Franken Berry and Count Chocula away. One mini-monster in specially marked boxes of monster cereals.

"[Monster Cereals Boo Hooter]" (Unknown year)

To prevent Boo Berry from talking about his new cereal, Franken Berry and Count Chocula put him in a candelabra and then put a candle on top. He comes out the wick to talk about "the haunting blueberry taste." Boo Hooters in specially marked boxes. They're kazoos, why, what did you think?

"[Monster Bowl]" (Unknown year)

Boo Berry, Count Chocula, and Franken Berry are at the bowling alley. Boo Berry's "ball" is attached to a chain. "Boo Berry has blueberry flavored sweeties." Have fun with Monster Erasers.

"[Boo-Hoo]" (Unknown year)

Boo Berry says, "Boo!" Count Chocula asks, "Boo who?" Boo Berry answers, "Don't cry. It's me, Boo Berry, with my ghostly good cereal, Boo Berry." A bird spooks them both.

"Monsters of Stage" (1977)

Franken Berry, Count Chocula, and Boo Berry are appearing in the musical stage show *Scared Silly*. Boo Berry flies underneath the stage and then appears and says, "Boo," scaring Franken Berry and Count Chocula silly. "We scared you, but you can't scare us," sings Boo Berry in a decidedly un-Peter Lorre-like voice.

"[Turn-Off]" (1979)

Franken Berry is charging his batteries when Boo Berry appears and says, "Here's a switch. My ghostly good Boo Berry with blueberry flavored marshmallows to spark up breakfast." He thinks strawberry flavored marshmallows are a turn-off. They are scared away by a three-eyed creature.

"[Boo Berry and Count Chocula Ghost Story]" (1981)

Count Chocula tries to read two kids a ghost story, but he is interrupted by Boo Berry, "Bringing you my hauntingly delicious cereal with blueberry flavor and tasty marshmallows." Count Chocula says his cereal is better and an argument ensues, which is taken up by the kids.

"[Trix, Lucky Charms, Cocoa Puffs, and Monster Cereals]" (1982)

Trix cereal was introduced in 1954 as a sugar-coated version of the popular Kix. General Mills began experimenting with a rabbit puppet called Tricks as the Trix mascot in 1954, and the animated version debuted in a 1959 TV commercial, voiced first by Mort Marshall and later by Bret Iwan. Cocoa Puffs, which was introduced in 1958, is basically Kix with chocolate flavoring. The animated cereal mascot, Sonny the Cuckoo Bird, was introduced in 1962. Originally voiced by Chuck McCann, Larry Kenney has played the role since 1978. Lucky Charms was created by General Mills Vice-President John Holahan in 1964 when he mixed Cheerios with bits of Brach's Circus Peanuts, a marshmallow candy. It was the first cereal with marbits, or marshmallow bits. Mascot Lucky the leprechaun's debut in 1964 was one of the most expensive advertising rollouts to that date including full-color ads in Sunday comics and comic books plus animated commercials featuring the voice of Arthur Anderson.

Tricks announces a contest. Grand Prizes include a Magnavox home video system and a Viewmaster projector and reel. All winners get a personalized director's chair. Boo Berry has one line, "The Monsters!" said in unison with Count Chocula and Franken Berry.

"[Boo Berry & Count Chocula Commercial]" (1982)

Count Chocula checks into a spooky hotel along with two kids. "Homey, isn't it?" says Boo Berry. He gets into an argument with the Count, until the portrait on the wall takes off its own frame and puts them in it, saying in a Jimmy Stewart-esque voice, "I picture a delicious breakfast."

"[Monster Marshmallows]" (1983)

An animation-live action hybrid spot to announce that Count Chocula, Franken Berry, and Boo Berry now have monster sized marshmallows. "They're everywhere," says Boo Berry.

"[Count Chocula, Franken Berry, and Yummy Mummy Commercial]" (1982-1992?)

Animated kids are having Count Chocula, Franken Berry, and Yummy Mummy, but not Boo Berry. "Scary bat marshmallows in monster cereals will change the way you eat breakfast," says a Peter Lorre-esque announcer. "Bat marshmallows in monster cereals. The spooky part of your complete breakfast will never be the same." Yummy Mummy was made between 1982-1992, and not again until 2013.

"[Igor the Spider]" (1990s-2000s?)

Count Chocula introduces Igor, his bug-eyed guard spider, who keeps an eye on his cereal, which is part of this complete breakfast. "And a tasty treasure!" says Igor, in a decidedly Peter Lorre-like voice.

"[Monster Mash]" (1990s)

Will the new chocolatey marshmallow in Count Chocula cereal be Frankenstein (actually Frankenstein's monster), the Mummy, the Swirled Ghost, or the Werewolf? It's all of them! Boo Berry appears but does not speak. "Frankenstein" speaks in a Karlovian voice different from Franken Berry. Oddly, Franken Berry also appears but does not speak.

"[Monster Mash 2]" (1997?)

Similar to the above, except Casper the Friendly Ghost is one of the new chocolatey marshmallows.

"[Monster Mash 3]" (1997)

Similar to the above, but there's a tie-in to the direct-to-video movie *Casper: A Spirited Beginning* (1997).

"[Monster Mash 4]" (1998?)

Similar to the above, but now with Wendy the Witch marshmallows also. Possibly a tie-in to the prequel, *Casper Meets Wendy* (1998).

"[Scooby-Doo]" (1998?)

Count Chocula, Franken Berry, and Boo Berry see Scooby-Doo (qv) and Shaggy in their crystal ball and as marshmallows in their cereals for a limited time only. Boo Berry has no lines.

"[Special Marshmallows]" (2000?)

Similar to the above, but this time the marshmallows are shaped like bats, moons, books of magic, and bubbling cauldrons.

"Marshmallows & Masks" (2000)

The monster cereals now have marshmallows shaped like bats, moons, books of magic, and bubbling cauldrons. "But that's not all. For a limited time, you can get free, spooky monster masks you can cut out of these specially marked boxes," says the announcer. Boo Berry appears but has no lines.

"The Monsters Go Disco" (October 2009)

In 2009, the Monster Cereals made a comeback with both a CD and this music video. The voices are from the original "flexi-disc" record that was free on the back of boxes in 1979 called "Monsters Go Disco". Boo Berry speak-sings the lines, "Discos here" and "Discos there" and giggles insanely.

Manny Galán did the layouts and Pat Giles did the color. Now owners of their own Pat-Man Studios, working on the Monsters video was a dream come true for them, having been fans since childhood.

"Up until I met Pat, I hadn't met another adult who had kind of like the almost addiction, such a pervasive obsession with these characters that I had. It was our collective goal to do more with the Monsters, we saw them as the gem in the treasure chest that kind of really needed to be polished and brought to light again," says Galán. "Nothing in my career has ever replaced that feeling of 'Oh my God, my drawings are on the front of Count Chocula, Boo Berry, and Franken Berry.' It was like, I had made it. I knew that it was such a huge achievement personally."

Their first big collaboration was the style guide for the Monsters. "The Monster Cereals style guide was the most fun because it was that kind of thing that really helped to codify the characters in a way that captured their look and feel from the 70s but also kind of updated them, made them modern. It really helped a lot in creating energy around creating new products with the characters, beyond the cereal," says Giles. Of this video, he says, "It was so thrilling to animate something that I had only heard the voice of when I was a little kid and always had pictured what the castle would look like or what they'd be doing. I had pictured them as playing cards sitting around on a Saturday night, and they're bored so they all decide to go out and go disco dancing, which was of course the rage in 1979."

Galán continues: "We ended up going off the rails in the storyboards. We gave Boo Berry a set of abilities that he hadn't had before, where he could change his form to suit the story. He could turn into a doorway so the Monsters could walk through it and go right from their castle and transition to the disco, for example."

"The Monsters Go Disco" (October, 2009)

Animation with the soundtrack from a "flexi-disc" record from the backs of Monster Cereal boxes in 1979. Another Saturday night and Count Chocula and Franken Berry ain't got nobody. They are playing cards in Monster Mansion when Boo Berry materializes and says, "Fellas, what are we going to do to cure our Saturday night blues?" Count Chocula suggests they go disco. Boo Berry produces a deck of cards and tosses them at Franken Berry and the Count, saying, "Discos here, discos there," and giggling insanely. This video ends before the song starts.

"[2015 Monster Cereals–Blippar]"

Since 2010, the Monster Cereals have been made and sold only seasonally around Halloween. In 2014, General Mills hired DC Comics to create new designs for the cereals and the Boo Berry design was done by Jim Lee. The following year, General Mills partnered with Blippar to bring the Monsters to life through augmented reality. Emily Daigle, General Mills associate marketing manager, said, "This year, we are excited about our partnership with Blippar as it allows us to take a deeper look at the Monsters' past in such a memorable way. We can't wait for fans to experience the fun." Fans could download the Blippar App, open it, and hold their phones in front of specially-marked boxes of Monster cereals to see the characters lurch off the box and utter a "phrase of fear." Boo Berry's is, "Ready for a ghostly good fright?" Using the app on the back of the box unlocked vintage commercials. In addition, Target offered exclusive packaging featuring a cut-out castle, and Walmart had glow in the dark, cutout masks of the Monsters.

GIGGLE RATING: Looks, Five Giggles; Voice, Zero to Five Giggles.

AVAILABILITY: Streaming on web.

MTV
"[Ident]" (1990s)
MTV was originally an initialism for Music Television and this pay-TV channel played mostly music videos. By the mid-nineties, MTV played 36.5% fewer music videos. In this ident, images of Peter Lorre from *M* (1931) are digitally manipulated. Hans Beckert, seen from behind, runs down the street, mumbling. Instead of an "M" on his shoulder, he has an MTV logo. The spot is fondly remembered today, even though few got the reference.

GIGGLE RATING: Five Giggles.

AVAILABILITY: Streaming on web.

Weetabix
"Big Shots" (1991, UK)
Weetabix is the British version of the original Australian Weet-Bix, a whole grain wheat breakfast cereal that comes in palm-sized biscuits. This commercial was animated for Passion Pictures by Chuck Gammage, who contributed animation to *Who Framed Roger Rabbit* (1988), which also has cartoon bullets in a live-action setting.

An old-timey car pulls up in front of a restaurant and three gangsters get out. They enter, draw their guns, and fire at three people sitting at a table. The bullets are caricatures of Edward G. Robinson, James Cagney, and, in a fez, Peter Lorre. "Let's get 'em, boys," says Robinson. "Sure, boss," says Cagney. However, they come to a halt when they find out their targets have been eating their Weetabix. "I guess I'll give it a miss," says Lorre. He stops in mid-air and changes course, shattering some wine bottles and hitting a wall before falling onto a table and hiding amongst the condiment shakers, still completely undamaged, like a magic bullet. Cagney and Robinson also come to bad ends. At the end, an announcer says, "Say, have you had your Weetabix?" in a bogus Humphrey voice.

GIGGLE RATING: Five Giggles.

AVAILABILITY: Streaming on web.

Cartoon Network and Boomerang

Cartoon Network (or CN), an American basic cable and satellite television channel owned by Turner Broadcasting System, was founded on October 2, 1992 to provide an outlet for the extensive library of animation media mogul Ted Turner had acquired, including the MGM cartoon library, the pre-1948 color Looney Tunes and Merrie Melodies shorts, most Harman-Ising Merrie Melodies shorts, the Fleischer Studios/Famous Studios Popeye cartoons, and Hanna-Barbera Productions. Cartoon Network UK was launched in 1993, and Cartoon Network Asia began in 1994. Boomerang started as a programming block and spinoff of CN and gradually became its own brand. It is a pay television channel and a streaming service owned by Turner Broadcasting System, and specializes in animated programming owned by Warner Media. Only spots with original animation, not footage repurposed from any series, are included below.

"[Cartoon Network Asia]" (1995)

An ad for Cartoon Network Asia featuring Jess Harnell as Morocco Mole. Unseen by this author.

GIGGLE RATING: Unknown.

AVAILABILITY: Unknown.

"[ID Velma and Morocco Mole]" (Unknown year)

An ident for CN. Velma Dinkley from the Scooby-Doo franchise (qv) and Morocco Mole crawl along the ground searching for their glasses. They put on each other's spectacles and fall in love, apparently.

GIGGLE RATING: Looks, Five Giggles; Voice, N/A.

AVAILABILITY: Streaming on internet.

"[Boomerang Commercial]" (Unknown year)

Features Maurice LaMarche as Morocco Mole. Unseen by this author. A black and white still can be found online.

GIGGLE RATING: Based on the still and the Maurice LaMarche impersonation, we'll give it Five Giggles.

AVAILABILITY: Unknown.

"tooned4(life)" (2001)

The first installment of a series from Cartoon Network UK, this spot posits that Velma Dinkley and Morocco Mole never appear together because they are one and the same. Morocco giggles insanely. Other Cartoon Network UK ads featuring Morocco Mole were unseen by this author.

GIGGLE RATING: Five Giggles.

AVAILABILITY: Streaming on internet.

Nickelodeon

Nickelodeon 3D Movie Maker (1996) "Official Trailer" (1996?)

Promotional video for *Nickelodeon 3D Movie Maker* (1996) (qv), featuring Ren.

GIGGLE RATING: All characters are amorphous blobs and Ren gets One Giggle for Looks. Voice, Four Giggles.

AVAILABILITY: Streaming on internet.

Chapter 4:
Video Game Lorre Tunes

AVAILABILITY: Some games are available free online. Others may be purchased wherever video games are sold.

Chip 'n Dale: Rescue Rangers (Franchise)
Based on the cartoon (qv). Players can be either Chip or Dale.

Chip 'n Dale: Rescue Rangers (1990)
Capcom.

The Rangers search for a lost kitten and encounter Fat Cat with his mechanical bulldogs and robotic rats. Wart throws his hat at the players.

GIGGLE RATING: Looks, Five Giggles; Voice N/A.

Chip 'n Dale: Rescue Rangers 2 (1994)
Capcom.

The sequel. Fat Cat breaks out of prison and has a rabbit plant a bomb in a restaurant as a distraction so he can steal an ancient urn from a cargo ship. Fat Cat gets away but the Rangers recover the urn. Wart operates a wrecking crane which has a spiked ball that releases objects which Chip 'n Dale throw at him.

GIGGLE RATING: Looks, Four Giggles. The eyes in the first version are more googly. Voice N/A.

Quest for Glory (Franchise)

Called a "rich, narrative-driven, role-playing experience" by co-creator Lori Ann Cole, the series consists of five hybrid adventure/role-playing games, each building on the last. The objective is to turn the player character into a Hero, and the original title was *Hero Quest*, but Sierra failed to trademark the name and they had to change it when Milton Bradley successfully trademarked an electronic version of their game *HeroQuest* (1989). Celebrity caricatures abound, including Boris Karloff, Laurel and Hardy (as French Foreign Legionnaires), and Redd Foxx and Demond Wilson from *Sanford and Son* (1972). Ali T. Fakir, the peddler, is based on Groucho Marx. Coincidentally, Groucho was considered to play Ali Hakim, the peddler in *Oklahoma!* (1943). Another peddler in the game, Alichica, is based on Chico Marx. He lives in Freedonia.

Quest for Glory II: Trial by Fire (1990)

Sierra Entertainment. Directed by Corey Cole, Lori Ann Cole. Written by Corey Cole, Lori Ann Cole.

The Hero arrives at the gates of Raseir, where he is met by Khaveen, captain of the Raseirian Guard, who makes it clear he is watching the Hero. Signor Ferrari is the mysterious proprietor of the Blue Parrot Inn in Raseir, a front for his criminal dealings. He looks like Sydney Greenstreet, is named after Greenstreet's character (who also owns an inn called the Blue Parrot) in *Casablanca* (1942), and, like Kasper Gutman in *The Maltese Falcon* (1941), as he says, "for seventeen years, I have sought the black bird," a falcon carved out of onyx worth a fortune, but also lost to the ages amongst three wooden replicas. He usually delegates the dirty work to his henchmen, like Wilmer (who, unlike the homonymous twink gunsel of Kasper Gutman, is a large and noisy man) and Guillermo Ugarte. Ugarte is named for Peter Lorre's character in *Casablanca* (1942), whom he resembles. Ferrari introduces the Hero to Ugarte, who sells the Hero information. "Khaveen has sent the word out to his men that you are to be watched at all times. It seems that, ah, Someone is very interested in your actions. You should be aware that Khaveen does not usually greet strangers at the gate. You were expected." The next day, Ugarte, who is also a water smuggler, is arrested and sent to the dungeons.

Ferrari has the Hero steal the black bird, but it turns out to be one of the ebony copies. Ferrari closes the Blue Parrot and he and Wilmer resume their search elsewhere. Ugarte, who got out of prison through unknown means, joins them.

GIGGLE RATING: Looks, Five Giggles; Voice, N/A. Characters speak in titles.

Quest for Glory IV: Shadows of Darkness (1994)

Sierra Entertainment. Directed by Corey Cole, Lori Ann Cole. Writing Credits: Corey Cole, Lori Ann Cole. Produced by J. Mark Hood, James W. Thomas. Cast: John Rhys-Davies (Narrator), Jennifer Hale (Katrina), Gregg Berger (Dmitri Ivanov the Burgomeister), Jeff Bennett (Ad Avis/Bonehead/ Dr. Cranium/Igor), Cathianne Blore (Anna), Hamilton Camp (Lorre Petrovich/The Chief/Punny Bones), Cam Clarke (Domovoi/Gypsy Davy/ Nikolai), Jim Cummings (Boris Stovich), Bill Farmer (Leshy), Joan Gerber (Gypsy Magda), Jess Harnell (Franz), Mitzi McCall (Bella Markarov), Diane Pershing (Erana/Rusalka), Stu Rosen (Yuri Markarov), Neil Ross (Erasmus/ Ivan), Susan Silo (Baba Yaga/Fenris/Olga Stovich/Tatiana the Queen of the Faery Folk), Russi Taylor (Tanya Markarov).

The Hero arrives with no explanation in Mordavia. Lorre Petrovich, also known as the Chief, is the Chief Thief of Mordavia. He is the uncle of Ugarte, and looks like an older version of same. He attempted to steal a statue from the Dark One Monastery basement and, like Gregor Samsa in *The Metamorphosis*, was transformed into a cockroach but still with the face of Peter Lorre. "After I became such as I am, many members left. One thief said that I was no longer fit to be Chief! After I showed him how fast I could throw daggers with these feet, he didn't say much. Never said anything again, as a matter of fact, heh, heh. The ones that left said they felt 'uncomfortable' around me. Fools! Do they think this is some sort of Brotherhood of Man? This is a Brotherhood of Thieves! They SHOULD be uncomfortable around me! Soon it was just me and two others. They decided to explore the castle after the new owner moved in, and never returned. So now there is only me and you." With the hero's help, he returns to his human form. "Wonderful! Wonderful! I won't have to scuttle in shadows all the time. I won't have to have unsavory eating practices. Thank you, thank you so very much." Lorre sends word to his nephew Ugarte in Silmaria, calling him "a little sneak." Ugarte hopes to win the Chief Thief contest and earn his uncle's praise. In addition to Camp, whose credits include *The Tick* (1994) (qv), the cast includes Lorre impersonators Cam Clarke, Jim Cummings, Jess Harnell, and Neil Ross.

FUN FACTS: Lorre's knife-throwing is a possible nod to *Mad Love* (1935). There is an Igor character who does not sound like Peter Lorre.

GIGGLE RATING: Five Giggles. The Kafkaesque blattid is a nice touch.

Quest for Glory V: Dragon Fire (1998)

Sierra Entertainment. Written by Lori Ann Cole. Produced by Jay Usher. Cast: Stephen Apostolina (Cerberus #3), Carol Baxter (Queen of Atlantis), Beau Billingslea (Rakeesh/Shakra), Marc Blancfield (Pretorious), Steve Blum (Abduel/Andre/Kokeeno/Magnum Opus/Parrot/Salim), Steve Bulen (Abdim/Bruno/Cerberus #2/Erasmus/Minos), Michael Carvin (Banker), Wendy Cutler (Erana/Sarra), Mari Devon (Ann Agrama), Elisa Gabrielli (Nawar), Marabina Jaimes (Sibyl), Joyce Kurtz (Julanar/Katrina), Roy Lee (Cloud/Weaponer), Diane Michelle (Budar), Larry Moss (Logos), Greg O'Neill (Mobius/Toro), Stephen Poletti (Fenris/Marrak), Ian Ruskin (Head Of FACS), Michael Sorich (Abdum/Cerberus #1/Ferrari/Guards/Guardian), Doug Stone (Abdull/Arestes/Gort/Ugarte/Wolfie), Greg Tomko-Pavia (Narrator), Ariana Weil (Elsa).

Ferrari, Ugarte, and their squad reach Silmaria where Ferrari opens the Dead Parrot Inn. He also buys a parcel of land that becomes the site of Gnome Ann's Land Inn, run by Ann Agrama. After the assassination of the Chief Thief of the Silmarian Thieves Guild, Ferrari enters the Chief Thief Contest against the Hero and Ugarte. "There is speculation that one of your competitors is the murderer," says Ugarte. "I'd watch my back if I was you." Ferrari says Ann Agrama owes him mortgage payments, so the Hero trades the real black bird statue for the deed. Later, the Hero steals it back from Ferrari, replacing with a fake, and uses it to win the Chief Thief Contest.

FUN FACT: Lorre Petrovich is mentioned but not seen or heard.

GIGGLE RATING: Four Giggles. Not a great likeness or voiceover. Doug Stone's credits include the video game *Tiny Toon Adventures: Buster and the Beanstalk* (1996).

Quest for Glory II: Trial by Fire (2008)
AGD Interactive LLC. Directed by Christopher T. Warren. Written by Corey Cole, Lori Ann Cole.

A Video Graphics Array fan remake of *Quest for Glory II: Trial by Fire* (1990).

GIGGLE RATING: Looks, Five Giggles; Voice, N/A.

Ren & Stimpy (Franchise)
Ren & Stimpy, Space Cadet Adventures (1992)
Imagineering. Written by Bob Camp, John Kricfalusi.

From the manufacturer: "Activate your viewscreen and prepare to blast off for adventure in the amazing year 400 billion with Commander Ren and his faithful companion Cadet Stimpy. Explore vast alien worlds with our heroes as they roam the endless uncharted regions of space struggling to defeat intergalactic evil. Is there intelligent life in the universe? No, you eediot! Only Ren and Cadet Stimpy, two space cadets who'll boldly take you where no higher mammal has gone before. The question is, will you know how to get back?"

GIGGLE RATING: Looks, Four Giggles (it's black and white); Voice, N/A.

The Ren & Stimpy Show, Buckeroo$! (1993)
Imagineering.

Based on the episodes "Space Madness", "Robin Höek", and "Out West" (all qv).

GIGGLE RATING: Looks, Five Giggles; Voice, N/A.

Ren & Stimpy: Stimpy's Invention (1993)
Sega Enterprises USA. Written by Bob Camp, John Kricfalusi, Will McRobb, Vincent Waller. Cast: John Kricfalusi (Ren Höek), Billy West (Stimpson J. Stimpy Cat).

Not based on the episode of the same name. Stimpy invents a Mutate-O-Matic, which falls into the wrong hands.

GIGGLE RATING: Five Giggles.

The Ren & Stimpy Show: Veediots! (1993)
Gray Matter, Nintendo of America.

Based on the episodes "The Boy Who Cried Rat", "In the Army", "Stimpy's Invention", and "Marooned" (all qv).

GIGGLE RATING: Looks, Five Giggles; Voice, N/A.

The Ren & Stimpy Show: Fire Dogs (1994)
Argonaut Games. Writing Credits: Bob Camp, John Kricfalusi, Will McRobb, Vincent Waller.

A video game adaptation of the episode "Fire Dogs" (qv).

GIGGLE RATING: Looks, Five Giggles; Voice, N/A.

The Ren & Stimpy Show: Time Warp (1994 Video Game)
Sculptured Software Inc., Nintendo of America. Directed by Jeff Peters. Written by Bob Camp, John Kricfalusi. Voices: Billy West.

Ren and Stimpy must stop Muddy Mudskipper from changing history and ruining space and time.

GIGGLE RATING: Four Giggles.

Ren & Stimpy: Quest for the Shaven Yak (1994)
Sega of America. Written by John Kricfalusi. Star: John Kricfalusi.

Created only for Sega Game Gear, this was one of the most popular titles of the year.

GIGGLE RATING: Looks, Four Giggles; Voice, N/A.

Nickelodeon 3D Movie Maker (1996)
Viacom New Media. Directed and Produced by Michelle Weiss. Cast: Charlie Adler (Ickis), Carlos Alazraqui (Rocko/Spunky), Gregg Berger (The Gromble), Christine Cavanaugh (Oblina), Paul Christie (Stick Stickly),

David Eccles (Krumm), Tom Kenny (Heffer Wolfe), Mr. Lawrence (Filburt Turtle), Gary Owens (Powdered Toast Man), Harris Peet (Muddy Mudskipper), Billy West (Ren/Stimpy).

Often abbreviated as *3DMM* (1996), this program, based on BRender, a 3D graphics engine created by Argonaut Software, enabled users to place 3D characters into pre-made environments and add action, sound effects, music, text, speech, and special effects. Microsoft provided another 3DMM program under license from Nickelodeon featuring actors, props, and scenes from *The Ren & Stimpy Show* (1991), *Rocko's Modern Life* (1993), and *Aaahh!!! Real Monsters* (1994). This was later made available as an unofficial, third-party expansion pack. A demo version, which does not allow the opening or saving of movies, features Ren and Stimpy and a spaceship.

GIGGLE RATING: Looks, One Giggle; Voice, Four Giggles.

Nicktoons Memory Challenge (1998)

Projector Skeleton Macromedia, Inc.

Flash game that is free and downloadable. Six characters from Nickelodeon, including Ren, are chosen in random order. The object is to copy the order correctly and have another character added on to the end. Only the backgrounds are animated, and no characters talk.

GIGGLE RATING: Looks, Five Giggles; Voice, N/A.

Ren & Stimpy's Crazy Cannon (2007)

Addicting Games.

Shoot Stimpy out of a cannon. Voice clips from the show are used.

GIGGLE RATING: Five Giggles.

Ren & Stimpy in Robin Höek (2007)

Addicting Games

A browser game based on the episode "Robin Höek" (qv).

GIGGLE RATING: Looks, Five Giggles; Voice, N/A.

Nicktoons MLB (2011)

Black Lantern Studios (Nintendo 3DS version), High Voltage Software (Wii version). Directed by Douglas Carrigan. Writing Credits: Stephen Hillenburg (characters), John Kricfalusi (characters). Cast: Dante Basco (Prince Zuko), Eric Bauza (Stimpy), Corey Burton (Powdered Toast Man), Jim Cummings (Ultra Lord), Tim Dadabo (Fanboy), Grey Griffin (Kitty Katswell), Debi Derryberry (Jimmy Neutron), Jack De Sena (Dudley Puppy), Brian Doyle-Murray (Flying Dutchman), Chris Edgerly (Ren Höek), Bill Fagerbakke (Patrick Star), Melissa Fahn (Gaz), Keith Ferguson (Danny Phantom), Jessie Flower (Toph Bei Fong), Nika Futterman (Chum Chum), Jeffrey Garcia (Sheen Estevez), Ben Helms (Aang), Richard Steven Horvitz (Invader Zim), Bob Joles (Mr. Nesmith), Tom Kenny (SpongeBob SquarePants), Matthew Yang King (Perch Perkins), Carolyn Lawrence (Sandy Cheeks), Mr. Lawrence (Larry the Lobster), Mae Whitman (Katara).

Nintendo.com: "A dugout full of Nicktoons including SpongeBob, ZIM, Dudley Puppy, Fanboy, Chum Chum, Aang, [Ren and Stimpy,] and more team up with superstars from all 30 MLB clubs in this epic baseball Showdown! You will swing for the fences in out-of-this-world Nicktoons venues and realistic MLB ballparks and collect over 50 in-game baseball cards complete with character bios." When he steps up to the plate, Ren says, "I can do this."

FUN FACTS: Dudley and Kitty from *T.U.F.F. Puppy* (2010) (qv) appear, but not the Chameleon. Frequent Lorre impersonators Corey Burton and Jim Cummings are in the cast.

Crash Bandicoot (Franchise)

This franchise was created by Andy Gavin and Jason Rubin for Universal Interactive Studios and Sony Computer Entertainment. Originally, it was exclusive to PlayStation video game consoles. It now comprises eighteen games and has sold 50 million units. Crash is an anthropomorphic eastern barred bandicoot, a small marsupial endemic to Tasmania and southeastern Australia. In the game, he is from the mythical Wumpa Archipelago. He was genetically enhanced by the series' main antagonist, Dr. Neo Cortex, but he escapes after a failed experiment in the Cortex Vortex and fights against Cortex and his plans for world domination. Dr. Neo Cortex's right-hand man is N. Gin (sometimes spelled "N-Gin"), an insane cyborg with a missile stuck in his head from an unfortunate accident in the defense industry. He is short and rotund, with one big eye and one really big eye, and he giggles insanely. Need I add that he sounds like Peter Lorre? In most games, his voice has a robotic echo. Peter Lorre impersonators who don't impersonate Lorre here include Maurice LaMarche, Lex Lang, and Jess Harnell.

Crash Bandicoot 2: Cortex Strikes Back (1997)

Naughty Dog. Directed by Andrew S. Gavin, Jason Rubin. Written by Andrew S. Gavin. Produced by Mark Cerny, Andrew S. Gavin, Shuhei Yoshida. Cast: Clancy Brown (Dr. Neo Cortex), Brendan O'Brien (Crash Bandicoot/Dr. Nitrus Brio/Dr. N. Gin/Tiny Tiger/Komodo Moe), Vicki Winters (Coco Bandicoot).

Cortex has a master crystal to power his Cortex Vortex. "But Doctor Cortex, to reach full power we need not only your master crystal, but also the remaining twenty-five slave crystals from the surface. How do you expect to retrieve them when we don't have any earthbound operatives left?" asks N. Gin. Cortex orders Crash to give N. Gin the crystals Crash has gathered. "Like Dr. Cortex said, give the twenty crystals you've collected to me!" says N. Gin. He tries to take the crystals by force, using a heavily armed mech, which Crash sends into the vacuum of space. "Doctor Cortex will be very displeased with your resistance! Prepare to suffer his wrath!"

GIGGLE RATING: Five Giggles. The character design is great, and so is the voice. Brendan O'Brien is the son of actor Edmond O'Brien.

Crash Bandicoot: Warped (1998)

Naughty Dog. Directed by Andrew S. Gavin, Jason Rubin. Written by Andrew S. Gavin. Produced by David Bowry, Grady Hunt, Shimizu. Cast: Clancy Brown (Dr. Neo Cortex/The Great Uka Uka), Brendan O'Brien (Crash Bandicoot/N. Gin/Tiny Tiger/Baby Dr. Neo Cortex), Mel Winkler (Aku Aku), Michael Ensign (N. Tropy), William Hootkins (Dingodile).

N. Gin builds an advanced mech, and tells Crash, "So, Crash Bandicoot, we meet again. Uka Uka and Dr. Cortex want me to teach you a lesson. Well, I've made a few modifications to my mechanics since our last encounter, so back off, or be deleted!" When he confronts Crash's sister Coco, he falls out of the mech and screams, "Aaargh! Not again!"

GIGGLE RATING: Five Giggles.

Crash Team Racing (1999)

Naughty Dog. Directed by Andrew S. Gavin, Jason Rubin, Daniel Arey. Written by Andrew S. Gavin. Produced by Andrew S. Gavin, Grady Hunt. Cast: Clancy Brown (Dr. Neo Cortex/Uka Uka), Brendan O'Brien (Dr. N. Gin/Tiny Tiger/Pinstripe Potoroo), David Anthony Pizzuto (Nitrous Oxide/Komodo Joe/Papu Papu), Mel Winkler (Aku Aku), Michael Ensign (Dr. Nefarious Tropy), Hynden Walch (Coco Bandicoot), Billy Pope (Crash Bandicoot).

N. Gin is a playable character in a violet high-acceleration cart. After his defeat, he opens an auto parts store in Toledo, Ohio, which sells Clear-the-Road missile systems. "One for the road!"

GIGGLE RATING: Five Giggles.

Crash Bash (2000)

Cerny Games, Inc., Eurocom Developments Ltd. Produced by Jon Williams. Cast: Clancy Brown (Dr. Neo Cortex/Uka Uka), Anna Garduno (Coco Bandicoot), Sherman Howard (Aku Aku/Dingodile), Brendan O'Brien (Crash Bandicoot/Dr. Nitrus Brio/Tiny Tiger/Papu Papu/Komodo Moe), David Anthony Pizzuto (Komodo Joe/Nitrous Oxide).

From the back of the jewel case: "Crash and his friends are back in a knock-down, drag-out arena rumble. That's right. Get ready to ride, race, jump, throw and battle it out to the finish. Blow stuff up. Toss TNT. Duke it out in a jungle. It's just a good old-fashion bandicoot brawl." N. Gin launches balls randomly at players.

GIGGLE RATING: Looks, Five Giggles; Voice, N/A.

Crash Bandicoot: The Wrath of Cortex (2001)

Traveller's Tales. Directed by Jon Burton. Executive Producer: Jon Burton. Cast: Clancy Brown (Dr. Neo Cortex/Uka Uka), Corey Burton (Dr. N. Gin/Dr. N. Tropy), Debi Derryberry (Coco Bandicoot), R. Lee Ermey (Wa-Wa, The Water Elemental), Mark Hamill (Py-Ro, The Fire Elemental), Jess Harnell (Lo-Lo, The Air Elemental/Computer), Brendan O'Brien (Tiny Tiger), Kevin Michael Richardson (Crunch Bandicoot) (as Kevin Michael Richards), Thomas F. Wilson (Rok-Ko, The Earth Elemental) (as Tom Wilson), Mel Winkler (Aku Aku).

N. Gin attends a bad guy's convention. "Need I remind you that Crash always finds a way to defeat us? Maybe he's just too good for us!"

GIGGLE RATING: Five Giggles. Corey Burton's credits include *Duck Dodgers* (2003), *Jackie Chan Adventures* (2000), *The Sylvester & Tweety Mysteries* (1995), *Timon & Pumbaa* (1995), *Animaniacs* (1993), and *Chip 'n Dale Rescue Rangers* (1989) (all qv).

Crash Bandicoot X/S aka Crash Bandicoot: The Huge Adventure (2002)

Eurocom Entertainment Software. Cast: Brendan O'Brien (Crash Bandicoot).

N. Gin pilots a mech similar to the one in *Crash Bandicoot 3: Warped* (1998). Later, he is merged with Cortex and two other characters to become Mega-Mix, who is on the space station when it explodes.

GIGGLE RATING: Looks, Five Giggles; Voice, N/A.

Crash Nitro Kart (2003)

Vicarious Visions. Written by Dan Tanguay. Produced by Karthik Bala, Todd Masten, David Robinson. Cast: Kevin Michael Richardson (Crunch Bandicoot/Advisor) (as Kevin Michael Richards), Mel Winkler (Aku Aku), Debi Derryberry (Coco Bandicoot/Polar), Steve Blum (Crash Bandicoot/Emperor Velo) (as Steven Jay Blum), Dwight Schultz (Dingodile/Fake Crash), Quinton Flynn (Dr. N. Gin/Nitrous Oxide), Michael Ensign (Dr. Nefarious Tropy), Clancy Brown (Dr. Neo Cortex/Uka Uka), Paul

Greenberg (Geary/Pura), Marshall R. Teague (Krunk/Velo Minion) (as Marshall Teague), Tom Bourdon (N. Trance).

N. Gin, a playable character, has been slightly redesigned. His cyborg eye is black with a red dot instead of an eyeball and a pupil. He gets stranded on another planet, but eventually returns home. "Earth! We made it, ha ha ha!" he giggles insanely.

GIGGLE RATING: Looks, Four Giggles; Voice, Five Giggles.

Crash Twinsanity (2004)

Traveller's Tales. Written by Jordan Reichek. Produced by Kirk Scott. Cast: Lex Lang (Dr. Neo Cortex), Mel Winkler (Aku-Aku/Tribesman), Michael Ensign (Dr. Nefarious Tropy/Tribesmen), Susan Silo (Madame Amberley/Nina Cortex), Debi Derryberry (Coco Bandicoot/Young Dr. Cortex), Alex Fernandez (Uka-Uka/Farmer Ernest), Dwight Schultz (Dingodile/Rusty Walrus/Papu Papu/Tribesmen), Quinton Flynn (Dr. N. Gin/Victor/Moritz/Penguin).

N. Gin controls the Mecha-Bandicoot, a 40-foot robotic version of Crash. It has a chainsaw, rockets, and plasma blasts. "Dr. Cortex gave the twenty crystals you collected to me!" He giggles insanely.

GIGGLE RATING: Five Giggles. Quinton Flynn's credits include *Robot Chicken* (2005), *Timon & Pumbaa* (1995), and *Animaniacs* (1993) (all qv).

Crash Bandicoot Purple: Ripto's Rampage (2004)

Vicarious Visions, Inc.

N. Gin appears as a trading card.

GIGGLE RATING: Looks, Five Giggles; Voice, N/A.

Crash Tag Team Racing (2005)

Radical Entertainment. Co-produced by Tim Bennison, Vlad Ceraldi, Joel DeYoung. Writing Credits: Chris Mitchell (dialogue), Jordan Reichek (story). Cast: Amy Gross (Nina Cortex), Bill Farmer (Old Man/Park Drones), Chris Coppola (Park Drones/Adult Male), Charles Dennis (Park Drones), Chris Williams (Crunch Bandicoot), Danny Mann (Ebenezer

Von Clutch), Debi Derryberry (Coco Bandicoot), Duane R. Shepard Sr. (Stew), Jess Harnell (Crash Bandicoot/Park Drones), Lex Lang (Dr. Neo Cortex), Nolan North (Dr. N. Gin), Quinton Flynn (Chick Gizzard Lips), Roger Jackson (Willie Wumpa Cheeks/Park Drones) (as Roger L. Jackson), Shanelle Workman (Pasadena Possum).

Once again, N. Gin is a playable character and he is redesigned to look more zombiefied. He convinces Cortex to help look for Von Clutch's Power Gems so he can use Von Clutch's theme park as a base.

Quotable quotes:

"Okay, this is scaring me."

"It's like my father always said to me, 'SHUT UP N. GIN, YOU FREAK!'"

"Up in the sky! IT'S A COMPLETE MANIAC!"

"I, uh, think I wet myself."

"Oh, the glory of the skies!"

"Oh that impact was regrettable."

"Not my paint! I spent forever on that!"

"Villagers with torches couldn't get me, what chance do you have?"

"Take that, father! What? Did I say father?"

"Oh, the insurance company is never going to go for that one."

"Don't fear the reaper! I need more cowbell. I DON'T HAVE A COWBELL!"

"SWEET MEXICAN WALNUTS THAT HURTS!"

"Back! Or I will shower you with sharp things!"

"Hit me harder! For I like it!"

"Finally! I made a friend!"

"What's the matter, little baby, you need your bottle, LITTLE BABY!?"

"Your mother is the speed limit now!"

"It's high school all over again. Ouch."

"Head rocket, ENGAGE!"

"No one can resist my good looks, I mean weapons."

"I'm happy, I'm actually happy. IT HURTS!"

"Take up a slower sport, like full contact [pause] duck hunting or something with a duck!"

"Hee hee hee hee hee! That's right, tough guy! Unless you want to buy all-new stationery, YOU RESPECT THE MASTER!"

GIGGLE RATING: Five Giggles. Nolan North's credits include *Be Cool, Scooby-Doo!* (2015).

Crash Boom Bang! (2006)

Dimps Corporation.

N. Gin has a cameo appearance in the Silhouette Quiz.

GIGGLE RATING: Unknown.

Crash of the Titans (2007)

Radical Entertainment. Written by Chris Mitchell (story). Produced by Kirsten Forbes. Cast: Jess Harnell (Crash Bandicoot), Lex Lang (Dr. Neo Cortex), Greg Eagles (Aku-Aku), John DiMaggio (Uka-Uka), Amy Gross (Nina Cortex), Debi Derryberry (Coco Bandicoot), Chris Williams (Crunch Bandicoot/Tiny Tiger), Nolan North (Dr. N. Gin).

N. Gin's weapons factory is a version of the Statue of Liberty modeled on him. He communicates to his workers via the PA system: "Attention filthy monkeys! I have lost my toast recipe. Repeat, my family recipe for toast has been lost. The butter supply arrives shortly but I'll have nothing to put it on! Somebody help me! I wrote the recipe on a little post-it note, but can't find it. Also, Crash Bandicoot has been sighted, yada yada yada, peace out, homies."

Quotable quotes:

"AAAAAHHHH! Thank you master! Hee hee."

"AAAAAHHHH! Thank you again! Hotter than the first!"

"Oh, come on! He didn't even have a cup!"

"Crash, you fool, you're too late. It's time to drop the Doom Hammer on you. Eh, the Doom Hammer of Doom. Upon you—and uh, LET'S JUST DANCE, BABY!"

GIGGLE RATING: Five Giggles.

Crash: Mind Over Mutant (2008)

Radical Entertainment. Written by Chris Mitchell. Produced by Greg Goodrich. Cast: Jess Harnell (Crash Bandicoot), Lex Lang (Dr. Neo Cortex), Greg Eagles (Aku-Aku), John DiMaggio (Uka-Uka), Maurice LaMarche (Dr. Nitrus Brio), Debi Derryberry (Coco Bandicoot), Chris Williams (Crunch Bandicoot), Amy Gross (Nina Cortex), Nolan North (Dr. N. Gin), Mark Hamill (Znus).

N. Gin attacks Crash and flees to Wumpa Island, where Crash catches up to him. N. Gin reveals he's been collecting information on the Bandicoot family, hoping to be rewarded with Wumpa Island by Cortex. "I've been watching you and your delicious sister!" After he is defeated, he is told to leave the island, and he does, reluctantly. His voice is also heard in the credits, and in the Nintendo DS version, he is a piece of concept art.

GIGGLE RATING: Five Giggles.

Crash Nitro Kart 2 (2008)

Polarbit AB.

In this game for iPhone, N. Gin is a playable racer and has gone back to his classic look but is less detailed.

GIGGLE RATING: Looks, Four Giggles; Voice, N/A.

Crash Bandicoot N. Sane Trilogy (2017)

Vicarious Visions. Directed by Dan Tanguay. Written by Andrew S. Gavin. Produced by Kara Massie. Cast: Corey Burton (Dr. N. Gin/Dr. N. Tropy/Baby Cortex), Debi Derryberry (Coco Bandicoot/Tawna), John DiMaggio (Tiny Tiger/Uka Uka), Greg Eagles (Aku Aku), Jess Harnell (Crash Bandicoot/Pinstripe Potoroo/Ripper Roo), Maurice LaMarche (Dr. Nitrus Brio/Lab Assistant), Lex Lang (Dr. Neo Cortex), Dwight Schultz (Papu Papu/Lab Assistant).

Remakes of *Crash Bandicoot* (1996), *Crash Bandicoot 2: Cortex Strikes Back* (1997), and *Crash Bandicoot 3: Warped* (1998).

GIGGLE RATING: Five Giggles.

Yu-Gi-Oh! (Franchise)
Yu-Gi-Oh! Capsule Monster Coliseum (2004)

Konami. Cast: Dan Green (Yami Yugi/Yugi Muto), Gregory Abbey (Tristan Taylor) (as John Campbell), Karen Neil (Ishizu Ishtar) (as Karen Neill), Madeleine Blaustein (Solomon Muto), J. David Brimmer (Odion Ishtar), James Carter Cathcart (Weevil Underwood).

From UK.PlayStation.com: "Your monsters are contained in capsules (rather than the cards you might expect), which need to be opened up. Once you've sent them into action, the battles take place in 3D which allows you to check out your favourite creatures in brilliant detail."

Weevil Underwood giggles insanely. "Long time no see! Yugi, if you want to get your grubby little hands on the tournament title, you'll have to go through me!" Yugi agrees. "How about right now?" asks Weevil. Yugi wins. "This is a nightmare!" says Weevil. "Noooooo! How could I lose?"

GIGGLE RATING: Five Giggles.

Yu-Gi-Oh! Duel Links (2016)

Konami. Cast: Clay Adams (Jesse Anderson) (as Christopher C. Adams), Amy Birnbaum (Tèa Gardner/Bonz), J. David Brimmer (Odion) (as Michael Alston Bailey), Kate Bristol (Additional Voices), Darren Dunstan (Maximillion Pegasus), Daniel J. Edwards (Mako Tsunami), David Errigo Jr. (Additional

Voices), Wayne Grayson (Joey Wheeler/Syrus Truesdale), Dan Green (Yugi Muto/Yami Yugi), Laurie Hymes (Jess), Matthew Labyorteaux (Jaden Yuki) (as Matthew Charles), Ted Lewis (Yami Bakura/Bandit Keith), Emlyn Elisabeth Morinelli (Alexis Rhodes) (as Anna Morrow), Karen Neil (Ishizu Ishtar) (as Karen Neill), Ryan Nicolls (Zachary), Scott Rayow (Zane Truesdale) (as Scottie Ray), Sam Riegel (Rex Raptor/Para/Arkana) (as Sam Regal), Alyson Leigh Rosenfeld (Yubel/Additional Voices), Jonathan Todd Ross (Yami Marik) (as Todd Garbeil), Tara Sands (Mokuba Kaiba), Sean Schemmel (Dr. Vellian Crowler), Erica Schroeder (Mai Valentine/Mickey), Eric Stuart (Seto Kaiba/Dox/Bastion Misawa), Billy Bob Thompson (Weevil Underwood).

A free-to-play, digital collectible card game for Windows, iOS, and Android devices, based on the trading card game of the same name. "I can't wait to swat you down," says Weevil. He giggles insanely. "You're about to get stung! I hope you're not allergic."

FUN FACT: A spinoff anime series was produced in 2006 without Weevil Underwood.

GIGGLE RATING: Five Giggles. Billy Bob Thompson played Scud in the movie *Yu-Gi-Oh! The Dark Side of Dimensions* (2017).

Frankenweenie (Franchise)
Frankenweenie: Electrifying Experiments (2012?)
Edgar E. Gore appears in a still picture and does not speak. Free to play on the Disney website.

GIGGLE RATING: Looks, Five Giggles; Voice, N/A.

T.U.F.F. Puppy (Franchise)
T.U.F.F. Puppy: Unleashed (Unknown year)
Online Flash strategy game on Nickelodeon's official website based on the series *T.U.F.F. Puppy* (2010) (qv). The Chameleon is a member of D.O.O.M. here, replacing Ollie. There is no voice acting.

GIGGLE RATING: Looks, Five Giggles; Voice, N/A.

Mighty Magiswords (Franchise)
MagiMobile (2016)

"The app is a landing page for a multi-story world," said Cartoon Network COO Rob Sorcher. "I haven't seen that done anywhere else. Usually apps are extensions of content and multi-story worlds. This was designed as part of the original master narrative—not created after the show." It was the first children's entertainment franchise app to use audio content recognition (ACR) technology.

ZP appears on the splash page, but not in animated form. It is not known if his voice or animated image is used. The app is no longer available on iTunes, and the Android version is apparently not playable anymore. Unseen by this author.

GIGGLE RATING: Looks, Four Giggles; Voice, N/A.

Surely You Quest (2018)

From the website:

"Help Vambre and Prohyas win Princess Zange's adventuring tournament by collecting and upgrading Magiswords in *Surely You Quest* [2018]!

ENTER THE TOURNEY

Every adventurer in Lyvsheria is competing to prove who's the best. Vambre and Prohyas want to win, but they'll need every Magisword and special trick they've got.

GATHER MIGHTY MAGISWORDS

Discover and collect an awesome array of Magiswords–including some that have never been seen before!

TAKE ON ALL CHALLENGERS

It's casual combat with a strategic twist! Simply tap on enemies to defeat them, but if you choose the right Magisword for the job, you'll get huge bonuses, and every Magisword has special abilities that can change the tide of battle.

BECOME MIGHTY HEROES

Explore the amazing land of Lyvsheria and uncover all of its secrets. Beef up your Magiswords collection as you become an ace adventurer in *SURELY YOU QUEST* [2018]!"

From the game: "Zombie Pumpkin starts talking nonsense that confuses the target." ZP says, "I'm so–ohh."

GIGGLE RATING: Four Giggles.

Chapter 5:
Other Lorre Tunes

Direct-to-Video Lorre Tunes
Tamagotchi Video Adventures (1997)

7th Level Productions. Directed by Dan Kuenster. Story: Susan Deming, Dan Kuenster, David Lewman. Produced by Susan Deming. Cast: Susan Deming, Paul Eiding, Jennifer Hale, Tom Kenny, Maurice LaMarche, Gail Matthius, Susan Silo, Frank Welker, Billy West.

Tamagotchi is a keychain-sized virtual pet simulation game named after a small alien species that lays an egg on Earth, which the player has to raise the egg into an adult creature. Over 44 versions of the game have been produced, along with a movie, an anime series, and this video.

Tamagotchi go to Earth to select an object for the Tamagotchi Museum that best exemplifies the planet. Two Tamagotchi, the cunicular Mimitchi and the canine Pochitchi, bring back a console television, which doesn't work, so they remove its guts and imitate Ren ("You eediot!") and Stimpy (qv), respectively, in the frame. Billy West is actually a voice actor for this video, along with Lorre impersonators Tom Kenny, Maurice LaMarche, and Frank Welker. It is not known who plays Mimitchi.

GIGGLE RATING: Five Giggles.

AVAILABILITY: On VHS.

The Monster University Halloween TV Special (2010)

Created, Written, Animated, and Performed by Professor Mike Von Hoffman. Special Thanks to Boris Karloff, Bela Lugosi, and Peter Lorre.

This was a DVD sold on Monster-University.com, which is now defunct.

A hunchback is a bell-ringer and also a projectionist and he shows us eight monster cartoons. These cartoons pay homage to Frankenstein's monster, Dracula, the Mummy; and, in live action footage of Lon Chaney, the Phantom of the Opera. In "Bad Brain", a green Peter Lorre-esque figure sings, "Bad brain/Well maybe it's true/Bad brain/Didn't mean to hurt you/ And it happens again/My fingers round your throat in the rain." Hoffman says this song was inspired by Lorre's performance in *M* (1931).

FUN FACT: Hoffman put out a three-page comic of "Bad Brain".

GIGGLE RATING: Looks, Five Giggles; Voice, Five Giggles.

AVAILABILITY: The DVD is out of print, but a digital download is available at https://payhip.com/b/BtiL

Monster High: Frights, Camera, Action (2014)

Mattel Playground Productions, Nerd Corps Entertainment. Directed by William Lau. Written by Audu Paden, Dan Serafin. Produced by Margaret M. Dean. Cast: Kate Higgins (Frankie Stein), Salli Saffioti (Clawdeen Wolf/Cleo de Nile), Debi Derryberry (Draculaura), Marcus Griffin (Clawd Wolf), Jonquil Goode (Twyla/Clawdia Wolf), Karen Strassman (Elissabat/Veronica von Vamp), Audu Paden (Ghoulia Yelps/Manny Taur/ Vampire Dignitary #1/Captain/Bodyguard), Evan Smith (Deuce Gorgon/ Gil Webber/Scarantino/Edweird/Alucard/Security Troll/Studio Executive), Laura Bailey (Lagoona Blue/Honey Swamp/Headless Headmistress Nora Bloodgood), Cam Clarke (Hoodude Voodoo/Ygor/Heath Burns/Mr. Rotter/Crow #1/Vampire Dignitary #1).

Monster High is an American fashion doll franchise created by Mattel in 2010 with characters inspired by horror movies. An animated web series launched the same year on YouTube, which resulted in a number of direct-to-videos. Some of these, like this one, were shown on Nickelodeon after their initial release.

The monsters are watching a movie where Veronica von Vamp, in the Vampire Majesty series, plays a vampire about to be crowned queen. Dracula's daughter, Draculaura razzes the movie because it is inauthentic since vampires haven't had a queen in 400 years. A gem called the Vampire's Heart was supposed to lead searchers to the new queen, but no one has found her. The meaner monster girls tease her about her royal status.

At Lord Stoker's study in his Transylvanian castle, his short, tubby, hunchbacked, craven assistant, Ygor, scuttles in. In a voice like Peter Lorre's, he says, "Master! The Royal Court of Vampire Dignitaries seeks audience with you at once!" The dignitaries want to know how the search for the queen is going. They think, quite rightly, that Stoker is stalling so he can remain in charge and they give him one week before he is fired. Stoker lies and says he has found a queen using The Vampire's Heart. "No, no," says Ygor. Stoker silences him by stomping on his foot. "Her coronation is next week," Ygor corrects himself. When they are alone, Stoker asks Ygor if Ygor has lost his mind. "No, Ygor still keeps it in this little jar." The Vampire's Heart was stolen 400 years ago by Stoker's niece, Elissabat, who then disappeared. Stoker plans to appoint a puppet queen so he can maintain control. He chooses Draculaura, whom he thinks will be a pushover. Stoker shows up at Monster High with a fake Vampire's Heart, which lights up around Draculaura, thanks to batteries and a remote control operated by Ygor. Stoker takes Draculaura and some of her friends back to the castle in Transylvania.

In Lord Stoker's study, Draculaura discovers the fake heart and realizes that she is being used as a puppet. She and her friends discover that Elissabat is the real queen and they try to find Elissabat on a quest that that leads them to Londoom, New Goreleans, and finally Hauntlywood, with Ygor in hot pursuit, although falling down a lot. "I heard the Vampire Majesty movies are clawsome," he tells Stoker, giggling insanely. "I would really like to see my first boo-vie." Stoker decides to fly out himself. The gang meets Veronica von Vamp, who reveals that she is really Elissabat and bans Stoker from ever holding office again. Ygor gets to go to the movies. "Clawsome." He giggles insanely.

GIGGLE RATING: Five Giggles.

AVAILABILITY: *Monster High: Frights, Camera, Action!* (Blu-ray + DVD + Digital HD with UltraViolet.) Also on Amazon Prime.

Scooby-Doo: Frankencreepy (2014)

Warner Bros. Animation. Directed and Produced by Paul McEvoy. Written by James Krieg. Cast: Frank Welker (Scooby-Doo/Fred Jones), Mindy Cohn (Velma Dinkley), Grey Griffin (Daphne Blake) (as Grey DeLisle Griffin), Matthew Lillard (Shaggy Rogers), Diedrich Bader (Mrs. Vanders), Dee Bradley Baker (C.L. Magnus/Mr. Burger), Eric Bauza (Daphanatic/Rock Dude), Jeff Bennett (Iago/Shmidlap) (as Jeff Glen Bennett), Corey Burton (Baron Basil/ Ghost of the Baron), Candi Milo (Gypsy/Lila), Kevin Michael Richardson (Cuthbert Crawley/Inspector Krunch), Fred Tatasciore (Frankencreep).

Scooby-Doo (qv) became popular again with reruns on the Cartoon Network, and beginning in 1998, Warner Bros. Animation began producing at least one direct-to-video movie a year. This was the twenty-third.

Cuthbert Crawley, who claims to be Velma Dinkley's family lawyer, contacts her. Velma thinks it's an internet scam, like a super suit with a tiny FBI agent inside. Fred insists they meet him, though, and the gang goes in the Mystery Machine. Crawley tells her she has inherited the family castle of her great-uncle, mad scientist Baron Basil von Dinkenstein in Transylvania, Pennsylvania, but anyone who gets too close to the Baron's legacy will lose what he loves the most and be utterly destroyed. When they come out of the office, the Mystery Machine is destroyed, ostensibly by the Baron's ghost, who wears a metal mask. Freddie decides they should go to Transylvania by train to avenge the loss of his love. On the train, Velma tells them about the von Dinkenstein curse. Ever since the Baron's monster was destroyed, the town has been cursed.

When they arrive in Transylvania, they find they are not welcome due to the curse. A craven hunchback with bad teeth says, "Come with me", in a Peter Lorre voice and giggles insanely before taking them off in his coach. "Me Iago. All generations von Dinkensteins have hunchbacks for servant. Bad posture bring good luck." He explains the origin of the Baron's mask. The Baron cobbled together a monster, and the villagers destroyed it in a fire, which disfigured the Baron, who cursed the town.

They arrive at the castle, and the housekeeper, Mrs. Vanders, shows them the monster, who is encased in a block of ice. He's "part furry, part scaly, all ugly." Velma decides to prove it's a hoax and she orders everyone out but Iago. Mrs. Vanders hypnotizes her.

The rest of the gang goes to the festival in the village. The villagers start to move in on them, but they are rescued by Iago. "Quickly, you come. Iago take you to castle now," he says. Velma has gone insane. She is now convinced the monster can be brought to life, and does so, even as the villagers are battering down the door. She succeeds, and the monster escapes. The Baron's ghost says each will lose what he cherishes most. Daphne loses her figure, Shaggy and Scooby lose their appetites, and Fred loses his ability to solve mysteries. Fat Daphne follows the Baron down a tunnel, and Fred follows her. Shaggy and Scooby chase the monster until Velma shoots him with a tranquilizer dart. Then, she shoots Shaggy and Scooby.

Velma plans to take the brains of Shaggy and Scooby and put them into the monster. Iago interrupts her. "No, Mistress! It wrong to take brain." She stomps on his foot to get him out of the way. Shaggy and Scooby chew through their bonds and escape. Velma releases the monster, who pursues them. Velma gets unhypnotized and meets up with Shaggy and Scooby, who have reunited with Fred and Daphne in the tunnels. Iago enters and says, "Hurry! Gas is everywhere into the tunnels and seeping up into the castle! We must flee the gas!" They escape in his coach, which has been redecorated to look like the Mystery Machine, but the castle blows up. The villagers celebrate the success of their plot, but the gang survives. Shmidlap, a tiny FBI agent in a super suit exposes the whole conspiracy and feds round up the baddies. They would have gotten away with it, too, if not for those meddlesome kids.

FUN FACT: The cast includes frequent Lorre impersonators Frank Welker and Corey Burton.

GIGGLE RATING: Five Giggles. Jeff Bennett's numerous credits include *Quest for Glory IV: Shadows of Darkness* (1994), *The Sylvester and Tweety Mysteries* (1995), *Looney Toons: Back in Action* (2003), *Duck Dodgers* (2003), and *T.U.F.F. Puppy* (2010) (all qv).

Computer Software
Comedy Store Celebrity Guests 2 (Unknown year)

Apparently animated, voice actor Gary Gillett plays Peter Lorre, Jimmy Stewart, the Tasmanian Devil, Walter Cronkite, and Yakov Smirnoff. Unseen by this author and nothing else is known about it. Gillett's credits include *What's New Scooby-Doo?* (2002).

GIGGLE RATING: Unknown.

AVAILABILITY: Out of print.

Ebook
Frankenweenie: An Electrifying Book (2012)

This ebook is a companion to the movie *Frankenweenie* (2012) (qv) and includes original sketches and an animated 3D rendering of Edgar "E" Gore.

AVAILABILITY: iTunes/iBooks.

Internet Lorre Tunes

Unless noted otherwise, titles, usernames, dates, and descriptions (where in quotes) are verbatim from the internet, with minor changes in punctuation and formatting in some cases. This is the wild and woolly world of the web.

AVAILABILITY: Streaming on the net.

Crash Bandicoot: Monster Truck (2007)

The Animation Picture Company. Directed by Jamie Dixon. Written by The Altiere Bros. Produced by Dan Chuba, Michelle Eisenreich. Cast: Lex Lang (Dr. Neo Cortex, N. Gin), Jess Harnell (Crash Bandicoot), Debi Derryberry (Coco).

To promote the game *Crash of the Titans* (2007) (qv), four short web movies, each about three minutes, were produced, including this one. They were originally available for viewing on the Crash Bandicoot official website.

Dr. Neo Cortex has completed his new mutatorizer and tells N. Gin to bring in the test subject. "Way ahead of you," he says. It works, but he needs someone to lead the mutants, so he brings in Crash Bandicoot from a field where Crash is tossing a disc with Coco. N. activates the mutatorizor on Crash, but it dies. "Dead batteries," says N., and Crash escapes to fight the mutants. Interruption of the mutation process may result in unpredictable powers. "The bandicoot has developed super strength!" says N. While Cortex is searching for batteries, Crash escapes back to the field on the back of one of the mutants, a real monster truck.

GIGGLE RATING: Five Giggles. Lex Lang often plays Neo Cortex in the Crash Bandicoot franchise (qv). This is the only movie appearance of N. Gin to date.

AVAILABILITY: Free download on the Xbox 360 video service or streaming on the web.

Grand Theft Auto: Nickelodeon City SamuraiClinton (Uploaded February 1, 2007)

"A bunch of Nickelodeon characters are pissed by the producers sending their royalties to pay to the casino instead. In response, they rob a casino. Made with *3D Movie Maker* [1995] . . . It seems that it is a common misconception that *Nickelodeon 3D Movie Maker* [1996] (where the Nickelodeon props originated) is a game. It's a movie making program, not a game. Because people keep saying game in the comments. WOW, this is the first time any videos of mine have broke 100K views! Ironically, this video fell out of the first page of results for searches of the keyword Nickelodeon. This video is also the most popular *3dmm* [1995] animation on YouTube. The most amazing thing about this video is that it's my most popular one, yet it was filmed in less than a day. It just so happens that this video just bobbed back into the first page of results for the keyword 'nickelodeon'. Anyway, for all those who like this video, you should check out my other videos too!!!!!!!!! Even though a superior remastered version of this has been released, this old version is going to stay for posterity purposes!" Ren is played by Carl Daisy and Clinton Moore.

GIGGLE RATING: Looks, One Giggle. Voice, Zero Giggles, and it took two guys to do it, so divide that in half.

dialogue animation(peter lorre) lgkizzle (Uploaded Feb 27, 2007)

Brief 3-D animation. Dialogue is Peter Lorre and Raymond Massey in *Arsenic and Old Lace* (1944). Dr. Einstein is blue (this may be the lighting) and has big eyes. He drinks from a glass, not a flask.

GIGGLE RATING: Looks, Four Giggles; Voice, Five Giggles. It's Peter Lorre himself.

Grand Theft Auto: Weinerville SamuraiClinton (Uploaded June 1, 2007)

"A sequel to *Grand Theft Auto: Nickelodeon City* [2007]. Made with *3D Movie Maker* [1995]. a gang of Nickelodeon characters have encountered a new gang of mutants from the ocean that are trying to overthrow the aging gang of old cartoons. After the first few days of release, this short has gotten several views! A sequel has just been released."

GIGGLE RATING: Looks, One Giggle; Voice, Zero Giggles.

Grand Theft Auto: Nick Rebellion (part 1) SamuraiClinton (Uploaded August 30, 2007)

"A sequel to *Grand Theft Auto: Weinerville* [2007] made with *3D Movie Maker* [1995]. In part 1, Rocko and Heffer bust out of jail when Doug Funnie rams the tank into the wall. Later, he sends them to Kenan and Kel's place to discuss recruiting them to join their gang . . . Anyway, this is my first YouTube video to make use of tracks from APM Music. I used those tracks when I first discovered that APM tracks from Ren and Stimpy were available as a ZIP file compilation of MP3s. Also, I recently updated the tags on this since I want to appeal to a wider audience, and besides I spanned the tags across 3 different parts of this video since the character limit was less then. Now since it is increased, I squeezed in more tags."

GIGGLE RATING: Looks, One Giggle; Voice, Zero Giggles.

Grand Theft Auto: Nick Rebellion (part 2) SamuraiClinton (Uploaded August 30, 2007)

"In part 2 of *Grand Theft Auto: Nick Rebellion* [2007], Kenan, Kel, and Doug somehow manage to free Ren and Stimpy from Weinerville, and they end up being chased by imps, and eventually Spongebob outsmarts them."

GIGGLE RATING: Looks, One Giggle; Voice, Zero Giggles.

Grand Theft Auto: Nick Rebellion (part 3) SamuraiClinton (Uploaded August 30, 2007)

"Part 3 of *Grand Theft Auto: Nick Rebellion* [2007]. In this part, Pete Wrigley and his younger brother whose name is also Pete who happen to be from the 90s TV series *The Adventures of Pete and Pete* [1992] notice that Kenan, Kel, Ren and Stimpy don't have a vehicle anymore. After that, they see Doug Funnie's gravestone at the cemetery. Also, Spongebob and Patrick end up in a weird relationship after Spongebob is caught in firey wreckage."

GIGGLE RATING: Seriously? What do you think?

Blacksad–Ivo Statoc pencil test Javier Tedin (Uploaded September 21, 2007)

Description Google-translated from Spanish: "Character from the comic *BLACKSAD* by Juanjo Guamido, with the voice of Peter Lorre from the film *The Maltese Falcon* [1941]." *Blacksad* is a comic album series set in 1950s America rendered in a film noir style, with all the characters anthropomorphic animals. Ivo Statoc, a frog, is the richest and most powerful businessman in the city and a murderer. A movie based on the series was announced in 2006, scheduled for release in 2009. What, if anything, this pencil test had to do with the movie is unknown.

GIGGLE RATING: Looks, Five Giggles. Like the frog in the actual comic, there is a resemblance to Peter Lorre, accidental or not. Voice, Five Giggles.

Space Dementia SamuraiClinton (Uploaded October 6, 2007)

"Made with *3D Movie Maker* [1995]. Ren and Stimpy go on a voyage in the uncharted regions of nebulae consisting of weird planets on weird solar systems until a strange obstacle hits their space ship. Inspired by the classic Ren and Stimpy episode 'Space Madness' [qv]."

GIGGLE RATING: It's no *Grand Theft Auto: Nick Rebellion* (2007).

M [1931] *Movie Titles remake* hknb43c (Uploaded December 28, 2007)

"Cross between a teaser and movie titles for the 1931 Fritz Lang movie." Peter Lorre's name is in the credits.

GIGGLE RATING: N/A.

dR.LORRE EXPLAiNS TCP/IP eean2000 (Uploaded April 15, 2008)

"A BRiEF EXPLANAtiON OF thE TCP/IP PROTOCOL" Horror music plays under the titles. There is a shot of a castle. A short, bug-eyed man explains Transmission Control Protocol/Internet Protocol.

GIGGLE RATING: Looks, Two Giggles; Voice, One Giggle.

Peter lorre.... springhart (Uploaded July 31, 2008)

"Painted this at Facebook paint program VIMAGI. bout an hour hour and a half with my right hand and a mouse (im lefty)". The artist records himself painting a portrait of the titular character.

GIGGLE RATING: Looks, Five Giggles; Voice, N/A.

Le Click - Call Me (Nickelodeon 3DMM [1996] *music video)* SamuraiClinton (Uploaded on September 11, 2008)

"This music video to the classic Eurodance song 'Call Me' by Le Click is a recap of *Grand Theft Auto: Nickelodeon City* [2007], *Grand Theft Auto: Weinerville* [2007], *Grand Theft Auto: Nick Rebellion* [2007] and other *3dmm* [1995] shorts."

GIGGLE RATING: (qv).

Merrill Markoe presents: Quickdraw Noir zontarmozinky (Uploaded September 6, 2009)

Writer-comedian Merrill Markoe took "Choo-Choo Chumps", an edited episode of the Hanna-Barbera animated series *Quick Draw McGraw* (1959) (qv), set it to a Peter Lorre voice track from the original German-language version of *M* (1931), and then wrote her own subtitles in this glorious mash-up.

GIGGLE RATING: Looks, N/A; Voice, Five Giggles.

Nick 3D Movie Maker Poop: Let's Get Some Tacos dab414gnorts (Uploaded January 28, 2010)

Wikipedia tells us, "YouTube Poop, or YTP, is a type of video mashup created by editing preexisting media sources for humorous, annoying, confusing, shocking or dramatic purposes and occasionally containing mature content. YouTube Poop videos are traditionally uploaded to the video-sharing website YouTube, hence the name." This, then, is *Nick 3DMM* (1996) Poop. Ren slides around the room on his butt, actually sliding through the couch. "Let's get some tacos." The user promises, "Descriptions, tags, and correct titles will be added soon." I can't wait.

GIGGLE RATING: Looks, One Giggle; Voice, Zero Giggles.

Peter Lorre Dialogue Test: Rough Patrick Stannard (Uploaded September 26, 2010)

"Still in its keys and breakdowns, this is an early shot of a Dialogue test I am doing from a Peter Lorre scene from a radio drama. The end may be a bit hard to see as he gets cut off at the end and much of the second half is going to be revised. I am pretty happy with the first section of dialogue, and will begin tightening the frames down and in-betweening very shortly." Dialogue is from the radio show *Beyond Good and Evil* (1947) written by Ben Hecht and Doug Whitney. A large murine creature in a jail cell talks to a little man.

GIGGLE RATING: Looks, Zero Giggles; Voice, Five Giggles.

Peter Lorre Dialogue Test Patrick Stannard (Uploaded October 14, 2010)

"The final cut of a week long endeavor in independent animation. After finding some lovely dialogue from an old radio drama featuring Peter Lorre, I set out to try and explore the stretchier side of animation. What I was focusing on in this test was specific emotion, appealing facial expressions, and clear posing."

GIGGLE RATING: Looks, Zero Giggles; Voice, Five Giggles.

Nickelodeon 3D Movie Maker [1996]*: Sample Videos* sp19047 (Uploaded June 17, 2011)

"This video basically shows off all the sample videos in *Nickelodeon 3D Movie Maker* [1996]. Their only purpose was to introduce the characters or a tutorial towards a unique prop. Prepare for some awkward videos, because they're everywhere. Enjoy it, for a laugh or two." Ren is seen, and also heard in actual sound clips.

GIGGLE RATING: Looks, One Giggle; Voice, Four Giggles.

Ren and Stimpy dance to ending theme SamuraiClinton (Uploaded on June 27, 2011)

"OK, so this is a video where Ren and Stimpy dance to the ending theme of their series. Ren and Stimpy's dancing animation from this was filmed on *3DMM* [1995], while the background was synthesized with some QB64 programming along with a combination of other effects done in post-production to pull off digital psychedelia at its fullest."

GIGGLE RATING: Looks, One Giggle; Voice, N/A (thank goodness).

Let's Play Super Paper Mario: Part 8: Peter Lorre as Boomer VerticalSandwich (Uploaded on Oct 22, 2011)

"We tackle level 2-1, meet a new pixl, and I keep my word to my viewers and make him Peter Lorre." A gamer records himself playing and voices one of the characters as Peter Lorre.

GIGGLE RATING: Zero point zero.

3DMM: Ren and Stimpy Unmask! wileyk209zback (Uploaded January 4, 2012)

"Something I made on Microsoft's (Nickelodeon) *3D Movie Maker* [1995], based off the awful Ren and Stimpy episode 'Aloha Höek,' [qv] a boy is horrified to learn the true secret of his two favorite cartoon characters: they're really human spies from Russia in disguise! Chaos ensumes!"

GIGGLE RATING: Looks, One Giggle; Voice, Chaos ensumes!

Nickelodeon 3D Movie Maker [1996] *sample videos (MY versions!)* wileyk209zback (Uploaded September 10, 2012)

"These are all the sample movie files included with Microsoft's *Nickelodeon 3D Movie Maker* [1996], and since they weren't as good as MY films, I thought I'd give them my OWN touch. I think they are a lot better this way :)" Actual Billy West voice clips used.

GIGGLE RATING: Looks, One Giggle; Voice, Four Giggles.

Monsters Go Disco Animatic Spaceprince72 (Uploaded October 7, 2012)

"We were going to try and animate a Monsters Cereal [qv] short using the audio found on a flexi disc on the back of COUNT CHOCULA, FRANKEN BERRY and BOO BERRY cereal boxes in the late 1970s. This is an unfinished animatic starting during the second scene after the monsters decide they are going to enter a Disco contest. It's followed by an unfinished dance sequence. Watch carefully for cameos by FRUIT BRUTE, YUMMY MUMMY, the SILLY RABBIT [Tricks] and LUCKY the LEPRECHAUN."

"What are we waiting for?" says Boo Berry. "Let's go disco!" At the disco, he says, "Create your groove!" pointing up in the air like John Travolta in *Saturday Night Fever* (1977).

GIGGLE RATING: Five Giggles.

MONSTERS GO DISCO Original Edition Spaceprince72 (Uploaded October 7, 2012)

"This is a second, variant version of the MONSTERS GO DISCO flexi disc remix. Music by Jeff Elmassian at ENDLESS NOISE and the visual edit by David Gioiella at NORTHERN LIGHTS." Boo Berry is seen, and also sings or raps the lines, "Discos here" and "Discos there."

GIGGLE RATING: Five Giggles.

Ren and Stimpy pitch Marlboro Cigarettes! (*3DMM* [1996] film)
wileyk209zback (Uploaded December 20, 2012)

"Something I came up with on *Microsoft's (Nickelodeon) 3D Movie Maker* [1996] after seeing *Ren and Stimpy 'Adult Party Cartoon'* (2003) [qv], where our favorite nineties cat-and-dog cartoon duo can often be seen smoking cigarettes! So this is like their version of the famous Winston Cigarettes commercial with the Flintstones! And yes, that is me voicing the two of them." Wow, I thought it was Billy West.

GIGGLE RATING: Looks, One Giggle; Voice, Zero Giggles.

A Peter Lorre Like Person Meets Dracula VS ZOMBIES!?!
Chris Deaton (Uploaded October 29, 2013)

"A short Halloween animation written, directed and animated by Christopher Deaton. Music by Stephanie Deaton. Ashlyn Deaton as the voice of Dracula, Petter Lorre and the Zombie. Animated, edited, etc. using Blender 3D. Audio recorded and edited using Audacity. Celtix was used for Pre-Production. Also used GIMP and MuseScore." A Peter Lorre-like person walks down a staircase and Dracula comes out of the cellar door. Dracula summons a zombie to take over the world.

GIGGLE RATING: Looks, Five Giggles; Voice, One Giggle.

Character Animation Daniel Fox (Uploaded August 15, 2014)

"Shot 2: Edgar This is an animation I did in class. I created everything besides the audio, using 3D Studio Max, ZBrush, and Photoshop CS4. The audio file is an excerpt from a Peter Lorre film." A bald man with huge ears squats in a corner, holding a disembodied head. He looks at the camera, then back at the head, then back at the camera. "I want you to meet a friend of mine. A very good friend of mine. The be–the best friend I ever had." He speaks to the head. "What was your name, friend?" The speech is from *Tales of Terror* (1962).

GIGGLE RATING: Looks, Zero Giggles; Voice, Five Giggles.

iMac G3 with CompactFlash and Nickelodeon 3D Movie Maker! [1996] Alex Perrier (Uploaded on December 3, 2014)

"The children's game *Nickelodeon 3D Movie Maker* [1996] by Microsoft Kids runs well on an iMac G3 with a CompactFlash card and Microsoft Virtual PC! Featured here is a brief look at the CompactFlash setup, making cards as easy to swap out as RAM! Afterwards, my creative skills are put to the test to create a short movie in only a few minutes." Actually made with the demo version. Sound clips from the game are used.

GIGGLE RATING: Looks, One Giggle; Voice, Four Giggles.

3DMM [1995]: *Stimpy's TV gets blown up by Doraemon* Valyou (Uploaded on September 24, 2015)

Doraemon is a popular children's manga and anime series. The Japanese expansion pack was released only in that country. "Third *3D Movie Maker* [1995] animation. Put a little less into this, but I put a lot into Cowboy Skeltal anyways. In this universe, Doraemon is hitlerrific or something, and Doraemon Land has loads of explosives hidden around in case Doraemon really feels like blowing it up. Planned obsolescence.
EXPANSIONS USED: * Base 3DMM
Nickelodeon Expansion
Doraemon Expansion
Ren and Stimpy music pack
* other stuff i forgot"

GIGGLE RATING: Looks, One Giggle; Voice, Four Giggles.

Mighty Magiswords (2015)

As we have seen, this show began life as minisodes on the Cartoon Network App. Below is listed all the app content with Zombie Pumpkin Magisword, including web shorts, vlogs, and a music video.

"Zombie Reasonable" Cartoon Network
(Uploaded on September 1, 2015)

A three-minute short. The Warriors find ZP in Transylberia right where he was supposed to be, but Hoppus steals him away. Disgusted that ZP seems to do nothing, Hoppus throws him back. Prohyas gets ZP to lead him to a small pumpkin, which ZP eats. "Oh yeah." ZP spits seeds of the undead at Hoppus. Now that Hoppus sees ZP does something, Hoppus wants ZP back. Unable to get ZP, Hoppus slices ZP in half. However, ZP has the power of zombie regeneration.

"No Robots for Old Men" Cartoon Network
(Uploaded October 1, 2015)

A three-minute short. Vambre traps Old Man Oldman, Robopiggeh, and Grup in a succulent prison with Cactus Magisword and leave ZP behind to keep them company. "You guys are dumb," says ZP.

"Walkies" Cartoon Network (Uploaded September 12, 2016)

A five-minute short. Prohyas has a whole closetful of Magiswords, which burst through the door and fall on him. "You know Magiswords can shrink, right?" asks ZP.

"Flashback Farms" Cartoon Network
(Uploaded November 11, 2016)

A five-minute short. Prohyas recalls growing up with Vambre. ZP appears but has no lines.

"Zombie Pumpkin Magisword" Cartoon Network (Unknown year)

"It's time to meet: Zombie Pumpkin Magisword!" A parody of rap music videos with stock footage and new animation.

Mighty Magiswords Vlogs Cartoon Network (Unknown year)

The term "blog", a short form of "weblog", was coined in 1997 for a website consisting of posts often in a diary-like form. The term "vlog", for "video log", followed in 2000. Only the vlogs with ZP are listed below. Vlog titles in brackets are made up by the author.

"[Colors]"
ZP discusses his favorite colors with Prohyas. "You know what color I really like? You color."

"[Impressions]"
ZP does an impression of Prohyas. "Hey there, Duder. Hey. Hey. Yeah." His voice does not change.

"[Pretty]"
ZP is asked if he finds any girls pretty. "I don't know. That's a hard question."

"[Celery]"
ZP reveals he has conversations with Celery Magisword. Celery does not talk, ZP says, "But I pretend."

"[My Day]"
ZP talks about his day. "My Day, a story by Zombie Pumpkin Magisword."

"[My Dream]"
ZP talks about his dream, an antelope made of cotton candy. "You made me hungry."

"Prohyas Vlogs About Magiswords"
Prohyas asks ZP what he does to relax. "I think about squirrels."

CN Anything App
Cartoon Network ordered and finished fifteen *Mighty Magiswords* (2015) microshorts for the CN Anything App, which is not available in the United States. The player is told to "choose your magisword" to help the Warriors for Hire achieve their goal in each case. The segments air out of order and some clips can be found in promos.

"Prohyas vs. Tree-J" Segment 5 Production code 125/126 (Unknown year)

Prohyas tries to get Tree-Jay, a treen disc jockey, to pipe down. ZP shoots some seeds at him, which burn him and make him talk more loudly.

GIGGLE RATING: Four Giggles.

A Fire at Rocko's House! (3DMM) [1995] wileyk209zback (Uploaded on July 8, 2016)

"Here's an amusing idea I got for another *Rocko's Modern Life* [1993] *3D Movie Maker* [1995] episode! It's Rocko's birthday, and he's celebrating with many other Nicktoon characters. But when the candles on Rocko's cake set the house on fire, it's total chaos!" Ren speaks in sound clips.

GIGGLE RATING: Looks, One Giggle; Voice, Four Giggles.

Ren and Stimpy in space... again! (3DMM [1995] *movie*) wileyk209zback (Uploaded on Aug 11, 2016)

Made with *Nickelodeon 3DMM* (1996), loosely based on "Space Dogged", Season 5, Episode 3 of *The Ren & Stimpy Show* (1991) (qv). Actual sound bytes of Billy West mixed with dialogue not by West. Then Ren and Stimpy dance to "Happy Happy Joy Joy" and crash down.

GIGGLE RATING: Looks, One Giggle; Voice, Zero to Four Giggles.

Inside Out (N3DMM [1996] Edition) Chae Cook Media (Uploaded on Aug 28, 2016)

"CAST: Stimpson 'Stimpy' J. Cat as Joy Rocko as Sadness Ren Höek as Anger Filburt Turtle as Disgust Ickis as Fear" Sound clips from the game.

GIGGLE RATING: Looks, One Giggle; Voice, Four Giggles.

The Happy Undertaker Brian Horgan (Uploaded November 10, 2016)

"Personal animation test. Dialogue from the great Peter Lorre, rig from iAnimate." A fat, grinning mortician gets up from behind a lopsided casket made of old boards and giggles insanely. "Anybody would be proud to rest in this coffin." The line is from *The Comedy of Terrors* (1963).

GIGGLE RATING: Looks, Zero Giggles; Voice, Five Giggles.

TUFF PUPPY (2010) characters as HUMANS Butch Hartman (Uploaded October 19, 2016)

Butch Hartman shows what the characters from *T.U.F.F. Puppy* (2010) would look like as humans. Contains stock footage of the Chameleon. The drawing process of humanizing the character is animated, but the humanized character is not. He has big eyes and rotten teeth.

GIGGLE RATING: Looks, Five Giggles; Voice, Five Giggles.

Peter Lorre Lino Cristofaro (Uploaded December 21, 2016)

"CG model created with Maya and Mudbox." Brief video of a Dr. Lorre-esque figure. The camera revolves around him, but he does not move or speak.

GIGGLE RATING: Looks, Five Giggles; Voice, N/A.

The Nicktoons Movie: Teaser/Promotional Trailer CheckABookout (Uploaded on May 30, 2017)

Made with *Nickelodeon 3DMM* (1996). Ren is a passenger in a car driven by Stimpy. "Hey, watch where you're driving, you eediot!" says Ren, definitely not played by Billy West, John Kricfalusi, or even Chris Edgerly.

GIGGLE RATING: Looks, One Giggle; Voice, Zero Giggles.

Stimpy's Nickelodeon Phobia (3DMM) [1995] wileyk209zback (Uploaded on August 4, 2017)

"At last, it's finished! Here's something I made for my brother billdeco08. It is a goofy little *3D Movie Maker* [1995] Ren and Stimpy episode where Stimpy develops a fear of Nickelodeon's old 'Opera' station ID, while at the same time, Ren is terrified of the infamous Pinchface." Some spoken dialogue and insane giggling by Billy West, but mostly surtitled.

GIGGLE RATING: Looks, One Giggle; Voice, Four Giggles.

lori and pryce comedy of terrors [1963] carlyquinn (Uploaded September 3, 2017)

"i decided to finally animate something productive so heres my ocs [original characters] :V audio is from the movie *The Comedy of Terrors* [1963] w vincent price and peter lorre" Lorre and Price are animated as gray creatures with fangs. Price's character is short and fat while Lorre's is tall and thin.

GIGGLE RATING: Looks, Zero Giggles; Voice, Five Giggles.

Phil Hartman's Flat TV "The Monday Night Mystery Theater: The Luther Krupp File" (2019?)

Phil Hartman made this recording about a dysfunctional nuclear family and the radio and TV shows they listen to in the late 1970s or early 1980s as a sort of sizzle reel in his salad days before he became a star on *Saturday Night Live* (1975). The tapes were lost for years and only found after his murder in 1998. His brother, John Hartmann (Phil changed the spelling of his surname for show business purposes) released it as a CD in 2002. In 2013, Worker Studios teamed up with Paul Hartmann, another brother, to develop it as an animated film. Brian Lemay is the director and concept designer. The movie was unfinished at press time, but renderings of the set, props (including a statue of a black bird), and characters can be seen online. Hartman's voice acting can be heard on the CD or Audible.com.

In this film noir parody, "Fingers" Purcell, a dog-beating, purse-snatching, child-molesting drunk and snitch is murdered and has his tongue ripped out. Fingers' bloated corpse is a dead ringer for Sydney Greenstreet. Luther

Krupp, a Peter Lorre double, is caught red-handed by Chick Hazzard, Private Eye. Krupp starts off speaking calmly but becomes more and more agitated. "I didn't want to do it. I had to do it. It was in the contract. I needed the money. It's hard for an immigrant to find work. I begged them, please, let me just shoot him, but oh no, he was a squealer! He was a squealer, they said I had to, I had to pull, I had to pull out his tongue! You think I wanted to? I had to! It was in the contract, don't you understand? They even gave me these sandpaper gloves so I could get a good grip!" The police arrive and Krupp tells them Purcell pulled out his own tongue so Krupp shot him. The police send Krupp home.

GIGGLE RATING: Five Giggles.

Chapter 6:

Trivia

GOMEZ IN CHARLES ADDAMS' THE Addams Family, which debuted as a single-panel cartoon series in the magazine *The New Yorker*, was modeled on Peter Lorre. A live-action television series debuted in 1964 on ABC-TV with John Astin as Gomez. Astin did not resemble Lorre and made no attempt to imitate his voice. Gomez' first animated appearance was on the third episode of Hanna-Barbera's *The New Scooby-Doo Movies* (1972), "Scooby-Doo Meets the Addams Family" aka "Wednesday is Missing", where Astin repeated his role and the character stayed true to the Charles Addams model. After the episode aired, fans wanted more animated adventures featuring the Addamses, and Hanna-Barbera obliged with *The Addams Family* (1973). Gomez remained true to the Charles Addams model, but was played by Lennie Weinrib imitating Astin. In *The Addams Family: The Animated Series* (1992), the character was off-model from the original and played by John Astin imitating Lennie Weinrib sideways. In 2010, Illumination Entertainment, in partnership with Universal Pictures, announced a stop-motion animated film based on Charles Addams' original drawings, co-written, co-produced, and possibly directed by Tim Burton. However, in 2013, it was announced that Metro-Goldwyn-Mayer would produce an animated film based on the original drawings called *The Addams Family* (2019), with Oscar Isaac voicing the role of Gomez, not in imitation of Peter Lorre. In video games, no Gomez to date has followed the Charles Addams model or sounded like Peter Lorre.

Sydney Greenstreet makes a rare, perhaps unique, animated solo appearance in the Bugs Bunny cartoon *Slick Hare* (1947). Humphrey Bogart orders fried rabbit and gives waiter Elmer Fudd twenty minutes to get it. As Elmer chases Bugs through the restaurant, Bugs literally runs into Greenstreet and bounces off the man's gut.

Cut Man appears in *Captain N: The Game Master* (1989), Season 1, Episode 5, but he looks and sounds completely different from any of his other iterations and in fact is renamed "Cuts Man". Scott McNeil (qv) voices Cut Man in the series *MegaMan: NT Warrior* (2001), but it is a different character design and he does not sound like Peter Lorre. (In *Salty's Lighthouse* (1998), McNeil also redubbed Zug.) Elinor Holt plays Cut Man in *Mega Man: Powered Up* (2006) and puts her own spin on the character. Other games with Cut Man are not voiced and not discussed here. The series *Mega Man: Fully Charged* (2018) does not include Cut Man at all. At this writing, there is a forthcoming movie listed on IMDb called *Mega Man* (Unknown year). It is unknown if Cut Man appears or if this is live-action.

In *Robot Chicken* (2005), Season 4, Episode 11, "We Are a Humble Factory" (July 26, 2009), Boo Berry is mentioned but does not appear in the sketch "Who is Boo Berry?"

Anonymous commenters on the internet have stated that Klaus Heissler, the East German Olympic skier turned goldfish on *American Dad* (2005) is played by Dee Bradley Baker with a Peter Lorre voice. Baker and show co-creator Seth MacFarlane did not respond to requests for information. To my ears, it sounds like Baker is doing an authentic East German accent, and not imitating Lorre. As of May 2018, the show had broadcast 247 episodes over fifteen seasons, and has been renewed for two more seasons.

Addicted to Bad Ideas: Peter Lorre's 20th Century (2008?) is a "cabaret punk-rock operetta" written by the World/Inferno Friendship Society and directed by Jay Scheib, with twelve songs about Peter Lorre. It was originally inspired by Warner Brothers cartoons and the novel *Pandaemonium* by Leslie Epstein, whose father and uncle wrote *Casablanca* (1942); and "greatly informed by" Stephen D. Youngkin's biography, *The Lost One: A Life of Peter Lorre*.

In *Igor* (2008), the title character has big eyes like Peter Lorre, but John Cusack makes no attempt to imitate him, nor do any of the other actors playing any of the other Igors, although I had to watch the whole movie for due diligence.

In *Foodfight!* (2012), Wayne Brady as Daredevil Dan, a chocolate squirrel, says, "You despise me, don't you?" Although he is quoting Peter Lorre from *Casablanca* (1942), he does not imitate Lorre, and, mercifully, I did not have to watch the whole movie.

In November 2019, General Mills launched a website called WorkWithTheMonsters.com, which solicited pitches from filmmakers, actors, agents, writers, and producers for movies with Boo Berry, Franken Berry, and Count Chocula, and said:

> We're calling all filmmakers, actors, agents, writers, producers, animators, tastemakers, dealmakers, movers and shakers.
>
> We want to work with you to bring great stories to life. From mythical fables to magical journeys. Fairy tales to folk tales. Cliffhangers to nail-biters. Heroic sagas to cosmic battles. Binge-worthy dramas to historical epics. Blockbusters to indies. Serials to sequels.
>
> Together, let's captivate the hearts and minds of teens and adults.
>
> This isn't a contest. This isn't a pitch for free ideas.
>
> We humbly submit this brief to you, Hollywood.

At this writing, it is impossible to say what form the movie will take or even whether or not it will be animated.

Epilogue:

The Late Peter Lorre

PETER LORRE'S POSTHUMOUS CAREER, AS performed by animated and living surrogates, is already longer than his actual one. In a few years, it will be longer than his lifetime. It shows no sign of stopping, as new generations are delighted by the impersonators, even as the memory of Peter Lorre himself slips further and further away. What will happen then? Will mimics mimic other mimics, like clones of clones?

Clones. I think Peter would like that. [Giggles insanely.]

Bibliography

Articles, Print And Web

@CartoonNetPR. "New MagiMobile App Transforms Mighty Magiswords into a Connected World by Encouraging Fans to Watch, Engage and Collect"

Andreadis, Kosta (November 2, 2014). "Revisiting *Quest for Glory I & II*" ign. com/articles/2014/11/03/revisiting-quest-for-glory-i-ii

Annyas, Christian. "Saul Bass–*Around the World in Eighty Days* (1956)" annyas. com/screenshots/updates/saul-bass-around-the-world-in-eighty-days-title-sequence-1956/

articles.chicagotribune.com/2005-09-11/news/0509110323_1_stop- motion-puppet- dead

Barrier, Michael. "FUNNYWORLD REVISITED, An Interview with Bob Clampett" michaelbarrier.com/Funnyworld/Clampett/interview_bob_clampett.htm

Carozza, Kyle. "Kyle and Luke Talk About Toons #79: Throw Peter Lorre Into It" ognetworks.tv/c/kyleandluke/show/921a9050133e11528f224ac45d782b04?fbclid=IwAR0WEbU_zRHKK63gyCM4t9jYzOg3agLSKLBvUFbAO-e38y1xtqAeP4uof 9ZM

Film Threat. "CLEFT-O-MANIA: Screen veteran Kirk Douglas is a big chin-spiration at Spümcø Studios". *Film Threat.*

Garland, David. "Pulling the Strings: Gerry Anderson's Walk from 'Supermarionation' to 'Hypermarionation'". *Channeling the Future: Essays on Science Fiction and Fantasy.*

Geraghty, Lincoln (Editor). *Television.*

Gilligan, Beth. "*Around the World in 80 Days* [1956]: The End Credits" notcoming.com/saulbass/caps_around80days.php

Goodman, Martin. "Cartoons Aren't Real! Ren and Stimpy In Review" *ANIMATIONWorld Magazine.*

Halladay, Ashley. "The Monsters are alive!" blog.generalmills.com/2015/08/the-monsters-are-alive

Hunt, Kevin. "From fandom to the Monsters front lines" https://blog.gener-almills.com/2018/10/from-fandom-to-the-monsters-front-lines/

Komorowski, Thad. "The Clampett-Freberg-Lorre Connection"cartoonresearch.com/index.php/the-clampett-freberg-lorre-connection

La Rivière, Stephen. "Voice Actor Robert Easton Discusses Stingray". Published on September 7, 2014. https://www.youtube.com/watch?v=b01Zq_4Jm48&app=desktop

Lukovitz, Karlene. "General Mills Uses Blippar To Bring Monster Characters To Life On Boxes" mediapost.com/publications/article/256846/general-mills-uses-blippar-to-bring-monster-charac.html

Mellor, Louisa. "Robin Williams interview: *Happy Feet 2, Call Of Duty*, playing bad guys and more" denofgeek.com/us/movies/18392/robin-williams-inter-view-happy-feet-2-call-of-duty-playing-bad-guys-and-more

Morioka, Lynne. "The ultimate guide to Lucky Charms" blog.generalmills.com/2014/03/lucky-charms/monsterhigh.wikia.com/wiki/Igorpeterlorrebook.com/world01.html

Sibley, Brian. "*Around the World in Eighty Days* (1956)" artofthetitle.com/title/around-the-world-in-eighty-days/

"YouTube Poop". en.wikipedia.org/wiki/YouTube_Poop

Zachary. "How A Hip '90s Reboot Of Yogi Bear Helped Kill Saturday Morning Cartoons" throwbacks.com/90s-reboot-of-yogi-bear/

Books

Adamson, Joe. *Bugs Bunny: 50 Years and Only One Grey Hare*. Henry Holt & Company, 1991.

_____ _____. *Tex Avery, King of Cartoons*. Da Capo Press, 1985.

Archer, Simon; Hearn, Marcus. *What Made Thunderbirds Go! The Authorised Biography of Gerry Anderson*. London, UK: BBC Books, 2002.

Barrier, Michael. *Hollywood Cartoons: American Animation in its Golden Age*. Oxford University Press, USA, 2003.

Bass, Jennifer and Kirkham, Pat. *Saul Bass: A Life in Film & Design*. Laurence King Publishing, 2011.

Beck, Jerry. *Looney Tunes and Merrie Melodies: A Complete Illustrated Guide to the Warner Bros. Cartoons*. Holt Paperbacks, 1989.

_____ _____. *Looney Tunes, The Ultimate Visual Guide*. DK Publishing (Dorling Kindersley), 2003.

_____ _____. *The Animated Movie Guide*. Chicago Review Press, 2005.

Canemaker, John. *Two Guys Named Joe: Master Animation Storytellers Joe Grant &*

Joe Ranft. Disney Editions, 2010.

Clark, Danae. *Negotiating Hollywood: The Cultural Politics of Actors' Labor.* University Of Minnesota Press, 1995.

Collier, Kevin Scott. *Milton the Monster: Horror Hill Epitaph.* CreateSpace Independent Publishing Platform, 2018.

Culhane, Shamus. *Animation: From Script to Screen.* St. Martin's Griffin, 1990.

_____ _____. *Talking Animals and Other People.* St Martins Press, 1986.

Cohn, Art (ed.) *Michael Todd's Around the World in 80 Days* [1956] *Almanac.* Random House Inc. 1956.

_____ _____. *The Nine Lives of Michael Todd.* Forgotten Books, 2018.

Frank, Sam. *Buyer's Guide to Fifty Years of TV on Video.* Prometheus Books, 1998.

Hahn, Matthew. *The Animated Marx Brothers.* BearManor Media, 2017.

Horn, Maurice (ed.) *The World Encyclopedia of Cartoons.* Chelsea House Publications, 1979

Komorowski, Thad. *Sick Little Monkeys, The Unauthorized Ren & Stimpy Story.* BearManor Media, 2013.

Lawson, Tim and Persons, Alisa. *The Magic Behind the Voices: A Who's Who of Cartoon Voice Actors.* University Press of Mississippi, 2004.

Lenburg, Jeff. *The Encyclopedia of Animated Cartoons.* Checkmark Books, 1991

_____ _____. *The Great Cartoon Directors.* Da Capo Press, 1993.

_____ _____. *Who's Who in Animated Cartoons.* Applause Books, 2006.

Maltin, Leonard and Beck, Jerry. *Of Mice and Magic: A History of American Animated Cartoons.* Plume, 1987.

Mangels, Andy. *Animation on DVD, The Ultimate Guide.* Stone Bridge Press, 2004.

Ohmart, Ben. *Welcome, Foolish Mortals: The Life & Voices of Paul Frees.* Bear Manor Media, 2004.

_____ _____. *Mel Blanc: The Man of a Thousand Voices.* BearManor Media, 2012.

_____ _____ and Bevilacqua, Joe. *Daws Butler, Character Actor.* BearManor Media, 2010.

Petty, Miriam J. *Stealing the Show: African American Performers and Audiences in 1930s Hollywood.* University of California Press, 2016.

Sandler, Kevin S. (ed.) *Reading the Rabbit: Explorations in Warner Bros. Animation.* Rutgers University Press, 1998.

Scheimer, Lou with Andy Mangels. *Creating the Filmation Generation.* Two Morrows Publishing, 2012.

Sennett, Ted. *Masters of Menace: Greenstreet and Lorre.* Dutton Books, 1979.

Thomas, Sarah. *Peter Lorre: Face Maker: Constructing Stardom and Performance in Hollywood and Europe.* Berghahn Books, 2012.

Todd, Michael Jr. and Todd, Susan McCarthy. *A Valuable Property: The Life Story of Michael Todd*. Arbor House Publishing Co., 1983.

Womack, Kenneth. *The Beatles Encyclopedia: Everything Fab Four*. Greenwood, 2014.

Youngkin, Stephen D. *The Lost One: A Life of Peter Lorre*. University Press of Kentucky, 2005.

____ ____; Bigwood, James; and Cabana, Raymond Jr. *The Films of Peter Lorre*. Citadel Press, 1984.

DVD

Around the World in Eighty Days [1956] *Special Edition* (2004). Intro by Robert Osborne, audio commentary by Brian Sibley.

Behind the Looney Tunes: A Cast of Thousands (2006)

"The CooCoo Nut Grove "(1936). Audio commentary by Michael Barrier.

"Homer Simpson in: 'Kidney Trouble'" in *The Simpsons, The Complete Tenth Season* (2007). 20th Century Fox. Commentary by George Meyer.

Mad Monster Party Special Edition (2009).

Websites

BCDB.com
BehindTheVoiceActors.com
Fandom.wikia.com
hardcoregaming.net
ign.com
IMDb.com
Ebay.com
Intanibase.com
lparchive.org
Toonopedia.com
VoiceChasers.com
Wikipedia.com
WorkWithTheMonsters.com
YouTube.com

Bibliography

Notes

Prologue

"In the early twentieth century" Petty.

"I am without a question of a doubt" Youngkin, *The Lost One: A Life of Peter Lorre*.

Chapter 1

Credits are compiled from the cartoons themselves, and from IMDb and BCDB. Discrepancies are noted. Synopses are my own unless otherwise indicated, and are deliberately Lorre-centric.

"Warner Bros. was the cartoon studio" *Behind the Looney Tunes: A Cast of Thousands* (2006).

"a Negro boy" Maltin.

"Bosko in whiteface" Sandler.

"Leon's argument" michaelbarrier.com/Funnyworld/Clampett/interview_bob_clampett.htm

"Gossamer" The orange monster is sometimes known as "Bruda" and fans dubbed him "Rudolf."

"a gem carved in celluloid by a star." Cohn, *The Nine Lives of Michael Todd*.

"The limited animation technique" Sibley.

"the cost of a B picture" Cohn, *Michael Todd's Around the World in 80 Days [1956] Almanac*.

"One of my favourite actors of all time" Mellor.

"You don't find me unattractive, do you?" Youngkin, *The Lost One: A Life of Peter Lorre*. "He's inspired by Peter Lorre" articles.chicagotribune.com/2005-09-11/news/ 0509110323_1_stop- motion-puppet-dead

Chapter 2

"Blabbermouse" Blabbermouse is variously spelled as one word or two. I have used the spelling on the nameplate on the desk in this episode.

"*The Dick Tracy Show* (1960)" IMDb dates the show to 1961, BCDB dates it to 1960. IMDb credits Blanc as Flattop, BCDB credits Frees and Blanc as Flattop. Anonymous internet sources credit Benny Rubin as Flattop, which seems unlikely. Similarly, some sources say Paul Frees played "Go Go" Gomez and B.B. Eyes, some credit Blanc.

"Snaggletooth" In later episodes, Snaggletooth was referred to as Snagglepuss' cousin.

"One possibility was underwater." Archer and Hearn.

"looks and sounds like Lorre." Some anonymous internet sources say X-2-Zero is based on Lorre's *Casablanca* (1942) co-star, Claude Rains, to which I say, "Oh, pooh." Easton himself, in an interview, said he based the voice on Lorre's.

"bête noire" Garland.

"It took about four weeks to animate each film" Womack.

"The producers, the animators, and everyone" Lawson.

"*Waldo Kitty* [1975] was one of our three [parodic] shows for the fall" Scheimer.

"a mistake on many levels." Ibid.

"Krool" Sometimes spelled "Cruel" by anonymous internet commenters. It is never spelled out in the credits or on the show.

"Chip 'n Dale" is variously punctuated. This iteration is taken from the DVD cover.

"that he thinks Republicans are commies" *Film Threat*.

"*Yo Yogi*" Different sources give different airdates.

"You don't see it coming at least" Meyer.

"Singapore" Anonymous sources on the internet claim Chuck Powers, who was also the voice director for the Singapore dub, played Yami Bakura in a Peter Lorre voice. I have heard samples, and to me, he doesn't sound like Peter Lorre. Emails to Mr. Powers about his intent went unanswered.

"Genius is the twin brother of madness" tvtropes.org/pmwiki/pmwiki.php/Trivia/TheRenAndStimpyShow

"1972" Anonymous internet sources say Boo Berry was introduced in 1973, but General Mills says 1972. Presumably, they would know.

"What I had to do to make it cute" Carrozza.

Chapter 3

"A Well, I want to have my name changed to Peter Lorie" Youngkin, *The Lost One: A Life of Peter Lorre*.

"Q Anyone ever call you Bob Hope?" Ibid.

"to cash in on the reputation established over a period of years by Peter Lorre"
     Op. cit.

"Up until I met Pat" Hunt.

"It was so thrilling" Ibid.

"We ended up going off the rails" Op. cit.

"This year, we are excited about our partnership with Blippar" Halladay.

Chapter 4

"rich, narrative-driven, role-playing experience" Andreadis.

"The app is a landing page" @CartoonNetPR.

Chapter 5

"YouTube Poop, or YTP" en.wikipedia.org/wiki/YouTube_Poop

Chapter 6

"cabaret punk-rock operetta" peterlorrebook.com/world01.html

"greatly informed by" Ibid.

Index

About the Author

MATTHEW HAHN IS THE AUTHOR of *The Animated Marx Brothers*, an award-winning filmmaker, a published cartoonist, a lifelong rescuer of animals, and a pioneering Maryland craft brewer. He endowed Freedonia/Marxonia, an annual Marx Brothers festival held at State University of New York-Fredonia, with his wife Cheri. They live outside Washington, DC, with Thelma Todd.

CPSIA information can be obtained
at www.ICGtesting.com
Printed in the USA
LVHW041612190123
737484LV00008B/574